RALPH W. YARBOROUGH, THE PEOPLE'S SENATOR

FOCUS ON AMERICAN HISTORY SERIES
CENTER FOR AMERICAN HISTORY
UNIVERSITY OF TEXAS AT AUSTIN
Edited by Don Carleton

Organized in 1991, the Center for American History at the University of Texas
at Austin was established to administer the University's vast collection of letters,
books, photographs, oral histories, newspapers, and other documentary materials.
Today it stands as one of the nation's premier historical research institutions.
The Center's holdings focus on the history of Texas, the South, the Southwest,
and the Rocky Mountain West, and on media history (including broadcast news,
photojournalism, and newspaper history) and Congressional history. The Focus
on American History Series will include books that draw extensively from these
important collections.

Ralph W. Yarborough,
THE PEOPLE'S SENATOR

PATRICK COX ★ *Foreword by* SENATOR EDWARD M. KENNEDY

 UNIVERSITY OF TEXAS PRESS, *Austin*

Requests for permission to reproduce material from this work should be sent to
Permissions, University of Texas Press, P.O. Box 7819, Austin, TX 78713-7819.

⊛ The paper used in this book meets the minimum requirements of
ANSI/NISO Z39.48-1992 (R1997) (Permanence of Paper).

LIBRARY OF CONGRESS CATALOGING IN PUBLICATION DATA
Cox, Patrick, date
Ralph W. Yarborough, the people's senator / Patrick Cox ; foreword by
senator Edward M. Kennedy.
     p.   cm. — (Focus on American history series)
Includes bibliographical references and index.
ISBN 0-292-71243-X (hardcover : alk. paper)
1. Yarborough, Ralph Webster, 1903-   2. Legislators—United States—
Biography.   3. United States. Congress. Senate—Biography.   I. Title.
II. Series.
E840.8.Y3   C69   2002
328.73'092—dc21   2001003575

To those who provided support and guidance and the encouragement to undertake and complete this task:

Dr. Lewis L. Gould, my advisor and the distinguished professor who directed me in this effort; my wife, Brenda Cox, and daughter, Lauren; my mother, Doris Varnon, and my stepfather, the late Beven Varnon, with special regards for Opal Yarborough and the family of the late Senator Ralph Webster Yarborough.

Contents

Foreword

When President Kennedy wrote *Profiles in Courage* in the 1950s, one of the stories he told was of Texas' great nineteenth-century senator, Sam Houston. If my brother were writing today, he might well have selected Ralph Yarborough as a Texas Profile in Courage for the twentieth century. A man *of* the people who fought *for* the people, he inspired a living legacy of Texas officeholders who went into public service to follow in his footsteps. Determination defined Ralph Yarborough. He could be beaten, as he was the three times he ran for governor, but never be beaten down. He knew his cause was justice and progress for all, and he always found the courage to pick himself up and keep on campaigning for what he knew was right. People were depending on him and he never let them down.

With each early defeat, more and more people heard his message of help and hope, and the election day finally came when the trickle of his early support became a tidal wave that swamped the established special interests and he was elected to the United States Senate.

I had the privilege of serving with Ralph on the Senate Labor Committee. It was a real learning experience to watch Ralph go up against entrenched power and make large waves. He sponsored more legislation than any other member of the Texas delegation, and he was indispensable in shepherding the social initiative of the New Frontier and the Great Society through the Senate and into law. Whenever Senate issues involved health, labor, science, education, veterans, or the environment, Ralph was in the thick of the debate. Being from Massachusetts, I often wondered if he drew special inspiration from the fact that his middle name was "Webster." If he hadn't been a senator, John F. Kennedy and Lyndon B. Johnson would have had to invent him.

Ralph was a man who looked to the future and had a vision of a better quality of life for all Americans. He believed in President Kennedy's commitment to those basic principles and honored him with his support. And when Bobby ran in 1968, and I ran in 1980, he was there for us too—just as he always was for the people of Texas.

Ralph Yarborough was a loyal friend and a tower of integrity. He was a shining example to all of us who serve in public office. "Discouraged" was not in his vocabulary. He taught us never to give up or give in and that with a courageous attitude, victory was always possible next time or next year. In his biography of this greatly respected and much beloved giant of our time, Patrick Cox shows us why Ralph Yarborough truly was "The People's Senator."

SENATOR EDWARD M. KENNEDY

Acknowledgments

I first heard Ralph Yarborough in 1968 when he appeared with fellow U.S. Senator Eugene McCarthy at a political rally one warm summer evening in Houston's Hermann Park. I was an impressionable high school student and, like many others in the 1960's, trying to understand the Vietnam War. I was old enough to know that our U.S. senator was breaking ranks with his president over the issue. The park was filled with Yarborough supporters and others interested in the 1968 presidential campaign. A large presence of uniformed police and a small group of people taunting both Yarborough and McCarthy also gathered under the evening sky. Although I failed to fully comprehend the significance of Senator Yarborough's appearance with Senator McCarthy, I do recall an evening of rousing speeches followed by a great debate among my friends about the presidential race.

Two years later, Ralph Yarborough lost his U.S. Senate seat and failed in his comeback attempt in the 1972 Democratic primary. During these years, I attended the University of Texas in Austin, and it was fairly easy to see Yarborough during these campaigns. I interviewed him in his office in the Brown Building for a research paper I was writing on the Big Thicket, the important environmental area that Yarborough wanted for a national park and still sought after he left the Senate. Yarborough was more than willing to talk to a young student about not just the Big Thicket but about Texas politics. I told him about family members in East Texas, and he surprised me with a recitation of election returns from small, piney woods counties. At the time, I had no idea of the magnitude of his accomplishments or his lasting contributions to the Texas political culture. He struck me as an extremely knowledgeable and open man, strong in his opinions yet willing to spend hours with a young college student with nothing more to offer than an interest in a subject close to his heart.

Many years later, Dr. Lewis Gould and I met in his office at the University of Texas at Austin in 1993 to discuss my dissertation topic in American history. Dr. Gould mentioned that Ralph Yarborough had recently donated his papers to the Center for American History. By this time, I knew of Senator Yarborough's accomplishments in the U.S. Senate and his role in recent Texas politics. That conversation with Dr. Gould opened the door for this book on Ralph Yarborough's life and provocative career.

During the years of research and writing, I received tremendous support from the Yarborough family and many others who knew and worked with the senator. As I began my research at the Center for American History, I discovered that while there were volumes of materials from the 1950's through the 1970's, very few files contained information on his earlier career. Fortunately, after meeting with Senator Yarborough and his wife, Opal, they granted access to all his remaining files in the Yarborough law office and home. These included records and correspondence dating back to the early 1920's. Our agreement allowed access to this area of his life, previously unavailable to anyone who was not part of the family, and provided me with an early picture of Ralph Yarborough and an understanding of the motivation that propelled him into the leadership of the postwar liberal movement in Texas. Unfortunately, before I completed my interviews with him, Senator Yarborough passed away on January 27, 1996, at the age of 93. However, I knew he was grateful that an assessment of his contributions and place in history was underway.

Numerous members of the Yarborough family helped me in this research. These included his niece Grace Billie Presley. "Grace Billie" is the unofficial family historian and recorded stories of the Yarboroughs along with descriptions of life in Chandler at the turn of the century. Ralph's younger brother Donald also served as a fountain of information. He provided a number of personal stories and escapades in which the brothers participated. At several Yarborough family reunions during the 1990's I spoke with Ralph's sisters, cousins, nieces, and nephews, who politely responded to all of my questions. I extend my appreciation for the encouragement I received from Yarborough's family, including Judge Jack Hardee, Brooks Hardee, Dr. Clare Yarborough, Mr. and Mrs. Jackson Spear Yarborough, Mrs. Nell Mallet, Mr. and Mrs. William Randolph Smith, Mr. and Mrs. Chester Bryant, Commander and Mrs. Clayton Spikes, Ms. Dorothy Sloan, Mr. Richard Harrison, Dr. Oren Murphy, Clare Yarborough, Mrs. Ann Yarborough, and Mrs. Donald Yarborough. Mr. and Mrs. Sidney Mallet Jr. graciously showed me their Chandler home, where Ralph Yarborough grew up.

I am also very grateful to DeAnna DiCuffa, longtime administrative assistant to Senator Yarborough. Her years of invaluable assistance directed me through files at Senator Yarborough's law office and home. Without her direction, many of the letters, memos, photos, and documents would still be gathering dust in some forgotten file cabinet.

The staff of the Center for American History, under the direction of Dr. Don Carleton, was a model of cooperation and assistance. During my research on the Yarborough Papers stored at the Center, the staff provided guidance and tolerated any type of question. The staff of the Special Collection at the University of Houston, the Lyndon B. Johnson Presidential Library, the Houston Metropolitan Research Center, and the Woodson Research Center at Rice University also gave me generous assistance, and my appreciation goes as well to the Texas State Archives, the Texas Law Library, the Lower Colorado River Authority Archives Division and the Legislative Library at the Texas State Capitol, the Henderson County Clerk's office, the Henderson County Historical Society, the *Athens Daily Review,* and the Murchison Library in Athens, Texas. I also extend my gratitude to my editors at UT Press, Bill Bishel and Carolyn Cates Wylie. And special thanks go to Lois Rankin for her invaluable review.

Finally, I owe much appreciation to my family. My mother, Doris Varnon, provided some of the earliest encouragement to pursue my historical interests. Likewise, I received important critiques from my late stepfather, Beven Varnon. His editing during his final months helped complete this effort. At times I became so involved in work that my wife believed I became Fred MacMurray's absent-minded professor. My wife, Brenda, and my daughter, Lauren, stuck with me during this marathon that lasted even longer than one of Ralph Yarborough's best stem-winders. Brenda and Lauren demonstrated their love and commitment to me for these many years, and for that I will always be more than grateful. Just as Ralph Yarborough's family supported him in the lean years and those in which he made his greatest contributions, Brenda and Lauren gave their best to me.

Introduction

As the sun cast its final golden rays on a warm, muggy evening in 1993, more than a thousand people gathered on the grounds of the picturesque, white colonial Texas governor's mansion to spend a few moments with a political legend. Senator Ralph Webster Yarborough, whose decades of public service dated to the 1930's, smiled and patiently greeted well-wishers. The once spry, seemingly unstoppable campaigner now wore a hearing aid and sat in a lawn chair with his walking cane propped nearby. Opal Yarborough, his wife and greatest supporter since their 1927 marriage, sat beside him in the shade of the green-and-white tent next to the mansion. Although his once great voice had grown weaker, his eyes still sparkled. His enthusiasm seemed just as strong as during his campaigns for governor and senator. As his admirers greeted Ralph and Opal, they talked about politics and the "good old days" that covered his nine decades in Texas. A few of his oldest friends called him "Judge" in recognition of his tenure on the bench in Travis County. Although he won only three of nine statewide races during his long career and never attained his cherished goal of presiding over the state from the governor's mansion, Ralph Yarborough inscribed a record of achievement during his fourteen years in the U.S. Senate that may never be equaled by any other Texan.

"The People's Senator" best describes Ralph Yarborough. He is the acknowledged "patron saint of Texas liberals." In spite of his prominent position in modern Texas and national politics, Yarborough remains in the shadow of his more famous counterparts, Lyndon Johnson and Sam Rayburn. How Yarborough became the successful, modern champion of Texas liberals is a story that originated in rural East Texas and followed a career which spanned nearly the entire twentieth century. His ascent in the liberal wing of the Texas Democratic party began prior to his campaigns for governor during the 1950's and lasted through his last race for the U.S. Senate in 1972. With the exception of Jim Ferguson, no Texan, not even Sam Houston, ran more statewide campaigns than Yarborough. His legacy influenced and inspired others long after his final campaign.

Yarborough charted his own path, apart from his contemporaries. His rivals included Lyndon Johnson, Lloyd Bentsen Jr., and governors Allan Shivers, Price Daniel Sr., and John Connally. A host of other modern Texas leaders made up the rest of the mix. Yarborough began developing his political philosophy with his work as a young assistant attorney general to James Allred. Antitrust law and protection of public lands and natural resources became the focal point of his public career in the 1930's. These early pursuits revealed Yarborough's evolving belief in the necessity for government to play a role in protecting "the little guy" against unethical and dishonest practices.

World War II interrupted his promising political career. The postwar conservatism that replaced the New Deal reform movements never influenced Yarborough. His three unsuccessful races for governor in the 1950's merely increased his desire for elective office. His popularity increased with each loss, but the fruits of victory always seemed to be just out of reach. Others would have quit—but not Yarborough. The governor's office might have eluded him, but victory finally came after the hard-fought 1957 special election for U.S. Senator.

Yarborough's social and economic views more closely resembled those of national Democrats of this era rather than those of traditional, conservative southern Democrats. His frequent clashes with the Texas congressional delegation sometimes damaged his effectiveness. But during his fourteen-year tenure in Washington, D.C., Yarborough sponsored more legislation than any senator who served the state of Texas in our nation's capitol. Nearly all of President Lyndon Johnson's initiatives that involved public schools and universities, veterans of the armed services, the environment, health care, and many other domestic issues carried the name of Yarborough as a sponsor or earned his active support. If LBJ was the grand architect in the design of the Great Society, then Yarborough earned the title of chief engineer. His legislative work and tireless commitment steered a major portion of the president's programs through the political process into law.

Yarborough's contributions to the political culture of Texas rival his legislative accomplishments. In more recent times, Texas has developed the reputation of producing only conservative political leadership for the highest levels in state and national government. Yarborough never fit that mold. He followed the strong populist, antiestablishment streak that has been present since Sam Houston in the early days of the state. Along with preserving this legacy, Yarborough inspired two generations of Democratic officeholders. His large following rivaled that of Lyndon Johnson. A litany of conservative leaders that included Allan Shivers, Price Daniel Sr., John Connally, and countless others sparred with Yarborough on everything from major policy issues to mundane, personal matters. However controversial Yarborough's politics were, few questioned his integrity or his sincerity. Had he replaced Adam in the Garden of Eden, Eve would still be holding the apple while Yarborough defiantly argued with the serpent.

Yarborough's life offers a window into the dramatic changes in Texas and the nation during the twentieth century. He is an excellent study of a regional political figure devoted to traditional democratic ideals: the restoration of fairness, justice, and economic opportunity for Americans. His vision of economic liberalism combined the ideals of Jefferson and FDR to include a vibrant economy based on small farms and businesses, a well-educated and organized work force, and a strong government presence as referee and rule maker. He was also a man of action and impatience who believed that his knowledge, energy, and enthusiasm would overcome all obstacles and serve him well in his aspirations to elective office.

Along with his distinctive, modern philosophy, Yarborough cloaked himself in the populist-styled traditions of the pre-television political era. A common element of this leadership style was its ability to entertain people while transmitting a political message. Yarborough's evangelical style resembled that of twentieth-century Texas governors James "Farmer Jim" Ferguson and W. Lee "Pappy" O'Daniel, the controversial yet dominant politicians of their respective generations. Yarborough's speaking ability together with his keen mind enlivened and energized his whirlwind campaigns that often seemed more like old-time religious revivals. However, he differed politically and personally from Ferguson and O'Daniel. Yarborough provided true leadership and results on plain pocketbook issues whereas they had merely lined their own pockets at the expense of meaningful reform.

Beneath the public persona was a man driven by the urge to succeed and implant his vision on Texas and the rest of the nation. His intense devotion and desire sometimes exposed a temper that stung his closest advisors and staff members like a whip. Even his closest friends threw up their hands and lost their patience. Yet Yarborough always offered a courteous greeting and friendly nod to all. Whether he met a constituent in his Senate office or talked with a family who stood for hours in the sun to shake his hand, Yarborough displayed a genuine compassion for people. Campaigns and public appearances became like oxygen to him. He never tired of driving the back roads of Texas making speeches and shaking hands. The internal drive that propelled him forward through rough political waters often swamped his devoted followers along the way. His obsession with hard work and his willingness to take on seemingly insurmountable tasks continued throughout his career. His determination and hands-on approach to all issues, no matter how small, reflected both his legal training and his domineering personality. He never wanted to be outworked by anyone. He firmly believed that any disadvantage, most often a lack of money for his political campaigns, could be overcome by his hard work, unsurpassed knowledge, and power of persuasion.

Ralph Webster Yarborough, "The People's Senator," was one of a kind. He made a difference during a time of monumental change in the state and the nation. His remarkable story makes him a true Texas legend.

RALPH W. YARBOROUGH, THE PEOPLE'S SENATOR

1   *It Was a Joyous Boyhood*

The Texas in which Ralph Yarborough grew to adolescence in the early twentieth century was bound to Old South culture and politics. Ralph's paternal grandparents, Harvey Yarborough and his wife, Margaret Ann, moved from Sumpter County, Alabama, to East Texas in 1848, settling among the marshy, chocolate-colored creeks and dense forests of Smith County. Like most southerners who made their way to Texas, they came to farm, bringing a small number of slaves with them. As an Alabama volunteer in the Mexican War, Harvey had served as a first lieutenant but never saw action. In the Civil War, he followed many of his East Texas neighbors in enlisting with the Confederate forces. He became captain of a company of Smith County light infantry. Known thereafter as Captain Yarborough, he remained in Texas and worked as a gunsmith in the Tyler arsenal. After the war, in 1871, Harvey joined in the founding of the Tyler Tap Railroad, the first railroad to serve that community.

Margaret Ann Miller of Mississippi, who married Harvey in December 1846, was an activist for much of her adult life, stepping beyond the established social boundaries for women. Along with two other women, she was chosen as a delegate to the 1869 Baptist General Convention in East Texas. Male delegates challenged the trio because women were not supposed to be eligible to serve as voting delegates. However, Margaret Yarborough and the other women challenged the rule, pointing out that the constitution and bylaws provided that "persons" were qualified as delegates. They eventually were seated, but a male majority changed the bylaws at the convention to provide that thereafter only men could serve as delegates.[1]

Ralph Yarborough's maternal grandfather, Andrew Jackson (A. J.) Spear, married Margaret Ann Walton, who was a descendant of George Walton, a signer of the Declaration of Independence from Georgia. A. J. and Margaret Ann moved to Henderson County in 1871, where A. J. became a large landowner near Chandler and also owned a gristmill in the small community. He too served in the Confederate forces.[2]

Charles Richard (C. R.) Yarborough, Ralph's father, was the seventh of Harvey and Margaret Ann's ten children. He married Nannie Jane Spear, the daughter of A. J. and Margaret Spear, on June 13, 1889, in Tyler, Texas. Once C. R. and Nannie moved to the East Texas community of Chandler in 1903, they remained there and resided in the same house for the rest of their lives. Nannie Yarborough died in 1950 and C. R. lived to be a centenarian, passing away in 1964.[3]

The small town of Chandler resembled other rural communities in East Texas in the early 1900's. Located on the banks of the Neches River in the northeastern part of Henderson County, Chandler counted for 350 inhabitants in a county with a population of 19,750 in 1900. Athens, the county seat, was fifteen dusty, dirt-road miles from Chandler. As in the antebellum days when his grandparents moved to the area, large forests teeming with wildlife and meandering creeks crowded Yarborough's boyhood hometown. The minimal industrial activity in Henderson County took place in a few brick and tile factories, along with noisy sawmills, cotton gins, and gristmills scattered throughout the peaceful county. Chandler had a post office, the Cotton Belt train station, two general stores, and several other small businesses. The town doctor saw his patients in the rear of the drug store, which also served as the soda fountain and ice cream shop. Once the Yarboroughs moved to Chandler, they quickly became involved in the community's public life. C. R. Yarborough served as a member of the city council of Chandler and as its elected mayor. He was president of the local school board and later, in the 1920's, was elected justice of the peace. C. R. and Nannie farmed and relied on their crops and livestock for their income. But their interests kept them continuously involved in Chandler's business and political activities.[4]

Ralph Webster Yarborough was born on June 8, 1903, at the Yarborough home in Chandler. He was the seventh child of C. R. and Nannie and the first to be born in Chandler, for the family had moved to town from their nearby farm only a few months earlier. C. R. and Nannie moved to Chandler because they believed that education was essential for their sons and daughters. "We had to walk a mile or more to school from the farm, and Mama and Papa did not like that, so they bought a house in Chandler," Yarborough recalled. The Yarborough family was typical of the more-successful small landowners. A white picket fence enclosed the house and yard to keep stray dogs and other animals away from Nannie's rosebushes. The afternoon sun shone in on an L-shaped front porch covered with honeysuckle vine. The south porch bene-

Charles and Nannie Yarborough moved their family from the farm to their home in Chandler in 1903. From left to right are Charles, Nannie holding Ralph, Sunshine, Grandmother Yarborough, Grace, Orelia, Nell, Harvey, and Jewell. Courtesy Opal Yarborough.

fited from the prevailing summer breezes from the Neches River Valley. The family raised chickens, cattle, and hogs for meat and dairy cattle for milk and butter. The Yarboroughs used a large iron pot, a relic discarded by the Confederacy, for scalding the hogs during "hog killing time" in the cooler autumn days. Two acres were dedicated to providing fresh peaches, watermelons, and cantaloupes. The Yarboroughs were the first family in Chandler to have a claw-foot bathtub and a gas light fixture in their home. Although they were not rich, their large family was more secure than most families in East Texas during this time of widespread sharecropping and rural poverty. The home, which remained in the Yarborough family throughout the long life of C. R. Yarborough, also served as his office and the family political headquarters.[5]

GROWING UP IN CHANDLER

C. R. and Nannie Yarborough raised their children with an emphasis on education and participation in religious activities. The Yarborough sons and daughters also worked in the gardens and took care of the animals. As a child, Ralph picked cucumbers from the garden to sell at a large pickling vat near the Chandler railroad station and sold peaches from the family's orchard. He drove a mule team on weekends to move lumber from the woods to the saw-mills. Ralph also worked alongside his brothers chopping wood or looking after the chickens, hogs, cattle, and horses. When he was older, Ralph walked the short distance to the commercial area of town, where he worked at the *Chandler Times* newspaper. He inked the hand presses and earned a dollar per week. These many tasks helped the Yarboroughs support a large family and taught the children to be resourceful and independent as they continued their formal education.[6]

Not all of the young Yarborough's time was taken up with school and work. The Yarborough household was not extremely strict, so the children had time for recreation. Hunting, fishing, and exploring the forests and river bottom lands surrounding Chandler drew Ralph and his brothers Donald and Harvey on many adventures where they likened themselves to characters from Mark Twain's stories. Also, local politics and community affairs engaged young Ralph. His interest in law came from watching his father. Though C. R. never attended law school, he served as a legal advisor to people in Chandler. To keep up with the cases and procedures, he purchased a set of law books and stayed abreast of the news. R. T. Craig, a longtime family friend and publisher of the Chandler newspaper, said that C. R. performed practically all the community's legal work and "was generally looked upon as a fountain of information on any question that arose." His decisions in settling local disputes were most always accepted as final. C. R. held the law and public service in high esteem and imparted those attitudes to Ralph.[7]

The young Ralph matured in a household where knowledge of history and citizenship comprised an essential part of life. C. R. presided over daily supper-table discussions about Civil War battles and leaders, political events, school assignments, duties on the family farm, and current legal cases in Chandler. Out of these talks came Ralph's love of history, along with his dedication to service in the community. Yarborough was close to both parents but seemed to be more attuned to his father, who served as a model citizen for not only his children but the rest of Chandler. C. R.'s legal acumen focused on land transactions, which gained him a reputation for honesty and reliability. As Ralph watched and listened to his father, he learned legal terminology and about the frequent difficulties encountered in the exchange of property. His early knowledge of deeds and Spanish land grants later proved valuable to him when he became one of the best-known land attorneys in

Texas. History, law, public service, and enjoyment of the outdoors became lifelong pursuits for Ralph Yarborough.[8]

During his youth Ralph was exposed to the most emotionally charged political controversy of the day: alcohol and drinking. With the demise of Populism at the turn of the century, Texas Democrats became the only political party, but political divisions occurred over moral issues and personalities. "Prohibition was debated between the Drys and the Wets with a vim and a vigor that touched everyone in all of those small towns," Yarborough recalled. Families fought and communities divided over the imposition of prohibition—the banning of the sale and consumption of alcohol. The county seat of Athens remained a "wet" area during this period while the antiliquor "dry" forces dominated Chandler and the other small communities of Henderson County. C. R. and Nannie were strong dry supporters. Dry advocates believed that liquor contributed to the leading social ills of the day: alcoholism, crime, poverty, illiteracy, child abuse, and mental illness. During one local-option election in the county in 1909, a wet supporter complained he was "forbidden to make an anti speech in Chandler on pain of death." The liquor question remained volatile and played a major role in political life during the first two decades of the twentieth century. As an adult, Ralph refrained from drinking and led a temperate personal life long after alcohol consumption ceased to be the defining issue in the state's politics.[9]

While people eagerly debated prohibition in this era, few questioned segregation or sought to improve the plight of African Americans. Jim Crow laws held East Texans, like the rest of their southern neighbors, in an iron grip during the early twentieth century. Custom and law isolated whites from blacks in nearly every facet of life except for labor. Like many white families, the Yarboroughs employed local African Americans for domestic and farm work. During the harvest season, the Yarboroughs frequently hired several black men, provided meals, and housed them in a small structure behind the main home. African Americans in the community lived isolated in one northside neighborhood, where they attended their own churches, maintained separate schools, and coped with life as best they could. The Yarboroughs were paternalistic but not cruel in their dealings with local African Americans. They were far more concerned with prohibition and educational issues that involved their children than changing racial boundaries. But C. R. and Nannie taught their children to be tolerant, and they never participated in or condoned harsh attacks or physical violence against their African American neighbors. Though lynchings occurred frequently in many East Texas communities, none were recorded in Henderson County.[10]

Work and public affairs were important to the Yarborough boys, but so were outdoor activities. Ralph began to fish and hunt almost as soon as he could walk. Living near forests and the Neches River offered him many opportunities to appreciate nature's beauty. The boys frequently hunted ducks, which became a lifelong passion for Ralph. They fished the quiet creeks and the sandy banks of the Neches River. Wildlife was abundant in East Texas in the early 1900's, but unrestricted hunting eliminated some species altogether. One of those, the passenger pigeon, was hunted to extinction; the last recorded sighting of the passenger pigeon in the area was in 1898. A well-known hunter, Joe Boyd, interviewed by Yarborough in the 1930's, described the last time he saw the passenger pigeons: "On a cold morning in winter, there were nine of them in a peach tree facing the rising sun, with their breast feathers fluffed out against the cold. The sun shining on their red breasts made them look like nine large golden red apples in the tree. I will never forget the sight." Yarborough wrote down the account and undoubtedly added his own descriptive language. But it was the thrust of the story that was important to him. He would later recount the demise of the passenger pigeon in his Senate speeches on protecting the country's natural resources.[11]

Throughout his legal and political career, Yarborough's devotion to hunting and fishing provided a reprieve from his hectic professional life. Nearly every fall, even with an overbooked schedule, he looked forward to these expeditions with friends and family members. His concern for conservation and resource protection stayed with Yarborough. He emerged as a champion of national parks and wilderness areas, endangered species, and conservation while serving in the U.S. Senate.

Ralph began to show his leadership and oratorical skills in his teen years. The Yarboroughs raised their family in the Baptist Church. Singing schools were held for young people and Ralph became a prominent vocalist. "When Ralph was called on to lead, he led with confidence and skill, as he swung his arm and forefinger in time with the music," recalled his niece Grace Billie Presley. But at the time his voice was changing, and his father discouraged him. While his singing career never blossomed, Ralph's ability to captivate an audience with his voice had emerged.[12]

Like most boys, Ralph had a favorite dog who literally grew up with him. "Ring," a devoted dog who went hunting with the male family members, sat in the road each day waiting to greet Ralph as he came home from school. Ring lived to the ripe old age of 15. One day, Ralph found Ring under a sycamore tree in front of the house where he had quietly passed away. Although he was distraught at the passing of his favorite dog, Ralph rounded up the children in the neighborhood for a memorial service. As he laid Ring to rest in the orchard and placed flowers over his grave, Ralph praised his dog in a oration worthy of Marc Antony's praise of Caesar.

Old Ring, poor old dog, hero of ten thousand battles is dead. His life was a long and valiant one. If all the squirrels which he has treed were in a pyramid over his grave they would reach to a height of 30 feet with a 10-foot-square base. If all the opossums which he has treed and killed were in a stack they would astonish us and if all the snakes, mice, rats, gophers, and moles were in a stack and could be seen by everybody, the people out of gratitude would raise a monument over his grave. He was never known to harm a man or any domestic animal with the exception of the house cats who were his sworn foes. His service to mankind was great. Let all who pass the last resting place of this noble animal honor him.

Public speaking and the ability to sway an audience with emotion were assets that Yarborough capitalized on throughout his long career.[13]

Yarborough also developed a keen interest in the Civil War during his youth. Confederate veterans residing in Chandler during the early 1900's captivated the young Yarborough's imagination. Ralph met many participants in the war, including a private from Pickett's division at Gettysburg. The old soldier painted a vivid picture of the climatic battle. He said when the muster roll call was held the morning before the famous attack his company had sixty-three men. That evening there were only four, as all the rest were killed or wounded. Yarborough recalled words from the survivor of the famous attack: "You would hear the orders to go forward, men were falling all around, but you couldn't see much because of the smoke." Another soldier amazed Ralph when he first heard a "Rebel yell," which was "the wildest, shrieking yell that raised the hair on the back of my neck." The young Yarborough saw these elderly southern veterans as community leaders because of their military backgrounds. But he also recognized many more veterans who gave up their livelihoods in the "Lost Cause" and suffered for years from the physical and economic impact of the war. Yarborough, who later would champion the rights of military veterans as a U.S. senator, saw firsthand the problems of the former Confederate soldiers. However, his admiration for these Civil War veterans influenced Yarborough's first career decision. Following graduation from high school, Yarborough obtained an appointment to the U.S. Military Academy at West Point.[14]

THE STRUGGLE AT WEST POINT

Ralph excelled in his school work and graduated as valedictorian from the small Chandler High School in 1918 at the age of fifteen. The following year he attended Tyler High School, where he graduated from eleventh grade as salutatorian.[15] Yarborough's desire to continue his education and his infatuation with the Civil War resulted in some ambitious plans. With his father's assistance, Ralph obtained the recommendation of Congressman John Young (D-Texas) for an appointment to the U.S. Military Academy in West Point, New York. The Academy accepted him, and in August 1919 Ralph left his boyhood home for the banks of the Hudson River to join the "long gray line." Yarborough became a private, third class, in Company E under the command of Captain Freeman "Fritz" Cross, a World War I veteran. Many changes were underway at the Military Academy that year. Brigadier General Douglas MacArthur was only recently appointed superintendent of West Point. The Corps and its new leader were thrust into an uncertain situation immediately following the end of the Great War in Europe.[16]

Yarborough was a "plebe," or incoming member, initiated in the summer of 1919 by older cadets before fall classes began. These upperclassmen included many young men who had witnessed the carnage in the trenches of Europe. Alongside those veterans were new cadets like Yarborough who had never ventured more than a few miles away from their boyhood homes. Yarborough was in an early group of "Augustines," eighty new entrants who lived in the "Beast Barracks" and "toiled up the hill to renounce life, liberty, and the pursuit of snaking for a long year of Plebedom." In the first week, the young plebes learned to eat in West Point fashion (which meant sitting at rigid attention while eating), to work on police details, to salute all officers and all upperclassmen, and to "sound-off, step out, and pick up." The plebes also felt the pain of corporal punishment. Yarborough and his fellow class members spent their time at Plebe Camp learning military drills, routines, and discipline to prepare them for their years at West Point.[17]

Yarborough made it through the tough initiations of the Plebe Camp, but his tenure at the Academy lasted only one year. Yarborough never provided specific reasons for departing West Point after his freshman term. He excelled in history and in courses involving military logistics but struggled with mathematics. His decision to leave may have been based on the rigid and often abusive cadet life, the long distance from home, and a lack of exposure to advanced courses in the rural schools of East Texas. Prior to arriving at West Point, Yarborough had never left Texas, and the largest city he had experienced was Dallas. Although he excelled in the small public schools in Chandler and Tyler, he probably was not prepared for the Academy's rigid competition and discipline. Also, with a diminished role for the army in peacetime, the prospects of a professional military life might have appeared less glamorous than Yarborough previously believed.[18]

Other factors of a less personal nature may have contributed to his un-happiness at West Point. The Academy was in a "state of disorder and con-fusion" immediately after World War I. Morale problems, lack of funding, disorganization, and a hostile environment greeted MacArthur, Yarborough, and all newcomers in 1919. MacArthur wanted to revitalize and reorganize the Academy, but ran into stiff resistance on many fronts. Hazing was at its worst and a congressional investigation was underway as a result of the death of a cadet. MacArthur also wanted the curriculum to focus on the so-cial sciences in an effort to produce officers with substantial knowledge of national and world affairs. That curriculum would have suited Yarborough, who already had demonstrated interests in law, history, and government. But the new superintendent ran into resistance from the faculty, which wanted only courses on strictly military and technical subjects. MacArthur's efforts to modernize the Academy and clean up its image eventually succeeded. But the turmoil in the first year undoubtedly had a negative impact on Cadet Yarborough.[19]

Later in his life, Yarborough appreciated his one year of education and training at West Point. This background helped him gain a better position as an army officer in World War II. Unlike his childhood, the months at West Point and the next two years were not days Yarborough remembered with great fondness. To him, as to many other young people, the years immedi-ately following the horror of World War I were a time of readjustment and uncertainty. In retrospect, his decision to leave West Point signaled a depar-ture from his childhood dreams of a military career and forced him to look at other alternatives for which he was better suited.

TO EUROPE AND BACK

After leaving West Point, Yarborough returned to Chandler in the sum-mer of 1920. However, employment prospects there were almost nonexistent. He left to work in the wheat fields of Oklahoma and later that summer found a job in a flour mill in Enid. Returning home in the fall, he hoped to find a better opportunity. Luck was on his side, for a local school needed a teacher. The nearby Delta Common School District trustees offered him a job at their one-teacher school for one school term on the condition that he obtain his state teaching certificate. After a summer in the scorching wheat fields, working in a school with a roof over his head undoubtedly had great appeal. The Delta board members knew that Yarborough had left West Point but were willing to take a gamble on him. Yarborough and his family were well known and he had an excellent reputation in school. He passed the Second Grade exams on the first attempt and earned his First Grade Certificate a mere four weeks later. Yarborough made a "decent salary" of $125 per month while teaching in the one-room school for the six-month term. There Yarborough discovered the challenges and the pleasures of working in an underfunded yet relatively independent atmosphere. His experience was quite similar to that of Lyndon Johnson, who began his career teaching in a small, rural school in South Texas.[20]

Yarborough discovered he enjoyed teaching and receiving a regular paycheck, so he decided to enroll in Sam Houston State Teachers College in Huntsville. Although it was the middle of the term in the spring of 1921, Yarborough persuaded college officials to admit him. (The credits he earned at the college eventually would apply toward admission to the University of Texas Law School in Austin.) But as the session at Sam Houston drew to a close, Yarborough once again decided to look for another job. While attending classes at Sam Houston, he had encountered many war veterans who served in Europe. These veterans told Yarborough that he could attend universities in France without any credentials from American colleges or high school. At the age of nineteen, Yarborough decided to forsake teaching and join Ernest Hemingway, F. Scott Fitzgerald, and thousands of other Americans of the "lost generation" who went to Europe in the early 1920's. Obtaining his passport, Yarborough left Huntsville for Galveston, where he boarded a ship for New Orleans. There he found a job on the French liner *Missouri* bound for Le Havre, France, by way of Wilmington, North Carolina. The freighter carried cotton but also transported beef. Yarborough took advantage of his background and Texas accent. He wangled a job taking care of the cattle to pay for his passage to Europe.[21]

Yarborough arrived in Le Havre in October 1921. He first went to Paris, where he attempted to enroll at the Sorbonne, but the university would not accept him because he was not fluent in French. After viewing the sights of Paris, Yarborough decided to move on as the cost of living in the French capital had nearly exhausted his meager funds. He heard that he could find work in Germany, so he purchased a ticket on the Paris-Berlin Express. But on the train he discovered that prices in Berlin were the same as in Paris and New York—very high. When the train stopped the next day in the town of Stendhal, Germany, Yarborough found that it reminded him of Austin. Many Germans remained hostile to foreign visitors from victorious nations, "but they did not take it out on a stray American," Yarborough recalled.[22]

Yarborough found a Stendhal home with room and board for $5 per month. He went to a private school for eight months, where he became fluent in German. One day he found *Transatlantic Trade,* an English-language magazine published in Berlin by the U.S. Chamber of Commerce. The United States still had not recognized the German government, and the Chamber of Commerce served as its unofficial embassy. Yarborough wrote the Chamber to place an ad seeking employment in the magazine. The editor of the publication saw his letter and offered Yarborough a position. "I went to Berlin and was employed to proofread all the magazines and letters they sent out in English," he recalled. For the first half of 1922, Yarborough lived in Berlin with an elderly German couple who also worked at the magazine. Within six months, Yarborough decided he longed for East Texas. After receiving money from his father, he resigned his position and departed for London, where he found work on a ship bound for America. Once again his Texas background helped him find a job, for he worked his way to New York on a boat loaded with polo ponies. "After all, once they found out I was from Texas, they just assumed I knew how to handle horses," the young traveler confessed.[23]

The journey to Europe opened the world to Yarborough. He witnessed firsthand the depravations of war and the sufferings of a conquered people. He saw the economic, social, and political chaos that gripped Europe and especially Germany in the early 1920's. He came to know of the bitterness many Europeans felt about the slaughter and political outcome of World War I. The time he spent in Europe as a young man undoubtedly brought home to him the widespread hardships and sufferings of people. Texas had its own poverty, racism, and poor living conditions, but even these conditions sometimes paled in comparison to the problems Europeans faced in the aftermath of "the war to end all wars." His experiences in war-ravaged Europe and later military service on the Continent during World War II provided Yarborough with a unique perspective which strongly influenced his future political decisions.

"I WON'T MARRY A MAN IN POLITICS"

After Yarborough returned from Europe, he once again went back home to Chandler. In August 1922, the Delta Common School trustees were again looking for a teacher. He signed a contract to teach the 1922–1923 term at the one-room school for the same amount he previously earned—$125 per month. Yarborough passed his exam for a permanent teacher's certificate. While teaching at the Delta school, he made a decision which changed his life. He applied to the University of Texas Law School and was accepted in the spring of 1923. The following September Yarborough moved to Austin. Remaining in law school and completing the coursework would prove to be a challenge. Upon completing his first year of courses, Yarborough hoped to find a job with an Austin law firm. He was unsuccessful so once again he fell back on teaching in East Texas. In the fall of 1924, the Martin Springs School trustees offered Yarborough a position to serve as a teacher and as the principal for 120 students in grades one through nine. Yarborough along with one other teacher instructed students at the school, where he earned enough money that school year to return to his studies at the University of Texas Law School.[24]

In 1926, Yarborough still had not finished law school and was "broke again." Instead of returning to classroom teaching, he decided on another job. He went to the Panhandle town of Borger, the site of one of the great Texas oil strikes of the early twentieth century and as wild and dangerous as any boomtown. He quickly discovered that many men had been killed on the derricks. "I decided to spend the summer of 1926 working with a crew that built heavy oil-storage tanks, and I saved my money," he said. Recalling the excitement of the time, Yarborough remembered that "wells ran wide open and fires were common. Fights, brawls, drunkenness, and murder were common in the streets." The experience hastened his desire to return to law school and complete his degree. The Borger experience, his many different jobs, and his stay in Europe broadened Yarborough's knowledge of the world. He understood hard work, but he realized that working from sunup to sundown did not necessarily give a person wealth or security. These early years of manual labor and teaching in the small, rural public schools left lifelong impressions on him. The immediate impact was to push the eager Yarborough back to law school. He decided that wandering from town to town hoping for employment was no way to live. His older brother Harvey, who had preceded Ralph at the University of Texas Law School, encouraged him to complete his degree. Harvey, or H. J. as Ralph sometimes called him, served as a mentor to his younger brother in this instance and on many future occasions.[25]

Back in law school in the fall of 1926, Yarborough finally seemed to hit his stride. He was active in a number of organizations in his final year, having joined the Acacia fraternity, the Rusk Literary Society, and the McLaurin Law Society. The Rusk Literary Society was one of the largest and most visible forensic organizations on campus. The forty-three members of the group met each Saturday night to discuss topics ranging from economics and education to law and politics. Prominent Texans previously in the organization included U.S. Senator Morris Sheppard and Governor Pat Neff. Among those participating with Yarborough in the Rusk Literary Society was fellow classmate Percy Foreman, who eventually became a nationally known trial attorney. Foreman was the Rusk Literary Society president and Yarborough its vice president. Active participation in the literary society with some of the most competitive and articulate students on campus increased Yarborough's oratorical skills and his ability to think on his feet. Yarborough completed his coursework and graduated with Highest Honors from the Law School in 1927.[26]

Because of a lack of money, Yarborough borrowed from a number of sources to finance his law school tenure. But neither was the University of Texas wealthy in the early 1920's. Prior to the discovery of oil on university lands, the college relied on funds appropriated from the state legislature and on tuition from its students. Yarborough recalled that "many of the classes met in wooden shacks, built over the campus for emergency military classes in World War I," and he especially admired those professors who labored under difficult circumstances with little pay. He recognized that professors' salaries were insufficient and some left for other universities outside the state. "But most of the best ones were imbued with Texas, with a love for her history and culture, and put love of teaching here above the lure of more money at other places," he observed. Yarborough believed that strong personal commitment to a profession combined with hard work were necessities for success.[27]

Yarborough passed his exams and was admitted to the State Bar in September 1927. However, even more important to Yarborough, was his decision to marry. Yarborough returned to East Texas and married his longtime sweetheart, Opal Warren. Opal, the same age as Ralph, lived near Yarborough's home when the two were children. She and her family moved away when Opal was seven years old, but the Warrens returned to the area for her high school years when her father, Frank, became a local school superintendent. Opal and Ralph attended Tyler High School and graduated together. When

Ralph Yarborough as he appeared at the time of his 1927 graduation from the University of Texas Law School. Courtesy Opal Yarborough.

he returned to teach school in Henderson County, the relationship between the two became more serious. They became engaged in 1925 and remained so for three years, until he finished law school. "Next to being born, that was really the most important event of my life," Yarborough said.[28]

Opal was an intelligent woman and influenced Yarborough's decision to finish law school. With his engagement to her, Yarborough finally became serious about finishing his legal education and settling into a profession which would provide the couple a permanent home and a bright future. During their engagement, Ralph and Opal discussed his future as an attorney. He briefly considered entering politics and running for county attorney in Henderson County. Surprisingly, of the fifty-three University of Texas Law School graduates in 1927, three were from Yarborough's home of Henderson County. His two classmates hailed from Athens, the Henderson County seat and largest community, and both promptly announced for county attorney upon graduation. Analyzing the situation, Yarborough felt his chances of winning the office were slim because Chandler was a small town in the extreme northeastern part of the county. He also had no money so "it was extremely unlikely that I would prevail in any contest when they would presumably be well financed out of Athens." [29]

Political and financial considerations were important to Yarborough. But the most influential opinion came from Opal, who strongly objected to the race: "If you run, the wedding is off. I won't marry a man in politics." Love quickly overcame Yarborough's early passion for politics. Following the decision, the couple exchanged vows on June 30, 1928, in a ceremony at the Third Avenue Presbyterian Church in the nearby community of Corsicana, where members of both families could attend. They didn't have a wedding picture taken, but they had a Kodak camera and took individual pictures of each other. "The Yellow Rose of Texas" and "Tea for Two" were the songs the couple played over and over again during their honeymoon. Ralph had accepted his first position with the law firm of Turney, Burges, Culwell & Pollard in the border city of El Paso with a strong recommendation from Law School dean Ira P. Hildebrand, who noted that the El Paso firm offered a higher salary than firms in other cities. Since the young graduate was in debt and married, he wanted to work with a firm that could provide a higher salary than those in Houston or Dallas that offered $50 per month in starting salary. Yarborough readily accepted the offer of $150 per month and became the first law school graduate from Austin to work for the firm. His marriage to Opal and his new profession gave him a renewed sense of confidence, and his love for Opal and his commitment to the law would help him through many difficult times in the years ahead. [30]

As the newest attorney in the firm, Yarborough received the routine justice and county courts cases. He assisted the senior attorneys in district court cases and worked probate, titles, and mortgages. El Paso and the law firm were an abrupt change for Yarborough, who had spent so many years at so many different jobs. He had his own office and secretary, and the different types of lawsuits appealed to his broad interests in many subject areas. He took on a large number of assignments, worked long hours, and showed great enthusiasm for pursuing individual cases. His three years in El Paso also enabled him to become familiar with the people and the arid lands of Far West Texas. On weekends, he and Opal often traveled hundreds of miles to the cooler air of the Davis Mountains or to gaze at the majestic Guadalupe Mountains on the New Mexico border.[31] Years later Yarborough would sponsor legislation that made the Guadalupe Mountains a national park.

Yarborough's work on one land case served as a catapult for his career. W. W. Turney, a senior member of the firm, chose Yarborough to assist him in a major land ownership suit involving the Rio Grande, an ever-changing river. As the river altered its course, both the State of Texas and the United States would issue patents on what turned out to be the same tract of land. In the case that became known as *Crawford v. White*, Turney represented Z. T. White and other claimants with the Texas patents. While the case was being heard in court, Turney suffered a heart attack mid-trial. However, the judge refused to allow a postponement. That forced Yarborough, then a twenty-six-year-old junior attorney, to the forefront of the complex case. He studied the case for one night, finished the trial for Turney, and received a favorable verdict for their Texas clients on the point that in 1850 the Rio Grande boundary was set as a fixed boundary. However, the decision was appealed and the Texas Legislature also intervened. This unexpected chain of events pushed Yarborough into a new arena which changed his life and the future of Texas. He left for Austin to appear before the new attorney general of Texas, James V. Allred.[32]

James Allred had just taken office as Texas attorney general after winning it in 1930. Prior to his election, Allred had been a Wichita Falls district attorney who built his reputation on prosecution of corrupt public officials, the Ku Klux Klan, and bootleggers. He was known for his honesty and integrity. Allred had run an unsuccessful campaign for attorney general in 1926 but in the 1930 Democratic primary he won his race against the incumbent, Robert Bobbitt, whom Governor Dan Moody had appointed the previous year to fill a vacancy in the office. Yarborough had been a student of Robert Bobbitt's brother Frank in law school and supported Robert Bobbitt in his unsuccessful election campaign.

A few weeks after Allred took office, Yarborough appeared in Austin to testify before a legislative committee on the Rio Grande case. He delivered his testimony to State Representative Coke Stevenson's Public Lands Committee. After completing his presentation, Chairman Stevenson informed him that he needed to present his case to Attorney General Allred, who would decide on its constitutionality. Stevenson had political aspirations of his own and declined to make a decision on the controversy, a trait for which he would become well known when he served as governor during the 1940's. Yarborough made the trek to the attorney general's office to discuss the case. Upon completing his presentation to Allred, Yarborough believed he had won the argument. But Attorney General Allred told him he would take it "under advisement until the next morning." The following day, Allred told Yarborough that he supported the young attorney's position on the land case. After the decision, Yarborough said the attorney general took him aside "as he had another matter that he wanted to discuss." Informing Yarborough that he was aware Yarborough had been a "Bobbitt man" in the previous election, Allred then offered the young attorney a position in the Attorney General's office. Yarborough's legal presentation and his knowledge had made a dramatic impact on the new attorney general, who needed young, aggressive lawyers for his agency.[33]

Yarborough quickly accepted the offer, with Opal's agreement. He returned to El Paso and announced his decision to the law firm partners. With the blessings of his law firm, the Yarboroughs left for Austin and a new career. He was only twenty-eight years old when he joined Allred's staff on April 1, 1931. In the span of a few years, Yarborough had matured from an uncertain but promising young law student into a competent and forceful attorney. Yarborough worked long and hard for nearly four years for Attorney General Allred and became one of Allred's strongest supporters. The assignment also began a lifelong friendship and political association that involved Yarborough in statewide Democratic politics. The difficulties Yarborough encountered on the road from Chandler to Austin never left his memory. He made a dramatic recovery and came a long way after his childhood dream of a military career unceremoniously ended. While his journey during the years of uncertainty before his marriage and becoming an attorney often seemed aimless, the variety of jobs he held—from teaching in one-room schools to sweating in the hot Borger sun and writing amid the destruction in Europe—provided Yarborough with firsthand knowledge he never could have learned in the classroom. He knew the struggle of thousands of others who, as he had, daily faced the challenge of providing a substantial meal and adequate clothes for their families. Yarborough also came to understand clearly the shortcomings of the state's educational system and the lack of economic opportunity for Texans and other southerners. Yarborough's experiences planted images in his mind that he kept with him as he entered the Attorney General's office in Austin in 1931. The seeds of Yarborough's vision would soon mature under the guidance of Texas Attorney General James Allred.

2 The Million-Dollar Victory

Texans possessed a long tradition of strong suspicion when it came to large corporations, monopolies, and out of state businesses. This lack of trust dated back to the Republic of Texas and continued through the Populist era of the late nineteenth century. Public acceptance of business increased somewhat in the next century with the economic expansion during World War I and the boom of the 1920's. However, after 1929, as the national economy and personal fortunes declined with the onset of the Great Depression, people quickly began to move away from the idea that business and the economic cycle should direct the economy. More Americans believed their elected officials and the government had a special responsibility to respond to the economic downturn. In Texas, people began to look to their state government to respond and to protect citizens from businesses which many perceived as the primary culprits for the economic depression. Despite the discovery of oil and increased urbanization, Texas was still a rural, agricultural state in tradition and outlook. Although the state's urban population rose during the 1920's and new businesses and services increased, agricultural products, livestock, and oil and gas and other raw materials were the primary components of the state's economy. Texans retained a large measure of the populist, anti-corporation sentiments rooted in its past.

These old attitudes quickly resurfaced after 1930, when the economic downturn became a reality and not just a newspaper headline. At the national level, the tide turned against President Herbert Hoover as people realized the depression was getting worse. In Texas, Governor Ross Sterling stood by as one crisis after another hit the state. Tax revenues fell for the state and all local governments. Independent and local-government relief efforts could not keep up with the increased demands. Crime was on the rise, banks failed, and unemployment demonstrations began to occur in some Texas cities. Pleas for greater state support grew as unemployment increased and private businesses laid off workers and reduced wages. The economic hardships created by the depression opened the door for many political aspirants in Texas who sought to use government as the mechanism to regulate and stimulate the private sector economy. Foremost among them in Texas was James Allred as he rode into the Attorney General's office in April 1931.

Allred brought with him a group of attorneys who believed in this aggressive agenda. Ralph Yarborough emerged as an outspoken proponent for Attorney General Allred's enforcement against business abuses. As Texas attorney general from 1931 to 1935, Allred challenged many large corporations yet built a strong base of support among smaller, independent businessmen, two years in advance of Franklin Roosevelt's New Deal. Allred focused on the growing oil industry in Texas. Large corporations and smaller independent companies fought heated battles over oil and gas rights as new discoveries spurred growth in all phases of the industry. The state's efforts in these disputes, which included the fight to protect mineral rights on public lands, fell to the Attorney General's office. Its decisions played a large part in shaping the future political careers of both James Allred and Ralph Yarborough.

Allred's background was similar to Yarborough's. The son of a rural mail carrier and family farmer, Allred grew up in the small East Texas community of Bowie. As a young student he manned a shoe-shine stand in a barber shop and worked in a soda-pop bottling company and the local newspaper office. After graduation from high school Allred enlisted in the navy and after his discharge moved to Wichita Falls, where he worked for an attorney and began reading law. Allred left Wichita Falls to attend Cumberland University in Tennessee. He returned to Texas with a law degree and was admitted to the bar in 1921. Governor Pat Neff appointed Allred the Wichita Falls district attorney in 1924. There he became known as the "fighting district attorney" for his opposition to the Ku Klux Klan.[1]

Allred gained recognition for his drive, energy, intelligence, and public appeal. Yarborough and others described him as a leader who inspired intense devotion among his followers. Allred was not afraid to challenge some of the most powerful corporate powers in the state. He openly attacked the "special interests"—the business lobbyists who wielded immense influence over state government in Austin. Allred supported the broader mission of the Roosevelt administration and the New Deal, but he frequently opposed federal intervention in Texas, especially when it involved the oil industry. Allred believed that economic recovery during the 1930's depression depended on the creation of new opportunities for small businesses. From a practical standpoint, his stance helped him gain the support of the many independent oil producers and landowners. Allred staked his career on his ability to fight monopolies and promote competition in an open market. These ideas also formed the core of Yarborough's political beliefs. In adopting the Allred stance, Yarborough gained insight from the attorney general and later surpassed his mentor in putting these beliefs into practice.[2]

Linking his political and professional fortunes with Allred was an important decision for Yarborough. The first glimpse of Ralph Yarborough as a liberal reformer on public policy issues emerged during his four years as an assistant attorney general. The oil boom of the 1920's and 1930's brought prosperity to many but also introduced new problems for Texas. Yarborough assumed a number of controversial cases concerning state properties in which millions of dollars were at stake for Texas. The acreage that many once viewed as useless held immense untapped wealth in its underground petroleum assets. In Yarborough's mind, attempts to wrest the minerals from the state were especially odious because the money derived from them ultimately went for public education. From this point forward, Yarborough saw himself as a defender of the public interest and an education proponent.

CHALLENGING THE OIL AND GAS COMPANIES

Texas was unique among all the states in the union in that it retained so much of its public lands. Although Texas gave away or sold off most of the public lands by 1900 to encourage settlement and construct railroads, the state still held title to about one million acres of surface lands and slightly more than seven million acres of subsurface or mineral lands. In 1900, the Texas Legislature dedicated all lands remaining in the public domain to the Permanent School Fund. The General Land Office and its elected commissioner administered these public lands. The Land Office maintained responsibility for leases it issued and the income from these public-school lands. However, the Attorney General's office took responsibility for any lawsuits involving the public domain, so that when the law was unclear or other conflicts arose, the land commissioner sought legal opinions from the attorney general.[3]

By the 1930's, the issue of the oil industry and its impact on other Texas businesses vaulted to the forefront of the economic and political scene. During the 1920's, a number of strikes had increased oil production in Texas. With the discovery of the great East Texas oil field in the early 1930's, a flood of petroleum came onto the market. Production from the East Texas field alone amounted to one-third of the oil produced in the nation. The price declined to pennies a barrel, though, as supply quickly overwhelmed demand. With the collapse in the oil market, many operators ignored the Texas Railroad Commission and court orders in their efforts to stabilize the situation. Protracted litigation and fights between major oil companies and independent producers erupted. Governor Ross Sterling placed the East Texas oil field under martial law and sent the Texas National Guard to maintain order, until a federal court ruled in February 1931 that he acted without authority. By 1933, after several special legislative sessions, the Railroad Commission obtained the right to set production limits through the practice of proration, a government action to conserve the oil in the reservoir and to maintain a market price. Yarborough was first involved in "hot oil" cases (oil produced over the mandated allowable), but Allred soon placed him into another hot spot.[4]

In addition to the disputes in the East Texas fields, the other major action in Allred's office involved the state's control over the mineral interests and the income from millions of acres of public lands. The vast majority of this state-owned land remained in the sparsely populated, arid western counties of Texas. Once oil was discovered on these lands by private corporations and individuals, petroleum became the primary revenue source for the public schools. Royalties (a percentage paid to the land- or royalty-owner), bonuses (additional proceeds paid to the land- or royalty-owner for a successful well), rentals, and other receipts from oil and gas production on state-owned lands were deposited in the Permanent School Fund. The contribution was especially significant in a state that had never adequately funded its public schools and relied on ad valorem taxes to finance them. Instead of thousands of dollars, millions began flowing annually into the fund.[5]

Retaining income for the Permanent School Fund was not always simple because of competing political interests. In 1919, the state legislature attempted to change the policy by which the state administered its mineral-classified lands—properties where the state had sold the surface but retained the mineral rights. Many problems arose where private individuals owned the surface acreage while the state owned the subsurface minerals. Once oil was discovered, landowners persistently challenged the often inaccurate surveys and the existing laws, actions which endangered the state's title to the minerals. The state legislature passed the Relinquishment Act of 1919, which all but gave away the state's rights to the mineral lands. However, the Texas Supreme Court subsequently ruled that the legislature could not give away the assets of the School Funds and that the state should retain a 50-percent interest in the mineral lands. In order to undermine that decision, the major oil companies in Texas and many landowners attempted new actions to limit the state's interest to royalties alone and to specifically exclude bonuses and rentals from the 50-percent formula.

To counter this interpretation, Yarborough authored a 1932 attorney general's opinion which held that the state was entitled to one-half of all bonus and rental payments on the state's mineral lands—the same amount the court set forth in the decision on royalties. The memo provided not just the state's legal justification for the income but also preserved a significant portion of the state's interests in the valuable properties. Yarborough argued that the state maintained both a legal and a moral obligation to retain the ownership because the funds involved the Permanent School Fund and the school children of Texas. He noted that once oil production from these public holdings ceased, the only future benefits that remained would be the income earned from the principle of these funds. "A vigorous, fighting attorney general can render a more real service in public land suits than in any other one capacity," Yarborough maintained in his official opinion. He warned that the state's interests could literally be drained out from under the most valuable oil lands in only a few years. Allred agreed with Yarborough's position and stood firm on the 50 percent formula for all revenues from the land. Soon, many large landowners and oil company representatives descended on the attorney general's office and demanded that Allred "withdraw the opinion, fire the man who wrote it, and assign it to someone else to write who could see the light of day." Allred refused and stood by Yarborough's decision. The following year, Yarborough authored a similar opinion stating that the bonus and rental income from University lands should receive the same consideration as the Permanent School Fund lands, thus saving hundreds of millions of dollars for what eventually became the University of Texas System and the Texas A&M System.[6]

At the same time he was working on these far-reaching decisions, Yarborough took on a number of high-profile court cases for Allred. Some of these significant cases involved "vacant" lands in the Yates Oil Field in a sparse and nearly inaccessible location near the Pecos River in Far West Texas. A vacancy occurred as a result of surveying errors which essentially left untitled land between two or more surveyed tracts. This "vacant" land legally belonged to the state. But as a matter of practice, many of the vacancies were literally landlocked within the holdings of private owners, who used them without ever purchasing or leasing the property from the state. Others purchased vacancy tracts at a minimal price. In 1920, a few years before the oil strike in the Yates Field, the State of Texas sold two tracts comprising 3,593 surface acres of "vacant" land to Ira Yates for $3 per acre. In the Yates transaction, the state retained all of the mineral interests. The state also sold a number of other nearby tracts, some with the minerals and some without. As a result, both the state and numerous private landowners retained thousands of subsurface acres of mineral interest in a checkerboard manner. The inexpensive land suddenly became extremely valuable when the first oil wells began producing.

Ira Yates, a successful West Texas rancher, owned thousands of acres along the Pecos River, land that many believed the buffalo once refused to cross and the crows still refused to fly over. Most experts of the day never believed oil could be found as far west as Yates' ranch. But when the first wildcat well came in on October 26, 1926, Yates began selling leases from his front porch and became an instant millionaire. The Mid-Kansas Oil and Gas Company and the Transcontinental Oil Company obtained leases from Yates and brought in additional wells that raised production to over 9,000 barrels. By 1929, over 175 wells in the Yates Field produced over 41 million barrels of oil, making it one of the most prolific oil discoveries in the world. One of these individual mineral owners in the Yates Field, Fred Turner Jr., filed suit in district court of Pecos County in an effort to gain control of contested vacant lands and the valuable minerals. The district court declared that portions of the entire property were vacant land, but the decision was overturned by the El Paso Court of Civil Appeals. Attorney General Allred inherited the case when he took office in 1931. Texas Land Commissioner J. H. Walker explained to Allred that the state would suffer a considerable loss if the decision favored the private owners. Ironically, the state could actually gain land with no mineral rights but would lose lands with proven production. Walker told Allred the issue "will be decisive of nearly all the other cases involving lands in the Yates field." Because the contested area had already produced millions of barrels of oil by early 1931, the attorney general and land commissioner agreed that the royalty money would disappear forever if the state delayed the case.[7]

Allred assigned Yarborough to serve as the state's lead attorney. In July 1933 Yarborough filed in Travis County District Court cases against the Mid-Kansas Oil and Gas Company, Fred Turner, and other parties for title, possession, damages, royalties, and half of a "fair bonus" from the contested vacancy. The Mid-Kansas well, located in the richest part of the Yates field and pumping 200,000 barrels per day, was reputed to be the largest producing well in its day. Yarborough estimated that the Permanent School Fund's royalty interest in the Yates oil field was "more valuable than its royalty interest in all the rest of its proven Permanent School Fund oil land in Texas." Land Commissioner Walker estimated the value of the property to be $20 million. Yarborough believed the total was much higher, between $300 million and $600 million. Ultimately, Yarborough's estimate was prophetic—by 1989 the Yates Field had yielded over one billion barrels of oil, making it one of the largest sustained producers in the world.[8]

On September 23, 1933, District Judge J. D. Moore of Travis County entered a judgment of $1,073,500 against the Mid-Kansas Oil and Gas Company. Allred quickly proclaimed the state's victory "the largest money judgment every secured in a land case" when it made statewide headlines. The award was second only to the $1.6 million judgment secured for Texas in 1900 in the famous Waters-Pierce antitrust case. Of the 551 acres recovered in the settlement, approximately 520 acres were "proven oil land." The judgment included $700,000 in bonus money and retention of $^1/_{16}$ royalty for the state in all future production. At the time of the decision, the balance of the entire Permanent School Fund was slightly more than $40 million; thus the Mid-Kansas check represented a sizable increase to it. Notably, in the agency's press release, Allred specifically praised Yarborough's role in the monumental decision. To illustrate the impact of the decision, Yarborough declared that in 1933 more royalty money came to the Permanent School Fund from the Yates Field than from all other oil fields combined.[9]

The historic decision brought Allred and Yarborough widespread praise since the million-dollar settlement for the state generated another million dollars worth of publicity for the two. Coverage by the *Dallas Morning News,* the *Houston Chronicle,* and other leading pro-business newspapers in Texas indicated the importance of these suits and of the ongoing struggle over the future of the oil and gas industry. Editorials praised the attorney general for his "diligence" and contribution to public education. Houston Harte, publisher of the *San Angelo Standard Times,* stated that the victories by the Attorney General's office had an effect that extended far beyond the oil fields. Harte sensed a change in the public mood from one of deep pessimism to a more hopeful outlook. "We know that during the last few years people have lost confidence in each other," Harte noted. "They have lost confidence in banks, they have lost confidence in law enforcement, and up until the time that you [Yarborough] intervened in the Whiteside case [an earlier case involving the Yates Oil Field] many of us had lost confidence in the integrity of the State itself." In a reply to Harte, Yarborough stated that West Texas oil producers noted the price for crude oil improved following the decision. Knowing that the state attorney general was actively and successfully prosecuting cases undoubtedly resulted in more honest business transactions in the unstable oilfield economy. "I think we are making progress in the right direction, though we have considerable territory yet to cover," Yarborough explained.[10]

Other notable law suits Yarborough was directly involved in during this period addressed disputes with Humble Oil Company, Texas-Pacific Railroad, Phillips Petroleum Company, Shell Petroleum Company, and a number of small oil companies. All of these cases involved title disputes ultimately resolved by settlements or rulings by Texas courts that resulted in a victories for the state. During Allred's two terms as attorney general, the coffers of the Permanent School Fund continued to grow, as did his political reputation. Yarborough was in the middle of many of the widely publicized cases involving land and oil.[11]

Yarborough also directed suits for the attorney general against oil companies on behalf of the Permanent University Fund, the trust which provided money for his alma mater, the University of Texas. One of the most significant cases involved the state's attempt to recover royalty money. Similar to the Permanent School Fund, the Permanent University Fund drew its income from surface and mineral lands reserved as a trust for the benefit of the University of Texas and, after 1934, Texas A&M University. Prior to the 1920's, the fund's annual income came almost entirely from grazing leases issued by the Board of Regents. After oil production began on university lands in 1924, the situation changed dramatically as hundreds of thousands of dollars in royalties and fees came from the sparsely populated West Texas lands. R. L. Holliday, a member of the Board of Regents at the University of Texas in the early 1930's, closely followed the attorney general's intervention on behalf of the Permanent School Fund. Holliday suspected similar problems on the university-owned lands in West Texas. In a 1932 letter to the attorney general, Holliday complained about oil production reports from the Big Lake Field in Reagan County. Production was "well below the quantity of oil the producing companies are under contract to sell, and is costing the University several hundreds of dollars daily." In response to Holliday's request for redress of the situation, the attorney general assigned the case to Yarborough. In *The State of Texas v Reagan County Purchasing Company, Inc.*, the state claimed $575,000 for underpayment of royalties from the Big Lake wells.[12]

The eight oil companies named in the suit attempted to have the trial moved from Austin to Fort Worth in the hope of gaining a more favorable hearing. However, Yarborough argued against the move and succeeded in keeping the trial in Travis County. In preparing the university's case, Yarborough believed that the companies' method of averaging did not produce the "fair market price" as stipulated in the contract. The trial court and the Court of Appeals ruled in favor of the state. The Texas Supreme Court upheld the Reagan County case for the state and the university. Allred once again singled out Yarborough in the press release announcing the victory. The Reagan County suit generated as much news coverage in the state's newspapers as those over the Yates Field. Like the public school cases, the decision ultimately brought in hundreds of millions of dollars, this time to the Permanent University Fund.[13]

Yarborough's description of his effort on the Reagan County case offers insight into his work ethic. While preparing the case, he explained to his brother Harvey that many hours went into the 316-page transcript and the 715-page statement of fact. "I wrote an 85 page brief, cutting it down as much as I could, and even then I had to ignore about half of their propositions in order to keep the brief within the bounds of reason," the young assistant attorney general wrote in his letter. When C. R. wrote to Yarborough congratulating his son on the victory, he praised him for confronting the best politically connected attorneys in the state who "left no chip unturned to win their case." He told his son that "it demonstrates beyond question that you have acquired some ability in your chosen profession, for which I am very proud, indeed." The correspondence is indicative of the close ties that Yarborough retained with his older brother and father and which he maintained for years to come. Ralph counted on his older brother and father for timely advice, both legal and political.[14]

THE MAGNOLIA CASE AND MILLIONS FOR TEXAS SCHOOLS

The legal victories in the Yates Field and Reagan County cases were monumental and far reaching. These actions prepared Yarborough for the landmark case of *Magnolia v Walker*. Yarborough defended Land Commissioner Walker and the state in district court and before the Texas Supreme Court from 1933 to 1935. The final arguments before the state supreme court in February 1935 marked Yarborough's final appearance representing the Attorney General's office. He was already in private practice by early 1935 as Allred occupied the governor's office following his election victory in November 1934. In the final arguments, Yarborough was assisting the new attorney general, William McCraw.[15]

The Magnolia case began when the Magnolia Oil Company, a subsidiary of the Standard Oil Company of New York, leased thousands of acres from a private landowner. The state owned the minerals in one section of the land involved in the Magnolia lease, but Magnolia claimed that the state was not entitled to any bonus or rental proceeds because the land was acquired through the Forfeiture and Repurchase Acts of 1925 and 1926. However, Land Commissioner J. H. Walker challenged the company's position and canceled their lease for Magnolia's failure to pay one-half of the bonus and rentals due the state from production on the site. Magnolia then sued Walker and the state, and the land commissioner turned the case over to the Attorney General's office. Magnolia representatives and other oil company attorneys pressured Allred (then still attorney general) to side with them on the dispute and settle the case without a trial. After meeting with the private attorneys, Allred called on Yarborough, who advised the attorney general to pursue the case. Allred agreed and gave the case to Yarborough.[16]

In defending the land commissioner's actions, Yarborough maintained that the purchaser acquired the surface land but never obtained title to the minerals. This made the surface owner the state's agent on all payment issues. Magnolia attorneys countered that no portion of the contract between the surface owner and the lessee was reserved to the state, so the company believed that all bonus and rental fees went to the surface owner, who also was entitled to all royalties except the one-sixteenth royalty reserved for the state. The supreme court ruled that the state never intended for a private landowner to obtain the mineral rights and that the state also maintained its interests and percentage of the royalties. The court sided with Yarborough and declared that even when the state provided surface owners of mineral-classified lands a share of the income, the landowners were responsible because the state had no other way to enforce its leasing provisions. Yarborough said years after the case that it was the state's intent to obtain assistance from the landowner. "It was not the intent to give away half of the value otherwise accruing to the Permanent School Fund. . . . the surface owner was burdened with many continuing duties under the Act—he was not a mere free-loader," Yarborough explained.[17]

The decision affected not just this one lease, but the additional four million acres of public school lands. Estimates of the total value of the decision to the state in 1935 were placed at $20 million. The *Austin American* announced, "Oil Millions Awarded to Texas Schools by Supreme Court Ruling," and acknowledged Yarborough's role: "Ralph Yarborough . . . said he was unable to estimate the ultimate revenue that would accrue to the school fund, but believed it would approximate $20,000,000." Although the state did not receive a million-dollar check as in the Mid-Kansas settlement, this decision had an even larger impact, which few people realized in 1935. Yarborough and others in state government estimated the award to be approximately $20 million. In reality, the decision brought in far more. Instead of tens of millions, the agreement ultimately resulted in billions of dollars from the state-owned mineral lands. This monumental victory literally rivaled other major court decisions made in the United States in this century. The case made Yarborough the first "billion dollar attorney" in the state. From the mid-1930's onward, payments made into the Permanent School Fund brought in hundreds of millions of dollars until the fund exceeded $8 billion by the 1990's.[18]

The decision cemented Yarborough's reputation as one of the premier land attorneys in the state. Executives of the major oil companies also had taken note. Yarborough's victory occurred just after he left the Attorney General's office to enter private practice. C. R. Yarborough told his son that the *Magnolia* case would have a measurable impact on his career. "It means a great deal to you. It establishes your ability as a lawyer, not only in this State, but through out the nation. The most prominent lawyers over the nation will know about it, as well as a great many of the citizens." He added that the state should have paid him at least $10,000 and "if the legislature had any appreciation for what had been done for the schools of this State, they would make an appropriation to that effect. But of course, they won't do that." The words of praise were not surprising coming from a proud father who recognized his son's accomplishments and ability, but he also understood the long-lasting benefits to Texas, which traditionally short-changed public school funding.[19]

These cases and others during Yarborough's four years in the Attorney General's Office laid the foundations for the modern Permanent School Fund and the Permanent University Fund. They also enhanced Yarborough's legal skills and nourished his desire for involvement in state politics. Even though he was widely praised for his actions, Yarborough knew that these decisions, especially the Magnolia case, earned him the unrelenting hostility of the oil industry. The Mid-Kansas and the Magnolia cases became topics of subsequent political campaigns for Yarborough and Allred. During the 1980's, after his long political career had ended, Yarborough was still working on lawsuits involving the Yates Oil Field and the Permanent School Fund as a practicing attorney.[20]

In the course of his tenure at the Attorney General's office, Yarborough authored a number of official opinions to state officials which also had far-reaching effects. One of these was a 1934 decision on the offshore lands in the Gulf of Mexico which preserved the state's interests in those properties.

Land Commissioner Walker sought an opinion from the Attorney General's office following a request for an application to lease submerged land near Beaumont. The acreage was near existing production. The applicant based the claim on the premise that he had discovered a 2,200-acre survey that was vacant school-fund land. Yarborough disagreed and wrote that "submerged lands under the jurisdiction of the State of Texas are subject to lease for oil and gas to the highest bidder." In the opinion, Yarborough stated that individuals could not "discover" underwater land in the Gulf and attempt to claim it as a vacancy. Yarborough explained that the state always owned its submerged lands, which meant that all rentals, bonuses, and royalties from lease of these Gulf submerged lands belonged to the school fund and were "subject to lease for the development of oil and gas to the highest bidder." The ruling went largely unnoticed in 1934, but years later the decision became economically and politically important. After World War II, the federal government's attempt to claim the submerged lands resulted in a public outcry from the oil industry and state government. This "tidelands" dispute played a political role, driving a wedge between conservative Texas Democrats and the Truman administration.[21]

NEW FRIENDS AND FAMILY MEMBERS

Yarborough noted in later years that "I did not endear myself to the major oil companies by suing them and collecting millions of dollars from them." From the time he served in the Attorney General's office through his career in the U.S. Senate, very few oil and gas executives supported his political campaigns. Yarborough believed that he alienated this influential group because of his aggressive positions in representing the state's interests. In his future political campaigns, support from this sector came from only a handful of independent operators. Unlike Lyndon Johnson, who made efforts to pursue a liberal social agenda while appeasing the major corporate entities, Yarborough never saw the necessity to curry favor with the large oil and gas entities. However, many smaller, independent producers looked to Allred and then to Yarborough for protection against the major companies. One such individual was J. R. Parten, veteran of World War I, businessman and oilman, and a lifelong friend of Allred and Yarborough. In the 1930's, Parten was an independent producer working in East Texas. Parten took a public position opposing the attempts of large oil companies and the federal government to regulate production. Yarborough was impressed most by Parten's knowledge and ability to successfully challenge the larger companies and the Washington bureaucracy. "We in the Attorney General's staff were all proud to see him in the office. . . . He took a leading role in the fight over conservation and energy legislation before the legislature of Texas," Yarborough stated.[22]

Yarborough praised Parten as a man who distinguished himself from the rest of the crowd in the oil industry by his enthusiastic support in political campaigns. "He added judgment, prestige, and stability to an office and a campaign." As an independent, Parten demonstrated his ability to differ with the views advocated by Yarborough and Allred and yet remain a supporter. Yarborough recalled, "I was filing vacancy school land suits right and left, and collecting a good amount of money from them for the Permanent School Fund, not popular with oil men nor with Parten, so our personal visits were not very frequent at that time." However, after the Mid-Kansas case and as the Allred campaign for governor progressed in 1934, Parten observed to Yarborough, "that million dollar check is making the big difference in this race." The landmark victory and the publicity he received provided Allred the boost to win the governor's campaign while it forged a lasting relationship between Yarborough and Parten.[23]

Yarborough earned a name for himself as a young attorney general in these landmark cases by putting in many long hours. In spite of the time he spent on his work, Ralph and Opal established a solid marriage in their early years together, one that withstood the test of time. The couple's only son, Richard, was born on October 21, 1931. When the new baby arrived, the family was living in a small house only a few blocks away from the state offices. After his evening meal and talks with Opal and Richard, Ralph often returned to labor on cases until the early morning hours. He returned home only to rise before dawn, ready for another day's work. After his first year in the Attorney General's office, Ralph and Opal purchased their first car in the summer of 1933—a Chevrolet—from Kelly Saylor, an automobile dealer in Goldthwaite, Texas. When he made the purchase, Yarborough asked Saylor to postpone one installment of $41.65. "I am taking my vacation in the last half of August by car and will be unable to take a vacation and make my payment in the same month," he told Saylor. The Yarboroughs enjoyed a vacation that summer in Arkansas, thanks to Saylor's generosity, and Ralph made up the payment. While he attended law school, Yarborough had borrowed a total of several hundred dollars from the Students Memorial Loan Fund, his brother Harvey, and Ira P. Hildebrand, dean of the University of Texas Law School, to pay for his tuition and living expenses. By 1934 the young state attorney had repaid these loans acquired during the lean years. Yarborough insisted on paying all his debts to friends and family as a demonstration of his personal integrity, a policy he continued throughout his long political career.[24]

Throughout these years, Yarborough maintained his close relationship with his father. They frequently corresponded on events in Washington and economic and legal issues. As he had done before Ralph left home, C. R. Yarborough, even though he never attended law school, practiced law in the local courts of Henderson County, representing clients on property and contract issues. C. R. often sought Ralph's advice on difficult cases. When C. R. challenged an incumbent county commissioner in Henderson County, Yarborough provided political advice despite being immersed in the complex proceedings in the state Attorney General's office. The East Texas county's Democratic primary that summer of 1932 gave Yarborough a real taste of Texas-style politics at the grass-roots level.[25]

"THE BOTTOM WAS OUT OF THE BALLOT BOX"

C. R. Yarborough's challenge to the incumbent Henderson County commissioner involved questionable financial activities on the part of the commissioner. The campaign strongly influenced Ralph Yarborough's perspective on politics. Fighting a campaign on behalf of the people's interests versus those of the corrupt special interests, a useful, populist-styled theme, became a focal point of nearly all his later statewide battles. Ralph played a leading role in his father's campaign, and his tough, aggressive positions were evident in the race. During his father's campaign, his brother Harvey, who was five years his senior, became and would remain one of his trusted political advisors.[26]

Another important political relationship established during this campaign was the friendship of the Justice family. Attorney Will Justice of Athens and his son William Wayne Justice became Ralph's close friends after this campaign. The Justice and Yarborough families had a political and legal relationship prior to the 1932 race. Will Justice served as district attorney for Henderson County at the same time C. R. Yarborough served as justice of the peace. Justice was hailed as a very successful prosecutor during the 1920's and later as a practicing trial attorney. "There was no justice but Will Justice," according to a popular saying of the time. The families became political allies and their relationship solidified from events involving the C. R. Yarborough campaign.[27]

In rural counties in Texas in the early twentieth century, one of the most important elected officials in the community was the county commissioner. Four commissioners and the county judge presided over each county's fiscal affairs, thus controlling the purse strings for the limited number of public projects in local communities. The commissioners court set the ad valorem tax rate, adjusted the tax rolls, and funded all county offices and programs. One of the most visible functions of the county commissioner was the maintenance of the roads and bridges within their individual precincts. As in nearly all elections during this period, selection as the Democratic nominee was tantamount to election as no other party had nominees on the general election ballot for county races.[28]

In the spring of 1932, C. R. Yarborough decided to file for Henderson County Commissioner, Precinct 3. Having been justice of the peace for the area since 1922, he decided to move up the local political ladder. Ralph urged C. R. to make the race and said that he wanted to see his father "pour it on from start to finish and collect the requisite votes. That precinct has been in need of a good Commissioner for a long time." Precinct 3 included five small farming communities: Brownsboro, Leagueville, Murchison, Opelika, and the Yarboroughs' hometown of Chandler. None of the these were larger than 1,000 people, thus no single town could elect a commissioner at the expense of the other communities. With the onset of the depression, the county commissioner post appealed to C. R. Yarborough because it offered a steady salary and the ability to offer supporters a job working on county-maintained roads. Although the Yarborough family was not destitute, they struggled like nearly all other families in this era.[29]

The questionable financial activities in the county government motivated C. R. Yarborough to make the race. Ralph and Harvey assumed behind-the-scenes roles in the campaign, selecting the issues and composing the materials for their father. Adhering to their advice, C. R. released a strong condemnation of the county's activities coupled with a personal appeal for a new commissioner with honesty and integrity. Alluding to the often-sordid affairs of local elections, C. R. also called for a "clean, legal and honest election." His comments were directed to those involved in past elections where dishonesty occurred. By questioning election officials, the elder Yarborough directly criticized the local Democratic party structure. Henderson County had a history of voter fraud and illegal activities in recent contests. The Yarboroughs' concerns were prophetic, for election irregularities in this local race and also in the hotly contested 1932 governor's race determined the outcome.[30]

Voters went to the polls in the Democratic primary that steamy summer on

July 23, 1932. In the primary campaign, besides C. R. Yarborough, two others had filed for the office: incumbent County Commissioner Harold C. Turner and a second challenger, J. Saylors. Also on the Democratic primary ballot that year was a hotly contested gubernatorial election involving incumbent Governor Ross Sterling and former governor Miriam A. Ferguson. Voters also had to decide on "submission" of a constitutional amendment to the U.S. Constitution which repealed prohibition. The Eighteenth Amendment, the "prohibition" amendment, was still a hot topic in Henderson County. Repeal of the Eighteenth Amendment passed by the wide margin of 3,244 to 1,781. Miriam Ferguson led all candidates for governor with 2,742 votes to Tom Hunter's 1,291. Ross Sterling trailed them with 722 votes, followed by the other candidates who received several hundred votes. In the Precinct 3 commissioner's race, incumbent commissioner Turner led the race with 437 votes. C. R. Yarborough edged out J. Saylors by 288 to 256 votes, narrowly making it into the second primary with the incumbent commissioner.[31]

The stage was set for the August 27 Democratic runoff election. Knowing that he was behind, C. R., with advice from Ralph and Harvey, decided to turn up the heat on the incumbent by focusing on specific financial transactions by the county commissioners. C. R. intensified his criticism of Commissioner Turner in a series of printed circulars and newspaper ads placed in the local weekly newspapers. A few days after the first primary, Ralph wrote a short letter to his father and enclosed a $5 donation. "I know that you should start campaigning immediately and should see every voter who voted for you, for Turner, and especially those who voted for the third man in the first primary, and try to hold all of your voters and get all the new ones that you can. Personal contact is the main thing in the campaign, in my estimation." The idea of seeing as many voters as possible in their own surroundings was advice that Ralph preached and practiced, especially in his own political career. People in rural Texas took a strong interest in their candidates and wanted to look them in the eye and hear what they had to say.[32]

The Yarboroughs decided to confront the established interests in the county when they singled out the Athens National Bank for the attack. The Henderson County commissioners selected the Athens National Bank as the official depository in early 1931. In less than a month, the bank folded and lost the county's money and many other individual funds. Bank failures in Texas and throughout the nation were common in 1932 and one of the many economic issues that propelled Franklin Roosevelt into the White House. Undoubtedly, many Henderson County residents questioned the timing of the bank failure, coming as it did immediately after the bank had obtained the county's deposits. In addition, the Yarboroughs wanted to know why a year after the Athens bank closed the commissioners had failed to collect the bond to cover the loss.[33]

Harvey told Ralph that he thought victory was possible because of the Athens bank questions. "I believe he [C. R.] will win this race unless he pulls some super boner between now and the time the polls close Saturday night." But Harvey issued a warning upon hearing from an election judge in Leagueville. C. R. Yarborough had confronted Sells Smith, the Leagueville election judge, and said, "Now Sells, don't cheat me." The judge stated on an earlier occasion to one of the Yarboroughs' friends that he would conduct a fair election, and "Papa made him sore by this statement," Harvey told Ralph. Although friends attempted to rectify this unintended insult, Harvey was uncertain of the success of their efforts. Harvey said that if the misunderstanding was not "straightened out, then Papa will lose practically all of the votes at Leagueville, as Smith will count them the way he wants to. He owns them lock, stock and barrel."

Election fraud in Henderson County became an open item of discussion following the first primary election. In addition to the Yarboroughs, supporters of Governor Ross Sterling were alarmed at the outcome and suspected wrongdoings on behalf of Miriam Ferguson in Henderson County. The *Athens Daily News* issued stories on illegal votes in the first primary and the concern of further fraud in the runoff election.[34]

With a torrid election for governor and the heated race for county commissioner, voters in eastern Henderson County flocked to the ballot box. Ralph left Austin and joined other family members as they walked door to door and visited the local stores and shops for the elder Yarborough. The runoff vote totals actually increased above those cast in the first primary. Miriam Ferguson, who narrowly defeated Governor Sterling in their race, won handily by a margin of 3,250 votes to 1,781 votes in Henderson County. Commissioner Turner defeated C. R. Yarborough by a vote of 551 to 525, a narrow 26-vote margin. The greater number of ballots indicated an influx of new voters or additional unregistered voters above those who cast ballots in the first primary. The Yarboroughs and many others felt that fraudulent ballots made their way into the ballot boxes. They immediately suspected fraud in the county commissioner's election.[35]

After the election, Ralph left Chandler for Austin and his job at the Attorney General's office. The day after the election, Ralph cited abuses in Murchison, where an election judge allowed ballots to be cast by as many as twenty-nine people who were under the legal voting age of twenty-one. In the meantime, supporters in Opelika and Leagueville publicly claimed that Yarborough should have won both those areas. Ralph analyzed the situation in a letter to his younger brother Donald: "Our disadvantage in any contest would be that the Athens' bankers have more money than we have and if it got down to a swearing contest, they could produce more witnesses than we could produce." Ralph obviously believed that the questions raised about the county's financial activities would lead those involved to pay off some local citizens. But even with those prospects, Ralph noted that "if the Leagueville and Opelika people will voluntarily get out and get affidavits from the majority of the voters in each box, why not contest it?" They could easily embarrass county officials and the business establishment in Henderson County. After hearing reports from friends and listening to his sons, C. R. decided to challenge the outcome in court.[36]

A few days later a bombshell dropped that confirmed the Yarboroughs' suspicions. Knowing that the election would be contested, the Opelika election judge went to check on the boxes holding the ballots that were stored in Athens. After inspecting them, he quickly contacted the Yarboroughs. "What in the name of God am I to do? The bottom was out of the ballot box and there are no ballots in the Opelika box," he exclaimed. To the Yarboroughs, this indeed was the smoking gun from the scene of the crime. They learned the ballot boxes were taken to the county seat after the first election and stored in the basement of one of the Athens banks. "Of course, the opposition would have access to said boxes," Harvey said to Ralph.[37]

In addition to the ballot tampering Harvey also warned Ralph that the district judge presiding over the case had a history that might not assist their father's challenge. Following a contested race for sheriff in a nearby county, Will Justice prosecuted a voter fraud case before Judge William Dent. The judge refused to open the ballot boxes even though Justice had affidavits of enough voters to change the result of the election. "Dent will do what the bank crowd at Athens wants him to do," Harvey warned. Furthermore, Harvey said that the same opponents had previously cheated Will Justice in a race for county judge. "They stuffed the ballot box at Opelika and Murchison when he ran for County Judge, didn't turn in the results until Monday, and changed enough votes in the meantime to count him [Justice] out," Harvey said. "[Justice] represented one of them several years later and they explained to him just how they stole it from him. He knows them." Even with this knowledge, the Yarborough family wanted Justice to represent their side in the case. They knew Justice had his own personal motivation to confront Judge Dent and the people of Henderson County.[38]

The case went to trial quickly. The first day of the trial, Judge Dent ordered delivery of the ballot boxes to the courtroom. According to the *Athens Daily News,* the suspicious Opelika box could not immediately be located. When deputies finally delivered it to the court room, "there was a gapping hole in the side that was large enough for one to reach their hand through." Surprisingly, ballots had once again appeared in the Opelika box, but a number were still missing. Will Justice questioned several voters from Opelika on the witness stand. They all testified they had voted for Yarborough but their ballots indicated Turner. Justice told the court that "there was not a legal ballot in the Opelika box." Calling the election judge by name, Justice declared "no man could hold an election in any such manner and then tell the honest-to-God man that it was legal." Following Justice's dramatic accusation, Judge Dent adjourned the trial amidst a great uproar from the packed courtroom audience. Another large crowd was on hand the next morning. Following examination of the Brownsboro and Murchison votes, the opposing attorneys launched into heated closing arguments on behalf of their clients. The Yarboroughs spent an anxious night awaiting the decision. The next day, Judge Dent ended the suspense and ruled in favor of Commissioner Turner. Although Turner's majority changed from a margin of twenty-six votes to a nine-vote margin, Judge Dent declared him the victor.[39]

The decision ended the active political career of C. R. Yarborough, who never ran for office again. Losing an election which they believed they won fairly on election day was a bitter pill for the Yarboroughs to swallow. For a family which so vocally trumpeted their honesty, integrity, and belief in the democratic system, the defeat had significant, far-reaching consequences beyond the immediate effect of the election's outcome. Politics were more than a hobby or passing interest to the Yarboroughs. It became a vocation and an important part of their everyday lives. Ralph and his brother Harvey demonstrated their ability to work together on political campaigns. Although they failed in their efforts to win the seat for their father, the sons showed a keen insight in recognizing an opponent's weakness. While they believed politicians should set positive standards for the community, misdeeds and shenanigans should not go unchallenged. They also recognized the difficulties in working the shadier side of electoral politics. One unsavory reality involved the wooing of local political bosses who controlled groups of voters. Although not as well organized as the political machines in South Texas during the early twentieth century, local patriarchs managed small numbers of votes throughout the county and the rest of the state. Every serious candidate had to compete for these local organizations.

Ralph Yarborough also understood that pocketbook issues were a driving force in local politics. He believed that when business and government cooperated to deprive people of their income or their rights, society and representative government were threatened. Yarborough maintained that the honest people of Texas needed protection from these unscrupulous activities. Because business could not play a role as a disinterested party, public officials and government had to play a strong role as regulator and overseer of the economy. Ralph followed this guide in his father's election and during his tenure as an assistant attorney general.

Yarborough's four years in Allred's office defined his political and legal personality. When he entered the Attorney General's office in 1931, he was a competent and talented young attorney who knew little of the political process but brought to the office the youthful enthusiasm and drive which he demonstrated from his earlier years as a student and teacher. Allred's judgment and confidence in selecting Yarborough to the position proved to be well placed and fruitful for both his own career and for Yarborough's future endeavors. The legal victories over the oil companies led Yarborough to believe that under the right circumstances, even the mightiest of corporations could be successfully challenged and defeated. (For the rest of his life, he kept a worn copy of the 1932–1934 *Attorney General Report* on which he had inscribed "Won" beside each case he successfully prosecuted, 127 in total.) Ability, evidence, and willpower could overcome the resources of corporate opponents on the level playing field of the courtroom. Yarborough felt the same principles could be applied in the political arena as well. If he were allowed to select a clear-cut case of corporate or government malfeasance, then he could also win in the court of public opinion.

This background contributed the essence of Yarborough's makeup as an economic liberal during the 1930's. Liberalism in that era meant that one focused efforts on reform of the capitalist system without destroying the foundations for free enterprise. Capitalism left totally unrestrained by government led to uneven distribution of wealth, unemployment, poverty, and the abuse of power by large corporations. Not only did these run counter to the basic moral beliefs of fairness and compassion, they also violated individual rights and undermined democracy. The liberals of the 1930's believed that people as a whole were honest and industrious. However, individual economic improvement and the right to earn a living and own property could not be insured by good intentions and laissez faire capitalism. The state and public institutions served as the instruments which could oversee society and ensure its prosperity. In classic Jeffersonian terms, this arrangement required a well-educated citizenry and economic opportunity. These pillars supported the democracy and the economic system which were the foundation of American society. This society and its entire form of government was in peril as a result of the unbridled capitalism which had run American society off the road and into the ditch of economic despair.

For southern liberals Yarborough and Allred, the invocation of moral obligations in the pursuit of economic liberalism was justified. The Progressives who preceded the political generation of the 1930's invoked morality with religious overtones in pursuing their causes. The economic liberals of the 1930's did not totally abandon the moral crusades of the 1920's, especially issues involving alcohol, but the focus of moral salvation was no longer the town saloon. The 1930's liberals painted the corporations with the same brush used by their predecessors when they attacked proponents of alcohol as the purveyors of corruption. Economic reform and reorganization were the hallmarks of the crusade which refocused public efforts on the legitimate problems in society. Public outrage, government involvement, and mitigation of the problem was the proper course of action.

3 *A Man Who Had to Earn His Way*

Ralph Yarborough left the Attorney General's office in early 1935 a devoted disciple of James Allred. As a result of his work in the state agency, many prominent Texans recognized Yarborough's ability as an attorney. He made a name for himself in legal circles by virtue of his participation in the courtroom victories as one of Allred's top assistant attorneys general. In the years before World War II, Yarborough emerged from Allred's shadow to become a political leader in his own right. Initially, he relied on Allred for appointments to influential positions in government. The first of these was an appointment to the first board of directors of the newly created Lower Colorado River Authority (LCRA) in 1935. Yarborough's service on the board came at a critical time and was an important milestone in establishing his personal career and public persona. Following his year on the LCRA board, Governor Allred named Yarborough judge of the 53rd District Court in Travis County. From this point on, Yarborough embarked on his own, independent political career, one that brought him initial electoral success followed by a disappointing loss for statewide office in 1938.

In the early 1930's, most Texas cities received electricity from privately owned companies. Few rural residents had electric service because it was not profitable for the companies to extend power lines into the countryside. Utilities prices and access to electric power became a rising concern in the 1930's. Allred believed that Texas needed a regulatory agency to oversee the activities of investor-owned companies. As Allred pointed out during his campaign for governor, utility company lobbyists had ample influence with the Texas Legislature to make sure that the corporate interests they represented were protected by state lawmakers. In Allred's view, all of these factors contributed to discrimination against the majority of Texans and thwarted competition. As governor, he planned to promote public power as an alternative to the investor-owned utilities and hoped to gain more leverage with the legislature in the battle with the private utilities. To highlight his position on public power, Allred supported the creation of the Lower Colorado River Authority (LCRA), a state-sponsored project to control flooding and generate electricity in Central Texas along the Colorado River. In promoting a project that combined public power with flood control in Central Texas, Allred selected a popular initiative to advance the cause of a large, multipurpose public policy program. The new agency became a reality at the same time Allred became governor.[1]

Electricity generated from hydroelectric power—that is, from generators powered by the flow of water from massive dams—was widely encouraged in Texas and other arid western states. In addition to the need for a reliable source of cheap electricity, residents of Central Texas wanted some relief from flooding. Seasonal flooding on the Colorado River was a major headache for the residents and the communities along the waterway, especially in Austin, the state's capital. The Colorado River basin drained 41,000 square miles with an annual runoff of over two-million acre feet as it flowed from the dusty High Plains of Texas southeast to the marshy bays of the Gulf of Mexico. The Colorado River basin, the second largest in Texas, encompassed a greater area than the Tennessee River basin, which flowed through seven different states. The Tennessee River was the target of a simultaneous effort by the federal government, which sought flood control and a new source of electrical power for the impoverished people of the South.[2]

Until the advent of the New Deal, most large-scale water development and conservation projects in the American West and South were hazardous ventures. With the onset of the depression during the Hoover administration, the likelihood of private funding for these multimillion-dollar projects diminished as quickly as jobs did. By 1932, only the federal government had the necessary resources to complete such massive projects. With the exception of Hoover Dam on the Colorado River in Nevada, large reservoir projects around the nation remained on the drawing boards. Following Franklin D. Roosevelt's election in 1932, the picture changed dramatically. With the support of congressional representatives and senators from the South and West, a new commitment from the federal government for large construction projects began. Dams and reservoirs were high on the list of priorities because they provided thousands of jobs and literally contributed a concrete addition to the New Deal legacy.

Floods and the damage they caused had always been one of the most difficult problems residents of Central Texas faced. The history of flood control efforts there illustrates the nearly insurmountable problems involved in securing private capital and political support for a multimillion-dollar project. The failure to ensure the safety and endurance of the dams in Austin was a continual source of frustration and embarrassment to civic leaders in the capital city. From the late 1800's until the 1930's every dam and hydroelectric plant constructed on the Colorado River near Austin eventually washed away in a seasonal flood. The dams were too small or poorly engineered to withstand the force of the spring floodwaters washing down from the Hill Country into the river. The most ambitious effort called for construction of a single dam between the communities of Llano and Burnet upriver from Austin. The Hamilton Dam was to be two miles long and 137 feet high with an expected completion date in 1933. However, in April 1932 the national depression brought down Insull, the construction company working on the project. Moreover, company owner Samuel Insull was indicted for fraud and embezzlement and the project was put in receivership. The uncompleted Hamilton Dam stood as a stark reminder of the failed dreams and the depression that now gripped Texas and the rest of the nation.[3]

Taming the Colorado River was a much greater task than the city government, the state, or a private company could achieve in the early 1930's. Many state and community leaders believed that only massive federal assistance would make the project feasible. Once the federal government began to take an active lead in funding new water development projects in the South and West, Governor Allred needed supporters with the ability to work with the Roosevelt administration and the Texas delegation in Washington. He turned to his trusted friend for the task, calling on Yarborough to join a select group of appointees to achieve what no group had previously obtained—approval of a full-scale plan and financing for a Colorado River dam system.

The LCRA was an agency in the making for several years in the early 1930's. In 1933 the Texas Senate passed the first bill to establish an agency for the purpose of constructing and managing multipurpose dams on the Colorado. However, private utility interests and some state representatives from areas around the headwaters of the Colorado River defeated the measure in the House of Representatives. The following year the Roosevelt administration pledged a $4.5 million loan to complete the unfinished project provided that the Texas Legislature create a public agency to build and operate the system. This stimulus along with Allred's support helped proponents achieve passage of the measure to create the LCRA during the 1935 legislative session. Even before passage, Governor Allred had begun the work to organize the new agency.[4]

A few days before Allred officially left his office as attorney general, Ralph Yarborough resigned his position as assistant attorney general. On January 1,

1935, he announced the formation of a law partnership with Henry Brooks, the former district attorney of Travis County and Yarborough's law school classmate. In February, Allred announced Yarborough's appointment to the LCRA's first board of directors, referring to him as "an authority on state land matters and public ownership." In the initial appointments to the board, the governor, the attorney general, and the land commissioner each made three selections. The first job of the appointed board was to receive the $4.5 million public works loan and grant secured by Congressman J. P. Buchanan (D-Austin) for completion of the half-finished Hamilton Dam. The structure was renamed the Buchanan Dam in recognition of the Central Texas congressman's efforts.[5]

Along with Yarborough, Allred appointed J. R. Key of Lampasas, a businessman, and C. R. Pennington of Abilene, a well-known civic leader from West Texas. The other six members were Tom Ferguson and Roy Fry (Burnet), Roy Inks (Llano), A. J. Reinhard (Fort Worth), Fritz Engelhard (Eagle Lake), and Raymond Brooks (Austin). The board gathered for their first meeting on February 19, 1935. Governor Allred, Land Commissioner James Walker, state senator James Hornsby (author of the law that created the LCRA), and a number of local dignitaries attended the inaugural session of the agency. Following the session, everyone met on the steps of the Travis County Courthouse for their group picture. Standing in the back row behind Governor Allred, the 34-year-old Yarborough still looked as if he were in his twenties. With his dark hair, medium height, and boyish looks, Yarborough stood out among the group of older leaders and the governor. Although Yarborough was the youngest board member, his experience as assistant attorney general had prepared him for the initial battles over control of the LCRA.[6]

BUILDING THE LCRA

At its first meeting, Yarborough took the lead in organizing the board of directors and requested an opinion on the constitutionality of the act that created the LCRA and its authority. The young director also told the board that the new agency needed information from the Highway Department concerning the location of roads leading to Buchanan Dam. The $4.5 million loan for completion of the dam was still pending with the U.S. Department of the Interior, so the board hoped the flurry of activity would spur approval.

The board faced its first battle over selection of its chief counsel. Congressman J. P. Buchanan told the board that the Public Works Administration

(PWA), the New Deal agency that sponsored public works projects to provide jobs and stimulate the economy, wanted a ruling from the Texas courts on the constitutionality of the LCRA. Congressman Buchanan recommended the board employ former state senator Alvin Wirtz to represent the agency in the legal proceedings. Also, the congressman directed the board to send all information to his office. This set the stage for the first political struggle of the new agency.[7]

Wirtz had strong knowledge of the complex world of water law and finance, but he had not escaped criticism. He had been a state senator from Seguin in the 1920's and later represented Insull Corporation. After Insull's failure, Wirtz became the receiver for the unfinished Colorado River dam project. In 1934 he moved to Austin to establish his own law firm after allegedly being forced out of Seguin by disgruntled farmers who believed they had been cheated out of their lands by his dam projects on the Guadalupe River. Although Wirtz lobbied for the creation of the LCRA, he represented some of the largest and most influential corporate utilities in the state: the Texas Power Corporation, the Houston Natural Gas Company, Lone Star Gas Company, and the United Gas Public Service Company. Wirtz was by far the most knowledgeable and capable supporter of the project, but he carried with him the baggage of his political associations with Insull and the failed Hamilton Dam project. Although Wirtz was considered one of the ablest lawyers in Texas on public utility matters, concerns immediately arose over the possible conflict of interest in serving both private utility companies and the newest public power agency in the state. Yarborough was quick to question his nomination.[8]

The second problem for the board involved Congressman Buchanan's participation. Buchanan not only wanted Senator Wirtz appointed but also demanded oversight of all board decisions. The congressman knew the importance of the dams and electricity to the people of his district, and he wanted to make sure he received the political credit. The state might have created the LCRA but Buchanan and the individual board members all knew the funding for the massive project came from Washington, D.C. Thus the congressman was surprised when Yarborough challenged the selection of Wirtz. Yarborough said he opposed the appointment of any attorney "who represents gas and electrical utilities at the same time he is representing this Board." Yarborough undoubtedly was aware of Wirtz' controversial background.[9]

The state legislation creating the LCRA required that before appointment any prospective board member had to show no involvement with private utilities for the previous three years. Yarborough believed the same criteria should be applied to its legal counsel. Knowing he was going against Congressman Buchanan's recommendation and that Senator Wirtz had considerable political influence, Yarborough nonetheless argued that the board was setting important precedents and that the legal counsel should meet the same litmus test required of board members. Yarborough urged the board to request an opinion from the attorney general as to whether any attorney representing "both gas and electrical utilities would be disqualified under either the letter or the spirit of the law from serving as counsel." Yarborough's stand illustrated a course he was beginning to follow in his policy decision-making process—his moral compass provided his political direction in critical public policy situations.[10]

The majority of the board, however, adhered to the wishes of Congressman Buchanan and selected Wirtz as general counsel on a divided vote. Once Wirtz was chosen, the board agreed to request an opinion from the state's attorney general on the legality of the appointment. Attorney General McCraw subsequently responded that the law made no provisions on the appointment and that the confidential relationship between the board and its attorney protected the agency. In this case, political expediency proved to be beneficial for the LCRA, but it would not be the last time Yarborough would raise this type of objection and challenge the majority of the LCRA board.[11]

The controversy over the selection of Wirtz as general counsel quickly faded as major problems emerged. Financing issues and political opposition were to be the most difficult. In retrospect, the selection of Wirtz proved fortunate, for he became an important legal and political asset in the LCRA's upcoming battles. Wirtz undoubtedly recognized Yarborough as a force on the board with whom he needed to work, and the tension from the appointment subsided as they worked together, though Wirtz never considered Yarborough a close confidant. Events moved forward; the next task the LCRA faced was to secure the promised funding from the PWA for construction of the dams. Nevertheless, at its March 27 meeting the board decided to hire an engineering firm and complete the unfinished dam with a hydroelectric plant even though the money was not yet committed for the expanded project.[12]

YARBOROUGH MEETS LYNDON JOHNSON

Yarborough first became acquainted with Lyndon Johnson through his work with the LCRA. After the March board meeting, Wirtz traveled to Washington, D.C., to work with Congressman Buchanan and the PWA on the final loan approval. Wirtz relied on the assistance of Johnson, his young friend in the office of South Texas congressman Richard Kleberg (D-Kingsville). The eager Johnson helped Wirtz set up appointments and meetings for the LCRA delegation. The Washington trip capped off the new agency's efforts: The PWA approved a $20-million loan for the LCRA projects. Later that year, Johnson became the director for Texas of the National Youth Administration (NYA) and appeared in that capacity at the LCRA's October 8, 1935, board meeting. Johnson explained that a number of young men who resided in the immediate area needed jobs and that the LCRA's construction project could provide employment opportunities for them. Along with other directors, Yarborough recognized the NYA's popularity and the previous work Johnson performed for the LCRA while in Washington. The LCRA board unanimously agreed to Johnson's proposal.

The initial year of the LCRA marked a political exchange between Yarborough and Johnson which lasted until Johnson's death in 1973. In these early years both young men were friendly and cooperative as they worked on the common goals of the LCRA and the New Deal programs advocated by FDR. However, years later, the relationship changed when the political stakes grew larger for both.[13]

EARLY ACCOMPLISHMENTS OF THE LCRA

The LCRA proceeded with plans which included completion of Buchanan Dam and construction of three to five additional dams on the Colorado River between Burnet and Austin. Previous loans and commitments from the bankrupt Insull company were paid. Money was allocated to purchase land for the dams and reservoirs and for camps for the new workers. A fish hatchery was also planned on the shores of the future lake to be created by Buchanan Dam. Finally, a new highway was also included in the project. The announcement of the LCRA plans came at a momentous time. Torrential rains hit Central Texas in the spring of 1935. On May 19, the river crested at twenty-six feet, the highest level measured in Austin in its recorded history. The flood caused an estimated $13 million in property damage to the capital city and other Colorado River communities. The landmark disaster is best illustrated by a photo taken during the storm. The dramatic shot captured a two-story frame structure, which the floodwaters washed into the river, falling over the spillway of the only dam in Austin.[14]

The LCRA projects provided thousands of jobs and a spark of energy for the people of Central Texas. After years of faulty starts, the efforts under the LCRA proved to be a tremendous economic stimulus. In less than a year, the LCRA had over $11 million in construction underway or scheduled. The agency hired a total of 800 people by the end of 1935. Over 4,000 were expected to be employed once the project was in full swing. Also, the board and management looked after the welfare of its employees, establishing a forty-hour work week and other benefits. The timing was critical as unemployment in Austin rose through 1934 and local resources were nearly exhausted. The political stock of Congressman Buchanan, Ralph Yarborough, and other leaders associated with the LCRA improved as the dollars began flowing into the region. Yarborough and many other Texans lined up in 1932 to obtain a Roosevelt-Garner bronze medallion for one dollar and so become part of the "Shareholders of America" who contributed to Democrats' election efforts. Those symbolic investments paid handsome dividends as federally funded building programs initiated by the LCRA, the University of Texas, and the City of Austin provided a much needed stimulus to the Central Texas economy.[15]

The LCRA's first year proved to be a political testing ground for both the agency and Yarborough. Once established, the LCRA quickly became one of the most active state agencies in the nation during the 1930's. The LCRA's early success set the stage for an expanded role for the federal government in Texas as state leaders witnessed the impact of the federal contribution in this one organization. Many now realized the importance of increasing federal and state cooperation, especially when it came to large capital projects that offered thousands of people jobs. Yarborough clearly understood this new state-federal relationship. Thanks to his experiences on the LCRA board, he believed that the federal government was now the first place to look for answers to previously insoluble problems. Large, publicly funded initiatives offered solutions and relief to citizens on a scale that the private sector could not provide. The LCRA served as a model in which a public agency provided solutions to long-standing problems through increased economic activity. The political influence Texans possessed in Congress and in the Roosevelt administration helped Yarborough and others in their efforts; this was the best possible scenario for addressing the problems created by the Great Depression.

Yarborough demonstrated on several occasions that he could at times be difficult to work with on political issues, especially if he believed a point of ethics or a procedure involving issues of character had surfaced. (His opposition to Buchanan and Wirtz are particularly noteworthy in this respect.)

The young Yarborough steadfastly believed that leaders in positions of public trust needed to maintain a spotless reputation. Although his devotion to the public interest, his legal skills, and his good reputation were indisputable, Yarborough also earned a reputation as a man who could be difficult to work alongside, one who might act independently with little consultation from friends and supporters who frequently sought the same outcome. Yarborough discovered that even though he could command the moral high ground in a political battle, he could lose it as a result of poor timing and lack of support from his allies. The young attorney added to his professional and political reputation independent of the Attorney General's office despite a few notable reversals, and in the end he proved that he could swim in the treacherous waters of state and national politics.

Throughout the rest of 1935, Yarborough remained an active LCRA board member. His years of experience in land matters and the law proved to be a valuable asset to the agency during this first year. In spite of the difficulties over personnel issues, the board worked in unanimity on nearly all other major issues. By the time the major projects were completed, the LCRA had faced many more obstacles and set a positive example of a government agency working in partnership with the private sector. Yarborough's term of service with the LCRA ended after the first year. Yarborough resigned his position as LCRA director at the January 2, 1936, meeting. He had already agreed in late December to accept Allred's appointment as judge of the Fifty-third District Court in Travis County. His final action was to name the second dam on the Colorado River after Roy Inks, a board member who unexpectedly passed away during his first year of office.[16]

The board members of the LCRA were local heroes, having succeeded where many others had failed. Yarborough eventually established a good working relationship with the influential Wirtz, but one cannot help but wonder how events might have changed if Wirtz had become a confidant of Yarborough's and supported his political career in the manner in which he supported Lyndon Johnson's. When Congressman Buchanan, the financial godfather of the project, unexpectedly died in 1937, Johnson jumped at the chance to seek his seat, with Wirtz as his motivator and financial backer. Running on his credentials as a supporter of FDR and the New Deal, Johnson won the special congressional election, a victory that led him to Washington and on to national prominence. Yarborough, whose reputation and political abilities were equal and more widely recognized in these early days, remained in Austin. Through his term on the LCRA and as a student of history, Yarborough came to realize that a shift in power was underway as more and more people looked to Washington instead of Austin for solutions to their economic and social problems. However, at this time Yarborough's interests centered on the state and his own legal and public career. Following his year on the LCRA board, the young attorney moved into a different political arena as judge of the 53rd District Court of Travis County.

TRAVIS COUNTY DISTRICT JUDGE

When Ralph Yarborough first joined the Attorney General's office in 1931, the state district courts in Travis County were the site of the decisive legal battles between the state and the leading Texas corporations. As one of Allred's leading prosecutors, Yarborough spent many hours in the courtrooms at the Travis County Court House prosecuting the oil and gas companies. The young attorney learned that the trial court made crucial public policy decisions affecting government and business in the early 1930's. An expanded governmental presence depended to a large degree on the abilities of those attorneys and judges during this time. The judicial system defined the pace and the limits of New Deal legislation and, in Texas, the courts served as the final arbiter in many landmark decisions which expanded the powers of government in the lives of everyday citizens. Yarborough understood the critical role the courts played, so when newly elected Governor Allred offered him a state district judge appointment, he never hesitated. As judge of the 53rd District Court, he set a new course of independence and legal precedents.

Yarborough succeeded Judge Charles A. Wheeler, who had abruptly resigned in December 1935 because of his dissatisfaction with the salary. In an effort to curb expenses, the Texas Legislature had reduced salaries of district judges from $5000 to $4000 a year. In his resignation letter to Governor Allred, Judge Wheeler contended that the lower pay "compels district judges to either borrow money for living expenses, or discount their warrants from one to two and one half percent." But the district judge's salary did not deter Yarborough. The $4000 annual salary was the same amount paid to the governor and the attorney general in 1936 and much more than he made as an assistant attorney general or earned in private practice. White collar workers in area businesses earned a base salary of $60 per month.[17]

Yarborough believed he could make even more of a name for himself than he had as an assistant attorney general. Serving as a district judge would offer him a variety of cases on which to work and increase his legal expertise. He also knew that once he received the appointment he would have to begin an election campaign within a few months. Like most other state officials, district judges ran for election every two years.

The appointment provided Yarborough several days of news coverage in the Austin press and other newspapers around the state. The *Houston Chronicle* noted that Yarborough, who had been in "some of the most important land cases in Texas jurisprudence," took the position "of one of the most important judgeships in the state." Only thirty-two, he was one of the youngest men on the bench in the entire state. The news story noted his contributions in the cases that involved the Yates Oil Field and acknowledged his participation in the million-dollar settlement with the Mid-Kansas Oil Company. Yarborough took the oath of office on January 8, 1935, from Judge J. D. Moore, the presiding judge of the third administrative judicial district. In a brief speech Yarborough called upon the members of the bar for their assistance. Besides Opal and their four-year-old son, Richard, a host of attorneys and friends from Travis County attended the ceremony. The group included former state representative George Mendell, an Austin attorney who had already announced for the judgeship in the upcoming election. According to newspaper accounts, Mendell was one of the first to congratulate Yarborough. Before Yarborough presided over a single case, he knew that he had a strong opponent who planned to watch his every move.[18]

The first major case tried before Judge Yarborough involved the Community Natural Gas Company of Wichita Falls. The Texas Railroad Commission filed an order against the company in February 1935 to reduce the gas rate the utility charged its customers from 67.5 cents to 61 cents per thousand cubic feet. The Wichita Falls City Council then passed a city ordinance that ordered the company to lower its charges to its customers. The utility company responded by filing suit against the city and the state. It challenged the valuation of its property by the city, the amount of gas required for its reserves, and whether an annual return of 7 percent was a fair and reasonable return on their investment. Attorneys for both sides argued the case for eight weeks before a jury in Judge Yarborough's 53rd District courtroom. The jury ruled in favor of the company's statement on the property value and its gas reserves but agreed with the state that the 7 percent return on the investment was fair as a reasonable return.[19]

Several days after the jury's decision, Judge Yarborough set aside the jury's decision and entered a judgment upholding the Railroad Commission's lower rate of 61 cents per thousand cubic feet. He also ruled that the company's customers were entitled to a refund of the difference, from 1933 to 1936, between that rate and the higher rate which the utility collected during those years. In making his decision, Judge Yarborough said he entered the decision "solely on the basis of the plaintiff's evidence and that the findings of the jury did not enter into consideration." Prior to 1933, Yarborough noted, the gas rates were 32 cents per thousand. Yarborough further noted that the company would earn a profit of 29 cents per thousand at the rate established by the Railroad Commission and that during the trial the gas company had testified that they entered into a contract with Lone Star Gas Company to deliver gas to Wichita Falls for 40 cents per thousand cubic feet. "Evidence shows that the Lone Star Gas Corporation, a holding company, owns all of the Community Natural Gas company's stock and most of the Lone Star Gas Company stock. Hence, the Lone Star Gas Company has made a contract with itself." Yarborough concluded that the company had to pay the 32-cent rate. The customers received an average refund of $4 per year and ended up with the lower 61-cent rate set by the state and the city of Wichita Falls.[20]

The impact of this decision went far beyond this one corporation. The opinion was important in that it gave the Railroad Commission virtually full control over gas rates throughout Texas. Until Yarborough's decision, the commission's jurisdiction on this regulatory issue was in doubt. Thus, within weeks of taking office, Judge Yarborough quickly gained the attention of the legal community and the oil industry. While he based his rulings on factual evidence and law, the young jurist showed his independence and a willingness to take political risks. He also delivered a lengthy presentation on the judgment in the courtroom which established a precedent he frequently followed on succeeding lawsuits of statewide importance. Yarborough's judgment in the Wichita Falls gas case gave clear indication that his judicial actions would move toward additional regulatory power and responsibilities for government. The decision also indicated that the young district judge was unafraid of confrontations with major oil companies. He previously pursued the oil companies as a young assistant attorney general under Allred. Now, he planned to continue that battle as district judge.[21]

Many of the state's major newspapers covered Yarborough's decision. The *Dallas Morning News* reported that he set aside the jury's verdict and that the judgment was considered a complete victory for the state. The report went on to say that Judge Yarborough believed the company had failed in its presentation to sufficiently show that the Railroad Commission's order was unjust and unreasonable. "On several points the court held company testimony at war with itself," the *Morning News* reported. Wichita Falls gas company spokesman and vice president Chester May announced the utility's plan to appeal the decision in favor of upholding the findings of the jury. He characterized

Judge Yarborough's ruling as "unfair and unjust." The ruling remained, for the case was never appealed.[22]

Judge Yarborough found another controversial issue which impacted many Texans. Yarborough, a devout Southern Baptist, never drank alcoholic beverages. While he did not sermonize extensively on alcohol consumption, he took a strong position against public drinking. "The drunken driver is a menace to life and property," Yarborough declared as he suspended the drivers licenses of two young offenders. Hoping to impress others in the community in addition to the two teens, Judge Yarborough delivered a lengthy message on the subject. "The slightest loss of control over your muscles and your car becomes an instrument of destruction and might kill someone. If you insist on drinking go home and stay there until you're sobered up and let some other person drive your car," he lectured. The sentence imposed and the public censure in the court earned him the critical praise of the local newspaper. In a May 24, 1936, editorial entitled "Judge Yarborough Sounds a Warning to Drinking Drivers," the *American Statesman* commended him for his actions.

Another case on morality and community standards which came before Judge Yarborough's court in his first term ultimately led to the end of pari-mutuel gambling. "Yarborough Closes Wires to Bookie Shops," the Austin newspaper told its readers in May 1936. Judge Yarborough filed an injunction which banned Western Union, the American Telegraph and Telephone Company, and Southwestern Bell from leasing equipment to operations he labeled "bookie shops." The decision prevented anyone from using the wires or telephones to distribute information on horse races. Everett Looney, special counsel for Governor Allred in the case, called the decision a "death blow" to the bookies of the state. The injunction halted what was estimated to be a $30 million a year business, "considerably more than is bet under the legalized pari-mutuel system." Legal betting at Texas race tracks in 1936 amounted to $22 million according to state calculations. Yarborough's decision foreshadowed the eventual demise of legalized gambling on horses in Texas during Allred's term as governor. The 1937 ban on pari-mutuel gambling lasted nearly fifty years in the state.[23]

GREECE, LINCOLN, COWBOYS — YARBOROUGH'S INTEREST IN HISTORY

During his years as district judge, more people became aware of Yarborough's historical interests. Ever since he was a child and saw Buffalo Bill

Cody's Wild West Show in Tyler, Yarborough maintained an interest in American history. Some of his most influential childhood memories included the recollections of Confederate veterans. His interest in history helped him in his college and law school studies and in research for cases as a practicing attorney. By the time he was district judge in Austin, Yarborough was well versed in history and literature. He appeared before many civic organizations and authored columns and stories on the development of the area and the nation.

Yarborough's range of knowledge extended well beyond Texas and the Civil War. Yarborough impressed members of the Austin Exchange Club with his knowledge of the history of insurance when he informed them that as early as 900 B.C. insurance was used to cover maritime losses in Greece. The young judge provided a lengthy, detailed history of the evolution of the industry, similar to his thorough legal briefs and decisions. Yarborough noted that the first life insurance policy of record dated to 1183, when Robert Martin, a London alderman, insured his life with businessmen of that city. Whether or not the group was surprised to learn that insurance was available in the Middle Ages, many were undoubtedly startled to hear a lecture on the early years of the profession from a thirty-two-year-old district judge.[24]

One of Yarborough's lifelong interests centered on interpretations of the American Civil War. He explained to another business group that a primary reason the North won the Civil War was Abraham Lincoln's service as a "professional politician." Yarborough maintained this was a compliment "but at one time or another he [Lincoln] was on both sides of nearly every question in the North." Lincoln easily bested his counterpart Jefferson Davis. "Lincoln proved to be the better leader because he endeavored to secure the support of every person who came to him while Davis on the other hand appeared cool and distant," Yarborough surmised. He said Lincoln showed his political skills when he persuaded the Border States to remain in the Union and maneuvered the South into firing the first shots of the Civil War. The young district judge criticized Davis for his decisions early in the war, one of them being the failure of the South to fight an offensive war instead of a purely defensive war in 1861. Yarborough was unafraid to voice his opinion before his pro-southern audience in an era when the Civil War and its outcome were still hotly debated. A devout southerner, he frequently used Lincoln as a model for his own political decisions throughout his career.[25]

For Yarborough history served as a means of developing his own perceptions and understanding of society. He researched history just as he studied law, spending a great amount of time and energy in the pursuit. He committed a mountain of facts and figures to memory, a habit which served him well throughout his career. His articles and writings provided him with an additional forum to increase his visibility and expand his influence. After Yarborough became district judge, he steadily increased his appearances at civic functions in Central Texas. As his visibility rose, he attracted the attention of the public and of the press and other opinion makers outside the legal community. One writer from the *Houston Chronicle* described him as "a walking encyclopedia." An Austin newspaper reporter declared, "There are very few subjects, apparently, on which Judge Yarborough is not thoroughly posted and he can talk for hours particularly on history, economics, government, changes in law practice, and on the constitution." Continuing his description, the reporter said, "A visit to his office any day on the fourth floor of the courthouse reveals that he has a library on assorted subjects that will excite the curiosity of any visitor." The interests the young judge demonstrated in the 1930's provide insight into the interests and work habits he maintained for years to come. It was not uncommon for him to be reading well after midnight and to rise early the next morning—another habit that he carried into his later public career, along with returning to his office after supper to continue working.[26]

Yarborough displayed an ability to work with reporters and editors in his early professional years. Attorney General Allred allowed Yarborough and other assistants to author press releases and provide information on important cases to the media, and Yarborough expanded his efforts to court the press as a district judge in Travis County. An *Austin American* editorial complimented him on his access and ability to clarify complex legal questions: "On every newspaperman's run there are persons who help not only to make the news but help the newsman to compile his information." The report described Yarborough as "one of the ablest men ever to grace a district court bench." Judge Yarborough also had "a fine sense of news values, and is a valuable aid to any newspaperman who happens to handle the affairs of his court." In one case when the reporter was not in the courtroom, Judge Yarborough telephoned his verdict to the *Austin American* and explained its meaning. The reporter noted that Judge Yarborough always took copious notes during trials and "kindly gives the reporters any important highlights of the testimony and fills in the gaps for the newsmen."[27]

This "kindness" brought Yarborough increased exposure in the newspapers. Yarborough understood early in his career the importance of media relationships. In his first political campaigns, he used this knowledge to his advantage. The initial cases before his court in 1936 made headlines and increased his visibility leading up to the summer Democratic primary election. Yarborough seized the opportunity to utilize the local Austin newspaper to enhance his image as an aggressive, knowledgeable judge who welcomed the opportunity to take on the toughest cases as he prepared for his first election campaign in 1936.

"WOMEN AND THE BLUE-SHIRTED BOYS PUT ME OVER"

Ralph and Opal enjoyed their days with their young son Richard in the mid-1930s. The Depression created difficulties for everyone but life seemed much better in Austin than other areas of the state. The city of 75,000 spread from tree-covered limestone hills in the west to rolling prairies on the eastern side of town. The background of the scenic hills enhanced evening sunsets of a purplish hue which inspired the famous author and former resident O. Henry to describe the town as the "City of a Violet Crown." The broad, tree-lined streets presented well-kept homes spread among the many government offices and buildings. The pink granite capitol dome and the University of Texas Tower dominated the skyline. The serenity of the community masked its sometimes turbulent political life. In a city whose main discourse centered on education and government, Austin's air was always filled with politics, a subject of great interest to the city's well-informed populace.

Yarborough announced for election to the 53rd District Court of Travis County promising that he would pay "diligent attention to the people's business." News accounts related the story of his growing up in Chandler, his jobs as a laborer in the wheat and oil fields, and his service as a teacher in public schools. The million-dollar Mid-Kansas victory and his other cases on behalf of the public schools were featured and his success in securing funding for Buchanan Dam as a director for the LCRA was lauded. Finally, stories noted that in his present brief stint as district judge he had "already won an outstanding reputation" and was "a man who had to earn his way."[28]

In his campaign Yarborough promoted himself as a seasoned judge who was "Old Enough to Have Mature Judgment . . . Young Enough to Handle a Hard Job" and stressed his incumbency. He also touted his graduation with highest honors from the University of Texas Law School and highlighted the millions of dollars for the state from land suits while he served in the Attorney General's office. Yarborough enlisted strong support from the political and legal community in the capital city. They included assistant attorneys general, former governor Dan Moody, Allred campaign manager Claud Wild, and other well-known lawyers in Austin such as Charles Betts, Henry Brooks, and Hardy Hollers. This support was important, for Yarborough faced a respected attorney with strong support in the legal community.[29]

Yarborough's opponent in the race, George Mendell, a former state representative and longtime Austin resident, had attended the University of Texas and studied law under former Texas governor Oran M. Roberts. He was admitted to the bar in 1895. Mendell reminded the voters in Travis County of his three terms in the legislature. "If you know me I want you to vote for me . . . and I will do my best to make you 'A Just Judge,'" he said. As a state representative, Mendell took credit for a number of improvements in state properties which benefited the city of Austin. Mendell said he filed injunctions to prevent members of the legislature from creating jobs for themselves. Following his three terms in the legislature, Mendell worked for twenty-five years as the general counsel for the Retail Merchants Association of Texas. Mendell offered his broader experience in contrast to Yarborough's brief record in public office.[30]

As the election neared, Mendell's campaign ads in the local newspaper stated that Yarborough's supporters included a group of "state officeholders, temporarily residing in Austin while drawing their state salary checks." Mendell said no judge "should embarrass the attorneys who will try cases before him by soliciting their votes or endorsements." Mendell claimed that Yarborough solicited all 195 members of the Travis County Bar Association and obtained an endorsement from fewer than half of them. However, no attorneys were listed in Mendell's ad except for Judge James A. King. Aside from this one attack by the Mendell campaign, the candidate made no other comments about Yarborough or his campaign. Mendell relied on his reputation and previous record as an elected official in his race for district judge. In doing so, Mendell underestimated the energy Yarborough devoted to the race.[31]

Yarborough replied to his opponent's charges with a critique of Mendell's record during the 1917 session of the Texas Legislature. Mendell had opposed a "mother's pension bill" that provided funds to widows with children under the age of sixteen, which passed despite his opposition. He also voted against legislation that gave injured workers coverage under the Texas Workmen's Compensation law. Most important, Mendell "bitterly opposed" women's suffrage and voted against the measure in 1917. Another strategy in Yarborough's election effort focused on his devotion to the Democratic party and its leaders Franklin D. Roosevelt and James Allred. In May 1936 Yarborough attended the local party conventions and the state party convention.

He delivered the keynote address at the Travis County Democratic Convention, in which he presented a plea for party unity and for a pledge to reelect Roosevelt and Allred. Even though the race for district judge was mannerly by most political standards, Yarborough demonstrated in his first political campaign that he would quickly respond to any attacks from a political opponent. He showed even more enthusiasm when he zeroed in on a political opponent's weakness. The young politician was no shrinking violet when it came time to strike a blow at the opposition.[32]

Yarborough knew Mendell was wealthy and could raise more money for the contest, so he concluded early on that even though he spent many hours on the bench in the courtroom, he would simply outwork his opponent. Yarborough also decided to take his campaign directly to the people. "And that's what I did. I got up next to the people. I went to churches, and socials, and parent-teacher meetings. I went into shops all over this town. Hot places. Places where you wonder how the men can stand it," he recalled. Yarborough appeared before many professional organizations and groups to deliver speeches. He told a group of students at the University of Texas and the Young Men's Business League of Austin that Texas gave away its valuable resources at the expense of future generations. Millions of acres of lands that should have been retained for public education and the state's universities were "squandered or carelessly disposed of."

Yarborough compared his campaign effort to his days in the Borger oil fields. He remembered the long hours and the hard work required to build oil storage tanks. "A lawyer has a tendency to bury his nose in the law books and forget the working man, who sweats all day for relatively little pay," he said in one election-eve interview. And the working men represented by organized labor responded to Yarborough's campaign. The Austin labor committee endorsed Yarborough as a candidate "who can and will serve Organized Labor best."[33]

Just as he had served as an advisor and critic in their father's race in 1932, Harvey Yarborough assisted his younger brother in his first campaign, working with Ralph on everything from overall campaign strategy down to the size of the print on his campaign cards. Early in the race, Harvey advised Ralph to research Mendell's voting record as state representative. "In the final showdown, the principal weapon they will fight you with will be your age, that you are too young," Harvey said. "Therefore, be careful not to take any hasty action for fear it might not portray deliberation and mature thought." Yarborough's campaign materials, news releases, and speeches reflected most of the suggestions offered by his brother in Dallas.[34]

In addition to printed flyers and newspaper ads, Yarborough used radio in his first election campaign. In the 1930's, candidates and their supporters began to purchase time on local radio stations. *Austin American* reporter Henry Brooks, who served alongside Yarborough as an LCRA director in 1935, spoke for him on the radio, describing the newest judge as young, hard working, and from a family of modest means. Brooks praised Yarborough's record at the University of Texas and for earning his own money "as a common laborer in the wheat fields of Oklahoma and in the oil fields of Texas." Brooks spoke of Yarborough's role in the million-dollar settlement from the Mid-Kansas Oil Company and noted that Governor Allred appointed Yarborough to the bench because he was "one of the most experienced land attorneys in Texas, so adjudged by his colleagues and contemporaries."[35]

Yarborough's first campaign for public office previewed his strategy for subsequent statewide races. He relied heavily on his background and his climb up the professional ladder. He was not wealthy, but his connections with Allred proved to be almost as beneficial in his early years. He relied on Allred's network of friends and supporters to form the backbone of his own organization. The million-dollar judgment for the Permanent School Fund provided strong testimony of Yarborough's professional abilities. The well-known decision promoted the image of a public servant who was unafraid to tackle difficult issues. When criticized, he counterattacked in a relentless manner and would not back down from a confrontation. He seldom hesitated to focus on his opponent's weaknesses. Always frugal, he utilized free media as much as possible.

Yarborough relied greatly on his family and friends to shoulder the burden of financing his campaigns. The close political relationship with his brother Harvey was evident throughout this campaign and future races. Following the district judge election, Ralph thanked his brother Harvey for the "suggestions on literature, on speaking, and on many other points . . . I am not putting that out for consumption in Austin for reasons which are obvious to you." Opal Yarborough, who remained behind the scenes in the political campaigns, nonetheless played an active role. In a letter to one of his supporters, Yarborough noted his wife's involvement and credited her work on his behalf among women in the county: "She ran me out every morning before I could get in bed from the night before, and managed my campaign among the lady voters." He concluded, "'the women and the blue-shirted boys' put me over."[36]

With his older brother's assistance, Yarborough actively planned and worked on all of the details of the campaign. He firmly believed that he could outwork any opponent and literally talk to more people and shake the hands of more voters. "This was my first race for public office and it convinced me that the best of all methods for any candidate is to go to the people," he remarked. "Let them look you over and you look them over. It'll do you both good." From the personal appearances to the media plan, Yarborough emerged as a candidate who exercised an active, hands-on approach to the election campaign. He personally maintained lists of voters he called on the telephone or visited. He kept separate lists of personal letters he mailed to individuals and sent thank you letters to supporters and friends after the election was over. As Ruth Shirley, a state employee, told him, "I didn't get to do much electioneering for you because everyone I'd talked to was already for you—and vehement about it." He thanked reporter Buck Hood for coverage during the campaign. "Your 'news' article published on the back of the front page of the Sunday *American Statesman* two weeks before the election was one of the most effective things done on my behalf during the campaign," Yarborough wrote. Yarborough assumed the roles of both candidate and campaign manager. He demonstrated that he was willing to accept advice, but he was reluctant to delegate too much authority to others in the campaign. While this was a successful combination in a local election campaign in 1936, the approach would cause him problems in later statewide campaigns, in which all of Texas had to be covered.[37]

The July 25, 1936, Democratic primary election was a total victory for Yarborough, who won a majority in every election precinct. Yarborough defeated Mendell by 11,077 votes to 4,895 votes. His margin rivaled that of incumbent Congressman J. P. Buchanan's victory over his primary opponent, and he easily outperformed other local candidates in contested races. Yarborough also polled several thousand more ballots than Governor Allred did in the area. However, the popular governor who appointed him to the bench faced four challengers in the gubernatorial primary. Mendell's vote against women's suffrage while in the state legislature probably hurt the challenger the most. By 1936 women were active in Democratic party politics and at the voting booth. Although no polls provided evidence that women preferred Yarborough in this race, the election results indicated solid approval for the young district judge. According to his records, Yarborough spent only $1,182, most of it on advertising and mailings.[38]

Yarborough's initial campaign victory set him on a course of public service and campaign politics that he pursued for the next thirty-five years. With the exception of his military service during World War II, Yarborough devoted most of his time and resources to the political process and the Democratic party. His first effort resulted in a complete victory over an opponent who was no easy mark. But Yarborough's record, his active campaign, and his reputation as a man with a future made him an unbeatable candidate in 1936. Equally important, Yarborough had made the transition from an appointed officeholder to a man who could win an election. He enjoyed campaigning and demonstrated that he was an effective officeholder. His first victory kindled the fires for future efforts.

As resounding as the 1936 victory was, it may have led Yarborough to make some false assumptions about running a political race in Texas. Personal contact was undoubtedly important in political campaigns in the 1930's. In local races, which involved a small area and concentrated population, the candidate had an opportunity to visit with many voters and know them on a first-name basis. Those circumstances changed dramatically when a candidate campaigned for statewide office, especially in a state as large as Texas. An organization, strong financial support, and the effective use of the media were essential in the 1930's for a man with larger ambitions for public office. Personal charisma and ability were important to the voters in Texas. Often the most qualified candidate failed to gain the party's nomination because of an inability to capture the attention of the voters and the press in Texas. Yarborough's impressive victory in the district judge's race took him one small step in this direction but not far enough to attract the widespread attention and financial backing necessary to capture a statewide office. Yarborough proved that he was a tough and able campaigner, but in a sense his victory in this campaign may have been too easy. Not surprisingly, he decided to follow the path of his political mentor, James Allred, who moved from district attorney to statewide official within a few years. Shortly after taking his oath as district judge in 1937, Yarborough decided to jump into the attorney general's race in the upcoming 1938 Democratic primary.

4 The Hamburger Campaign

The sweeping Democratic victory of 1936 gave Democrats a commanding presence in Washington, D.C., and in Texas. In Austin, the state's capital, Governor James Allred led a formidable group of Texas Democrats united behind President Roosevelt and the New Deal. District judge Ralph Yarborough, fresh off his first victory to elective office, became a strong proponent of the economic and social initiatives advocated by FDR and Allred. But by 1938, politics and the domestic agenda began to shift in Texas and the rest of the nation. While New Deal legislation fostered liberalism in Texas and the rest of the South, it also generated a tremendous counter-reaction among the wealthy and the larger corporate interests. In Texas, the core members of this conservative coalition included the major oil and gas corporations—the primary group Allred and Yarborough had battled to achieve their greatest legal victories in the early 1930's. By 1938, a combination of events and circumstances led to a political shift all the way down the ballot and thwarted the ambitions of Yarborough and other liberal candidates.[1]

Political concerns in 1938 focused primarily on economic matters, but some new personalities took the political stage. At the national level, the scope of the New Deal programs, Roosevelt's ill-fated plan to expand the Supreme Court, and the active involvement of the federal government in business became a divisive issue for Texans. The political rift in Texas between Democrats who identified themselves as New Deal, FDR supporters, led by Allred, and the more conservative group headed by Vice President John Nance Garner increased after 1936, though the breach between conservatives and liberals was overcome when their shared desire to funnel federal dollars into the state was in play. By 1937, the country was suffering reverses in the economic progress made during Roosevelt's first presidential term. Reductions in relief programs and public works coupled with a downturn in productivity translated into a recession that erased many of the gains earned in the previous four years. Business lobbyists representing the major oil companies and private utilities, who remembered the lawsuits pursued by Yarborough as an assistant attorney general, saw him continue in this direction as district judge. His activist approach on the bench indicated his adherence to the New Deal and its politics.[2]

A number of Yarborough's contemporaries began following different political paths after 1937. Lyndon Johnson, with whom Yarborough cooperated while serving on the LCRA board, came into the picture again. Johnson ran in the special congressional election following Representative Buchanan's unexpected death in 1937. Yarborough, who may have entertained thoughts of running for the open seat, supported Johnson in his efforts. Johnson ran as a strong proponent of FDR and the New Deal but accommodating business interests was also part of his underlying strategy in moving up the political ladder. Central Texas voters demonstrated in this election that despite some concerns about the New Deal's accomplishments, FDR and his programs maintained widespread support. For the short term, the philosophical and strategic differences of these two future Texas leaders remained closely aligned.

Future governor Allan Shivers was serving as a member of the Texas House of Representatives when Yarborough and Johnson won their first elections. Recognized as one of the rising stars in the state legislature, Shivers represented the Gulf Coast community of Port Arthur and southeast Texas. Shivers worked his way through the University of Texas in the early 1930's. After he returned home to Port Arthur he ran for the state senate with the support of organized labor and was elected. In his 1938 reelection campaign, Shivers campaigned on his legislative accomplishments, which favored older citizens and working people. After 1938 Shivers' marriage into a prominent local family and business opportunities lured him in a more conservative direction as he rose through the political ranks. Yarborough, Johnson, and Shivers began their political careers with somewhat similar backgrounds and political philosophies, yet within a few years each took a different path, which led to dramatic changes for the state and nation in the 1950's.[3]

The sudden emergence of W. Lee "Pappy" O'Daniel in the Texas governor's race significantly altered the political terrain in 1938. O'Daniel had never run for public office but was widely recognized throughout the state as the radio personality who promoted flour with the accompaniment of a popular band, the Lightcrust Doughboys. He was a Republican but filed in the Democratic primary when Governor Allred announced he would not seek a third term. O'Daniel campaigned on the "Golden Rule" and called for the "throwing out of the politicians of Austin." His campaign consisted of platitudes and country music as he barnstormed through the state. A total of thirteen Democratic candidates filed for governor. The group included Railroad Commission chairman Ernest O. Thompson, Attorney General William McCraw, Wichita Falls oilman Tom Hunter, and Karl Crowley, former assistant postmaster general of the United States. With no incumbent running and a large field of candidates, a record numbers of voters, of all political persuasions, turned out to cast their ballots in the primary that summer.[4]

Yarborough decided to run for attorney general soon after he won the district judge election. His official announcement was more than a year away, but he needed the time to organize his first statewide campaign and raise money. The young district judge had increased his court schedule and also launched new, groundbreaking grand jury probes. Moreover, in July 1937 Governor Allred appointed Yarborough presiding judge of the third judicial district in Texas. As such, Yarborough administered the case load for eighteen district judges in thirty-three Central Texas counties. He believed that his hectic schedule would further his political aspirations and result in more statewide headlines.

AN ACTIVIST JUDGE

District Judge Yarborough and his fellow judges were sworn in on January 1, 1937, by Susette Meyer, a graduate of the University of Texas Law School and member of the Travis County Bar Association, who thus became the first woman to administer the oath of office. As part of their oath, each man pledged to uphold the constitution and promise that "they had never fought a duel," a pledge then still required of Texas officials. Judge Yarborough presided over a state district courtroom that witnessed a parade of everyday problems ranging from petty quarrels to major issues of the day. One of his first cases in January 1937 tested the constitutionality of the state's cigarette tax law. Former governor Dan Moody represented a distributor who claimed the state legislature acted unconstitutionally when it gave authority to the state comptroller to collect the cigarette tax. In his decision that favored the state, Yarborough compared the case to other instances where the legislature gave power to administrative agencies to administer commerce. In a local burglary case, Yarborough allowed prosecutors to submit to a jury testimony from Austin merchant Henry Petri against a defendant accused of stealing liquor (though the evidence had been consumed). What made the case unusual was the death of Mr. Petri before the case came could come to trial. The local newspaper reflected some of Yarborough's subtle humor when it reported "Deceased Man's Testimony Heard in Burglary Case."[5]

In several small, seemingly insignificant cases, Yarborough challenged the community's culture of racism and segregation. Yarborough refused to accept the guilty plea entered by Jessie Mae Lott, who was described as "a negress" in the *Austin Statesman* on May 27, 1937. The accused had informed the prosecutor that she would plead guilty, but she took the witness stand and declared her innocence. With no other witnesses to support the theft charge, Yarborough accepted Lott's plea and ruled in her favor. That same day Yarborough dismissed the case involving another African American resident, this one charged with cattle theft. These cases are some of the earliest recorded indications of Yarborough's changing views involving members of the minority community. He was not prepared to openly challenge segregation and Jim Crow laws but was ready to use his judicial position to confront some of the most prevalent abuses in southern society. Nearly every officeholder and the vast majority of white Texans in the 1930's opposed any change in the racial status quo. Dismissing a few misdemeanor charges against several black defendants did not significantly alter a way of life for African Americans in the South. However, Yarborough's decision was one small step toward hope and equal justice in the minority community and a large step in his own character development.[6]

Yarborough received several accolades during this period of his life. He was elected the first president of the University of Texas Law School Ex-Students Association in July 1937. The new organization he helped organize served as a network for graduates of the university. In November 1937 he was appointed to serve on the advisory editorial board of the *Texas Law Review*, the only publication of its type in the state. Yarborough was frequently called upon to make speeches on relevant events of the day or historic occurrences. In an Armistice Day speech on November 11, 1937, at the University of Texas, Yarborough departed from local politics and history and turned his attention to events overseas. "America and the world are faced today with a grave problem—the problem of peace," he said. "We won the world war and the world all but lost democracy." Yarborough said the nation needed to broaden its efforts to maintain security and prevent another world war. Yarborough cautioned Americans listening to the propaganda of other nations to attempt to understand its true meaning. He warned Americans to be wary of the rise of fascism and nations who suppressed democratic governments by force of arms. "America can't cram democracy down the throats of other nations with bayonets," he warned. "We should educate them to democracy by setting the example for them, by keeping our government democratic, ruled by the people, a peaceful people, and make America a governmental light to the world." But as he advocated peace, Yarborough warned of alliances with other nations with a "too proud to fight" attitude. At this point, Yarborough realized that international political events were changing in Europe and Asia in ways that could affect the United States. His speech reflected his first public recognition of potential problems for the United States from aggressive totalitarian governments. He knew that people in Texas were affected not only by events in Washington, D.C., but also by activities in Berlin and Tokyo.[7]

As he searched for an early boost prior to his official campaign for attorney general, the young jurist seized on an issue which served many other aspiring politicians during this period—an attack on big business monopolies. In January 1938 a new grand jury panel assembled in the 53rd District Court whose purpose was to investigate violations of Texas antitrust laws. The chairman of the new panel was Dr. Walter Prescott Webb of the University of Texas. Webb was a nationally known historian whose monumental history of the American West, *The Great Plains*, was widely read. A more recent book of Webb's attracted Yarborough's attention and undoubtedly resulted in Webb's selection as chairman of this special panel. Webb's *Divided We Stand* provided an interpretive economic history of the nation that included severe criticism of business monopolies and antitrust practices. According to Webb, the nation was divided into three distinct cultural and economic regions— the North, South, and West. The North exercised "economic imperial control" over the other two sections, which resulted in widespread poverty and concentration of wealth. Webb's theories supported what many southerners and westerners believed and often discussed, whether in small coffee shops or the halls of the nation's Capitol.[8]

Yarborough made ample use of the new grand jury and its well-known foreman. In a dramatic opening, the judge told the panel that in earlier days a grand juror had to be concerned with assassination by outlaws. Those threats were no longer present but, Yarborough pointed out, modern grand jurors needed "a new type of courage, that to investigate the enforcement and observance of all laws, including the anti-trust laws." Yarborough's instructions closely followed Webb's theme of economic exploitation as he complained about giant monopolies that were a detriment to Texas, the South, and the West. "Many are headed in the money centers of the industrial mart, the East. Any monopoly is detrimental to the welfare of a whole people, because the monopolist is unjustly enriched with an unearned increment." Yarborough believed the investigation would be an ongoing probe continuing over many grand jury sessions. "It will take united and long efforts by our people to scourge these monopolies from Texas," he declared.[9]

At least one newspaper noted the political significance of the new grand jury panel: The *Austin American* reported that the "trust busting" charge was interpreted as a prospective platform for Yarborough's attorney general candidacy. When Yarborough delivered his instructions to the grand jury the courtroom was packed, with several prominent lawyers in attendance. Yarborough announced that this grand jury had exceptionally broad powers since the Travis County Grand Jury had the authority to indict persons living in any county in Texas. In addition, any person living outside the state could be charged with a crime if the jury determined they formed a conspiracy to violate the state's antitrust laws.[10]

The jury's wide-ranging power to investigate issues of trusts and monopolies drew the attention of the business community. With Yarborough as presiding judge and Webb as the grand jury foreman, the direction of the panel was clear. Webb's positions on economics and business were well known from *Divided We Stand* and Yarborough had equated violations of the antitrust laws with burglary and theft in his public presentation to the grand jury. In placing so-called white collar crimes on a par with the kinds of violations associated with common criminals, Yarborough wanted to convey to the grand jury— and, more importantly, to the general public and the press—that price-fixing and other crimes by business were no different from stealing by a common criminal.

Yarborough believed his grand jury troops would follow him against a strong, almost invisible enemy. But in his zeal for the task, he picked a very wide front for his attack. Rather than select one particular aspect of business, the grand jury was supposed to simultaneously advance in every direction. As a result, the panel could examine everything from the cost of milk charged by a small dairy to the price of oil set by large corporations. While the monopoly issue garnered much attention from the state's media, Yarborough's field of vision was somewhat too wide for a group of twelve grand jurors to effectively cover. Ironically, the widespread attention the grand jury received might have hurt Yarborough with some potential supporters within the business sector of Texas. Many of these leaders may have been hesitant to lend him political support for his upcoming campaign. But that was the risk Yarborough took. He believed that any losses he suffered among the business community would be offset by gains among the general population. His populist position in these hard economic times also appealed to the traditional Texas suspicion of out-of-state monopolies.

The grand jury had only a short time to conduct its work. The panel issued its report after less than two months' investigation. In place of indictments, the jury issued a statement censuring "deliberate and continuous flaunting" of the antitrust laws of Texas. The grand jurors said that "many witnesses have come before us from various sections of the state, and there have been numerous complaints as to alleged unlawful practices." Some witnesses told the panel they feared reprisals for appearing. The report urged the state legislature to fund a full-time auditor and investigator to assist with inquiries of this type. Because the grand jury also performed its regular duties, the members said they were handicapped in the monopoly and trust investigation "due to a lack of proper machinery and facilities necessary to thoroughly investigate matters of such magnitude as this has proved to be." [11]

The grand jury report stated that officials from other states submitted information showing that price fixing was prevalent throughout the nation. Recorded instances included identical bids submitted to federal, state, or municipal agencies even though in some cases as many as twelve different companies were competing for the contracts. The report noted that in one case the bids were identical to the "fourth decimal point." So frequent were these examples of identical bids that the grand jury concluded that they were not coincidences but were "clearly the result of collusion and price-fixing in order to stifle legitimate competition." Within one unnamed Texas industry, the panel found that price-fixing agreements were actually written into their contracts. In asking for state funds to combat the problem, the grand jurors wanted more investigative resources and enforcement of the laws already on the books. The panel equated the problems with burglary, theft, and embezzlement. "We feel that we have accomplished something worth while if we have done nothing more than awaken an apathetic public to the realization that the penal provisions of our antitrust laws are being violated, and that public necessity demands that this deliberate and continuous flouting of our laws cease." [12]

The grand jury investigation garnered statewide publicity but failed to produce the overall result Yarborough desired, though the investigation certainly put the business community on notice that their affairs would be subject to scrutiny. Price-fixing and illegal activities were shown to exist within various business sectors, but the grand jury failed to determine the extent or frequency with which these practices occurred in the state. The investigation with its widespread press coverage may itself have acted as a deterrent to the illegal practices, but the grand jury issued no substantive charges because of the short duration of the panel, its lack of resources, and the wide focus assigned to its members.

If the corporate establishment viewed Yarborough with suspicion based on his previous activities, the grand jury investigation sealed his reputation as a politician who was unafraid to attack vested interests. To the business establishment, he was the ultimate New Deal politician whose ideals were supported by legal knowledge and an energetic, articulate nature. For those who followed politics, Yarborough's positions were as clear as the summer sky. He wanted the support of the FDR-Allred faction of the Texas Democratic party in 1938. While he may not have obtained the desired results of having a well-known oil company or bank singled out in the grand jury report, he was pleased to have a statement that furthered his own political ideas and goals.

THE 1938 ATTORNEY GENERAL CAMPAIGN: "COLONELS OF MONOPOLY"

Ralph Yarborough worked at his customary fast pace during 1937. When he had any spare time while on the bench, his speaking commitments and service on legal and university committees filled it. Yarborough made dozens of public appearances and speeches. These included appearances at high school commencements, service clubs, veterans organizations, awards dinners, and Democratic party functions. Yarborough headlined many of these events since by this time he was noted for his ringing oratory. During the depression, Texans still viewed political speeches as a form of entertainment that ranked alongside radio and movies. Yarborough's entertaining mix of history, current events, and politics kept the attention of his audiences as well as any of the best preachers on a Sunday morning.[13]

With the attorney general's position wide open in 1938, a number of potential candidates considered running in the July Democratic primary. Among those attorneys and politicians from around the state evaluating their prospects in 1937 the most prominent were Ralph Yarborough of Austin, Lieutenant Governor Walter Woodul of Houston, former secretary of state Gerald Mann of Dallas, and Speaker of the House Bob Calvert of Hillsboro. Other possible candidates included Senator G. H. Nelson of Lubbock, Senator Franklin Spears of San Antonio, and former assistant attorney general Everett Looney of Austin.

Yarborough undoubtedly could have run for a higher court position, but the attorney general's office beckoned to him. The *Austin Statesman*, Yarborough's hometown newspaper and strong supporter, reported in August that the young judge was definitely in the race. In mid-August newspapers around the state began to focus on Yarborough as a potential candidate. Political prognosticators were certain that the young district judge from Travis County was ready to jump into the fast-moving waters of statewide politics.[14]

Yarborough officially announced for attorney general in Houston in early January 1938. He chose Houston rather than Austin because it was the largest city in the state, with over 300,000 people, and was the home of Lieutenant Governor Woodul, who would also be on the ballot. The offices of Gulf, Humble, Shell, and other petroleum companies Yarborough challenged in the courtroom crowded the downtown skyline. The city was a microcosm of the state. Its wealthiest families lived in stately mansions among the live oaks in River Oaks. Nearby, the African American residents lived on unpaved streets in ramshackle "shotgun" houses. In his announcement, Yarborough declared that "I will stand on my record and I will insist that my opponents stand on theirs" and professed that he wanted to be the "people's lawyer." Adopting a theme from Jim Hogg and James Allred, Yarborough said the voters wanted an experienced attorney who represented "the people's side in a courtroom." The candidate allowed that not everyone would agree with his views, but no one would have trouble understanding his positions. He added, "the man who will sidestep and straddle before election will duck and dodge duty afterward."[15]

Most correspondence Yarborough received congratulated him on the decision to run for attorney general. At least a few of his friends and political advisors had urged patience, primarily because of Walter Woodul's presence in the race. Mike Hogg, the son of former Governor Jim Hogg, told Yarborough that Woodul, "while a very fine gentleman personally, is unfit for the job of attorney general, and yet he is going to be mighty hard to beat." Nearly all of the correspondence applauded Yarborough's service as assistant attorney general of the state, and his record as judge during his brief term on the court was generally recognized as exceptional. Woodul's political knowledge might be formidable indeed but not enough to nudge Yarborough in another direction. The young district judge was determined to overcome the odds just as he had done earlier in his career when he successfully battled the major oil companies.[16]

Even with his driving ambition and work ethic, Yarborough realized that he faced long odds in the race. In October 1937 he wrote to a friend in Houston that Woodul was definitely the man to beat in the campaign: "From what I hear traveling over the state, I believe that the race is between Walter Woodul and me. I find some support for Gerald Mann and occasionally a supporter for one of the other candidates in the race, but generally they are either undecided or for Woodul or me, or sometimes for Mann." Yarborough noted that Woodul was strongest in the Gulf Coast region while Mann had support in the Dallas area. Yarborough told another friend in Houston that he was not going to attempt to pull support from any of the oil companies in the state for the campaign: "They are for Woodul tooth and toenail."[17]

Woodul's two terms as the leader of the Texas Senate provided him organization and drew financial support from around the state. Woodul had made it clear early in 1937 that he planned to run for attorney general. Getting the jump on other candidates was a good strategy, and the front-runner tag was his from the very beginning. His twenty years in political office gave him a clear understanding of the state electorate. One of his hometown newspapers described Woodul as a "stout, black-haired, moustached Houstonian that had the lieutenant governorship sewed up before his opponents knew what had happened." Born in Laredo in 1892, Woodul grew up in Corpus Christi and Alice. He served briefly as editor of the *Alice Echo* newspaper and later worked his way through college as a teacher, dishwasher, and stenographer. During World War I, he served in Europe in the Thirty-sixth Division and rose to the rank of captain. Following the war, he moved to Houston and began his law practice. He was elected to the state senate from Houston in 1928 and as lieutenant governor in 1934.[18]

Another well-known contender, Gerald Mann, was the "Little Red Arrow" of the SMU Mustangs football team in the 1920's and an Allred protégé. He grew up in the small East Texas community of Sulphur Springs, only a few miles from Yarborough's hometown of Chandler. His first job at Southern Methodist University was placing sod on the football field, and he later worked in boarding houses and waited tables. When Mann became the star quarterback of the 1927 Mustang team he received national recognition. Following graduation, he left Texas to attend Harvard Law School, where he earned his law degree. Governor Allred appointed the attorney–football hero his secretary of state in 1935. Later Mann obtained several million dollars in federal funds when he represented the state in Washington, D.C., while on the Texas Planning Board, created by the Texas Legislature in 1935 to secure federal dollars for state and local projects. In his campaign literature, he promoted his athletic reputation, clean-cut image, and professional accomplishments. He said "I had rather be a real attorney general for two years than a vacillating, shifting politician. . . . I had rather be a one-termer than a two-timer."[19]

The fourth major candidate in the race was Speaker Robert W. Calvert of Hillsboro. Calvert was born in Tennessee in 1905. He moved to Texas after the death of his father and was raised in the state's Orphan's Home in Corsicana. Calvert attended the University of Texas and its law school, where he earned his law degree in 1931. The voters of his Central Texas area elected him to the House of Representatives in 1932, and he became Speaker of the House in 1937. As Speaker, he worked for passage of old-age assistance and other legislation to benefit the underprivileged. In the 1938 race for attorney general, Calvert campaigned on protecting Texans from unfair business practices and reducing expenses of the Attorney General's office.[20] (Later in his career, Calvert was elected to the Texas Supreme Court as an associate judge and became chief justice in 1961, serving until his retirement in 1972.)

Woodul was the acknowledged leader at the outset and the other three candidates—Yarborough, Mann, and Calvert—understood that they battled for what would likely be a position in the runoff election. Mann was best known in Dallas and North Texas. Calvert and Yarborough drew their strength from the same areas—East Texas and Central Texas. Yarborough recalled years after the race that some influential friends tried to persuade the two candidates to pool their resources to defeat Woodul. In particular, J. R. Parten, the independent oil man who was one of Allred's strongest financial backers, urged an agreement. "Major Parten tried some political diplomacy, and suggested that Bob Calvert and I were drawing largely from the same people," Yarborough recalled. Parten recommended that "only one of us should run, or we would both be defeated." Yarborough listened to the advice, but neither he nor Calvert followed the suggestion.[21]

Yarborough spent the early months of the campaign touring hundreds of small communities. He made speeches, attended box suppers and pie socials, joined in singing at school picnics, and called on attorneys and small businessmen. Country people went to town on Saturdays to spend the day at the store and catch a western serial at the "Star" or "Texas" movie theater near the county courthouse. Yarborough made many appearances on courthouse steps for talks to small gatherings. He always stopped by the local newspaper office to leave his news release and offer an interview. The Mid-Kansas judgment served as his million-dollar calling card at all of his campaign stops. A dozen formal speeches and many more spontaneous ones were the norm for the energetic Yarborough. As election day neared, he began to draw large crowds, bands turned out to greet him, and in several towns streets had to be roped off to separate Yarborough from throngs of well-wishers.[22]

One campaign swing took Yarborough through the treeless High Plains, where he worked the crowds in towns where the jackrabbits and prairie dogs easily outnumbered the voters. The narrow paved roads often disappeared when strong winds blew dirt and sand across the Panhandle highways. Adverse weather and rough roads never discouraged Yarborough. Yarborough stopped in Borger, where he had spent the summer of 1926 building oil storage tanks. Borger had changed in the ten years since then. The boomtown of derricks and ramshackle buildings, where fights, brawls, and murders regularly occurred, no longer existed. Yarborough saw a community which was a "thoroughly civilized, respectable, quiet, peaceable, law-abiding, religious town. I didn't recognize it. I only knew I was there because the maps and signs told me I was there," he mused.[23]

Yarborough received favorable notices from reporters around the state. He appeared to campaign nonstop in his effort to individually greet as many voters as possible, a campaign style that became a Yarborough trademark for the rest of his career. At one small town in East Texas, a photographer captured a smiling Yarborough taking a break for a campaign "dinner" that consisted of a single hamburger; Yarborough was now on the "Hamburger Campaign" to the finish. The metaphor undoubtedly pleased him. Throughout the race, Yarborough wanted to portray himself as the candidate most closely associated with the common people, and the hamburger was the perfect symbol for his hard-working, low-budget campaign—straightforward, inexpensive, and available to everyone. His image defined, Yarborough was "the people's candidate."[24]

Yarborough began to pick up support from influential Texans, some of whom were previously mentioned as potential candidates. State senator J. Franklin Spears of San Antonio endorsed Yarborough, Ben Looney, another Allred assistant, dropped out of the race in favor of Yarborough, and Mike Hogg, son of former governor Jim Hogg, announced for Yarborough. Yarborough also gained the support of prominent newspaperman Boyce House of Fort Worth, whose popular column appeared in many of the state's newspapers in the 1930's. Yarborough's friendship with House began in 1938 and would last for many years. The popular writer traveled with Yarborough on some of his campaign swings around the state and in the 1950's worked on many of Yarborough's later campaigns. Yarborough also enlisted the support of his two brothers, Harvey and Donald. Harvey, a Dallas attorney, once again played an important campaign role, making appearances, raising money, and coordinating the radio speeches for his younger brother. His presence was felt throughout the campaign but seldom noticed by the press or political observers. Donald also spoke at rallies and raised money for radio programs. The political relationships the brothers first established during their father's county commissioner's campaign now were put to Ralph's advantage.[25]

Yarborough attempted throughout most of the spring and early summer to draw Woodul into a debate. As soon as money was available, Yarborough used the radio to broadcast his messages. He selected programs in Houston, Dallas, and San Antonio, the largest metropolitan areas and also the sites of the radio stations with the most powerful signals. All of the speeches contained a discourse on his family background, his education, and his record as assistant attorney general. He also devoted time to attacking Woodul's record and positions in each broadcast. In his speech of July 14, Yarborough said that Woodul's campaign manager criticized him for "waving the worn-out check of the Mid-Kansas case." Yarborough responded to that by suggesting, "instead of trying to belittle me, why doesn't my opponent wave a check that shows where he ever won as much as a thin dime in the courtroom for the taxpayers of Texas." Yarborough went on to claim that Woodul, while lieutenant governor, was "in the hire of sugar, sulfur, utilities and other monopolistic aggregations." He also charged Woodul with campaigning at the taxpayers' expense: "This is no time to elect as attorney general a man who— while holding public position—can make trips in air-conditioned coaches on a pass."[26]

Yarborough wanted to paint Woodul as a man of privilege who was far removed from the day-to-day problems of most Texans. He warned that in the final days of the campaign Woodul would spend an enormous amount of money to win the election. Commenting on the numerous Woodul signs posted along the highways, Yarborough lampooned them as "more-than-life-size posters in delicate pastel shades that were imported from Hollywood." Yarborough pointed out that Woodul had voted against women's suffrage and opposed the veterans' bonus. As chairman of the Texas Centennial Commission, Woodul even voted to omit Sam Houston's name on the monument cornerstone but to place his own there.

Noting his own efforts were similar to those of his hero, Sam Houston,

Yarborough drew a parallel between the situation then and now. "Sam Houston won freedom for us at San Jacinto by striking off the fetters of another nation," Yarborough declared, and he went on to equate Houston's battles with the ones Texans faced in 1938, telling his listeners that the enemies of labor, farmers, old people, school children, and the rank and file citizens threatened the state to such an extent that Texans would soon find themselves "strangers in the land of their fathers." Citizens could look forward to a life of "toil as peons in the domain that our forefathers freed a century ago." In closing his speech, he cried, "let us march shoulder to shoulder, with the Lone Star banner and Old Glory floating above us, and re-assert our freedom on July 23."[27]

Yarborough pounced on a little-noticed act by Woodul in an effort to gain further attention for his own campaign. During Woodul's term as lieutenant governor, he served as the acting governor when Allred was out of state. As honorary governor, Woodul bestowed the position of "colonel" as official commissions to citizens and his friends. Yarborough charged that Woodul presented these "glittering commissions as colonels to spokesmen and executives of monopolies that are draining Texas to enrich a few men in distant states." Yarborough said these "colonels of monopoly" were the ones which the next attorney general would engage in the courtroom. These included the New York president of a national mortgage-holding company, Wall Street bankers, and the Texas representative of the J. P. Morgan Company. Also a recipient of one of Woodul's commissions was one "Richard Whitney, who admitted stealing a million dollars of trust funds and is now a number in Sing Sing prison." If Woodul served as attorney general, Yarborough predicted, "the lobbyists that he has made colonels will flash their commissions like a passport and be ushered into his august presence while the plain people have to cool their heels in an ante-room for hours." Yarborough obviously enjoyed turning the honorary awards into a political weight around his opponent's neck. He seldom missed an opportunity in the closing weeks of the campaign to attack Woodul with his comic jibes and populist rhetoric.

For his part, Woodul ignored most of Yarborough's attacks and continued his campaign. He discussed his record and touted the support he had lined up in campaign stops around the state, which included five former attorneys general and most of the large daily newspapers.[28]

Funding the Yarborough campaign remained a major headache for the candidate and his supporters. Sidney Benbow, an attorney who served with Yarborough in the Attorney General's office, practiced law in Houston in 1938. Benbow volunteered to serve as a campaign manager and fund raiser.

A month before the primary, he noted the problems he and other supporters encountered in their efforts to raise campaign funds. Benbow complained to fellow attorney Elbert Hooper that he had "been turning heaven and earth trying to raise some money here for Ralph," but his solicitations went unanswered. Benbow noted that Yarborough focused a lot of his efforts in the small communities and failed to pay attention to gathering donations for his own campaign treasury. "Insufficient funds" was to become a familiar cry not just for this race but all other subsequent Yarborough campaigns. "Ralph made a serious mistake, as I told him early in the campaign, by not coming down here and spending a little time placating these boys who have a little money and are supporting him but are not hot." Benbow suggested that Yarborough make a personal appearance in Houston specifically to raise money from individual attorneys and other well-to-do activists. "The only thing I see for us to do is bring him down here and keep him hidden out. . . . and to go to some of these boys and cry on their shoulders and tell them he just has to have the money." Benbow commended Yarborough on his public appeal and speaking ability, but all would be lost if the candidate's message never reached enough people. Benbow believed that "it is a damn sight more important for him to get down here and help us raise some money in order that we could disseminate his message to the people over the radio and through the newspapers than for him to be going to these little country towns to pick up a few votes." Yarborough heard the pleas of Benbow and others who asked him to do the hard work of asking for money. Yet he was always drawn to the crowds and the handshakes at the small-town pie socials and the open air forums of the courthouse square and coffee shops, not to the back-room meetings in the corporate office buildings.[29]

Instead of focusing on raising money for the campaign, Yarborough chose to work on other aspects of the race. He took a direct, hands-on approach to the management of the operation. He wrote nearly all his speeches, whether they were for the radio or for a stem-winder on a courthouse square. The candidate also tried to respond to all of his mail, although campaign managers Sidney Benbow and Charles Betts wrote some letters on his behalf. Yarborough's involvement in the day-to-day activities of the campaign were indicative of the style he maintained throughout his long career. No detail was too small for him to review. Although this approach fostered a close relationship with people at the grass-roots level, he was often beset with a multitude of activities which could be delegated. Yarborough, however, never viewed this as a problem. To him, it was his signature: the personal commitment, the long hours, the hundreds of stops on the campaign trail, and the individual letters to friends and supporters that were the necessary part of his program. He always believed that hard work, a thoughtful discussion of the issues, and personal attention to detail could offset any financial advantage his opponent might have. If given the opportunity, Yarborough believed the power of persuasion would overcome any obstacle.[30]

As the 1938 campaign approached the July 23 primary date, the candidates made their final push. Yarborough made one last swing by car through the small communities of East Texas before wrapping up his campaign. By the time he delivered his final speech in Austin, he had appeared in 221 of the 254 Texas counties. Yarborough spoke on election eve before a rain-soaked crowd at Wooldridge Park across the street from the Travis County Courthouse. The driving rain diminished the crowd of 2,500 but failed to dampen Yarborough's enthusiasm. He sounded the familiar themes he had stressed throughout the campaign. Based on straw polls, Yarborough predicted he would lead in the first primary "by 40,000 votes" with support from East, Central, and West Texas.[31]

The July 23 primary failed to give Yarborough victory or even a place in the runoff. Woodul was first in statewide totals with 340,453 votes, followed by Gerald Mann as a close second with 328,538 votes. Yarborough was third with 220,964, followed by Calvert with 95,967. A fifth candidate, Lewis Goodrich, trailed with 53,285 votes. A total of 1,039,217 ballots were cast in the attorney general election, only slightly below the number of votes cast in the governor's race, which broke the record set two years before in the election that put Allred in the governor's office for his second term. The 1938 election was the largest primary turnout to date in Texas. The million-plus voters in the primary in fact exceeded the turnout for the 1936 presidential election in Texas.[32]

Woodul easily carried Harris County, including his hometown of Houston, by a large margin. Woodul had 32,529 votes compared to the 12,586 cast for Yarborough, who finished second in the county. Mann won Dallas County over Woodul but by a much smaller margin of 17,729 votes to Woodul's 11,379. Yarborough came in third with 8,314 votes. Woodul also placed first in Fort Worth, San Antonio, El Paso, Lubbock, Amarillo, Laredo, and Beaumont and was either first or second in nearly every county across the state. Yarborough won Austin and Tyler, gathering most of his support in Central and East Texas, where he placed first in 22 counties. He generally ran third to Mann and Woodul in other areas of the state.[33]

Yarborough took pride in his campaign that took him to 221 counties. Yet this approach may have hurt his campaign in the final analysis. Had he worked the areas where he ran the strongest and was best known, he possibly could have built up his margins to a level which placed him in the runoff election with Woodul. A more concentrated effort in East and Central Texas as opposed to his statewide efforts might have improved his vote totals. J. R. Parten's warning to his friend Yarborough early in the campaign that he and Calvert should unite forces might have been advice worth taking. Combined, the primary votes the two candidates generated would have been sufficient to qualify for a runoff. Certainly the lack of funds hurt the Yarborough campaign, but he proved to even his critics that he could personally campaign at a pace that left even the strongest supporters gasping for breath. Yarborough's oratorical skills, his dedication to the campaign, and his ambition certainly boded well for future political endeavors. All of Yarborough's exhaustive efforts failed to offset Woodul's advantages, though Yarborough's efforts placed him in better position for future campaigns. His strong showing of over 220,000 votes as a first-time candidate indicated to politicians and the press that he had a political future. He was no longer a local district judge and a former Allred assistant attorney general. Ralph Yarborough was now a recognized rising star in the Democratic party of Texas.

Yarborough incurred a sizable debt from the 1938 race which took him several years to pay off. At the conclusion of the campaign, Yarborough's records indicated he owed $3,202.04. Apparently, a number of debts incurred by supporters in the campaign were laid at Yarborough's door after the race was over. Outstanding amounts included bills from newspapers, printing companies, and telephone and secretarial services. He borrowed money several times from the Capital National Bank in Austin. He told Fort Worth printer Dudley Hodgkins six months after the election that "in each instance, however, I have assumed responsibility . . . I do not intend to see any printer lose any money on printing done on my behalf." Yarborough also rejected an offer from Hodgkins to reduce his bill after the printer proposed a $96.20 reduction. Yarborough thanked him for the offer but said, "I never accepted a discount on an obligation that I owed, and I feel that the same should hold true of the obligations incurred by others for matters to be used on my behalf." One of Yarborough's creditors expressed appreciation to him for his payment. Tucker Moore, a Fort Worth printer, wrote, "the character of man you undoubtedly are, by these convincing demonstrations in connection with this account, has won for you the unanimous support of this organization, when and if you should run again." Yarborough maintained a handwritten ledger of all the bills and the dates on which they were paid. The last bills paid were $121.51 to Southwestern Bell and $426 to Capital National Bank. He noted in his journal "pd. all debts in full, Dec. 12th, 1941."[34]

Yarborough was reluctant to raise money on his own behalf but never shirked paying his campaign debts. He always took pride in the fact that he had worked his way through school and that he managed to repay all of his loans, whether for law school or for his unsuccessful attorney general's race. At this point in his career, Yarborough relied on his own limited resources and support from his brother Harvey. Certainly no one in the Yarborough family could come close to matching the financial support Lyndon Johnson garnered in the late 1930's and early 1940's from his network of wealthy contributors. Later in his career, Yarborough received support from some independent oil men and bankers who subscribed to his liberal philosophy. J. R. Parten, the wealthy East Texas independent oil man and a large contributor to James Allred, became one of Yarborough's earliest financial backers. He provided some assistance in Yarborough's first campaign, but not a great deal when compared to the efforts made on behalf of James Allred.

Although Yarborough and Lyndon Johnson had similar political philosophies at this stage, they operated differently in the campaign finance arena. Johnson secured the support of Alvin Wirtz and Herman Brown to fund his political aspirations and never had problems raising money after his successful congressional election in 1937.

Yarborough maintained his support for Congressman Johnson throughout this period. Following the 1938 election, Yarborough served as president of the Travis County Bar Association in 1939. As the presiding attorney for the bar, he wrote a letter to Congressman Johnson recommending Judge Joseph C. Hutcheson Jr. as associate justice for the Fifth Circuit Court of Appeals. Yarborough wrote, "we liberals are extremely fortunate in having available for appointment to the vacancy the outstanding judicial intellect in the United States." The Austin-area congressman quickly replied and agreed to support Hutcheson. Johnson took the occasion to tell Yarborough, "I want to take advantage of this opportunity to tell you how much I appreciate your personal interest but, more than that, I feel deeply in your debt because of your real patriotism and service to mankind." Johnson added, "You are leaving something behind you when you are gone that will mean more than ordinary public service or material collections." No indications of any ill will between the two Democrats existed; Yarborough and Johnson saw eye-to-eye as solid Roosevelt Democrats.[35]

Yarborough showed no signs of being depressed after his defeat in 1938.

He was encouraged to continue his efforts and remain active by many supporters from around the state. Gerald Mann sang the praises of Yarborough as he pursued Yarborough's support against Woodul in the runoff election. The solicitation was successful. Yarborough announced his support for Mann (as did Calvert) and actively worked on behalf of the Dallas attorney to defeat Woodul. Yarborough wrote to one of his friends about his endorsement of Mann: "I believe that it would be a disastrous thing to the people of Texas for Walter Woodul to be elected Attorney General of Texas and have been doing what I could to help elect Gerald Mann. . . . I expect to make a radio speech for [him]."[36] In a statement for Mann's campaign Yarborough declared, "I believe the public interest will be best served by Mann's election." Mann placed Yarborough's endorsement and photo in a prominent position in his campaign publications prior to the runoff.

Mann, whose political philosophy and positions were akin to Yarborough's, told voters he opposed monopolies and trusts and favored old-age assistance programs. Following Yarborough's lead, he also attacked Woodul as a favorite of the large corporations and labeled the lieutenant governor an "imperialist." Governor-elect W. Lee O'Daniel endorsed Woodul in the runoff election, but the front-runner in July faltered in the stretch. Mann's support from Yarborough and Calvert, coupled with the absence of O'Daniel at the top of the ballot, resulted in an upset win for the "Little Red Arrow." Mann defeated Woodul by a vote of 493,678 to 364,167 and took office in January 1939.[37]

Yarborough returned to his position as 53rd District Judge with renewed enthusiasm. The legal and business community recognized him as an up-and-coming leader and he had a new friend, Gerald Mann, in the Attorney General's office. Just as his mentor James Allred had viewed his initial election defeat, the irrepressible Yarborough never saw his own as a setback. He had already experienced the pitfalls of Texas politics and learned that serving as the candidate and de facto campaign manager in his own race differed greatly from playing a supporting role for a popular statewide officeholder like James Allred. Yarborough learned firsthand the logistical and strategic problems in running for statewide office. Many candidates wilted in the heat and under the stress of working the expansive state, but Yarborough enjoyed the frenzied pace. He proved to himself that his oratorical skills, vision, and capacity for hard work were assets he could rely on in future campaigns. He also now understood that money for newspaper and especially radio ads was a political necessity but continued to place more value on making personal appearances, shaking hands, and delivering speeches. Yarborough was lucid and provocative as a speaker and knew that once a voter met and heard Ralph Yarborough, no doubt existed about the stands he took.

The political future appeared promising for Yarborough, but the gathering clouds of war soon changed the direction of his career and that of many others in Texas and throughout the rest of the nation. As Yarborough surveyed the horizon in 1939, neither he nor any other person realized the vast changes that would occur as a result of the nation's entry into World War II.

5   *We Saw the Worst*

Following the 1938 Democratic primary runoff election, Yarborough returned to his seat on the 53rd District Court in Travis County. His leave of absence for the primary enabled him to return to the judgeship in the fall of 1938. The opportunity also provided him a chance to renew his legal work and briefly forget the traumas of political campaigns. Yarborough served until 1940. At that point, he did not run for reelection and instead decided to enter private practice and await political developments. Two elections in the early 1940's piqued his interest—the special U.S. Senate election of 1941 and the regular election in 1942. In 1941, the death of U.S. senator Morris Sheppard, a staunch New Deal defender, opened the Senate seat. In both the special and regular elections, Yarborough enthusiastically supported the candidates most closely aligned with the New Deal and liberal politics—Lyndon Johnson in 1941 and James Allred in 1942. W. Lee O'Daniel, still riding high with his image as an entertainer/politician, defeated Congressman Lyndon Johnson in 1941. Johnson appeared to have won but changes in the vote totals in the days after the election changed the outcome. Whatever consideration Yarborough gave to running for Congress vanished as quickly as Lyndon Johnson's lead. During the regular election the following year, O'Daniel bested former governor Allred and managed to hold the position for the next six years.

Meanwhile, Yarborough's political future remained a source of political speculation. He was consistently mentioned as a likely candidate for attorney general once Gerald Mann left office. At one point, Governor O'Daniel hinted that Attorney General Mann was a likely candidate for appointment to the supreme court of Texas. "No sooner had the announcement gone out that Atty. Gen. Mann had been offered the supreme court appointment by Gov. O'Daniel, than friends began to call, write and wire Judge Yarborough, urging him to be a candidate for attorney general in the event Gen. Mann accepted the post," one newspaper account stated. An *Austin Statesman* editorial praised the two as men who were "capable, honest, fearless and consider the rights of the masses against special favors to the privileged few. Texas needs men like Gerald Mann and Ralph Yarborough in public service."[1]

Any thoughts Yarborough gave to again running for higher office quickly subsided with the onset of World War II. After the attack on Pearl Harbor on December 7, 1941, he decided to enter the armed forces and temporarily forego his political career. Concerns about the war replaced any thoughts of running for attorney general again. He told James McDuff, his nephew in the navy, that "the outbreak of the war has so changed the duties and obligations of all of us that I have not been able to get back into the swing of political things since the actual outbreak of the war." He had been too young to enlist in World War I. At age 38, he was now too old for the draft. But duty and patriotism were important to him and millions of other Americans. The conflict also rekindled some earlier dreams Yarborough had had when he believed he would follow a career in the military.

Yarborough requested applications from both the army and the navy in 1942. He rejected the army's initial offer in July 1942. As he explained to his nephew Russell Spikes, a naval officer in the submarine service, he turned down a desk job in Washington "in the hope of getting something more active." Yarborough wanted to be directly involved in the war overseas and waited for an offer that would take him into the conflict. He expressed his growing impatience for a position that would take him overseas. "Practice of law is much more interesting than being on the bench, but all civil life is dull compared to service in the military or naval forces in this world struggle."[2]

In the first year of the war, Yarborough received an offer to work as chief attorney for the Office of Price Administration (OPA) with oversight of petroleum production and distribution. His friend J. R. Parten had accepted a position with the OPA in Washington, D.C., to keep the oil flowing to the war effort. Yarborough rejected the OPA offer and, after considering the two main branches of service, decided to enlist in the army. But after waiting for nearly a year for a commitment, he received an offer to become an officer in the navy. Just as he was about to accept, the army came through. "I would have been highly honored to have had the privilege of serving with them, but felt it my duty to offer my services where the experience that I had would most likely be of benefit to our country," he explained in rejecting the navy's offer. The Department of the Army commissioned Yarborough as a captain in the Judge Advocate General's office based on his legal skills and his year at West Point. After a year of waiting for his combat assignment, on February 1, 1943, he left his wife, son, and Austin home for active duty.[3]

As he prepared for his departure, Yarborough received a congratulatory note from his brother Harvey, who enclosed a word of caution about political activities in the armed forces. "Remember this: the army is *not* liberal like the New Deal. It is the opposite, therefore if you have any New Dealish ideas you had better be very, very careful about *where* you express them," Harvey wrote. "I am, of course, thinking of your promotion to a higher grade in the army and not what is or will be of advantage after the war." Harvey knew his brother well.[4]

Yarborough left Austin in early 1943 with his captain's commission to study military law in the army's Judge Advocate General's School. After several crash courses over two months, he graduated in Ann Arbor, Michigan, on April 17, 1943. For the remainder of 1943, the army assigned him to Camp Swift in Texas, Fort Leonard Wood in Missouri, and finally the Pentagon. As judge advocate for his division, Yarborough performed a number of legal services for the men in the unit. He also participated in prosecuting cases brought by the military police. In one report, Yarborough listed what he called some of the "unusual cases" he took on in 1943. A staff sergeant crashed a jeep at Camp Swift. The sergeant's trip ended when he sped across the prairie and smashed the front of the jeep into a stump "which the rabbit succeeded in dodging." In another case, a soldier was tried for "painting the bar and furniture of a restaurant in Bastrop with red mercurochrome." Although the defendant claimed he was an artist, "the proprietor apparently lacked appreciation for artistic talent." Yarborough obviously saw the humor in these cases and recognized in them the soldiers' anxieties about the war. He too was anxious to leave for Europe. In 1944, their training completed, the newly organized Ninety-seventh Division boarded troopships to England in preparation for the invasion of Europe.[5]

In his shipboard correspondence to Opal while on his way to Europe, Yarborough wrote about Richard's schoolwork, their income taxes, the health of other family members, the books he read, the food they ate, and the shortage of some personal items. Yarborough was pleased to discover several other officers with similar interests. In the long periods of inactivity they discussed Abraham Lincoln, Andrew Jackson, Franklin Roosevelt, and other presidents. The musical *Oklahoma*, which he had seen in New York before his departure to Europe, impressed him very much, and he gave Opal an extensive critique of the production but admitted, "While I liked the show, I didn't enjoy it nearly as much as I would have had you been present." He reported that he did not get seasick, although he had spent several days in the bunk with a cold. Fortunately, his bed was next to the ship's doctor. "Of course

After his enlistment in the Army, Yarborough served in Europe until V–E Day, rising to the rank of lieutenant colonel. After Japan's surrender, the army appointed him military governor of Honshu Province. Courtesy Opal Yarborough.

the doctor was the one who brought the cold on board, and from whom we caught it!" The trip aboard ship was as enjoyable as possible given the circumstances, but he allowed that "after the war, I think I'll make my trips to foreign countries, if any, by air."[6]

Months after the Normandy invasion, the Ninety-seventh Division landed in France to become part of General George Patton's Third Army, which spearheaded the final drive across Europe in the early months of 1945. Ralph told Opal not to be alarmed if she did not hear from him for extended periods of time. "The government doesn't waste expenses on notifying relatives of a soldier's good conditions," he noted, using humor to reassure his wife. He said that it was "highly improbable" that he would become ill or wounded, "so no news is good news." Yarborough knew that keeping in touch with Opal and Richard during the long period overseas would be difficult. Letters from soldiers often took weeks to reach the States.[7]

As Yarborough crossed through northern France and Belgium in early 1945, he once again witnessed the ravages of war on the people, as he had after World War I twenty years earlier. As Yarborough moved east toward Germany with the American forces, he described the tremendous destruction from the recent battles in his letters. Homes, businesses, and churches were completely destroyed or stood as shadowy skeletons. Bombing knocked out rail lines and bridges, making travel as difficult for the American troops as for the enemy. Many roads were still blocked with concrete barriers and twisted steel after the Germans withdrew. He witnessed a panorama that he frequently admitted was difficult to put into words. Describing his activities and thoughts to his family, he often wondered how Europe and civilized people descended to levels so shocking and indefensible.

Yarborough also provided stories about the different places and people with whom he came in contact. As he made his way inland from the coast, he visited French towns which survived some of the awesome destruction. The shops were often bare or had only a few items to sell. At one town, he found a book store still in operation. Always the avid book collector, Yarborough purchased a French history of the American Civil War for twenty-six francs.

After a twenty-four-year absence, Yarborough spent several days in Paris and enjoyed its world-famous scenery and landmarks. When he ran low on gas, he went to the quartermaster's office in Paris and immediately noticed the Lone Star flag. There he met Colonel Aubrey Wilson, a Longview attorney who once appeared in Yarborough's district court. "The last time I saw you was in 1940, when you threw me out of your court on an injunction," Wilson said with surprise. Yarborough replied that he hoped that Wilson

would "return good for evil, and don't throw me out on my plea for movement of a few gallons of gasoline into my jeep." The two attorneys enjoyed
their reunion and Yarborough departed Paris with a full tank of gas.[8]

Patton's Third Army moved across the German frontier into the heart
of that nation with lightning speed in March 1945. Although Yarborough's
assignments as the division's legal representative often kept him out of the
combat areas, he stayed close to the front and witnessed firsthand some of the
great atrocities of World War II. In the most disturbing events of his wartime
experience, Yarborough participated in the capture of Allied prison camps
and the concentration camp at Flossenburg in the Bavarian forests. When
his unit liberated the camp, Yarborough was among the first soldiers on the
grounds. He recalled, "I saw the rawest part of that, and the hospital full of
people, some dying." He described the camp that first day of liberation:

> We were the first armed troops to enter and it was terrible. We saw the
> shoes stacked up, the dead bodies stacked like cords of wood, turned yel-
> low from starvation, the crematoria that had been used. We saw the worst.
> A man who had come into the hospital with a sore foot, and they just cut
> his foot off. The German doctor doing this was a civilian doctor. They did
> not use anesthetics. One inmate was telling me that he saw the doctors
> operating with cigarettes in their mouths, ashes falling where they may.
>
> General Eisenhower issued orders to every regimental commander
> serving in those camps to choose a representative group from every regi-
> ment division from Colonel on down to Private, different ranks and dif-
> ferent experiences, and send them through those camps to see what has
> happened there. He said that after the war, someone will rise up and say
> this did not happen, and I want those men to see what happened. That was
> a smart move of Eisenhower.[9]

The capture of the concentration camp was a memorable event for all of those
who participated, and the incident left an indelible mark on Yarborough. Like
many Americans, he joined the war out of patriotic duty and a desire to defeat
the fascist powers. Coming into contact with the horrors of the concentration camp revealed the full extent of the holocaust. Yarborough noted that
the mood of the American troops changed as they progressed into Europe
and began to uncover the "atrocities of the Hitler regime." He wondered
how many thousands of people had died in the camps. He also criticized the
clergy, noting that in all the German communities captured by the Americans, the churches "were going full blast, with a fat and well fed appearing

priest." Yarborough was truly offended that the German clergy knew of the atrocities without making any protest. The concentration camps provided the most graphic illustrations of the Nazi German's inhumanity. He also said that American soldiers frequently told him that if people witnessed what the troops saw after entering Germany, no one would ever question the motivation for fighting in the war.[10]

As the Americans moved through Germany, Yarborough found other examples of Hitler's atrocities. Yarborough's spent several days at a "displaced person's camp," a temporary location housing the slave laborers used to maintain Nazi wartime production. The camp had Russians, French, Italians, and Poles, most of whom worked years in the factories. "They were a glum, dispirited, unhappy lot of people," he commented. After talking with some of the newly liberated people, Yarborough learned that the Germans deported entire families from occupied areas for slave labor. Women were put to work on farms or performing domestic tasks and the men were assigned to factories, "much as slaves used to be divided up in the South when a slaver came to port." Several American soldiers discovered whips, clubs, and cat-o-nine tails used for punishment.

He was most impressed by the Russians, the largest group of people at the camp, who had "rustled" some wine and celebrated their new freedom. The Russians and some Poles sang, danced, and drank in a celebration that Yarborough said he would always remember. Most of the Russians at the party spoke German, so Yarborough conversed with them to learn the story of their travails. One of the Polish women, who observed that Yarborough was enjoying the festivities, became "jealous." When he told her that he was impressed by their music, the Pole remarked that "it was the only thing good about the Russians."[11]

Not everything was as painful as the liberation of the concentration and slave labor camps. While in Europe, Yarborough rose to the rank of lieutenant colonel and assistant division quartermaster. He spent most of his time in administrative duties with the division headquarters, which took him to many locations in France, Belgium, Germany, and Czechoslovakia. The countryside still had abundant wildlife. In one letter to Richard, he provided detailed descriptions of the deer, birds, rabbits, and even the dogs he saw as he traveled across France. The animal life undoubtedly reminded him of his childhood in East Texas. He said he kept up on the news on a daily basis reading the Paris edition of *Stars and Stripes*. The newspaper gave him "a pretty good summary of the doings of Congress and the President," an indication that his interest in politics had not diminished. He also said he was very busy in

April. "Through the night of the 15th, was swamped with helping soldiers fill out income tax returns." Even with the war in Europe, the business of the government continued, especially when taxes came due.[12]

On another occasion, Yarborough and a small group of officers "liberated" a German castle full of medical supplies. As they searched for a bridge, the group stumbled upon a medieval fortress which appeared to be unoccupied. When Yarborough decided to inspect inside the walls, they were surprised to find it occupied. "Five German women Red Cross workers came out and wanted to surrender," he said. Entering the castle, Yarborough discovered medical supplies piled fifteen feet high. The fortress was a central medical supply center the German army had quickly abandoned during their retreat. Yarborough said he learned that they had captured one of the largest stockpiles of medical supplies on the entire Western Front.

Later, his unit stayed several nights at a school in a small German town. He noticed that the science exhibits equaled those at the college level and exceeded any he had seen in Texas public schools. Yarborough said many educators were in his headquarters group and everyone admired the facilities. However, Yarborough could not locate a single volume of fiction on the shelves. The library contained books by "Himmler, Goebbels, Rosenberg and a number of lesser Nazi lights." Several of the books Yarborough looked at he described as "hymns of hate." He also noted one volume about the United States that said American society was a "Negroid Civilization." But in a later chapter, it stated that "Negroes are brutally and wrongfully treated in 'free' America." Although Yarborough made no other reference to the passage, he was undoubtedly aware that in part the cryptic remarks rang true, for he had seen evidence of discrimination against African Americans his entire life.[13]

Yarborough's division received credit for the capture of prime industrial areas of Germany: Siegburg, Solingen, and Dusseldorf. The unit spearheaded the drive all the way across the collapsing Nazi homeland, taking thousands of Axis prisoners. As the army moved east, the roads in Germany became more crowded with civilians and soldiers. He described it as "the greatest flood of human movement ever to take place in the history of mankind." People on foot and with handcarts carried what was left of their possessions. "Regardless of whether they be Russians or Poles or French or Dutch, they head west," Yarborough observed of European refugees generally. "The Americans came from the west—there lies liberty." As the war in Europe wound to a close, Yarborough thought of the difficulties in restoring the war-torn economies and democratic governments. He predicted that "unless there is food brought in from outside Europe, there will be famine here within another year." In Czechoslovakia, the formerly independent nation occupied by Hitler's armies in 1938, Yarborough and his fellow soldiers in the Ninety-seventh Division freed the cities of Cheb and Pilsen along with many other small towns and villages in the western region of that nation. He wrote that he came under fire and participated in battle on both sides of the Rhine and near Cheb. On VE Day (May 8, 1945) he was in Pilsen. Once victory was declared, he wanted to return home as soon as possible.[14]

Although the war was over in Europe, the conflict with Japan was still unfinished in the summer of 1945. The Ninety-seventh Division received orders to move to the Pacific Theater by way of the United States. This division along with many others were part of a massive buildup in preparation for the invasion of Japan. However, as the unit was crossing the United States for the Pacific, Yarborough and his fellow soldiers received the news that the atomic bombs dropped on Hiroshima and Nagasaki had dramatically ended Japanese resistance. Japan formally surrendered on September 2, 1945.

After the surrender, orders from President Truman dispatched the unit to Yokohama, Japan, as a part of the U.S. occupation forces assigned to the defeated nation. Yarborough enjoyed a brief but joyous reunion with his family in Austin before leaving with his division for California and the Pacific. They landed in Yokohama on September 24, 1945. From there they went by train to Miizugohara Air Base, sixty miles northwest of Tokyo. Ward Blacklock, a friend and fellow officer in the division, recalled that their commanding general disliked the assignment: "Since our general loved combat and hated occupation duties, he cut an order devolving on Colonel Yarborough from his military duties to deal with civilians." In other words, the order made Yarborough the military governor of Honshu Province, the seventh-largest area of Japan. The heavily populated region was the industrial heart of the nation and suffered widespread devastation from the thousands of tons of bombs dropped during the air attacks in the final months of the war.

While working in Japan, Yarborough toured many areas of the nation, including "atomized Hiroshima," his description of the city. In Tokyo, he said, the Japanese capital was "about 70% to 80% burned" from bombing attacks. "Every town or city I have seen of over 50,000 population is over 50% burned, usually 70% to 80%. Fire bombs were used, the residences were mostly of frame or stucco over a bamboo framework and they evidently burned with great speed when the fire bomb hit one." The devastation equaled the worst he saw in Europe.[15]

Yarborough spent eight months in Honshu working long hours in the struggle to rebuild and establish a democratic nation. As military governor

of the province, Yarborough approved all requests for businesses and industry to change from wartime production to peacetime manufacturing of con-
sumer items. Yarborough pushed through hundreds of these changes during
his tenure in the haste to return the Japanese nation to a self-sufficient industrial country. Yarborough was well prepared for the long hours and difficult
tasks as military governor. His previous government experience in Texas and
his service as quartermaster for the Ninety-seventh Infantry Division prepared him for the administrative headaches and long hours of negotiation.
Yarborough's penchant for hard work, his positive attitude, and his ability to
inspire the Japanese people contributed to his success as provincial governor.

Yarborough's headquarters in Honshu Province was a barracks building
that housed Korean prisoners of war who had been incarcerated by Japanese
troops and freed upon the arrival of American troops. While managing all
the civil affairs as the military governor of Honshu, Yarborough also worked
on repatriation of the Koreans. This included providing health care, housing,
and assistance for the Koreans to return home. Toward the end of his tour as
provincial governor, the former Korean prisoners of war saluted Yarborough
for his generosity and work on their behalf. At a ceremony outside their
former barracks, a delegation presented Yarborough a Korean flag with a
handwritten inscription: "This small present is made as a token of our heartfelt gratitude to you." Yarborough came home with the flag and kept it in his
office as a symbol of triumph over tragedy.[16]

Yarborough and the Ninety-seventh Infantry Division made history as the
only unit assigned to active duty in both the Atlantic and Pacific theaters
during World War II. Yarborough served under the most renowned generals of his day: Dwight D. Eisenhower and George Patton in Europe and
Douglas MacArthur in Japan. After spending nearly eight months in Japan,
Yarborough received his discharge orders in May 1946. He returned to Texas
with a distinguished wartime record. He had earned the rank of lieutenant
colonel and received eight medals of service and awards, including a battle
star and a bronze star. He received a superior rating from three different commanding generals for his wartime service and his term as military governor.[17]

Yarborough eagerly wished to return to civilian life in 1946. Since early
1943, he had seen very little of Opal and Richard and, even though he appreciated the opportunity of serving in Japan to assist in the restoration of the
war-torn nation, he longed for his life at home with his family in Texas. Opal
told him in her letters that many of their friends were already discharged and
he was among the last to come home. While Yarborough remained in Japan,
he rekindled his political interests, corresponding regularly with his brother

Harvey on his attorney general prospects. Upon his return he received encouragement from many of his friends to run for office. Some suggested he run for the Texas Supreme Court. Others wanted him to challenge Congressman Lyndon Johnson. In early 1946, when Attorney General Grover Sellers announced he would not seek reelection, several friends paid the $100 filing fee to enter Yarborough in the 1946 Democratic primary for the post. However, when he returned to Austin, Yarborough declined to enter the race. "Having been in the army of the United States for 40 months, and having just returned to the United States from Japan on May 26, I wish to spend some time with my family," Yarborough announced in a public statement.[18]

His decision was most likely the result of Opal's influence. Prior to returning home, Opal strongly questioned her husband's political future. While he was in Japan, she reminded him that he had previously stated that he "would never be running for another office." However, Opal noted, many of his friends now informed her that he planned a campaign as soon as he returned to Austin. If he chose to run again, Opal advised, he should run for attorney general "with the Governor's office as a future objective." Otherwise, she said "I do not see the advantage of it." She warned that it would be difficult to raise funds for any campaign because "the moneyed people feel that you are a radical, that you don't have your feet on the ground." She reminded her husband that they had been in debt from the unsuccessful 1938 attorney general race. Because he had not secured funds for another race, Opal objected to another campaign. Opal pleaded with her husband to obtain a discharge so they could resume their normal lives again. The Yarborough family like many others struggled with a lack of money during the war years. But in making his political decisions, she finally told him that he would "have to work this problem out alone." Opal's concerns, the years spent away from home, and the lack of money outweighed Yarborough's desire to reenter the political fray. Just as Opal had convinced Ralph not to run for office when they were first married, she once again exerted her influence in the political arena.[19]

In the remaining years of the 1940's, Yarborough reopened his Austin office and watched the changing postwar political scene. Returning to Austin in the summer of 1946, Yarborough joined the local VFW and American Legion posts. He also became the chief counsel for the Texas State Teachers Association. He continued to receive many solicitations from friends encouraging him to run again for a statewide office. When Congressman Lyndon Johnson chose to run for the U.S. Senate seat in 1948, a number of Austin citizens encouraged Yarborough to again consider the congressional seat. "I didn't even stop to look up the salary when offers of support came in (including an offer of withdrawal by Homer Thornberry in my favor . . . he is probably the leading candidate in the race). I couldn't walk out on my law practice at this time," Yarborough told his friend and fellow attorney Cooper Ragan. Thornberry, with Yarborough's support, won the election to succeed Johnson in Congress. Yarborough again was encouraged by friends to run for attorney general, or for Texas land commissioner. Other supporters urged his appointment to the Texas Supreme Court when a vacancy occurred during Governor Allan Shivers' first term of office as governor.[20]

As late as 1950, Yarborough told friends that he still had no firm plans to seek public office. He frequently expressed concerns over the conduct of state officials and offered public support to some political aspirants, but he remained behind the scenes. He was never one who could ignore current political events and their impact on Texas. As Cold War tensions escalated, Yarborough revealed some of his concerns. He told one longtime friend who encouraged him to seek the attorney general's office, "I agree with you that our State government needs improvement. I think that democracy will be strengthened generally by a strengthening and improvement of government at home." He added that he still thought about a campaign but conflict might occur with a former ally. "I served for over three and a half years in the army during World War II. Should we have an open, all-out, total mobilization war with Russia, I think that every one able to bear arms will be back in the service, or serving in some other capacity where he can be equally effective."[21]

Domestic political issues soon overcame international affairs. Increased opposition by conservative Texas Democratic leaders to presidents Franklin Roosevelt and Harry Truman during the 1940's carried over into the 1950's. The movement took root with a small group of "Constitutional Democrats of Texas" who opposed Roosevelt's New Deal policies. This dissension increased with the open break between Roosevelt and Vice President John Nance Garner of Uvalde. "Cactus Jack" split with FDR over the New Deal, and the Democrats replaced him on the ticket in 1940. With Garner's departure, Texas Democrats broke ranks over the issue of a third presidential term for Roosevelt. Roosevelt easily carried Texas and remained popular throughout the war. His conservative Texas foes muted their criticism during the war, but the smoldering embers of dissension became a new political wildfire after it. The split involved racial issues, the New Deal, and economic policies, and the division assumed the personalities of the leaders, as first the pro-Roosevelt and later the pro-Truman Texas Democrats aligned with national Democratic economic and social policies. Conservatives, who became known as "Texas Regulars" in this period, and liberals, who were the "loyalists," pulled out their political swords and kept them sharpened while the fighting raged in World War II. Yarborough, the staunch Roosevelt Democrat, remained in the liberal-loyalist camp.

The first true victim of this political struggle was not an elected official. University of Texas President Homer Rainey became the lightning rod for controversy in this emerging power struggle. During Pappy O'Daniel's term as governor, he appointed to the Board of Regents of the University of Texas conservative businessmen who attacked Rainey and his professors for their alleged liberal views that encouraged subversion. Rainey publicly defended the university and the professors accused by the board and characterized the assault as a witch hunt. Under attack by the ultraconservative regents, Rainey was fired for no specified reason on November 1, 1944, with only one dissenting vote from the board. New regents selected by Governor Coke Stevenson refused to reappoint Rainey, and the University of Texas subsequently was blacklisted by the American Association of University Professors and the Southern Association of Colleges and Secondary Schools. Yarborough was in the army but still voiced his complaints to Opal about Rainey's dismissal. He called the confrontation "tragic" and accurately predicted the debacle would harm the university and drive off other faculty members. In a letter to his wife from Europe, Yarborough criticized Governor Stevenson for his inactivity. He recalled the days in the early 1930's when he had first come into conflict with Stevenson as a House committee chairman. Yarborough now said Governor Stevenson, who stated he would not touch the "hot coffee pot," was deceitful in the Rainey firing. Yarborough also wrote his longtime friend J. Frank Dobie about Stevenson and the governor's failure to support Rainey or the University of Texas. "His coffee pot rule typifies his Texas office holding—which always put Coke's welfare ahead of the public welfare," Yarborough complained. Before Yarborough returned home from Japan, Rainey had entered the 1946 governor's race representing the loyal, Roosevelt faction of the Texas Democratic party. After a bitter primary, Railroad Commissioner Beauford Jester defeated Rainey. But the struggle for control between the liberal-loyalist and the conservative Democrats had just begun and would accelerate in the 1950's.[22]

The fight between these factions took on more significance with the actions of Allan Shivers, who ascended to the governor's office following Beauford Jester's death in 1949. Shivers easily won the governor's election in 1950. In preparation for the 1952 presidential election, Shivers began spreading the word through his supporters that he wanted an uninstructed (that is, uncommitted) group of Texas Democratic delegates that he could control at the 1952 Democratic presidential convention. By then Shivers' public disputes with the Truman administration had already made headlines. In particular, Shivers fanned the flames of the fight over disputed submerged lands in the Gulf of Mexico that became known as the Tidelands Controversy.[23]

The controversy over title to over 2.4 million acres of submerged lands in the Gulf of Mexico erupted after oil was discovered offshore of Texas. Both the state and the federal government claimed ownership. Texas based its claim to lands that extended from low tide to three leagues (10.35 miles) from shore on the 1845 treaty that admitted the state to the Union. Under the agreement, Texas retained its public lands after annexation, and for the next one hundred years the United States government recognized the three-league boundary. The Truman administration opposed Texas' claims, and U.S. Supreme Court decisions that went against Texas raised the stakes. State officials labeled federal attempts to claim the submerged land and its oil as "expropriation" and "a steal." The major oil companies, who had the most to gain by siding with Texas, helped Governor Shivers arouse public indignation in the late 1940's. Because a portion of the revenues from the submerged lands were dedicated to the state's Permanent School Fund, the ensuing hue and cry included accusations that the federal government and the Supreme Court were robbing the school children of Texas.[24]

Yarborough had authored the initial opinion that preserved the state's rights to these submerged lands when he served as an assistant attorney general in the early 1930's, and Texas Land Commissioner J. H. Walker issued the first submerged land leases based on Yarborough's opinion. In the late 1940's Yarborough once again became actively involved in the Tidelands issue, serving as a director of the State Tidelands Committee, a group formed to lobby Congress for legislation that upheld the state's claim to the three-league boundary. He made trips to Washington, D.C., in the early 1950's, testifying for congressional legislation that would overturn the Supreme Court's decision. Congress passed the legislation, but it was vetoed by President Truman a second time in 1952. Truman's veto and the well-publicized efforts by state officials and the oil companies to regain state jurisdiction over the Tidelands became a major issue in Texas politics in 1952. The confrontation also played an important role in the future of Governor Shivers and Ralph Yarborough.[25]

At a meeting of southern governors in Hot Springs, Arkansas, in November 1951, Governor Shivers listened as Sam Rayburn, Speaker of the U.S. House of Representatives, urged Democratic loyalty for the presidential nominee. The Texas governor refused to make a pledge and expressed public dissatisfaction with Rayburn's position. On January 12, 1952, Shivers announced for reelection as governor and reiterated his opposition to unqualified commitment to the Democratic national ticket. By elevating the loyalty issue in the race, Shivers not only believed that he could convince Texas voters to reelect him to the governor's office, he also hoped to control the party's process of selecting convention delegates and so maintain control over the sizable loyalist-liberal faction of the Texas Democrats. Most Texas Democrats and political writers in the state assumed Shivers had enough power to offset Rayburn's influence and the loyalist Democrats' presence at the grass-roots level. Shivers and his supporters criticized loyalist Democrats who planned to bolt from party conventions if a loyalty pledge was rejected, calling the ploy a "rule or ruin" strategy. The governor stated at his own press conference that the fight among Texas Democrats was over "Trumanism" and whether or not Democrats were going to allow the outgoing president to pick his own successor. Shivers later said the loyalist Democrats wanted to "capture the party organization in Texas and hand it over to the national machine."[26]

In the meantime, as events continued to deteriorate between the Shivers forces and the loyalist Democrats in the spring of 1952, Ralph Yarborough entered the picture. Yarborough prepared to climb back into the political waters and run for attorney general. He had postponed plans to run after returning home from the war but had never completely given up on the idea of running for attorney general, the position once occupied by his mentor, James Allred. It was one of the highest prizes for an attorney, especially for legal practitioners like Yarborough who excelled in the courtroom and thrived in the public limelight.

In January 1952 Yarborough made contacts around the state for a second attorney general race. But fate was about to move Yarborough to the forefront of the struggle between liberals and conservatives as they fought over the political and social agenda. While visiting the state capitol, he ran into Governor Shivers, who told Yarborough that he had heard about his potential candidacy. Yarborough related the conversation with Shivers hundreds of times in 1952, and in many of his future campaigns:

> He said he just wanted to tell me that I was wasting my time, that it wouldn't do me any good, that he had already decided who was going to be the next attorney general of Texas.
>
> As I looked the Governor in the eye, I knew in my heart what I must do. I knew the time had come to end dictation and boss rule in Austin. The

time had come for some red-blooded Texan to stand up and challenge this arrogant Austin machine that tries to hand-pick the candidates for public office. I determined I would not let this governor attack me from the rear. I resolved to meet him head-on. I set my sights on the Governorship itself.[27]

Modern Texas politics would never be the same.

6 *The Strong Acid Test*

The face of Texas changed considerably in the years following World War
II. Although in its agrarian, rural outlook the state maintained its "Texan"
image, the population and the state's commerce were in the midst of a major
transition. After 1950, nearly two-thirds of the 7.7 million Texans lived in
urban areas, making the 1950's the first decade in which more Texans resided
in urban areas than in the countryside. Most of the nation had a majority
of city dwellers by the 1920's, but Texas and the rest of the South lagged
far behind. The sudden change from rural to urban came as a result of the
rapid industrialization during World War II coupled with the expansion of
the petroleum industry. Farm jobs were fewer, and more opportunities in
the service, manufacturing, and construction industries lured people to Texas
cities during the war. The trend continued through the 1940's postwar economic boom and the into the evolving Cold War era. Most of the migration
to the state's urban centers came not from other states but from nearby rural
areas. Although classified as urbanites, these recently uprooted newcomers
brought with them their traditions, philosophies, biases, and political viewpoints. While the largest cities like Houston and Dallas touted their steel
skylines and sudden wealth, they were at heart mostly old, rural Texas, just
in a new set of clothes.

Texas during the decade of the fifties made a slow, uneven transition to
its new cosmopolitan image. The state's economy, now more strongly linked
to industrialization and urban centers, changed much faster than individual
attitudes. The political culture remained tradition-bound. Politically, Texas
remained a one-party state whose working classes and city residents went
largely underrepresented while minorities were merely seen and not heard. In
rural Texas, the railroad tracks separated whites from black and brown people.
In the new, urban Texas the separation continued, with African Americans
and Mexican Americans residing in divided communities defined by legal
and de facto segregation. In the early 1950's, racial segregation was the rule in

schools, public facilities, private businesses, and throughout the entire culture, in practice and by law. U.S. Supreme Court rulings began to knock down some barriers in the 1940's, beginning with the all-white Democratic primary, whose voters and candidates had represented only white citizens in the state. However, little changed, for "whites only" signs continued to appear in Texas communities, rural and urban, even in locales with few minority residents. With the exception of Mexican Americans tied to South Texas political machines, only a handful of minorities legitimately participated in the democratic process. Equal opportunity was as remote as a sudden freeze on a July afternoon for the state's African Americans and Mexican Americans. Texas and the rest of the South would face a test of these long-standing traditions and beliefs in the 1950's, but as the decade began, it was business as usual in politics and society.[1]

Political scientist V. O. Key noted in his monumental study *Southern Politics* that most people viewed Texas as a traditional southern state but one distinct from the states which composed the Old Confederacy. Texans were less concerned about keeping African Americans in their place than the rest of their southern counterparts. With a lower percentage of African Americans than in other southern states and a more diverse economy, Texas was by 1950 "more western than southern." According to Key, such issues as taxes, corruption, communism, water, and the respective roles of state and federal government all figured larger in the gubernatorial elections of the 1950's. Texans may have been somewhat more tolerant than many of their southern neighbors, but the issue that particularly dogged Yarborough during his gubernatorial campaigns in the 1950's involved race relations and integration. If, as Key noted, racism was not as overtly hostile in Texas, the concerns of white Texans about the role of African Americans and Mexican Americans in modern society nonetheless became a deciding factor in the politics. The gathering storm of civil rights changed the social and political atmosphere in Texas to one in which race suddenly became the most important issue.[2]

THE 1952 DEMOCRATIC PRIMARY

By 1952, Yarborough was aligned with the loyalist faction of the Texas Democratic party in spite of his differences with the Truman administration over the Tidelands issue. However, he was not part of the leadership of the loyalist faction of the state's Democratic party. The active supporters of Homer Rainey's unsuccessful race for governor in 1946 composed the original group of "Texas Loyal Democrats." These activists included former Allred supporter and independent oilman J. R. Parten, Dickinson banker Walter Hall, former state representative Fagan Dickson, Austin attorney Creekmore Fath, former suffrage leader and longtime Democratic activist Minnie Fisher Cunningham, former San Antonio congressman Maury Maverick Sr., and a number of others. What began as a philosophical battle and intraparty dispute evolved into a political free-for-all that drew Yarborough into the statewide leadership of the loyal Democrats. Yarborough decided to reenter politics and run for attorney general at the beginning of 1952, but prior to the planned attorney general campaign, his chance meeting with Governor Shivers on the issue changed his direction. His decision then to someday run against Shivers for governor led him into the leadership of Texas liberals and into the forefront of state and national politics.[3]

Allan Shivers, firmly aligned with the pro-business, conservative establishment of the Texas Democratic party before he became governor, had entered the legislature in the 1930's as a pro–New Deal Democrat. But by the time he became lieutenant governor after World War II, the conservatives counted him as one of their most promising leaders. Once he became governor after Jester's death in 1949, Shivers capitalized on the publicity generated by the Tidelands Controversy. He criticized the Truman administration and the U.S. Supreme Court decisions that favored federal ownership of the submerged lands off the Texas coast. In 1951 he accused the Truman administration of attempting to "nationalize" the oil industry and wanting to establish a "dictatorship over fuel production." Texas newspapers provided extensive coverage and editorials that commended the governor for his staunch opposition to the Truman administration's attempts to regain federal control of the disputed lands. Shivers confronted the national government on an issue on which even many loyal Democrats, including Ralph Yarborough, disagreed with the administration. In declaring the federal government's actions an invasion of state's rights, Shivers utilized the traditional southern argument against federal action. Shivers realized the popularity of this position with Texans. He expected to benefit from it should he have serious opposition in his reelection effort in 1952. In reality, although the Tidelands dispute threatened a significant amount of revenue for the state, the battle was more important to the oil companies than to the average Texan. The fact that the actual beneficiaries of the Tidelands were the major petroleum companies, who had the most to gain financially, seldom appeared in the state's newspapers. Shivers' moves set the stage for future opposition to federal initiatives and Supreme Court decisions that would have a significant impact on the everyday lives of Texans.[4]

Yarborough was sincere in his recollection of the 1952 capitol meeting with Shivers. His initial goal was to run again for attorney general as he had in 1938. But he was concerned about the opposition of John Ben Shepperd, a popular politician whom Shivers appointed as secretary of state and who had already received the governor's support in the race. Shivers and others knowledgeable of the Texas political scene warned Yarborough that a race against Shivers' well-financed associate would be a difficult task. However, many political columnists suggested that Yarborough was nonetheless a strong candidate because of his record and experience. Also, no other Democrat stepped forward to fill the shoes of James Allred and Homer Rainey. Thus most people were surprised when Yarborough announced on May 1, just five days before the filing deadline, that he planned to run not against Shepperd but against Shivers in the Democratic primary. Later, during a statewide radio broadcast Yarborough stated that he had been "threatened by Governor Shivers" while he was considering the race for attorney general. "There is no place in Texas for political dictatorship," he declared. He maintained that he felt "a change was needed" in the governor's office and denied that he was "persuaded to run by Washington or by the 'loyal' Democrats." While Yarborough undoubtedly was motivated by the reasons he stated, Speaker of the House Sam Rayburn and some of the loyal Democrats in fact had encouraged him to challenge Shivers.[5]

Speaker Sam Rayburn disliked Governor Shivers but did not want to publicly oppose the popular governor. Rayburn was concerned about the 1952 elections and worried that the Republicans, with Dwight Eisenhower leading the ticket, might capture both the White House and the House of Representatives (which would result in his being replaced as Speaker by a Republican as was the case from 1947 to 1949). He wanted a credible opponent to Shivers and discussed the issue with Democratic loyalist J. R. Parten at a Washington meeting in January 1952. Rayburn did not think that Shivers could be defeated in the primary, but he still wanted to force him to work for his reelection. Rayburn hoped that with a strong primary opponent Shivers would not openly break with the Democratic party and support the Republican presidential nominee. Parten suggested that Yarborough could be a possible opponent for Shivers. Parten had supported Yarborough in his first campaign for attorney general and knew that Yarborough was a loyal Democrat with statewide aspirations.

After Parten returned to Texas, he met with Yarborough to discuss the governor's race. But Yarborough turned him down because of the difficulty in raising money for the campaign and because he was more interested in the attorney general's office. Yarborough realized it would be difficult to run against John Ben Shepperd but running against Shivers at the height of his popularity was a truly vexing proposition. (Yarborough later revealed that Shivers' representatives contacted him with a proposal to support him for the Texas Supreme Court if he dropped out of the race with Shepperd.)[6]

Shortly before May 1, Yarborough met with Parten again. During the confidential meeting in Houston, Parten gave Yarborough a check for $5,000 and told him he would raise $50,000 for his campaign against Shivers. Parten also promised an endorsement from James Allred and the behind-the-scenes assistance of Speaker Rayburn. In addition, Yarborough understood he could count on the active support of the loyalist Democratic party members who were organizing around the state in preparation for the 1952 primaries and presidential election. Prior to Yarborough's May 1 announcement, the loyalists had no success in recruiting a candidate to challenge the governor, but they had never contacted Yarborough to run against Shivers.[7]

Parten's commitments, along with Rayburn's and Allred's support, helped in Yarborough's decision, but he still seethed over his treatment by the governor and his associates. He knew he would be outspent but believed that the majority of Texas Democrats were loyal to the party and would support a candidate with solid credentials, especially if they were given a clear choice. Yarborough had some organizational support throughout the state from his previous campaigns. He also assumed he would receive support from the loyalist Democratic faction, especially the small but well-organized group who called themselves "Democrats of Texas." What he lacked in resources he hoped to overcome with his own energy and tenacity. Furthermore, he believed events were working in his favor. The drought which would grip Texas for the early part of the decade was already causing difficulties, but the governor paid scant attention to the problem. The shift from a rural to urban majority of residents also worked in Yarborough's favor. His strength centered on the small communities of East and Central Texas. The core liberal-labor support was in the cities, which could be organized more easily at the grass-roots level than farm and ranch communities. Thus while Parten's commitment was a critical piece of the puzzle, Yarborough was already predisposed toward challenging Shivers.

Trends appeared to be moving in Yarborough's favor, but he faced a difficult task. The Democratic party precinct conventions held on May 3, shortly after his announcement for governor, took the pulse of Texas Democrats. Usually most precinct conventions in Texas were poorly attended, but in 1952 record numbers of people appeared at the grass-roots meetings throughout the state. Shivers' anti-Truman position was well known by this time. Many lobby and civic organizations around the state distributed information to potential voters touting business issues and candidates. These included pro-Shivers organizations such as the Texas Manufacturers Association and others formed by major oil and gas companies. They assisted the Shivers organizers in the local counties and most local officeholders who favored the governor. When the results from the May 3 meetings were tabulated, the "Shivercrats" (as they became known) had dominated meetings across the state. With the exception of a few urban areas like San Antonio, San Angelo, and Galveston, where loyalists and labor were well organized, the Shivercrats controlled the precinct meetings and selected an overwhelming number of delegates for the county conventions. Of the 1,152 precincts in the state, the Shivers forces won 1,009 compared to 143 for the loyalists. The message to Yarborough was clear. Governor Shivers had the organization necessary to win reelection—and to win with a large majority. In addition, because of his overwhelming victory at the precinct meetings, Shivers felt more secure in his public attacks on the Democratic loyalists who questioned his leadership. He also knew that Speaker Rayburn was in no position to counter his attacks. During campaign speeches he urged audiences to keep the party in the hands of the conservatives and the moderates. "I'm tired of a lot of ultra-intellectual parlor pinks and so-called liberal crackpots running the Democratic Party," the governor said.[8]

Ignoring the setback at the local Democratic conventions, Yarborough continued his low-budget, grass-roots campaign through the late spring and early summer of 1952. Following his typical campaign style, he lived on the road nearly every day, traveling from one small town to another, making speeches on courthouse lawns, giving radio and newspaper interviews, and constantly telephoning friends and supporters. He frequently gave as many as twenty speeches per day and delivered countless remarks to individuals and small groups at roadside cafes, gas stations, feed stores, and street corners. He always tried to work the crowd and shake as many hands as possible before leaving for his next stop. The temperature soared to over one hundred degrees as he tirelessly worked into the summer of 1952. He called for the elimination of waste and corruption in state government. He opposed any sales tax or state income tax. He pushed for better roads, schools, and soil and water conservation programs. Walter Prescott Webb, Yarborough's old

friend, provided him with information on the drought and its growing impact on the state. Another friend, J. Frank Dobie, urged him to attack Shivers
for betraying the Democratic party, Franklin Roosevelt, and Harry Truman.
Other than his call for a direct presidential primary to replace the Democratic party's convention system, none of Yarborough's ideas seemed to really
catch fire with the voters.[9]

Yarborough primarily relied on his family and longtime friends to assist
in his campaign. As Maury Maverick Jr. recalled, Yarborough seemed "des-
perately poor" during the gubernatorial campaigns. "We would give him a
free bed and the next morning I would give him five dollars to get gas money
to get his car from San Antonio to Austin." Other than the donations from
J. R. Parten, Walter Hall, and his own relatives, he accumulated very little
money for the campaign and only token support from the Democratic loyalists. As a result, he had to rely on volunteers to staff the headquarters and
assist his efforts throughout the state. Ralph's brothers Harvey and Donald
provided money and advice as they had done before. Opal Yarborough exhibited the dedication that became a standard for this campaign and many more
to come. She served by taking on a number of tasks at the campaign headquarters in Austin and at their home. She wrote letters, addressed envelopes,
answered the phone, mailed out literature, and helped coordinate the volunteers. She looked on these supporters, many of whom were young and getting
their first taste of a statewide political race, as part of her extended family.
"They're just like a very large family. They've all become fond of one another
from working together," she stated. The first Yarborough gubernatorial race
followed his patterns from before the war and served as an introduction to
future endeavors.[10]

Yarborough realized he was fighting an uphill battle and running out of
time. The precinct meetings indicated the strength and depth of the Shivers
forces. As he traveled from one town to the next, Yarborough frequently saw
local elected officials in courthouses and city halls who were sympathetic to
his candidacy, but many told him that they were afraid to support him for fear
of retaliation by the governor's office. Some indicated that Shivers' coordinators had actually threatened them with reprisals. With only a few exceptions,
all of the state's major newspapers endorsed Shivers. Only daily newspapers
in Austin and Waco refused to endorse him. Yarborough privately admitted
that he knew he was not going to win the race but was determined to make
a strong showing. On election day, the Shivers campaign rolled to victory by
a wide margin. Shivers defeated Yarborough 833,861 votes to 488,345. Yar-

borough won 36 percent of the popular vote and carried twenty-one counties, located mainly in East Texas.[11]

In a post-election analysis, Yarborough said he believed that in addition to all the organizational problems he confronted, another statewide campaign influenced the outcome: "The worst blow I had in my campaign occurred within forty-eight hours after I had announced." Attorney General Price Daniel, who had filed for the U.S. Senate seat vacated by longtime Senator Tom Connally, expected to run virtually unopposed, but Congressman Lindley Beckworth jumped into the race as a surprise candidate, much as Yarborough had with Shivers. Yarborough believed many of Price Daniel's supporters, especially the attorneys around the state, would have supported him against Shivers had they not been tied down by the Senate race. But Yarborough also admitted that Shivers had "the strongest political machine that I have ever seen in Texas."[12]

The Shivers and Daniel campaigns were well financed, followed the anti-Washington theme on the Tidelands issue, and counted on many of the same local campaign managers, who were usually influential attorneys. Daniel ran a better campaign and was a better speaker than his opponent. "Price Daniel helped Shivers as much or more than Shivers' speeches helped himself," Yarborough declared.

The challenger also said he had difficulty getting his messages into the urban areas of the state. He noted that most rural Texans stayed abreast of the candidates and issues through large farm organizations like the Farm Bureau or Farmers Union. The only urban residents who were clearly informed about the election (that is, received his message) were those families who were connected to organized labor. "Once you leave the labor groups and go into the unorganized white-collar workers, you reach a group that pays little attention to political issues until the last few days before the election," Yarborough noted, adding, "If they pay much attention, they are apt to fall for a Nixon cry story without realizing the issues." Along with the difficulties in reaching the postwar generation in the growing cities, Richard Nixon's infamous 1952 Checkers speech on national television left an impression on Yarborough.[13]

Even with one-third of the popular vote, Yarborough gained Shivers' attention. Yarborough said that until the last week before the election his crowds were growing and he believed he was gaining on Shivers. At the same time he realized the governor and his supporters were not sitting on their lead but were spending great sums of money to influence the outcome of the election in the final days. Yarborough stated that Shivers and Daniel together spent $50,000 in San Antonio shortly before the election, and the *San Antonio Light* reported that "$20,000 was seen to change hands on election day." San Antonio had a long history of elections delivered to the highest bidder. According to Yarborough, "everybody knew who had the money and who put it out," an oblique reference to the Shivers campaign. Bexar County favored Shivers over Yarborough by a two-to-one margin. Houston, Dallas, and Fort Worth also favored Shivers, but by smaller margins than San Antonio.[14]

In spite of his defeat, Yarborough remained convinced that he had forced Shivers to abandon his plan to denounce the Democratic presidential nominee at the party's national convention. In fact, Shivers had already met with Sam Rayburn and pledged his support for the national ticket. Rayburn, the chair of the convention, supported the Shivers delegation. During a nationally televised speech from the convention floor, Shivers pledged that he would support the party's nominee. The Texas primary election came just a few days after the convention. Yarborough's candidacy combined with the pressure from loyalist Democrats and Rayburn undoubtedly contributed to the governor's pledge to support the national ticket. After Shivers won the primary election, however, he denounced Democratic presidential nominee Adlai Stevenson of Illinois. Shivers announced that he planned to support Dwight Eisenhower because of Stevenson's opposition to Texas in the Tidelands case and because of his own anti-Truman and anti-Washington positions. Shivers claimed he never broke any pledges made at the Democratic convention because, he said, he had only promised to allow the Democratic nominees to be placed on the ballot in Texas. He maintained that he had never promised to endorse the Democratic nominee, even if his statements at the party's convention appeared to indicate that he would. Had Shivers revealed his true sentiments on national television, Yarborough believed, "we would have unseated him." Sam Rayburn also believed Shivers misled him.[15]

Race was not the focal point of the 1952 campaign, but the issue certainly loomed on the horizon. The state's newspapers and the Shivers campaign made the most of the governor's opposition to the Truman administration on the Tidelands issue. Shivers and other Texas Democrats also openly criticized the federal government on racial issues. In the late 1940's Truman proposed to widen federal jurisdiction on civil rights by strengthening the Fair Employment Practices Act. Many northern Democrats also pushed for congressional legislation which would restrict poll taxes and enact tougher anti-lynching laws. Southern congressmen consistently opposed these initiatives as they knew these measures were aimed at the Jim Crow laws and southern segregation. The 1948 Democratic National Convention passed a civil rights plank for the party. From the outset Shivers aligned himself with other southern governors in opposition to these proposals and made many public statements supporting segregation and states' rights. While these issues were not in the forefront of the 1952 election, Shivers frequently made reference to them.

Immediately after the election, Yarborough had been of the opinion that Shivers would learn from his mistakes. He thought that the governor now understood that he was vulnerable to attacks stemming from corruption within his administration and his negligence in dealing with the drought. Yarborough felt that after his attacks Shivers would work to keep his administration scandal-free and, to combat the drought, would "come out with a plan whether it's worth a darn or not," which he would announce on television and radio and in the newspapers. Yarborough also thought that Shivers would vote for Eisenhower but would not openly endorse the Republicans in the national election. None of this happened. Instead, Shivers' endorsement of Eisenhower ensured that the Republican nominee carried Texas in the 1952 November election, the effects of the drought worsened, and the Shivers administration produced a fresh crop of political scandals by 1954.

As a result of the 1952 campaign, Yarborough gained a group of core supporters who would follow him for years. Walter Hall backed Lyndon Johnson but felt Yarborough's political philosophy aligned more closely with his own beliefs. He realized Yarborough had faced long odds in 1952 but predicted a better future in 1954. Hall told Athens newspaper editor R. T. Craig, Yarborough's friend and former employer in Henderson County, "I want to see this man Governor."[16]

THE 1954 DEMOCRATIC PRIMARY

Shivers' popularity declined in the short time between his victory over Yarborough and the 1954 campaign. Shivers' support of Republican presidential nominee Dwight D. Eisenhower hurt the governor's image with many Texas Democrats. Many traditional Democrats were upset with the governor after his announcement to support the Democratic presidential nominee was followed by the switch to Eisenhower, and critics saw through his tepid explanation. The Tidelands Controversy, Shivers' main campaign issue, was resolved when Congress passed and Eisenhower signed legislation which gave Texas the valuable offshore lands. The drought in the state continued and became a greater concern as more Texans watched their productive lands crack from the lack of rain. Many farmers and ranchers saw their lands and their bank accounts evaporate simultaneously—and there was no end in sight. Strikes by organized labor and the rising concerns of Texas businesses with unions were unsettling. Finally, the specter of official corruption in state government emerged, setting the stage for a more contentious atmosphere in 1954. Shivers' misfortunes became Yarborough's opportunities. Yarborough could hardly believe how events had suddenly turned his way.

Other actions changed the political scene for the drama unfolding in 1954. McCarthyism and the Red Scare gripped the state for several years. The hysteria over communism coincided with the rise of right-wing political activity at the national and local levels. But the monumental Supreme Court decision in 1954 did more to shake the political establishment and churn the waters in Texas and the rest of the South that year and for many years to come. The *Brown v. Topeka Board of Education* decision provoked greater debate and social upheaval than the outlandish theatrics and emotion generated during the McCarthy era. The court's decision had two long-lasting consequences for Texas and her sister southern states. First, the judgment initiated a series of prolonged events to accomplish desegregation of public schools and eventually all public and private facilities. *Brown v. Board of Education* weakened and eventually overcame the "separate but equal" standard in place in the South since the turn of the century. Second, the decision again pulled racial relationships to the forefront in southern and national politics. The revival of racial segregation as a campaign issue in 1954 brought immediate change to the political landscape. In 1954, the U.S. Supreme Court's decision quickly elevated the governor's campaign to one of national importance. Texas, rather than setting its own agenda on issues like the Tidelands, now had to confront an initiative from Washington that changed the face of local communities. Some believed that society was upside down.[17]

The Supreme Court in its ruling accomplished what many national Democrats had failed to achieve since the days of the depression. Southerners had always maintained sufficient political clout to defeat measures which threatened to alter the established social order in their part of the country. White Texans and their southern neighbors were unified in their belief that the "place" of the African American population was God-given and politically justified. Although local laws and customs varied in tone, style, and enforcement throughout the South, white Democrats in the region consistently locked arms behind the shield of segregation and discrimination. Generations of leaders since the Civil War believed that they were united by a common, irrefutable resolution that the South "shall be and remain a white man's country."[18]

Governor Shivers felt comfortable as a "moderate segregationist." Prior to 1954, he opposed racial integration but did not engage in the vile race-baiting that many of his southern counterparts engaged in during the postwar period. Shivers maintained more interest in economic themes and promotion of business expansion. He described himself in news stories as "basically a conservative man, but one progressive enough to want Texas to have good schools, good highways and farm-to-market roads, and a good welfare program." He preferred to emphasize his role as the public leader of a state that was a rising star in the postwar South. Initially, he and his supporters wanted to focus on his accomplishments in funding public schools and mental health and link them with the growing prosperity and urbanization of the state. In a letter Texas businessman James Taylor, an Austin lobbyist and Shivers supporter, claimed that the future success of business and a sound economy in the state relied on the continuation of the governor's conservative policies. But in an ominous note of things to come, Taylor predicted that the expansion and "constructive leadership" could all come to an end should Texas elect a governor who "willingly accepts the support of the CIO-PAC and the NAACP leadership." Should Shivers be ousted in 1954, "it would take 50 years to recover from such a catastrophe."[19]

Not everyone agreed with Shivers' reputation as a racial moderate, especially since the description originated with white political scientists and historians. African Americans who lived in segregated Texas saw little distinction between the Lone Star State and other southern states. The Shivers administration provided more money for schools and health care than its immediate predecessors, but nearly all of it went to white Texans. Charles Graggs, a native Texan and graduate of Howard University, was a well-known civil rights advocate in the early 1950's. He spoke for many African Americans when he praised the *Brown* decision but feared opposition from southern political leaders who would lead the charge to preserve the status quo. Initially, many southerners and the press cautiously examined the *Brown* decision. The pause indicated a degree of uncertainty as opposed to immediate rejection. In an article entitled the "Strong Acid Test," Graggs wrote that the Supreme Court's action placed the burden directly on southern leaders. He accurately predicted that some "bitter, rebellious enemies" would take the lead fighting the decision. Singled out in this group were leading southern segregationists who became vocal advocates of "massive resistance," which involved total rejection and active opposition to integration. Those officials included Georgia governor Herman Talmadge, Georgia senator Dick Russell, Senator Allen Ellender of Louisiana, and Governor Allan Shivers of Texas. Graggs also included the state legislatures in Louisiana and Mississippi as the other major obstacles. Graggs said no one should be fooled. Governor Shivers and the other southerners "still preach segregation and worship at the shrine of Jim Crowism."[20]

The *Brown* decision changed whatever positive course Shivers might have considered in his efforts to secure a third term as Texas governor. By early May, Shivers and his campaign coordinators attacked the decision and likened it to a second Reconstruction. Shivers quickly discarded his moderate robes and replaced them with the shield of the Confederate flag. The governor and his campaign made continuous and expansive efforts to heighten fears and play on the racial prejudices of white Texans. Shivers announced for reelection in his hometown of Lufkin, a small city in East Texas. The governor declared that he was running against organized labor, northern liberal Democrats, communists, and the NAACP, but he focused his energy on the *Brown* decision, saying, "All my instincts, my political philosophy, my experience, and my common sense revolt against this Supreme Court decision." Shivers declared that integration of public schools would be a disaster for both whites and blacks. He proclaimed that he had "never resorted to demagoguery" or "tried to inflame the passions of the people for political gain." However, the governor and his cohorts consistently used the race issue for the duration of the contest.[21]

SCANDALS AND CHARGES OF CORRUPTION

Yarborough announced for governor in a televised speech in April, a month before the Supreme Court decision. "Something will have to be dug up on Shivers to get people interested," Walter Hall had remarked to him in a letter written months earlier. "Shivers has lost some ground since 1952, but I do not know that you have gained any," Hall warned. The challenger took his advice, keeping Shivers on the defensive from the outset of the 1954 campaign. Yarborough initially focused on criticizing Shivers' attempt to run for a third term, a violation of a time-honored tradition in Texas politics. He said that Shivers' unprecedented attempt represented a "power-mad political machine" that would stop at nothing to maintain its control and influence. "A vote against machine domination in Texas is a vote to stay on the free

Crowds gathered in courthouse squares and on street corners throughout Texas to hear Yarborough blast Governor Allan Shivers in the 1954 Democratic primary. Courtesy Center for American History, Russell Lee Collection (3Y152).

side of the iron curtain," Yarborough charged in his own attempt to capitalize on the anti-communist sentiment of the Cold War era. He described himself as a "traditional, sure-nuff Democrat" who, unlike Shivers, never conspired with Republicans. He claimed he would never run for a third term or attempt to establish his own "self-perpetuating political machine." Yarborough's announcement delivered a much stronger punch than his first one in 1952. Thirty-five television stations beamed his speech around the state. Yarborough recognized the power of the new medium and made several other televised broadcasts during the campaign. He also hit the road, preaching his message of better schools and roads, an expanded loan program for veterans, increases in pensions for older Texans, and more federal aid to combat the drought.[22]

Besides hammering Shivers on the third-term issue, Yarborough claimed that the governor tolerated fraud in the state's insurance industry. He constantly portrayed Shivers as a power-hungry politician whose corrupt admin-istration "allowed the influence peddlers and fixers to operate in Austin." Several insurance companies in the state were insolvent and others were under investigation. Texas maintained the reputation of having some of the most lenient insurance regulations in the nation. Yarborough specifically accused John Van Cronkhite, the governor's 1952 campaign manager, of receiving lucrative contracts sent his way by the Shivers administration. One of these clients was the Lloyds of North America Company, which became insolvent in 1953. However, Van Cronkhite continued to receive his payments and the company operated through 1954. Yarborough called for a wholesale investiga-tion into what he termed "the insurance mess." The challenger concluded, "it just goes to prove—when politicians become fixtures—their cronies become fixers." According to Yarborough, if the people of Texas allowed Shivers a third term in office, they should expect a continuation of the shady dealings and favoritism.[23]

Garland Smith, a South Texas attorney and chairman of the Texas In-surance Commission tipped off Yarborough to another potentially damaging charge that involved the governor. Documents showed that Shivers gave a sworn statement in a land suit in which he was involved with South Texas land developer Lloyd M. Bentsen Sr. In 1946, Shivers acquired an option to buy 13,500 acres of land in Hidalgo County from Bentsen's land company. Shivers obtained the option with a $25,000 promissory note. Seven months later, he sold the option back to Bentsen's company for $450,000. The ex-change occurred after Shivers' inauguration as lieutenant governor in 1947. When Shivers became governor, the State Board of Water Engineers issued a permit for irrigation water from the Rio Grande to Bentsen's company. Bentsen's company then subdivided the land, known as the "Texas Gardens," and offered it to farmers. However, the water rights sold with the property existed only during flood conditions and a number of purchasers filed suit against Bentsen's company claiming fraud. Shivers disclosed his participation with Bentsen as part of these lawsuits. Although the land transaction was legal and the water permits were issued years later, the quick profit Shivers earned and the circumstances surrounding the water permits smacked of fa-voritism and an insider transaction. More important to the Yarborough cam-paign, the affair clearly supported his charges of corruption and influence peddling.[24]

Yarborough initially believed the incident was too complex to explain, but he nevertheless issued a press release on the story with encouragement from J. R. Parten. He soon followed up with attacks in his campaign speeches. He called on the governor to explain the $450,000 profit since he never owned the land or the water rights and remarked in San Antonio that he had "never heard of another deal where so little was sold for so much." He pushed the issue in a statewide broadcast less than two weeks before the primary election. Yarborough explained that he originally learned of the $450,000 payment during a 1952 campaign stop in San Antonio for Adlai Stevenson. During the rally for Stevenson's presidential campaign he met a supporter in the Alamo, where he first saw documentation of Shivers' activities. Utilizing his oratorical skills as he would have before a jury, Yarborough solemnly intoned, "Inside the walls of the sacred Alamo . . . and near the spot by the door to the sanctuary where James Bowie died . . . he unfolded the papers . . . and on that hallowed ground explained to me the transaction through which the present Governor of Texas had been paid $450,000." Yarborough claimed that hundreds of people lost money "on sales of cactus land for citrus land." Yarborough predicted the day of retribution was close at hand and the people of Texas would punish the transgressors on election day. As he left the Alamo after the meeting, Yarborough described how he envisioned William Travis drawing the line in the sand to separate the patriots from the cowards at the climactic 1836 battle. "My last thought as I gazed on that hallowed spot, was that we will draw another line in Texas on another day of decision," he concluded.[25]

Shivers, incensed with this attack on his personal integrity, struck back at Yarborough. From the outset of his campaign, Shivers warned Texans to expect "a bitter race." He charged Yarborough with launching "the most vicious barrage of personal slander and abuse in the history of Texas politics." In response to Yarborough's charges in the insurance cases and the Bentsen land suits, Shivers labeled Yarborough's accusations "political poppy-cock." The governor noted that Yarborough evidently believed something was "wrong with this great American system of profit making." The state's newspapers provided no front page coverage of Yarborough's charges and editors dismissed the attacks. Thereafter Shivers largely ignored the insurance and land questions and went back on the offensive. At nearly every opportunity, the governor and his campaign hit Yarborough often and hard—especially in their attempts to link Yarborough to African Americans and organized labor.

Typical of Shivers' attacks was a statewide telecast from Palestine in East Texas. Shivers charged that Yarborough's "close political advisors are working hand-in-glove with the NAACP." He warned that after the *Brown* decision the NAACP "boastfully declared that it is going to end segregation in social activities and in residential areas." In fact, Shivers claimed that the

minority organization planned to integrate "every phase of daily living—
and it is going to do so as quickly as possible." Shivers told his audience
that he would actively fight any attempts to change the status quo. "You
know where Allan Shivers stands; and although my opponent refuses to say
where he stands I think you and I both know that, too." Shivers actually
played both sides of the race issue in the 1952 campaign. At the same time
Shivers pounded Yarborough for his affiliation with African Americans and
the NAACP, his campaign circulated a brochure entitled "The Big Lie" in
urban minority neighborhoods. The campaign literature noted that Shivers
opposed the Ku Klux Klan and wanted African Americans to know that
Yarborough favored segregation. While keeping this low-key effort going in
black neighborhoods, some Shivers supporters paid a black man to drive a
Cadillac through East Texas plastered with Yarborough stickers. He purposely stopped at gas stations manned by white attendants, demanded fast
service, and insulted the employees, claiming that he was in a hurry to return
to work for "Mr. Yarborough."[26]

Yarborough's response was less than candid. He attempted to avoid the
issue in spite of the governor's charges tying him to labor and the NAACP.
When the *Brown* decision hit the newspapers in May, Yarborough issued a
subdued statement saying that the Supreme Court decision "must be studied
to see how it will affect Texas." In the following weeks, his speeches, press
releases, and materials ignored the growing controversy even as Shivers increased his public criticism of Yarborough and the desegregation decision.
Finally, Yarborough responded on July 14 in a televised campaign program.
He said that he had always supported "states' rights," a code term well understood by southerners who opposed integration. Yarborough failed to provide
an interpretation of his version of states' rights, but the insertion of the phrase
into his speech clearly was intended to deflect some of the governor's attacks
on the race issue. In his personal appearances in the final week before the
election, Yarborough began making other statements on the controversy. He
said he still favored segregated schools and simultaneously criticized Shivers.
"We are at the present time in favor of these fair and equal facilities for segregation within the legal framework of the law," he remarked. He did not
issue a clear statement on integration until after the July 25 primary.[27]

Confronting the integration issue clearly made Yarborough pull back. He
knew that the small number of African Americans who participated in the
primary elections in the state supported him. Privately, he had been supportive of the positions taken by national Democrats who favored some type of
plan for integration, but he feared any pronouncements would harm his can-

THE STRONG ACID TEST ★ 113

didacy. He understood that most white Texans were not prepared to begin integrating public schools and other facilities in 1954. However, he antagonized some of his own liberal supporters because of his vacillation on the issue. Creekmore Fath, a key campaign advisor, knew from private discussions with some of Yarborough's trusted confidants that his reluctance to confront the issue was a concern and that it created discontent among many of his liberal admirers. After one heated, closed-door session on the issue before the election, Yarborough refused to budge. "I just figured it was the old Deep East Texas business, that this was something in Ralph's background that would take time," Fath commented. At the time, Fath and other close friends believed Yarborough may not have been totally committed to integration for more than just political reasons: "He didn't want to address it because he wasn't comfortable with it." Fath recalled that "Ralph said something to us like, 'it's easy for you all' to take the position that you are all taking supporting the *Brown* decision. None of you are running for office." Yarborough eventually revealed his unequivocal position in favor of *Brown* and integration, but that would take several more years and another campaign.[28]

The impact of Yarborough's decisions cannot be precisely determined, but when the votes in the governor's race were tallied on July 25, the results startled both campaigns and veteran politicians. Shivers narrowly led with 668,914 votes to Yarborough's 645,944 votes. Two other candidates, Cyclone Davis and J. J. Holmes, garnered only 36,000 votes. They drew just enough to force a runoff between Yarborough and Shivers. The election results that served as a stimulant for the Yarborough forces must have tasted like castor oil to the Shivers supporters. The two candidates were virtually tied, but Shivers knew his popularity appeared to be in a nose-dive as Yarborough's shot skyward. Shivers had a tighter organization and enjoyed the support of the big money contributors, but his momentum toward a third term appeared to have stalled. An internal election analysis provided to the Shivers campaign spelled out the bad news in precise numbers. Compared to 1952, Shivers gained votes in twenty-six counties but lost support in more than two hundred rural and urban counties in the state. Yarborough, however, gained votes in all but twenty-three counties. In the few places where Shivers gained votes, Yarborough was hot on his heels. For example, in Bexar County Shivers attracted 6,400 more votes than in 1952 but Yarborough more than doubled his numbers, picking up more than 13,000 votes. With the exception of the boss-controlled counties in South Texas, which backed Shivers, Yarborough's support increased throughout the state in both rural and urban counties. Yarborough votes actually surpassed Shivers in the pivotal areas of Central Texas

When the Dallas Morning News *advised voters to use a clothespin on one's nose when voting for Yarborough, Democratic women provided clothespins to Yarborough for "hanging out Shivers' dirty linen." Courtesy Center for American History, Russell Lee Collection (3Y152).*

and East Texas. Momentum shifted to Yarborough's side as concerns about the third term and corruption cut into the Shivers vote with the accuracy of a surgeon's scalpel. The governor's opposition to integration, however, allowed him to maintain his razor-thin lead over Yarborough. Shivers knew that every previous Texas governor forced into a primary runoff subsequently lost to the opponent. With only a month before the runoff election, both candidates and their supporters regrouped for the next frenzied month.[29]

"THE PORT ARTHUR STORY"

Yarborough immediately came out punching in the runoff round, confident that his hard-hitting campaign had Shivers on the ropes. As an invigorated Yarborough renewed his challenge, the growing crowds sensed this underdog had more than a fighting chance. Women in flowered dresses standing beneath the shade of umbrellas and men in short-sleeved shirts and wide-brim summer hats braved the searing August heat to see and hear Yarborough. As he stood on the courthouse steps or on makeshift platforms under a spreading oak tree, Yarborough pounded away at Shivers' "power mad politi-cal machine." The folded newspaper with its blazing headlines that he pulled from his coat pocket served as his official prop to illustrate his opponents' abuse of the public trust.

Yet even as his audience grew, Yarborough's stump speeches served as a sideshow in the larger production. The Shivers campaign set the tone for the second election, which justifiably ranks as one of the most sordid campaigns in Texas political history. Any thoughts of discussion of substantive issues were flushed down the drain after the first primary. The Shivers forces not only went to great lengths to personally attack Yarborough through a series of lies and innuendoes, they also mounted an intensive statewide campaign to fan the flames of racial animosity and fear of communist subversion. By means of television and radio ads, letters, handbills, telephone calls, and an army of Shivers' supporters, the word went out that Yarborough was a "negro lover" controlled by "labor bosses and the NAACP," and the governor's cam-paign provided evidence that every "colored" precinct in the state went for Yarborough by margins ranging from 10 to 1 to 20 to 1. The mountain of ma-terial went to every worker and volunteer in the governor's campaign. The culmination of Shivers' efforts appeared in a pamphlet and television program that became known as "The Port Arthur Story."[30]

"The Port Arthur Story," a landmark twelve-minute black-and-white film produced for television, depicted the Texas coastal city crippled and desti-tute because of a strike by the CIO, which conspired with northerners and African Americans. The Shivers campaign also produced an eight-page bro-chure, "Ask the People of Port Arthur—They Know," that amplified the televised account. In the film, a narrator explained how the once-thriving city of Port Arthur was now literally deserted and a community where "no-body smiled." As the camera pans empty streets and businesses, the narra-tor explains that the city was closed by communist-inspired organized labor as the harbinger of a larger plot to take over all Texas cities. Port Arthur was merely the first beachhead for this communist-based program of in-ternal subversion. The city was under the control of the union-dominated African American strikers. Nearly all of the African American pickets posed lazily outside a storefront or scowled and interrupted the scene as one white business owner attempted to explain the threats. All of the white business men and women in the film complained that their livelihood and commu-nity was destroyed by "outside organizers" and the "communist-dominated" labor unions. Following their pleas, Dave Smith, a "plain businessman" from Austin who told viewers the story, revealed that the plot to take over the state and its businesses came from out-of-state, communist-backed unions. But Governor Shivers and Attorney General John Ben Shepperd had discovered the ploy and were fighting this "invasion." Smith said that those who were trying to destroy democracy and business in Texas, "their henchmen and their pickets, are backing the opponent of Allan Shivers." Only the governor could save the state and "hold Texas for Texans."[31]

The campaign brochure developed to circulate after "The Port Arthur Story" aired on the state's television stations delivered a more provocative message. The brochure was an even stronger attempt to link Yarborough with the strike and integration. The fight in Port Arthur involved racial equality and race mixing, a long-standing fear in southern society. The brochure warned readers that this "war" over integration would soon impact their own communities. Photos showed white women and black men together, where they "mix daily on these picket lines. They drink from the same bottles and smoke the same cigarets." One photo pictured an African American woman in her car with her arm wrapped around a white woman, and another showed a black man and a white woman together. "They'd rather beat Allan Shivers than win the strike," the caption read. The final message stated that "these people" were Yarborough's primary supporters. The brochure and the film were blatant attempts to inflame racist attitudes with the implied "war" over integration and tag Yarborough as a proponent of the unpopular *Brown* decision and an advocate of radical change.[32]

Port Arthur remained in a divisive, prolonged strike between the CIO and retail merchants throughout most of 1954. The Syers-Pickle and Winn Advertising firm hired by the Shivers' campaign developed the idea of using the strike as the threat that linked integration with communism. Jake Pickle, a young protégé of Lyndon Johnson and a future Central Texas congressman, stated that his agency produced the film but others in the firm conceived the piece and went to Port Arthur. The film's opening depicted a forlorn city with closed stores and deserted streets. "Sure it was deserted," Pickle said. "It was 6 A.M." The film crew took pictures of the empty city early one Sunday morning. Otherwise, Port Arthur continued normal operations despite the ongoing strike. Pickle confirmed that "The Port Arthur Story" was intended solely to demonstrate Yarborough's link to labor and minorities and reduce his popular support. "Yarborough, who was a decent man, got mixed up in people's minds with Big Labor, outside interests, Communism and God knows what all," Pickle recalled, "just about every bugaboo that people worried about during those paranoid Red Menace years." In this election, "The Port Arthur Story" represented the culmination of all the Shivers campaign's efforts to smear Yarborough and overwhelm him in the final critical days before the runoff election. The precedent-setting campaign film appeared on television sets throughout the state—except for those in Southeast Texas. Years later, another participant who helped produce the film admitted he was instructed to "burn every copy after the election."[33]

Yarborough supporters across the state harbored concerns about Shivers' attacks even before "The Port Arthur Story" aired on television. Most of the worries centered on the racial issue rather than the antilabor or communist themes raised by their opponents. D. H. Biggers of Quemado, a small community north of Eagle Pass which had no African American residents, reported that he had a confrontation with some of "Shivers flunkies" on the integration issue. "Shivers is now playing it up that Yarborough is for Negro equality, and his political henchmen are going about the country screaming their heads off about what a dangerous man Yarborough is—favoring Negro equality." Another supporter provided what appeared to be an official document that contained a "warning" to voters from the "Citizens' Protective Committee." The committee predicted that if Yarborough won, blacks "will flock to the white schools and demand their children be enrolled." From the woodlands of East Texas to the arid plains in West Texas, evidence of a concerted effort to link Yarborough with African Americans and integration poured into his campaign office. In addition to the widespread and coordinated attacks, Yarborough's supporters also expressed their own frustration with the candidate. His position on segregation was unclear and many urged him to take a firm position on the issue before the runoff election.[34]

Yarborough finally responded in the waning days of the runoff campaign. In his crafted response, "Exploding the Big Lie," Yarborough charged that attempts to link him with "labor, labor bosses and 'pinkos'" was a complete fabrication. He said that the Shivers campaign was following an old propaganda trick of repeatedly lying "as often and as loud as he can until he hopes the people will come to accept accusation without proof as truth." The Yarborough campaign also released an affidavit stating that he had never accepted any money from the CIO or the NAACP. "You can't tell me groups of hundreds of thousands of Texans are communists or even weaklings who can be communist-dominated," he pointed out in defense of his followers. He also finally addressed the racial question. He said he was "against the mingling of our white and colored children in our public schools against the will of either race, and . . . I have never taken any contrary position in different parts of the state, as has my opponent." At an Austin news conference, Yarborough stated that he favored segregation but with "equal facilities for Negroes and whites." Shivers' attack stalled Yarborough's momentum by placing him on the defensive in the critical final days of the race.[35]

In his final media campaign prior to the runoff, Yarborough deleted any discussion of integration. The campaign produced a series of radio spots and one final television broadcast which appeared in every part of the state except for South Texas. In the last push before the runoff, Yarborough attempted to resurrect some earlier issues. He and other supporters in his ads disputed Shivers' charges of ties to organized labor or affiliation with any communist organization. Yarborough lashed out at Shivers for corruption in his administration. He attacked Shivers on the third-term issue, the $450,000 profit from the South Texas land deal, and the insurance scandals. Full page ads in the *Dallas Morning News* and other dailies also attempted to refocus on the questionable activities by the governor. He avoided any mention of the Supreme Court decision or integration. A last-minute attempt to respond came in his final press release. He once again stated that he opposed forced integration and favored "local control" of public schools.[36]

Yarborough was running his most expensive and organized statewide race to date, but he and his supporters could not overcome the massive attacks by Shivers' forces in the final weeks. Almost every major newspaper in the state endorsed Shivers. Shivers' campaign team bought an overwhelming number of television, radio, and newspaper ads. The *Dallas Morning News,* the strongest pro-Shivers publication in the state, published continuous, flattering stories about the governor while slamming Yarborough at every opportunity. Major business organizations around the state urged their members to vote for Shivers. Their speakers toured the state vilifying Yarborough as the candidate of "left wing labor bosses" and the "paid bosses of the NAACP." One pro-Shivers speaker claimed in a statewide radio broadcast that Yarborough supporters were from the "I Hate Texas Group, the Vote More Taxes Group, the Promise Anything to Get Elected Group and the What's In It For Me Group." Republican organizers also turned out to support Shivers as a result of his 1952 endorsement of Eisenhower. To its credit, the Shivers campaign was extremely well financed and organized. The strong coordinated effort probably would have been enough to defeat Yarborough. But the entire menu for the final Shivers banquet consisted of little more than demagoguery, race-baiting, and character assassination. As Governor Shivers said in one of his final campaign speeches, "we know that the CIO-PAC, the ADA [Americans for Democratic Action], and the NAACP don't want Allan Shivers to be governor."[37]

The Democratic primary set a new record for both its low campaign tactics and its high expenditures. For the entire 1954 campaign, Yarborough raised and spent nearly $280,000. The Shivers campaign spent over $1 million. State law required that contributions and expenditures be filed with the Secretary of State's office, but campaigns routinely avoided listing all of their individual contributors and the amount of money spent. Yarborough's list of contributions was more accurate than Shivers' but did not include all of the contributions from organized labor (which they were not required to report under the law at this time). The Shivers campaign may have actually been a multimillion-dollar campaign. Hundreds of thousands of dollars were spent in the final two weeks before the runoff election. Taking into account undisclosed contributions made by many of the state's businesses and other unreported activities, actual totals are difficult to tabulate. All in all, as election day approached, many people realized they had witnessed an unprecedented election even by the wild and unpredictable standards set by previous Democratic campaigns.[38]

The Shivers blitz before the runoff carried him to victory in the August runoff. Shivers defeated Yarborough by a vote of 775,088 to 683,132. Shivers and Yarborough each increased their statewide total from the first primary. Both candidates carried the same regions of the state they had in the first election, but Yarborough's totals dropped in North and Central Texas. Shivers maintained his margins in West and South Texas and on the Gulf Coast. He also carried many counties in the areas that he had lost to Yarborough a month earlier. Shivers kept his majorities in the largest metropolitan centers of Dallas, Houston, and San Antonio. Also, the state's Republican party canceled many of their own elections, thus potentially allowing as many as 100,000 GOP party faithful to cross over and vote for Shivers in the Democratic primary. As Yarborough observed, he lost to the "big money, the big smear, and the big lie." Comparing his fate to that of the Confederate Lost Cause, he allowed to his friends and supporters that they had been overwhelmed by the Shivers forces, but "I want to assure you that we went down fighting in the tradition of Hood's brigade, and we did not cry for quarter," Yarborough said in his post-election news release.[39]

Yarborough lost to Shivers because he was overwhelmed by the governor's organization and media blitz in the final weeks. He gained ground early in the campaign with his attacks on corruption and influence-peddling in the Shivers administration. But his hesitancy and his vacillation on the race issue contributed to his downfall in the 1954 campaign. The governor consistently attacked him on integration and simultaneously his underground campaign continuously worked the small-town cafes and businesses, linking

Yarborough to the NAACP. Also damaging to the challenger were Shivers' barbs that tried to tie Yarborough to organized labor and communist subversion, especially as they were illustrated in "The Port Arthur Story." However, many people knew Yarborough's military record and his own anti-communist rhetoric. On these matters Yarborough adequately responded to his opponent's assaults before the end of the runoff, but he never decisively or convincingly responded to the ever-present racial question. His inability to provide a clear position cost him votes in East Texas and Central Texas and reduced his numbers in other counties along the Gulf Coast.

The Shivers campaign used the red scare/labor-boss argument because it was a relatively new phenomenon in the early years of the 1950's. The communist conspiracy may have enticed some new followers into the Shivers camp in the summer of 1954. White supremacists throughout the South used the anti-communist message in their fight against integration and unions. The actual threat of a communist takeover backed by massive labor unions in the state was overstated. Texans might see these images on television, but once they went about their everyday affairs, very few ever encountered labor organizers and only those who suffered delusions conversed with communists during their morning coffee sessions. But the ongoing fear of racial integration was one instilled in Texas as an integral part of the culture. Texans could look under the bed every day for communists without ever finding one, but they could drive down the street and see African Americans or Mexican Americans in nearly every community in the state on a regular basis. Even in the remote areas of West Texas where the African American population was virtually nonexistent, the white community feared a sudden change in the social order. Long-standing traditions and physical boundaries kept people of color separate from whites everywhere in the state. Racial integration weighed on all Texans' minds during 1954 because of the uncertainty of the Supreme Court's decision and the inability to determine the impact it would have on everyday life.

Other outcomes from this election left a lasting impression on Yarborough. He came to believe that the state's major newspapers had slanted their news coverage to help his opponent. He understood that the editors sometimes chose candidates they expected to win and that their positions usually reflected the views of the newspaper owners and downtown business establishments. Many influential Texas newspapers in the 1950's were independently owned by leading families whose interests included other business enterprises in addition to publishing. Because many of his news releases and speeches went unprinted, Yarborough believed that the majority of the news editors took an active position in assisting his opponent's campaign. He frequently mentioned this problem to his family and close friends like Walter Hall. In one of his post-election assessments, he stated that of all the major dailies, only Amon Carter's *Fort Worth Star Telegram* provided objective coverage of the campaign. In contrast, the *Dallas Morning News* provided Governor Shivers extensive news coverage and editorial support from the outset. The *Morning News* consistently targeted Yarborough in its editorials and frequently depicted him as the tool of organized labor, radicals, and the NAACP. After 1954, Yarborough remained an outspoken critic of the *Morning News* for its harsh editorial positions and its lack of support for his efforts both as a candidate and later as U.S. senator.

Another casualty of Yarborough's first campaigns for governor was his cordial relationship with Lyndon Johnson. He had enjoyed a good relationship with Johnson dating back to the days when Yarborough served as a director of the LCRA. Yarborough supported Johnson in his first congressional race, in the unsuccessful 1941 U.S. Senate race, and in the infamous 1948 campaign against Coke Stevenson. Once Johnson was in the Senate, he had loftier ambitions—and also had to counter the popularity of Allan Shivers. Both men wanted to be at the top of the state's political mountain. Many of Johnson's supporters considered Shivers as his most formidable challenger on the mountain in 1954. Sam Low told Senator Johnson that according to a story he obtained from Yarborough, Johnson could expect a challenge from Shivers. Johnson aide Bobby Baker claimed that his boss was petrified that Shivers was going to be his opponent for U.S. Senate in the 1954 Democratic primary. Johnson might have viewed Shivers as a potential challenger, but he never actively assisted Yarborough. In fact, Johnson and many of his key supporters in the state sided with Shivers during the primary. Johnson's resistance to supporting Yarborough, coupled with his intraparty activities opposing the Democratic loyalists, raised problems for Yarborough, both political and financial. While Yarborough still trusted Sam Rayburn at this point, he became very suspicious of Johnson's behind-the-scenes maneuvers. The deteriorating relationship between Johnson and Yarborough dated to these elections. What began as a small cut became an open wound in subsequent years.[40]

Yarborough missed his first opportunity in 1954 to pass the "strong acid test." He would soon have a second chance and still another opportunity to pursue his quest to become governor.

7   *Coonskins and Coon Hunters*

The dust had barely settled from the 1954 campaign when jockeying for position began for the 1956 governor's race. Shivers' train of Republicans and conservative and moderate Democrats was losing steam and would soon lose its engineer. The governor remained in control of the state Democratic party, but his appeal declined significantly after his reelection. The integration issue hung over the governor and Texas like a shroud. The regular session of the legislature closed in June 1955 with much discussion but no consensus on how to address the thorny issue. A Texas Poll in the spring of 1955 showed 45 percent of Texans opposed to integration while 35 percent favored some form of gradual integration, which indicated a much larger percentage of moderates in Texas than in neighboring Deep South states. Meanwhile, Citizens Councils formed in several large cities to organize local opposition to integration. Klan activities were officially reported in twenty-two counties. A special statewide committee on integration issued a recommendation to "stop, look, and listen" before any school district attempted integration. The Texas Supreme Court invalidated provisions of the Texas Constitution that required segregation in schools. Even with the state court ruling added to the Supreme Court decision, the governor and the attorney general stated that local school districts were not required to formulate any plans for integration. While Shivers believed that his outspoken opposition to integration pleased most Texans, his support for massive resistance widened the gulf between the liberal-loyalist Democrats and other party leaders and elected officials.

Governor Shivers' defiance fell in line with the position of other Deep South governors who vowed to preserve the status quo and took increasingly harsh positions to enforce their hard-line views.[1] Shivers' opposition to integration gained further authority when President Eisenhower refused to endorse the 1954 Supreme Court decision and expressed reservations about the effects of federally mandated integration of the South. The prospect of support from Shivers and other southern Democratic leaders in the 1956 presidential election undoubtedly played a part in the Republican president's reluctance to endorse desegregation. Following the lead of national and state leaders, business-oriented conservatives and many moderates throughout Texas and the rest of the South joined with ardent segregationists to solidify control of state and local governments. Massive resistance was the order of the day. Southern political leaders who failed to take up the banner usually met with defeat. Even popular southern governors Jim Folsom of Alabama and Earl Long of Louisiana, "neopopulists" who attempted to expand state services to residents regardless of racial considerations, refused to embrace desegregation after the *Brown* decision, though they would not link arms with proponents of massive resistance. Because they did not do so and because racial politics dominated nearly every southern political debate, both lost popularity and were out of office by 1958. As support for massive resistance grew, southern politicians came to see taking any less extreme position on desegregation as sure death in terms of their future in elective office. As southern historian Numan V. Bartley noted, "the politics of massive resistance completed the devastation of southern rural liberalism."[2]

Other old problems stayed with Governor Shivers like an unwanted relative. His administration never proposed any plan or dedicated emergency funds to meet the ongoing drought that continued its ever-tightening grip on Texas. In the fifth year of substandard precipitation, every day without rain meant another lost farm or ranch. More scandals haunted the administration. The *Cuero Record,* a small weekly newspaper in south-central Texas, broke the story of fraud in the Texas Veteran's Land Program which involved a number of well-known officials. Designed as a benefit for Texas veterans to help them purchase acreage, the state-sponsored program was begun after World War II at the urging of Land Commissioner Bascom Giles. Once approved by the voters, a board composed of the governor, attorney general, and land commissioner oversaw the sale of bonds and the administration of the innovative loan program for returning veterans. The Land Commissioner's office maintained oversight of day-to-day operations. In a series of investigative stories, the *Record* revealed that many veterans, a number of whom were Mexican American or African American, purchased tracts at artificially high prices, with the state loan money ending up in the pockets of unscrupulous developers. In 1954 Land Commissioner Giles was reelected along with Governor Shivers and Attorney General Ben Shepperd. Once Giles' participation was exposed by the newspapers, he admitted his involvement in the schemes, refused to take his oath of office in January 1955, and subsequently served time in state prison. Because Shivers and Shepperd composed two-thirds of the Veteran's Land Board, many people assumed that they also were involved in the scandal, or at the very least never objected to the illicit loans.[3]

In addition to the veterans' program scandal, further political embarrassment ensued when a number of bankrupt insurance companies failed to take action to protect Texas policyholders. The governor's appointees on the insurance regulatory board were accused of accepting illegal gifts from the suspect companies while ignoring their unsound business practices and allowing insolvent companies to continue operations. Yarborough's campaign complaints about Governor Shivers' misconduct now seemed prophetic and contributed to the public's increasingly negative perception of Shivers. Every time a new scandal hit the papers, Shivers' popularity seemed to sink lower as his ship of state floundered in his final term. As Yarborough commented to Houston attorney W. A. Combs, the stories of "widespread corruption" verified his 1954 campaign charges.[4]

In early 1956 Governor Shivers, despite his political problems and declining popularity, still hoped that he could run once again for governor and control the state Democratic party. He criticized Yarborough, who he believed created his problems and would once again challenge him in the party's primaries. The governor said that charges of corruption were part of a "get Shivers" campaign that originated when the "communists" and his other enemies pledged to defeat him. Shivers also wanted to thwart the efforts of Sam Rayburn and Lyndon Johnson, both of whom had presidential aspirations in 1956. Shivers essentially engaged in a two-front political war, fighting Yarborough and the party liberals on one side and the Johnson-Rayburn moderate Democrats on the other. Had Shivers been politically stronger at home, he might have been successful, as he had been in 1952 when he controlled the party machinery and convinced a majority of Texas Democrats to support Eisenhower. But his bloody campaign victories over Yarborough, together with the rising tide of political scandals, were far too much for the governor to overcome. To many Texans, Shivers now came across as just another politician interested in his own personal gain. He seemed more interested in covering up wrongdoing than cleaning up his own problems. Early in 1956 a number of editorial writers urged the governor not to seek a fourth term. The governor announced on Texas Independence Day, March 2, 1956, that he would not run an unprecedented fourth time for governor. Shivers never admitted to backing down from a third challenge with Yarborough, and he continued his attacks on his political foe.

Even as Shivers withdrew from another battle with Yarborough, he believed he could take on Johnson and Rayburn and control the party's presidential selection process. Shivers and Johnson engaged in a lively exchange in their attempts to select delegates to the 1956 Democratic party precinct conventions. The local May 5 meetings attracted large numbers of Democrats. Shivers lost the war of words to the forces of Johnson, who emerged with a three-to-one margin of victory. Shivers, who had managed a victorious campaign with grass-roots Democratic support in 1952, fell victim to the accumulation of charges from Yarborough and the organized grass-roots efforts of Johnson and Rayburn. If Shivers had any doubts about the decline of his political fortunes, the May precinct conventions demonstrated that the end had come to his reign as king of the political hill in Texas.[5]

Democratic party liberal and moderate activists united behind Johnson and Rayburn in the fight to control delegates to the national convention. That unity ended because Johnson alienated many of the liberals with his own favorite-son candidacy for the 1956 Democratic presidential nomination. Yarborough broke his long-standing rule of staying out of the intraparty squabbles when he attended the 1956 state convention in Dallas. There Yarborough and Johnson each spoke to the assembled delegates. Yarborough received a greater ovation than Johnson during and after their speeches. However, the Johnson forces controlled the convention and he was selected to chair the Texas delegation to the national convention. Texas also pledged to support Johnson as a favorite-son candidate for president. Johnson's heavy-handed treatment of convention participants alienated the liberals, who were still suspicious of his motivations and intentions.

Following his second loss to Shivers in 1954, Yarborough had made a concerted effort to improve his strained relationship with Senator Lyndon Johnson. Throughout 1955, Yarborough corresponded with the Senate leader and praised Johnson's efforts on federal income tax reduction. He also touted Johnson's leadership role for the Democratic party and reminded him of Shivers' support for Eisenhower in 1952. Yarborough pointed out that the Shivercrats were weaker in the state because of the revelations of corruption in the Veteran's Land Board proceedings. "The trail does not lead into some canebrake; it leads to the Governor's office," he wrote to Johnson. Yarborough hoped that with the change of events Johnson's earlier support for Shivers could now be turned. Yarborough knew that he had little chance to persuade Johnson and his supporters to openly support his third attempt to become governor. However, Johnson's own political schemes as demonstrated by the fight to control the state Democratic party actually worked to Yarborough's advantage. He still bristled from the lack of attention, but he realized that Johnson and Rayburn now played a role in the strategy for his next campaign for governor.[6]

With Shivers discredited and out of the race, Yarborough suddenly emerged as the front-runner in the governor's race. As Shivers' star faded from the Texas political sky, Yarborough's grew ever brighter. J. R. Parten agreed with Yarborough's assessment of the situation and encouraged him to run as a "good middle of the road candidate." However, a few leaders among the Democratic loyalists were ready to find a new standard bearer for the 1956 campaign. Some feared that Yarborough, now a two-time loser in the governor's race, lacked the ability to clear the final hurdle and win the office.[7]

Yarborough was downcast after the 1954 runoff. His second loss to Shivers and his $70,000 campaign debt might have forced others out of politics. Yarborough had campaigned nearly continuously since 1952, giving almost as many speeches as the thousands of highway miles he put on his car. By 1956, though, he sensed that it was his two previous efforts that finally forced Shivers out of the political ring with a technical knockout. Yarborough realized his earlier defeats now made him stronger. All he had to do was make one more run for the nomination. After a brief lull, Yarborough resumed his ongoing crusade, taking it to old folks homes, barber shops, auction barns, and civic group meetings. Letters and telephone calls came into his home and his Austin law office asking him to run one more time. "They say they don't like a quitter, and they don't want me to quit," Yarborough remarked in one newspaper interview. Early polls indicated that without Shivers in the race, he would defeat prominent challengers including U.S. Senator Price Daniel, Attorney General John Ben Shepperd, Lieutenant Governor Ben Ramsey, and State Senator Jimmy Phillips. Yarborough needed little encouragement for by this time he was a virtual candidate, almost totally consumed with the routine of campaigning at his customary breakneck speed. He maintained his law practice in Austin but spent more time on the 1956 race for the governor's office, which he felt was finally within his reach.[8]

With no incumbent in the race, many Texas political leaders considered entering the governor's contest in 1956, but Yarborough and U.S. senator Price Daniel emerged clearly the front-runners and scared off most of the competition. Former governor and U.S. senator W. Lee "Pappy" O'Daniel entered the Democratic governor's campaign. O'Daniel re-created his hillbilly band, toured the state in a fire truck, and preached against professional politicians, big corporations, and "Daniel millionaires," thus following the same themes he successfully used in the 1930's and 1940's. Archconservative writer and former Jeffersonian Democrat leader J. Evetts Haley also joined the race. Other minor candidates included Ruben Senterfitt, a pro-segregation candidate, and J. J. Holmes, the only man who favored integration. Daniel, a longtime veteran of Texas politics, was Yarborough's heavyweight opponent.

Price Daniel was born in Dayton in Liberty County on October 10, 1910. He traced his descendants to Texas when the land was a colony of Mexico. Daniel attended public schools in Liberty and Fort Worth and graduated from Baylor University with a degree in journalism in 1931 and a law degree in 1932. He was admitted to the State Bar of Texas and returned to Liberty to practice law in the same location that Sam Houston had his law office. In addition to his law practice, Daniel was co-owner and publisher of the *Liberty Vindicator* and *Anahuac Progress,* two weekly newspapers. Daniel served in the Texas House of Representatives for three terms from 1939 until 1945. At the age of 32, he became Speaker of the House for the 1943–1945 session. At the conclusion of the session, Daniel waived his legislative exemption, joined the U.S. Army, and served in the Judge Advocate General's Office in the Pacific Theater. He left the military in May 1946 with the rank of captain. When he returned home, Daniel successfully ran for attorney general in 1946 and served for three terms. As attorney general, he was best known for his antitrust suits, a well-publicized campaign against organized crime, and the Tidelands battle with the federal government. He also represented the state before the U.S. Supreme Court when the University of Texas Law School refused to admit Heman Marion Sweatt, an African American postal clerk from Beaumont.[9]

In 1952 Daniel announced for the U.S. Senate against the longtime incumbent, Senator Tom Connally. Daniel hoped that once his intentions to run against Connally were known, Governor Shivers would then enter the race against the incumbent senator. Shivers, Daniel believed, would not run for a third term as governor. However, Daniel's strategy backfired when Shivers announced for reelection in 1952. After the governor's decision, Daniel received the backing of the state's conservative business establishment to unseat Connally. Daniel's popularity and the senator's age forced Connally's withdrawal from the Senate in 1952.

Daniel had joined with Shivers when he broke with other Texas Democrats and endorsed Eisenhower in the presidential election. Once he took office as the junior senator from Texas, Daniel continued to focus on the Tidelands issue and his anticrime interests.

Immediately prior to Daniel's announcement to run for governor in 1956, stories circulated that the senator and Shivers had made a behind-the-scenes agreement to trade offices, just as Daniel had hoped in 1952. Shivers and Daniel both made "states' rights" a main theme after the *Brown* decision and had virtually the same supporters from the conservative and moderate divisions within the Democratic party. One scenario circulating in early 1956 had Daniel resigning from the Senate to run for governor. In that event, Governor Shivers would have the responsibility to make an interim appointment to fill the position and could select himself for the position. However, the scenario had flaws. Daniel would have realized that, given the recent scandals involving the insurance companies and the Veteran's Land Board, such an agreement with Shivers would not serve his interests and that Yarborough would be primed for an attack accusing them of making deals in smoke-filled rooms. In any case, Daniel did not have to resign from his senate seat to run for governor and, moreover, had no real incentive to give up a secure position to run in a contested governor's race.

FIGHTING FOR VOTES — ROUND ONE

Declaring that he would "rather be governor of Texas than President of the United States," Daniel returned to Texas in 1956 to run for governor while keeping his Senate seat. He opened his campaign with a statewide television and radio address from Dallas on March 26. In his announcement, he vowed he "would not think of appointing [his] own successor" if elected governor. Emphasizing his pro-segregation and states' rights position, he said he intended to protect the people of Texas from "further federal encroachments." In a statement undoubtedly directed at Yarborough, he asserted that "no matter how much mudslinging and name calling may be done by the opposition, Price Daniel promises you to keep his part of a campaign on a high level — worthy of the dignity which should go with the office of Governor of Texas." In his campaign Daniel initially capitalized on his Senate sponsorship of a bill for stronger federal drug trafficking laws and his work for drought relief and water conservation. His campaign brochures pictured the senator, dressed in Western shirt and cowboy boots, with his wife and four children seated on a log beside a lake. As he toured the state with family members in his green and white Chevrolet, Daniel touted his Senate and attorney general record. He lauded his fight against "federal encroachments on the rights of States and the people as retained in the U.S. Constitution."[10]

Daniel was an excellent attorney but could not sway large crowds as Yarborough or O'Daniel could. He preferred to promote his image as a "home-town boy" and a soft-spoken, small-town family man. When he made speeches, he often kept his coat and tie on even with the summer sun bear-ing down on him. Both Daniel and Yarborough were accomplished attorneys from East Texas, but were about as much alike as piney woods cornbread and a Dallas country club martini. After the Democratic party precinct meet-ings in April, Daniel began to focus exclusively on Yarborough and ignore the other candidates. The integration issue continued to play a prominent role in the Democratic primary. Neither Yarborough nor Daniel supported integration, but Daniel clearly positioned himself as a stronger proponent of continued segregation.

As attorney general, Daniel had defended the state's refusal to allow He-man Sweatt to attend the all-white University of Texas Law School. Daniel's campaign manager, Joe Greenhill, said that many African Americans re-membered Daniel's role in the matter and resented him for it. In Congress, Daniel supported the Southern Manifesto, which denounced the *Brown* de-cision and urged states to resist integration. Daniel criticized the U.S. Su-preme Court's decisions on integration for "reversing decisions of a hundred years." Immediately before the election, he called for a constitutional amend-ment that would override the Supreme Court's decisions in favor of integra-tion. Without addressing Yarborough directly, he clearly identified his main opponent as the candidate of "left wing radicals" which included the CIO, the ADA, and the NAACP. Criticized by Yarborough for his support for Eisenhower in 1952, Daniel stated in June that he would back the Demo-cratic presidential nominee in 1956. In his final television appearance, Fess Parker, the actor who portrayed Davy Crockett in the popular Disney tele-vision production, was beside him. Parker said that Daniel was "cut from the same cloth and is the same kind of fighter" as Crockett, Houston, and other early Texas heroes. Throughout the campaign, Daniel essentially followed the Shivers campaign recipe of 1954, with a few new ingredients of his own. By early July, Daniel and Yarborough were still considered the top two candi-dates in the race. Neither had made large inroads into their opponent's base of supporters prior to the July primary.[11]

Yarborough waited until Daniel formally announced his candidacy to kick off his own campaign, though he had never really stopped campaigning since his second loss to Shivers. He selected the East Texas city of Nacogdoches to officially launch his third effort for governor on June 1, 1956. Yarborough addressed an enthusiastic crowd of more than one thousand people at the Nacogdoches Fair Park. The speech was on statewide radio thanks to some last-minute contributions totaling $800. He stressed that he would end "corruption" in state government and specifically referred to the insurance and Veteran's Land Board scandals. He called for a teacher pay raise and more state money for colleges and old-age pensions. He received the loudest applause when he stated he opposed the "forced co-mingling of white and Negro children in the schools." He said that he opposed the use of force to integrate local public schools and called for moderation. "I avoid stirring up hatreds, strife, and dissension. I do not denounce any race of people nor do I try to set class against class," the candidate told his supporters. Yarborough confronted the issue but wished to avoid it since he was more interested in whipping up a storm over the scandals in state government.[12]

Most of Yarborough's focus during the first primary centered on his calls to fight corruption and clean up state government. He sensed that the insurance and veterans scandals weighed heavily on the minds of Texans. He too ignored the minor candidates and aimed his criticisms at his main opponent, Daniel. At nearly every campaign appearance, Yarborough spoke about Daniel, the Shivers administration, and official corruption in one long breath. He utilized his well-refined public-speaking skills and was at his best at these outdoor rallies. Shedding his coat, rolling up his sleeves, and waving his arms, Yarborough worked his audience better than anyone since Jim Ferguson. He addressed people by their first name, recalled old families and local stories, and then peppered his opponent with charges of corruption. He likened the situation to his experiences during World War II, when people despite long odds fought for liberty against totalitarian governments. His pledges to "clean up the mess at Austin" provided him with a consistent message that allowed him to stay on the offensive and avoid the integration issue as much as possible. "Corruption in office was the main issue when I ran for governor four years ago and it is the main issue today," he repeated over and over. Yarborough believed that his charges made a strong impact on those he needed the most—the moderate voters in Texas. He enjoyed calling Daniel the "political buddy of Allan Shivers." With proof of government dishonesty now in hand, Yarborough's denunciation of the scandals offset whatever support he might have lost from his previous two defeats for governor. As the summer days wore on, Yarborough made sure that politically the heat increased faster than on the rising thermometer. His liberal and labor backers were firm, for they were not going to desert him over the integration question. Although he never raised sufficient funds to match Daniel's television and radio coverage, Yarborough raised enough money to remain competitive. The campaign used televised events other than paid advertising to obtain

Charles R. (C. R.) Yarborough (left), once a Henderson County justice of the peace, advised his son (right) on Texas politics. Courtesy Center for American History, Russell Lee Collection (3Y155).

coverage and moderate the effects of the state's major daily newspapers, all of which endorsed Daniel. Yarborough obtained free air time and even appeared as a spectator eating hot dogs alongside the fans at wrestling matches and rodeos.[13]

Yarborough also made many other personal appearances and stayed on the road through most of the race. With the help of his energetic supporters, he came up with more creative ways to grab attention. Yarborough countered Fess Parker's Davy Crockett with his own icon of popular culture: The campaign hired three young men who resembled Elvis Presley to form the "Cass County Coon Hunters." They sang "The Yellow Rose of Texas" from the stage during Yarborough's campaign stops. Yarborough enjoyed his campaign mail and spent many late-night hours reading comments and suggestions from supporters. Reading mail was important to him for various reasons, but the letters especially seemed to regenerate his spirit, not unlike the experience a teacher enjoys when past students express gratitude for what they learned in the classroom.[14]

When Governor Shivers announced he would not seek a fourth term in

March, he urged Democrats to approve state constitutional amendments "against unwarranted federal encroachment." The State Democratic Executive Committee (SDEC), still under Shivers' control, stirred passions further by adding three referendums to the July 28 ballot. With the governor behind the initiative, the SDEC voted to let Texas Democrats decide on three politically sensitive issues: integration of public schools, intermarriage between whites and blacks, and "interposition," the right of a state to invalidate a federal law. The initiatives were intended primarily to arouse voter passions concerning integration and assist the conservative candidates. The Shivers forces believed these volatile measures would draw more people to the primary, including Republicans.[15]

In the July 28 primary, Daniel led the other candidates but did not take a majority. Daniel carried 147 of the 254 counties and led Yarborough 622,000 votes to 460,000. W. Lee O'Daniel finished a strong third with 345,000 votes, followed by Haley with 90,000. Daniel's biggest support came from West Texas, the boss-controlled counties in South Texas, and the largest urban areas. Yarborough's support came from East Texas and the Gulf Coast region. In the referendums on the primary ballot dealing with segregation issues, Texas voters by a four-to-one margin supported stronger segregation laws, opposed intermarriage between races, and were for interposition to stop federal encroachment of states' rights.

Daniel raised more money and outspent Yarborough by a two-to-one margin. Yarborough's stand on integration did not hurt him with African American voters in the state; he won all of the large urban minority precincts. His margins ranged from three-to-one in East Texas cities to ten-to-one in Dallas and Houston. Minority boxes in a few smaller cities such as Waco actually favored Daniel by a small margin over Yarborough. Yarborough easily outdistanced all of his opponents for the small number of black voters in the Democratic primary. Only one aspirant for governor, J. J. Holmes, favored integration, and he finished last in the primary behind all other contestants, drawing barely 10,000 votes.[16]

THE DANIEL-YARBOROUGH RUNOFF, 1956 — ROUND 2

The three-week runoff campaign in the broiling hot summer of 1956 also turned out to be even hotter than the record-breaking temperatures. Daniel put Yarborough on the defensive when he released a telegram from twenty-six prominent Democrats who urged Yarborough to withdraw from the race for the sake of harmony and Democratic unity. Yarborough's response was, "I am not a quitter, and the 26-turncoat telegram is a confession of the sacred double cross." None of the "white flag bearers" were his supporters in 1956, Yarborough noted. He also replied to Governor Shivers, who stated early in the runoff his disdain for candidates who "dealt in personalities and wild, unsubstantiated charges." Yarborough claimed that the Shivers-Daniel team "has smeared me with their evil and false charges for years." Yarborough then fired back, claiming that Daniel's charges against him were a distraction to cover up millions of dollars "to buy his way into the second primary." He challenged Daniel to a series of debates around the state. He also began his own behind-the-scenes effort to capture the endorsement of former governor "Pappy" O'Daniel, who had finished a strong third in the first primary. O'Daniel announced his support for Yarborough, which provided a real shot in the arm for the runoff election. In broadcasts over seventy Texas radio stations the week before the runoff election, O'Daniel urged voters to support Yarborough against Daniel.[17]

In televised campaign programs during the runoff, Yarborough continued his assault against Daniel as the "hand-picked heir to the Shivers throne." Yarborough noted that Daniel, who sat as attorney general until 1952, never objected to any of the Veteran's Land Board loans or challenged any of the Texas insurance companies that became insolvent. Yarborough also criticized Daniel for the support he received from the Parr family and the machine-controlled counties in South Texas. "My opponent carried every border county controlled by a pistol-packing border boss," he said, noting that Daniel carried nearly every county in South Texas by margins of two to one or larger. In a parody of Daniel's complaint that Yarborough was backed by the NAACP, Yarborough charged that Daniel was backed by the TAAM, the "Texas Association for the Advancement of Millionaires." By this time, Yarborough and his family were aware of the claim supporters had heard from around the state—that Yarborough had deserted three different wives. Yarborough believed the falsehoods to be part of an organized smear campaign launched by Shivers and Daniel. He also complained about anonymous late-night telephone calls made to Opal at their Austin home.[18]

Daniel had assured voters at the beginning of the runoff election that he would not "descend to the kind of campaign he [Yarborough] conducts," and he announced that he would not debate Yarborough because he "so lightly regards the facts and the truth." Daniel denied that he had made any deal with Shivers in exchange for his support. A number of prominent supporters of Lyndon Johnson made public appearances on behalf of Daniel. One of them was from Johnson's Senate staff—J. J. "Jake" Pickle, whose Austin public relations firm had participated in the 1954 production of "The Port Arthur Story." Daniel disputed Yarborough's claims that he spent one million dollars and claimed only $12,500 in expenditures. Daniel renewed his charges that the NAACP actively worked for Yarborough and provided election returns with heavy Yarborough majorities from African American precincts as proof. Daniel also claimed he never solicited support from George Parr and "everybody knows that I'm the first man ever to send investigators into Duval County. I've fought Parr all the way." Daniel attempted to again emphasize his crime-fighting record as attorney general and senator, but nearly all of the news coverage centered on his denials of charges made by Yarborough.

In the final days of the campaign, Daniel continued his attacks on Yarborough's "smear" campaign while linking him with the NAACP and labor unions. He also tried to remind Texas voters of his lead in the first primary. Daniel must have sensed his campaign was suddenly out of tune just as Yarborough struck the right chords. Yarborough's exhaustive efforts, O'Daniel's endorsement, and Daniel's totally defensive campaign made the runoff outcome uncertain.[19]

While Yarborough jousted with Daniel in the media, his campaign staff focused on mobilizing his supporters for the runoff election day. By the summer of 1956, Yarborough had a large base of organized and devoted followers. What they lacked in money they made up in effort. Campaign organizers in the thousands throughout the state concentrated their efforts on getting supporters to the polls. Daniel's lead of over 100,000 votes in the first primary may have worked against him since many of his workers believed the front-runner would coast to a runoff victory just as Shivers had two years earlier. The Daniel campaign apparently overlooked the party precinct meetings held the night of the first election. For the first time, the loyalist-liberal faction actually won more counties than the conservatives and nearly obtained a majority of the delegates. These results were the best indication of the organizational strength of those united behind Yarborough.[20]

Saturday, August 28, dawned with campaign volunteers feverishly working in the summer heat from the isolated crossroads precincts to the large urban neighborhoods. As the runoff votes came in to the Texas Election Bureau that night, the lead changed hands as Daniel and Yarborough ran neck and neck. Daniel's campaign manager, Joe Greenhill, and his staff were very nervous. Greenhill and Jake Pickle manned the telephones as Daniel's tally margin dropped like the stock market on Black Friday. Yarborough's pre-election optimism was warranted, for he reversed the results from the first election and carried 146 counties to Daniel's 108. But votes continued to trickle in and late returns pulled Daniel back into the lead the day after the election. Daniel's votes totaled 697,932 to Yarborough's 695,209. With Daniel holding on to a narrow 2,500-vote lead the day after the election, he issued a victory statement and promised an administration of confidence and harmony. Yarborough refused to concede, believing his campaign workers had detected many "sizable errors." Specifically, the Yarborough campaign received reports of questionable tally changes from Webb, Limestone, Cass, Shelby, Caldwell, and Tyler counties. In Woodville, the seat of Tyler County, one county official told Yarborough "they burned 250 ballots here, right there in that wastepaper basket on the courthouse square." Allegations in the other counties told of marked ballots being thrown away or burned. In each reported occurrence, several hundred ballots, a small percentage of the total votes cast, were discarded. The differences were not enough to change any local races but when put together they amounted to thousands of votes. Yarborough's campaign workers went to observe the Austin airport in the midnight hours on Saturday night. Dozens of planes left with men carrying briefcases, all bound for county seats where ballots were tabulated. Yarborough and many of his supporters firmly believed that the election was stolen right before their eyes. W. P. Johnson summarized the sentiments of most ardent Yarborough enthusiasts when he wrote that the "damnable hellish GOP Shivers-Daniel corrupt party" stole the election. The votes became official the Tuesday after the election: Daniel won by 3,547 votes out of nearly 1.4 million ballots cast in the runoff election. Yarborough grudgingly conceded the race to Daniel a few days later and announced he would not contest the election.[21]

Yarborough's surprising comeback came as a result of his improved organization and his ability to link Daniel with the Shivers administration scandals. In 1956, a number of young campaign workers came up with a better communications network and "get out the vote" effort. The Yarborough campaign also took better advantage of the media and was able to obtain free coverage on many occasions. The Daniel campaign bought more television, radio, and newspaper ads, but the Yarborough network, together with Yarborough's campaign tactics, nearly pulled off an upset. In fact, Yarborough and his key campaign managers believed they actually won the race by 30,000 votes based on discrepancies in nearly a dozen counties.

Daniel was reported to be quite upset with the narrow margin of victory. The election results were the closest since the disputed 1932 runoff between

Ross Sterling and Miriam Ferguson. In many high-profile statewide races, candidates frequently questioned the integrity of the primary elections. Voting and tabulation in nearly every community relied on paper ballots and a few individuals responsible for the count. The system remained open to corruption throughout the 1950's, just as it had been for many years. Most precinct and county election officials were honest, but some, unduly influenced by politicians, businesses, and courthouse officials, altered ballots or return totals. C. F. Booker, a Galveston County election official, astutely noted what ultimately tipped the scale: in the runoff Republicans voted for Daniel in large numbers. "I firmly believe that this precedent was duplicated in every two-party precinct in Texas," Booker wrote. Yarborough's charges of fraud in this election were not just sour grapes—the late-night vote changes, combined with the Republican votes, were more than sufficient to alter the outcome.[22]

On the issues, the two primary leaders divided along the lines of Daniel's more conservative positions and the more traditional New Deal stands taken by Yarborough. The focus of the campaign quickly shifted in the runoff as both sides progressively leveled charges and counter charges. In the end, Daniel won by the narrowest of margins, receiving 50.12 percent of the popular vote. Beneath the surface of the 1956 election, the unresolved question of integration still lurked. Compared to the 1954 Democratic primary, the Daniel campaign was not as vitriolic as Shivers' in arousing the concerns of white Texans on racial issues. However, Daniel continued to maintain his outspoken opposition to integration and federal initiatives while blasting Yarborough as the candidate of the NAACP. In other races around the state, candidates who spoke for segregation and massive resistance generally won. Texas liberals criticized Yarborough for his position, but they consistently stayed with him through the governor's races. Yarborough was not afraid to publicly criticize his opponents for their shortcomings and questionable dealings. Yet at this stage of his career he was still unwilling to publicly confront the integration issue, which was to become a larger factor in efforts to modernize the state. The voices of dissent in Texas had not yet reached the level where they could be heard over the shrill screams of reaction.[23]

Throughout the 1956 campaign against Daniel, Yarborough's stand against "forced integration" in favor of "moderation" served as his attempt to find a middle ground between the dogmatic integrationists and the rock-solid segregationists. Yarborough was fully aware that Texas primary voters supported segregation four to one. Yet he saw a potential meeting place where moderates and liberals could join together to devise a gradual move toward integration that would take the state further into the national mainstream. Even as more Texas and southern political leaders embraced massive resistance in defense of segregation, Yarborough believed some yet-undefined opening existed that would allow him to capture the middle ground while holding his liberal base. Historian Dewey Grantham concluded that many well-known liberals of the day attempted a similar defense. Mississippi's William Faulkner, journalist Hodding Carter, and other prominent southerners launched initiatives in national magazines and northern newspapers to plead for tolerance and time as the school desegregation issue intensified. They also hoped to soften some of the harsher opinions of southerners held by people in the North. Yarborough's visibility and near-success gave a face to that image of moderation. His narrow defeat, alongside other elections in Texas and the South in 1956, represented the high-water mark of massive resistance to desegregation. Even as Daniel celebrated his narrow victory, cracks in the foundation were beginning to form in Texas and the rest of the South that would forever change the way of life there.[24]

After losing three straight campaigns, most political aspirants would retire to private life and look for another career. Yarborough, however, marched to a different beat and seldom missed an opportunity to defy conventional wisdom. He was visibly upset with the narrow loss to Daniel but also encouraged by the large number of votes he received and the ever-increasing efforts of his growing numbers of supporters. His base of traditional Democrats, labor, farmers, and small business owners was not one that would provide large sums of money for his political efforts. Only a few wealthy individuals such as J. R. Parten and Walter Hall consistently supported Yarborough with timely donations when the telephone company was ready to pull the plug or the electric utility prepared to shut off the lights. While many key supporters lacked money in their bank accounts to buy television advertising, they provided many hours of volunteer labor that could never be fully recognized. This base of activists expanded throughout the 1950's and remained committed to Yarborough in spite of his losses.

Fate also played a role in Yarborough's future. Before Price Daniel could take the oath of office as governor, he had to resign his Senate seat. Under Texas law, the governor could appoint a temporary replacement but then a special election had to be held. Lyndon Johnson, who won the 1948 special election in the historic race against Coke Stevenson, was the most recent beneficiary of this requirement. Yarborough had barely finished counting returns from the August runoff election when people began to contact him about the U.S. Senate seat. In one of the stranger developments in the unusual world of Texas politics, Yarborough's three ill-fated attempts to win the governor's office now placed him in an outstanding position to go to the U.S. Senate.

8   *Put the Jam on the Lower Shelf*

The ink had barely dried on the 1956 election returns before the race began for the U.S. Senate seat Price Daniel was vacating. A "Draft Yarborough" movement erupted even as Yarborough was considering whether to challenge the results of the Democratic primary runoff election that gave Daniel a razor-thin victory in the governor's race. Boxes of letters came to Yarborough reminding him that he was the "real winner" of the runoff election. Edyth Gilbert Barton, a student of Yarborough's from the 1920's, explained his supporters' sentiments best when she wrote, "don't give up; just keep holding on." In Wichita Falls campaign aide James Boren formed the first committee pushing a Yarborough Senate candidacy. Yarborough's local Harris County organization launched another and opened a Houston headquarters. Banker Walter Hall, businessman Billy Goldberg, former Houston mayor Neal Pickett, and a number of other longtime supporters began the effort. Within a week after the runoff, three other Democrats announced: State Supreme Court Justice James P. Hart of Austin, State Senator Searcy Bracewell of Houston, and U.S. Congressman-at-large Martin Dies. Other potential Democratic candidates included Attorney General John Ben Shepperd. Republican Thad Hutcheson announced for the office. Texas law allowed the governor to call a special election for a U.S. Senate vacancy and the ballot was open to both major parties. A candidate needed only a plurality to win the race since the law did not require a majority vote in a runoff election.[1]

Republicans and loyal Democrats united in a call for governor-elect Daniel to leave the Senate prior to the November general election. Although Republicans realized they were a small minority of the state's active voters in 1957, they hoped that a Senate race crowded with Democrats would allow Hutcheson to nose out the field in the winner-take-all contest. Daniel submitted his resignation to Governor Shivers on September 27 but gave a January 15, 1957, effective date. Shivers accepted the letter but never set an election date as speculation over the vacancy increased. Texans were not the only ones interested in the election to replace Daniel. National Democrats were very concerned. Lyndon Johnson, the majority leader, had a precarious one-vote majority in the Senate. A loss to a Republican would be disastrous to Johnson's presidential aspirations and the national party. Republicans and Democrats would have an equal number of senators, which would give Vice President Richard Nixon a tie-breaking vote as he presided over the Senate.

Johnson wanted a Democrat but preferred a conservative or someone he could easily dominate as opposed to the independent-minded Yarborough. Johnson and Speaker Sam Rayburn had already earned the wrath of the loyalist Democrats when they combined forces to seize control of the state party organization in 1956 and then supported party delegates promoted by Shivers and Daniel. In response, over one hundred liberals gathered in Austin to make plans for an independent campaign for Adlai Stevenson in the November election. Many of these activists distrusted Johnson for years to come, and for his part Johnson remained suspicious of them, referring to them as the "red hots."

Yarborough had joined with loyalist Creekmore Fath and others who announced their mistrust of the Johnson-Rayburn-Daniel coalition, and his public association with the party dissidents widened the breach between him and the Senate majority leader at a crucial time. As a result of the deepening divisions within their own party and the uncertainty of Daniel's replacement, Johnson and Rayburn focused on activities in Austin. They also began looking for a candidate other than Yarborough to take the soon-to-be-vacant position alongside Johnson in the U.S. Senate.[2]

Following Stevenson's loss to Eisenhower in November, the state's daily newspapers fanned the flames of discord between the rival Democratic factions. "Neither Johnson nor Rayburn want Yarborough to win that Senate race," Dick West of the *Dallas Morning News* stated. Both the Speaker and the Senate majority leader were "middle of the road" politicians who disliked the "wild eyed radicalism" of Yarborough's supporters and wanted to prevent Yarborough and the "extreme-liberal bloc to become stronger." The idea of having Yarborough alongside him in the Senate was far down on Johnson's list of preferences and probably gave the majority leader headaches when he contemplated having to work with the outspoken leader of Texas liberals. However, he certainly could not afford to publicly support any candidate in Texas who offended the mostly liberal national leaders of his own party. Following Stevenson's second defeat, Johnson believed he could be the party's presidential nominee in 1960, but only if he could find the middle ground between northern liberals and southern conservatives. In any case, his own aspirations aside, Johnson was not a politician who could resist throwing his weight into his state's turbulent political match.[3]

When the Texas legislature convened in January 1957, the special election issue jumped to the forefront. State Representative Joe Pool (D-Dallas), acting at the behest of Johnson and Rayburn, introduced a bill to change the Texas Election Code to require a candidate to receive an electoral majority in a special election; if no candidate captured more than 50 percent of the popular vote, a runoff election would be held. Pool's bill met immediate criticism from many Democrats and Republicans. GOP Senate candidate Hutcheson characterized it as an attempt to keep Republicans from elective office in Texas and described it as "immoral and probably illegal." In an unexpected move, Governor Shivers, only two hours before he left office, appointed Dallas businessman William A. Blakley as Daniel's temporary replacement in the U.S. Senate until a special election could be held. Blakley, the new senator, was a political unknown but admired in Texas business circles. He was a millionaire businessman whose appointment Shivers, Daniel, and Johnson all agreed upon. When Shivers announced the selection, he noted that Blakley would not run for the Senate seat in the special election. Upon taking office as the new governor, Daniel called for the special election to be held on April 2, 1957.

With the interim senator already out of the race, another well-known politician declared his interest in the race—Congressman Martin Dies (D-Lufkin), the rabid anti-communist conservative who rose to fame as chair of the House Un-American Activities Committee. Rayburn disliked Dies for his obsessive, McCarthy-like behavior. He, Johnson, and Daniel tried, unsuccessfully, to persuade Dies to withdraw in favor of Lieutenant Governor Ben Ramsey.[4]

In the meantime, Rayburn and Johnson worked from Washington on members of the Texas Legislature for passage of the Pool bill requiring a runoff if a candidate did not win an electoral majority. Yarborough knew Rayburn and Johnson pressured key members. The Speaker telephoned Yarborough as the Pool bill worked its way through the state legislature. When Yarborough revealed he had sixty-four members in the House opposed to the bill, the Speaker responded with a loud "hrrumph" and hung up the telephone. Yarborough realized he had made a mistake. The legislation passed the Texas House a few days later with over one hundred favorable votes.[5]

When the issue came to a vote in the Texas Senate, its fate was in the hands of a few uncommitted senators. One of these was Senator R. A. Weinert (D-Seguin), a Shivers stalwart who had never supported Yarborough. But

Vice President John Nance Garner, the crusty former Speaker and Vice President, supported Yarborough in his 1957 Senate race. Courtesy Center for American History, Russell Lee Collection (3Y155).

Weinert was a longtime rival of Alvin Wirtz of Seguin, one of Lyndon Johnson's main benefactors. Yarborough's relationship with Wirtz dated back to the formative years of the LCRA, when Yarborough had unsuccessfully opposed Wirtz for the position of LCRA general counsel. While Weinert may have opposed the Pool bill because he did not believe in "changing the rules during the middle of the game," he was also sending a message to Lyndon Johnson in the Senate. He described the move as nothing more than "gut-Yarborough" legislation. Weinert and a few other senators killed the Pool legislation. The bill's demise gave life to Yarborough. He was well-prepared for the winner-take-all April 2 special election.[6]

"THERE WASN'T A BIG SHOT DOWN THERE"

A total of twenty-two candidates filed for the winner-take-all April 2, 1957, election for the vacant U.S. Senate seat. Yarborough was in the fifth year of his nearly nonstop statewide campaign, so the people of Texas knew him well. Creekmore Fath and Mark Adams edited and designed "Yarborough, Portrait of a People's Senator," a mini-biography of the candidate. The booklet featured Yarborough's family, his years as district judge, his military service, and the campaigns for governor. "He is fighting a war in a cause he believes in his soul is just," the authors proclaimed as they portrayed the campaign as a moral crusade. Yarborough volunteers distributed thousands of these booklets door to door and placed them in barber shops, restaurants, union halls, service stations, and hundreds of other locations around the state. In his public appearances, Yarborough selected safe issues while his campaign workers concentrated on voter turnout. He called for budget cuts, favored an income tax reduction, and continued his longtime support for farm programs, soil conservation, and drought relief. He endorsed continuation of the oil depletion allowance for the nation's petroleum producers. Because this was a one-shot contest, Yarborough finally had the odds in his favor if he could maintain his base support and get them to the polls on election day.[7]

April 2, 1957, dawned as a stormy day throughout Texas as heavy rains, high winds, and sporadic tornadoes swept much of the state. Radio and television warnings cautioned people about leaving their homes in the unpredictable spring season. The sudden weather change was merely a harbinger for the election day drama. After the polls closed, volunteers in Yarborough's Austin headquarters listened to radios for reports and took telephone calls from the field. Volunteers crowded around the single black-and-white television set. First-time student assistants and veteran Yarborough supporters jammed the room to watch incoming returns from all 254 counties posted on the large chalkboard. A roar that rattled the plate glass windows burst from the building when the Texas Election Bureau announced Yarborough's victory. When the ballots were totaled, Yarborough had obtained 364,000 votes and 38 percent of the total vote—enough for a plurality and far ahead of the nearest challenger. Yarborough led the field of candidates in 172 of the 254 counties. Dies finished second with 290,000 votes, followed by Hutcheson with 216,000. Yarborough's long-suffering supporters went wild with jubilation. The beaming Ralph and an elated Opal entered his downtown office packed shoulder to shoulder with enthusiasts. As he jumped on a table to thank his voters, they realized the long crusade was over—victory was finally at hand. The celebration lasted long into the night. As one reporter described the tumultuous scene at Yarborough's headquarters, "there wasn't a big shot down there, it was just people."[8]

"Just people" greet Ralph and Opal at his downtown Austin headquarters after his first statewide victory wins him a seat in the U.S. Senate. Courtesy Center for American History, Russell Lee Collection (3Y155).

YARBOROUGH AND JOHNSON'S STORMY RELATIONSHIP

After the special election, Yarborough said, Lyndon Johnson remained distant and told him that no one should take office unless they captured a majority of the votes. In an interview years after he left the Senate, Yarborough noted, "That son-of-a-gun got elected on 27 percent," a reference to Johnson's first special-election congressional victory twenty years earlier. Yarborough wisely withheld any criticism of Johnson in the aftermath of his victory. The new senator believed that both he and Johnson relied on many of the same people. "I thought if I blast him I will run a bunch of them off," he surmised, so he remained silent after winning the election. J. R. Parten wrote to Johnson immediately after Yarborough's election, and Johnson assured Parten that he would "cooperate with him all I can." Yarborough realized the Senate majority leader exerted tremendous influence and would be assigning him to committees, but he grew impatient and blamed Johnson for the delay in his induction ceremonies in Washington as the Texas secretary of state withheld verification of the election results. Instead of a public confrontation, Yarborough called Speaker Rayburn for assistance. He complained to the Speaker that he had two automobiles which he had to sell to help finance the campaign. "I am walking. I would like to be sworn in," Yarborough pleaded. Rayburn offered his assistance and promised he would contact Johnson. Years after leaving office, Yarborough defined the difference between his dealings with Rayburn and with Johnson. "Lyndon Johnson would give you carrots one day and then stab you in the back with a sword the next day. He was treacherous as hell, but not Sam Rayburn. You could always trust Sam Rayburn." After his call to Rayburn, Yarborough's inauguration date was set.[9]

On April 29, 1957, Yarborough took the oath of office from Vice President Richard Nixon, with Senate Majority Leader Johnson looking on. Standing alongside him at the capitol ceremony were his wife, Opal, and son, Richard, both with broad smiles. The Yarboroughs moved to a small apartment in

Majority Leader Lyndon Johnson smiles as Vice President Richard Nixon administers the oath of office to Yarborough after the 1957 special election. Courtesy Opal Yarborough.

Washington close to Senator Albert Gore Sr. (D-Tennessee) and his wife. Yarborough and Gore established a close friendship and political relationship that lasted for his entire Senate tenure. A rented apartment seemed to many an appropriate choice. People across the political spectrum wondered aloud if Yarborough could withstand a challenge in 1958 from a well-heeled conservative opponent. Yarborough was considered vulnerable because of his previous frustration at winning a statewide election during the Democratic primary. Furthermore, others speculated about how Yarborough would adjust to the Senate with its focus on national issues. Most Texans still associated Yarborough with local and state matters. Also, Yarborough's ability to work with Senator Johnson and other southern Democrats was questionable, especially on the key domestic issue of the day. "The real test of Yarborough's qualifications for admittance to the southern fraternity possibly will be his willingness to participate in a filibuster against civil rights legislation," the *Dallas Morning News* observed only a few days after the election.[10]

The not-so-well-disguised feud between Johnson and Yarborough gave political insiders and the press many stories which illustrated the differences between the two senators. Johnson and his staff thought that the Yarborough group were mere "upstarts," expected to serve only a few months until the 1958 election restored a conservative Democrat to the Senate seat. Yarborough and his staff believed that Johnson wanted to work as if he were the only senator from Texas. After another delay from the majority leader's office, Yarborough finally received appointments to three committees: Interstate and Foreign Commerce, Government Operations, and the Post Office and Civil Service. In spite of the frosty relations with the majority leader, Yarborough and his new staff enjoyed a profoundly warm reception from other Senate Democrats. Had Yarborough lost the election to Hutcheson, an equal number of Republican and Democratic senators would have changed the organization of the upper chamber. Yarborough's election not only maintained Johnson's leadership position but also saved committee positions held by Democrats and legislative jobs dependent on the political party in control. As a result, many Democratic staff members expressed their gratitude and aided Yarborough's office in those first months.

"We had a lot of people pulling for us," recalled Jim Boren, who went to work on Yarborough's first Senate staff in 1957. The senator and the few who went with him were anxious to hit the ground running despite their lack of familiarity with Senate rules and protocol. Charles "Chuck" Caldwell also was a campaign worker who followed Yarborough to Washington, where he obtained a job in the Capitol Post Office. Majority Leader Johnson was not

particularly helpful, but others on his staff quietly aided Yarborough's new assistants. Congressman Jack Brooks, a Marine veteran representing southeast
Texas, and his staff were the most helpful in establishing relationships with
the close-knit Texas house members. "When you went through the political battles we had been through, you learned to keep your back against the
wall. Our cautious beginning turned out to be extremely wise," Boren recalled. In Yarborough's first office initially were Charlie Johnson, Jim Boren,
Lou Nora Spiller (former secretary to Texas senator Tom Connally), Sandra
Padilla, and Lyman Jones. Shortly thereafter, Chuck Caldwell, Bob Shirley,
Dave Shapiro, and Paula Brown came on board. All had participated in the
Yarborough Senate campaign except for Padilla, Brown, and Shirley, who
had worked in other Washington offices before coming to Yarborough's. Yarborough wanted to maintain control over everyday activities, just as he had
during the campaigns. He still wanted to read all the mail and sign all of his
letters. Yet the schedule was crowded, which led to problems that soon affected the performance of his office. Yarborough commented to Boren after a
trip to Texas, "every time I go home people are complaining to me about not
getting their mail. We've just got to do something about this mail." Some of
the letters waited on his signature for months as they piled up in stacks on
the credenza behind Yarborough's Senate office desk awaiting his individual
attention.[11]

YARBOROUGH BREAKS RANKS: THE SOUTHERN MANIFESTO

National politics and LBJ's presidential aspirations changed the agenda
and thawed the icy relationship between the two Texas senators in the summer of 1957. In his first one hundred days, Yarborough worked on drought-
and flood-relief bills, reducing the income tax, and restricting foreign oil im-
ports. The new senator boasted of cutting through government red tape to
obtain new heaters for the post office in Denison, an achievement a local
newspaper reported under the headline "Ralph Builds Fires Wherever He
Goes." The real political heat came from another area—civil rights. Pressure
came from northern liberals in both the House and the Senate to enact civil
rights legislation in support of integration of public schools following the
Brown decision against school segregation. The House of Representatives
passed a civil rights bill in 1956, and another was expected to pass in 1957.
For Johnson, support for monumental legislation on civil rights issues would
transform him from a southern Senate leader to a politician of national stat-

ure. Regardless of whether Johnson acted for political or moral reasons, he believed that the issue had to be addressed for the sake of the nation. For Yarborough, the civil rights issue proved to be a defining point in his career. He was truly uncomfortable with his public pronouncements about the Supreme Court decisions during the past two years on the campaign trail in Texas. He believed that he now had a moral imperative to support civil rights. He also knew that breaking down the racial barriers would provide a positive economic benefit for Texas and a political bonus for liberal Democrats. However, no one could be sure that a majority of Texans in 1957 would suddenly decide to reverse their thinking after a century of discrimination in the state.[12]

By 1957, little had changed in Texas and the rest of the South in the wake of the Supreme Court rulings. After the 1954 *Brown* decision, most elected officials in the state used anti-integration and racial ploys in their campaigns. Although a handful of Texas public schools ended segregation, the vast majority of districts and local school boards refused to take action. Few local officials had the political will to take the lead in erasing the long-standing color line because of hostile public confrontations and the unsuccessful integration of the high school in Mansfield, just southeast of Fort Worth, in 1956. From the governor and attorney general to the local county commissioners and school trustees, most elected officials in Texas locked arms in the campaign of massive resistance to integration.

Yarborough took his first bold step away from conventional politics when he refused to support the "Southern Manifesto." In 1956, 101 southern congressmen and senators signed a document that pledged resistance to the *Brown* decision and desegregation of public schools. The only senators representing former Confederate states who refused to support the Manifesto were Albert Gore and Estes Kefauver, both from Tennessee, and Lyndon Johnson. Johnson, as he eyed the national scene, believed that his chances for the presidential nomination depended on his support of some form of civil rights legislation which separated him from the die-hard segregationists. Yarborough also saw an opportunity to set himself apart from the same southerners but wanted to do so for moral and philosophical reasons instead of political ones. Yarborough gambled when he defied Johnson and ran for the Senate. Now, the stakes were higher as more than the relationship with Johnson was on the line. Yarborough could set his own independent course and placate many Texas liberals who supported him despite his earlier campaign opposition to integration. Most important, in spite of their many differences, Johnson and Yarborough could reverse the tenor and the spirit of Texas political leadership with their support for civil rights.

Texas would never break with its pro-southern traditions until its decision makers at the highest levels of government changed direction. Ironically, Yarborough's election gave both Texas senators the opportunity to step into the national arena and alter the course of history. Yarborough, in spite of his roots and his love for the region's history, was never burdened by extreme southern "nationalism." He was closer to the old Texas populism, which sought to unite working-class people, regardless of their race, while fighting a common enemy of entrenched, wealthy businessmen and large landowners. Times had changed, but Yarborough's departure from southern Democrats in the Senate marked his course. He recognized that Texas and the rest of the South risked further isolation from the nation. Continued resistance to integration might be noble in the eyes of the majority of the white population back home, but Yarborough realized a continuation of the politics of the past would lead to disaster and defeat. Nearly one hundred years had passed since the ill-fated attempt to establish an independent southern nation. Yarborough realized the time had come to set aside the Lost Cause and move Texas and the rest of the South into the national mainstream.

CIVIL RIGHTS BILL OF 1957

The Senate took up debate on the 1957 Civil Rights bill in early July. The proposal extended voting rights to minorities and gave the U.S. attorney general enforcement authority. Senator Richard Russell (D-Georgia) led the fight against the legislation, calling the proposal "the reimposition of post-Civil War Reconstruction." Russell received support from nearly every one of his colleagues from the states of the Old Confederacy. The glaring exceptions were from Texas and Tennessee: Johnson and Yarborough along with Gore and Kefauver. For nearly a month, the Senate debated provisions of the landmark legislation. Most attention concerned Part III, which allowed the attorney general to file civil suits against individuals for civil rights violations. Part III was eliminated in late July when southern senators equated the proposal with Reconstruction. They noted that the civil rights bill relied on an 1866 statute that gave the president the right to use armed forces. Opponents drew images of a new "force bill," whereby federal troops armed with bayonets occupied southern communities and pushed whites aside. In another key vote, the Senate added a guarantee for jury trials in all criminal contempt cases, not just those arising from the civil rights bill. The amended bill which became known as the Civil Rights Act of 1957 passed both the Senate and the

House in late August. In the key votes on the jury-trial amendment and the final bill, Yarborough and Johnson voted with the majority against the wishes of most of their southern counterparts. In doing so, they became the first Texas senators to vote for any civil rights legislation since Reconstruction.[13]

For all the attention the Civil Rights Act of 1957 received throughout the nation, it gained minimal results—African American voting barely increased. Few white southern leaders approved of the legislation. With no provisions for protecting other civil rights, the status quo continued in Texas and the rest of the South. Many northern liberals and civil rights activists agreed with Eleanor Roosevelt when she called the law a "mere fakery." However weak and ineffective the bill was, passage of the legislation nevertheless was significant. The 1957 bill was the first civil rights legislation to pass Congress since the Reconstruction era. The modern civil rights movement that began at the grass-roots level with court actions entered a new phase. The issue was now on the national agenda before the U.S. Congress and the president. Passage also demonstrated some cracks in the solidity of the Democratic South. Yarborough's support on the issue was an unrecognized bonus to Lyndon Johnson. The majority leader had an ally from his home state who deflected some of the criticism. Also, Johnson did not have Yarborough and the Texas liberals attacking him while he focused on his presidential aspirations. A united front presented by both Texas senators on this nationally important issue made its impact on Texans and other southerners. The previously unheard voices of moderation in the South suddenly became visible after 1957. A handful of businessmen, labor leaders, educators, and ministers began to view civil rights as an issue critical to the future of the South. The first cracks began to appear in the dam of massive resistance in the region. Yarborough and Johnson led the way for Texas.

SPUTNIK AND EDUCATION FOR DEFENSE

Two significant national events in 1957 influenced Yarborough's first year in the Senate. Hopes of making substantive progress in the South on integration following passage of the Civil Rights bill were dashed after the violent confrontation at Little Rock High School in September. When Arkansas Governor Orville Faubus openly challenged the hesitant administration, President Eisenhower federalized the Arkansas National Guard and sent additional federal troops to Little Rock. In spite of his reluctance, the president finally sent troops not just to preserve order but to establish his authority over the state.

The second crisis occurred when the Soviet Union launched Sputnik I, the first man-made satellite to orbit the earth. The small satellite caused a maelstrom of public reaction as the American public and press suddenly believed the Soviets had a wide lead in missile development and scientific education. People looking up at the night sky and seeing the tiny orbiting satellite flash by suddenly visualized nuclear missiles falling from the heavens. The news media bombarded the public with Sputnik's steady "beep-beep" radio transmissions. Critics throughout the land questioned the strength of the nation's defense system. The nation's lack of commitment to education emerged as the culprit. Public outcry called for action to correct the perceived second-class status of America's educational system that allowed the Soviets to overtake the United States.

Yarborough, the newest member of the Senate Labor and Public Welfare Committee, saw widespread apprehension as an opportunity to advance one of his lifelong interests—public education. Ever since he taught in the one-room schools of East Texas, Yarborough believed that education was one of the keys that unlocked the door for modernizing Texas. He and other Senate Democrats sensed that the Sputnik issue presented a political opportunity they could exploit at the expense of the Republicans. Democrats began an investigation that resulted in creation of the National Aeronautics and Space Agency (NASA). On the same front, Yarborough cosponsored the National Defense Education Act and successfully worked the legislation from the committee level through nearly eight weeks of hearings and final passage. The legislation provided $1 billion over seven years for loans and graduate fellowships and financial aid for foreign language, math, and science instruction. The law was the most significant federally sponsored program since creation of the land grant colleges in 1862. Like the Civil Rights Act, the Education Act was a first step toward bringing the federal government into a domain that heretofore was exclusively reserved for state governments. No senator wanted to be on the Education Subcommittee of the Senate Labor and Public Welfare Committee because integration was a hot-button issue with voters. Yarborough heard the warnings that it was a sure way to get in trouble with the folks back home but bucked the trend to back away. The Education Act was the first of many initiatives Yarborough participated in throughout his Senate years. He quickly became recognized as an expert on education by his fellow senators. Committee chairman Lister Hill of Alabama commended Yarborough's dedication to the long hours he served in hearing and negotiations.[14]

Yarborough also introduced other significant legislation that became part of his legacy and fulfilled his vision of a modern state. In 1958, he filed his first proposal to create the Padre Island National Seashore. The long, narrow barrier islands extend 130 miles in the Gulf of Mexico from Corpus Christi Bay south to the mouth of the Rio Grande. The mostly unpopulated stretch of fine sand with scenic dunes and a unique ecosystem is the longest beach of its kind in the United States. Yarborough worked on the legislation for the next four years before securing final passage in 1962. He also launched his first effort to extend veterans benefits to the men and women who joined the armed services after World War II. Yarborough believed that those who served during the Cold War deserved the same educational opportunities as those who served in World War II and the Korean War. Yarborough's work on his Cold War G.I. bill put him into frequent contact with Senator John F. Kennedy of Massachusetts. He developed a friendship and great admiration for Kennedy as the year progressed.

"THE JAM" VERSUS THE "THE FAKE COWBOY"

Yarborough faced two critical questions following his brief Senate tenure after the April 1957 special election. Should he remain in the U.S. Senate and, if so, how was he going to meet the challenge of a well-funded conservative candidate, especially if his challenger was former Governor Shivers or another well-known Democrat. Throughout the spring of 1958, Yarborough played a cat and mouse game with the press and with Texas Democrats over his future political intentions. He told the press that he had never been able to finance a campaign for longer than ninety days and stated it was "impractical" for him to make any premature announcements concerning his future plans for the 1958 Democratic primary due to his shortage of funds. Even Yarborough's sign at his campaign office in Austin displayed the message "Senator Ralph Yarborough, Candidate for _____?" In delaying his announcement, Yarborough wisely used his incumbency as he issued an appeal for donations. He forced the opposition and the press to speculate for months on his candidacy, thus gaining media exposure he never would have enjoyed otherwise. Democratic kingpin Ed Clark appealed to Walter Hall behind the scenes. Clark wanted Yarborough to run for governor "to save us from the worst mess in which we have ever gotten into. I refer again to one

P. Daniel." Clark said that Yarborough could easily defeat Daniel in a rematch. But now that he finally held a statewide elective office, Yarborough
realized even a newly obtained Senate seat provided more assurance than a
fourth attempt for the governor's office.[15]

In April, the wait ended. William Blakley, the wealthy businessman and
rancher from Dallas who briefly served as the interim senator, decided to run.
A nervous Blakley told the capital press in Austin that he intended to wage a
"vigorous" campaign for the U.S. Senate and make sure the "sovereign rights
of the state" were protected from the federal government. Blakley concluded
his brief announcement by declaring that he was unsure when he would actually begin campaigning because "I've first got to get out to the ranch. . . .
we're doctoring cattle right now."[16]

Though he appeared to be a reluctant candidate, Blakley was carefully
selected and supported by Shivers and the conservative faction of the Democratic Party. Congressman Martin Dies declared he would not run for the
office, thus eliminating a well-known conservative who would have competed
with Blakley for both votes and money. Based on a conversation with Shivers,
Blakley assumed other prominent Texas Democrats would support him, especially Lyndon Johnson, Sam Rayburn, and Price Daniel. In addition, Blakley
also hoped that Yarborough, who still had not declared his intentions, would
decide to make another attempt at the governor's office and return to Texas
in 1958. Blakley was born in Missouri and moved to Texas as a young man,
where he grew up and worked on a ranch. He served in the Army Air Corps
in World War I. After he returned to Texas, he married his high school sweetheart Villa Darnell and in 1925 moved to Dallas. There he studied law and
passed the bar exam and began investing and buying ranches in West Texas
and the Rio Grande Valley. He was also a large stockholder in Braniff Airways, but always tried to downplay his wealth. "I never struck it rich," he
said, "but after I got started I never went broke, either."[17]

Blakley, despite his business acumen, revealed his inexperience in navigat-
ing the treacherous currents of Texas politics. His belief that both Rayburn
and Johnson would openly support him indicated a lack of understanding
of how incumbent officeholders position themselves in elections with uncertain outcomes. Johnson, who had his share of disagreements with Yarborough, maintained his position as Senate majority leader only by virtue of a
slim majority of Democrats and wanted to appease northern liberal senators.
Furthermore, Rayburn wanted Johnson to be the Democratic nominee for
president, and they needed northern Democratic votes to win the nomination. Moreover, Rayburn disliked Shivers more than any other major politi-

cal figure in Texas, which now worked to Yarborough's advantage. Shivers, although he was still well-known in Texas, was no longer in office, which diminished his ability to deliver supporters and funding for Blakley. Thus Blakley had little chance of gaining any meaningful support from either Johnson or Rayburn.

Blakley's statements reflected his conservative beliefs, which stood in contrast to Yarborough's more liberal positions. "A vote for Blakley is a vote for freedom of individual initiative: freedom to work, to think, to pursue happiness," he proclaimed. The businessman said the federal government preempted the authority of the states in its attempts to protect personal and property rights. Blakley was a Democrat for Eisenhower in 1952 and again in 1956 but declared he would vote to preserve Lyndon Johnson's status as majority leader. His brochure, "The Story of Bill Blakley, Lawyer—Rancher—Businessman," featured the candidate in western garb—a blue-jean jacket, Stetson hat, and chaps—in an attempt to create the image of a plain-speaking Texan. But afterwards he was always pictured in a pressed white shirt with a black bow tie, even when he was standing next to his horse in front of a barbed wire fence. His appearance and his background soon became the focal point of Yarborough's campaign. Editor and Yarborough supporter H. M. Baggarly wrote, "we can think of none we would rather see in the race than William Blakley, millionaire Dallas resident, who is one of the world's richest men."[18]

Yarborough knew that a unified effort by Shivers, Daniel, and other conservatives would put him to the test in the primary. Although he had the advantage of incumbency, his hold was slippery. Yarborough had his bedrock group of supporters, especially now that they had tasted some of the fruits of electoral victory. But Yarborough also had antagonized many Texans and the state's editorial writers with his opposition to the Southern Manifesto and his support for the 1957 Civil Rights Act. During a radio speech in Austin on April 28, when Yarborough announced for the Senate, he warned that "we can expect the hate mongers to once more try to run class against class and race against race." In a return to his old populist style campaign, he attacked large corporations and the Eisenhower administration for the 1958 economic downturn and charged that the Republicans subscribed to the belief that what is good for General Motors is good for the country.

No one outside of the senator's organization claimed to have advance knowledge of Yarborough's decision to run for a full six-year term as U.S. senator. Announcement of the decision, described as one of the "best kept political secrets in Texas politics," had come as rumors were still circulating that he would leave Washington for a rematch with Price Daniel. R. C. Slagle, who managed Speaker Rayburn's campaigns, signed on as his state chairman, and Yarborough began his campaign with a veteran campaign staff and a stronger statewide organization than Blakley had.[19]

Blakley's campaign focused on the traditional conservative issues of limited government. He called for a national right-to-work law and opposed any federal aid to education as a back-door method of achieving integration. The Blakley camp centered their attacks on the "ultra-liberal" forces supporting Yarborough as they beat the drums in outrage against the AFL-CIO and the NAACP. Blakley charged that Yarborough's votes merely followed the agenda of these "influential" organizations. While campaigning in East Texas, Blakley said that he opposed integration because "God made people different colors" and "wanted them segregated." He complained that the ongoing economic recession was the result of "hobbles" on business and the recklessness of organized labor.[20]

Blakley campaigned throughout the state making speeches, holding rallies, and giving interviews. His appearances served up the traditional Texas campaign mix of politics, music, and barbecue. At a typical Blakley rally at Fair Park in Dallas, an estimated 10,000 people turned out for the entertainment and the food. Yarborough campaign manager R. C. Slagle began referring to their opponent's campaign as "Cowboy Bill's barbecue circuit," acerbically noting that when Blakley made his public appearances, he wore what *he* considered to be western dress (a white shirt with a black bow tie) so that people would "think of him not as a millionaire but as a Westerner, a man of Texas." Blakley was confident that his combination of a well-coordinated campaign fueled by well-heeled contributors would not tarnish his "cowboy" image.[21]

Yarborough remained in Washington while the campaign progressed. He wanted to impress on Texans that he was a full-time senator. Mindful of the three unsuccessful attempts for governor, Yarborough wanted to prove he could meet his responsibilities as an officeholder. He finally returned to Texas in late June, accompanied by his wife, Opal, and son, Richard. Yarborough had already established a reputation as a consummate campaigner, but this time he surpassed himself. Slagle remarked that "just like a mule, he never seemed to wear out." There could never be enough appearances and speeches, or hours in the day, to meet his needs. He traveled by car, campaigning after midnight and beginning with sunrise coffees the next morning. He consistently outpaced and wore out his drivers and volunteers. He said that he stayed in Washington "on the job to take care of problems" and labeled

"Put the Jam on the Lower Shelf" became Yarborough's slogan during his reelection bid to the Senate in 1958. Courtesy Opal Yarborough and Gulf Coast Texans for Yarborough, 1958.

Blakley a "half-time worker." Yarborough noted that during his months as an appointed senator, Blakley had maintained only a 55 percent voting record.

Yarborough's tactics were unchanged, but he stressed a new campaign theme for the Senate race: "Put the jam on the lower shelf so the little man can reach it." He credited a Colorado City resident who first used the term in a letter saying, "Senator Yarborough will put the jam on the lower shelf so the little man can reach it," and he affirmed, "That's exactly what I am working to do." As Yarborough campaigned in Texas, he posed often for photographs, usually in front of the truck that carried a desk and chair and a sign that said, the senate seat is not for sale. The truck carried a large jam bottle topped by a cowboy hat with the saying keep the jam on the bottom shelf. The new theme made an impact, as even his critics with the *Dallas Morning News* acknowledged, although editorial attacks labeled Yarborough as a "demagogue," and columnist Lynn Landrum warned readers that every Texan would "pay for his jam."[22]

In early July, Blakley continued his attacks on Yarborough, citing the incumbent's support of civil rights legislation and contributions from out-of-state labor organizations. In a Dallas television broadcast, Blakley accused Yarborough of favoring national civil rights legislation and receiving direction from the "labor bosses headquartered in Detroit, Pittsburgh, Cleveland, New York, and elsewhere." Yarborough responded that his votes were consistently in line with the Democratic leadership, and of course that meant that he was voting down the line with Lyndon Johnson. Yarborough said that on twenty-three occasions his votes were similar to those of Senator Johnson and Senator John McClellan (D-Arkansas). Yarborough emphasized his Democratic loyalty and asserted that had Blakley been U.S. senator he would have deserted the party and LBJ. Blakley's positions put him directly in the "Republican camp," Yarborough said.[23]

Yarborough began his own television campaign in early July with a statewide broadcast that repudiated Blakley's charges that he was a "controlled Senator." Without directly acknowledging his receipt of labor union contributions, Yarborough said that "his charge shows that my opponent thinks that all men can be bought" and that "a contribution means control. I wonder how many state Senators and governors he has controlled by contributions?" Yarborough revealed Blakley's opposition to federal subsidies for farmers while he obtained a subsidy for Braniff Airways, a company in which he was a major investor. Yarborough also raised questions about Blakley's contributions to state senators in Austin whose committees had jurisdiction over his insurance companies. "He should tell Texans whether he would consider it all right to take fees from insurance companies if he were elected a U.S. senator," Yarborough said. A short time later, Blakley admitted paying three state senators $12,300 in fees for "general legal work" but denied the money influenced the lawmakers. The themes were familiar to Yarborough and Texas voters because the circumstances reminded people of the insurance scandals in the Shivers administration.[24]

As the candidates traded punches in what seemed a repetition of Yarborough's earlier statewide campaigns, two events turned the tide for the incumbent. One centered on a personality issue that so often determined close Texas political races. The second was an international crisis in Lebanon. First, the Yarborough camp recognized that Blakley's "cowboy" image was a facade intended to cover up his wealth and profession. Yarborough called Blakley "Cowboy Bill," who rode west into the setting sun "following the reflection of gold cuff links in the sand." Well-known Texas folklorist and Yarborough supporter J. Frank Dobie lampooned Blakley in a well-publicized story entitled "Fake Cowboy." Dobie satirized Blakley's "western" campaign theme and questioned the authenticity of a cowboy who wore French cuffs and cuff links. Blakley never responded and sales of shirts with French cuffs never caught on in Texas that year.[25]

As the primary election date approached, events in Lebanon unexpectedly captured people's attention, in Texas and throughout the nation. Longstanding religious conflicts between Lebanese Moslems and Christians threatened to disrupt the government in the Middle Eastern nation on the Mediterranean. More importantly, instability in the pro-American regime posed a threat to the balance of power in the Middle East along with an escalation of the Cold War. Concerns over a potential armed intervention by the U.S. forces diverted attention from local politics. Speaking to the nation on July 15, President Eisenhower called the rescue of the Lebanese government the "gravest crisis to confront the country since Korea" and announced a plan to send five thousand U.S. Marines to the embattled nation. The decision originated with a request from Lebanon's president Camille Chamoun. The president blamed interference from the Soviet Union and President Abdul Nasser's United Arab Republic for the uprising which threatened Lebanon's independence. The crisis in Lebanon tilted the campaign scales in the incumbent senator's direction thanks to a timely reaction.[26]

Responding to the crisis, Yarborough stated on a campaign swing in West Texas that the nation faced "more dangerous times than any since Pearl Harbor." He added that it was no time for partisan politics. Yarborough left the campaign trail in Texas to return to Washington as the Lebanon crisis quickly unfolded. Yarborough's strategy was sound, especially when he could utilize his position and connections in Washington to his advantage. In Washington, he met with the Chief of Naval Operations, Admiral Arleigh Burke, for a well-publicized briefing. The Yarborough campaign obtained photos and films from the navy for a scheduled television broadcast. Yarborough later remarked that he told the admiral, "Sir, you have just won an election for me." He believed that a last-minute broadcast and appeal to Texans centered on the crisis of Lebanon would cement his victory over Blakley.[27]

Using information from the navy, Yarborough appeared in a live thirty-minute televised program in much of the state. He provided a brief description of the crisis as the film dramatically opened with U.S. Marines dashing through the surf onto the beach. A solemn Yarborough told viewers, "Tonight the flickering campfires of our Marines light the green and rolling hills of Lebanon, the same hills that sent the cedars that built King Solomon's temple." Yarborough spent most of the broadcast informing viewers of Lebanon's importance to U.S. Cold War strategy. In addition to seizing the initiative in this arena, Yarborough felt that the broadcast would head off any last-minute thrusts by Blakley. He believed his challenger had a "secret smear up his sleeves," a plan to attack him in East Texas and align him with the NAACP. In fact, some of leaflets of this nature already had been distributed by the Blakley campaign. Yarborough's staff sent copies of the racist appeals to their own supporters to motivate them.

This was not the only trick played by Yarborough's campaign staff. The scenes of Marines dashing through the surf that opened the televised message on Lebanon actually had taken place in North Carolina as part of a training exercise. At the time of the broadcast, no one had any film of the landings in Lebanon. "Had he [Yarborough] known that part of that last television show, he would have never allowed it," former campaign aide James Boren revealed. Deletion of the scene would have been made the broadcast less effective, so the campaign staff left the training-film segment in the show and never told Yarborough about the switch. Thanks to his timely, well-received message on Lebanon, the "wild-eyed liberal" now appeared as a competent member of the U.S. Senate. His calm and deliberate presentation of world events and their effect on the state made a dramatic impact on Texans in 1958.[28]

As part of the last-minute flurry before the election, Yarborough released a statement that Speaker Sam Rayburn, "the greatest Democrat of them all," cast his absentee ballot for Yarborough. In fact, Rayburn was working behind the scenes through most of the campaign to help Yarborough. Blakley offended Rayburn with a well-publicized attempt to donate $10,000 for the Speaker's library in Rayburn's hometown of Bonham. Senator Johnson declined to state his position on the race and remained aloof from the campaign, but Rayburn's endorsement of Yarborough sent a public message to Texas voters that many influential individuals heard firsthand from the Speaker. Rayburn and Johnson seldom publicly disagreed on major political issues and many translated Rayburn's endorsement as a tacit endorsement from the majority leader. Yarborough privately complained about Johnson's lack of support during the 1958 campaign. Johnson now realized that his national ambitions precluded some direct involvement in statewide politics, especially since many northern liberals and other Democrats outside of Texas wanted Yarborough back in the Senate.[29]

Yarborough handily defeated Blakley in the primary election. He totaled more than 761,000 votes to Blakley's 535,000 and took 220 of the state's

After his son Ralph wins reelection to the Senate, C. R. Yarborough administers the oath of office to him on New Year's Eve, 1958, in the family's Chandler home. The elder Yarborough, a former Henderson County justice of the peace and notary public, performed the ceremony in the room in which Ralph was born. Courtesy Center for American History, Yarborough Papers (3Y434).

254 counties. Yarborough carried nine of the ten largest urban counties in the state, defeating Blakley in the conservative strongholds by several thousand votes. Blakley managed to carry only Dallas County. Commenting on the surprising majority, Yarborough's media spokesman Bob Bray said, "we sure gave those professional hotshots a country lickin'." Blakley, who had the

words but not the appeal of Allan Shivers, failed to impress the voters as an effective politician on television or in person. In the November general election, Yarborough easily defeated Republican nominee Roy Whittenburg by a nearly three-to-one margin.

Yarborough's resounding victories after years of frustration were due to his maturation as a politician and also a matter of luck. He was definitely a resourceful, tireless candidate. Most of the state's daily newspapers supported Blakley, but Yarborough managed to overcome their longtime opposition through his own tireless efforts and a better-organized campaign. He also benefited from the accumulated scandals that finally damaged Shivers' conservative wing of the party. Yarborough was now the elected leader of the loyalist-liberal wing of the Democratic party and had expanded his support to include many moderate Democrats. He had the strongest and most devoted followers in the state by 1958. In addition, although Yarborough and Johnson had their personal differences, most Texans believed the two worked as a team and got things done for the folks at home.

After this election, Texas began slowly to drift away from its traditional role of supporting the Solid South and its massive resistance on civil rights issues. Yarborough and Johnson's break with other southern senators put them at odds with die-hard segregationists, but their leadership set a new standard of modified racial viewpoints for Texans to follow. The nationwide economic recession that began in 1957 and lasted through the following year also contributed to Yarborough's success since many people were suddenly more concerned about their pocketbooks than integration. The news of Sputnik and a White House scandal that resulted in the resignation of Eisenhower assistant Sherman Adams also influenced elections that year. Democrats around the nation won contested offices as millions of Americans apprehensively prepared for a Republican recession. Yarborough's gritty determination combined with his response to outside events provided him with a full six-year term in the U.S. Senate. In 1957 the Yarborough family enjoyed one of their best holiday seasons in years. On December 31, Yarborough returned to his boyhood home of Chandler, where his ninety-four-year-old father, Charles, administered the oath of office for the Senate and made his son promise to "do a good job."[30]

9 *Problems with Johnson and Rayburn*

Yarborough's first full Senate term coincided with the arrival of many new Democrats destined for major roles in the Kennedy and Johnson administrations. The Senate Class of 1958 included Robert Byrd, Tom Dodd, Gale McGee, Vance Hartke, Eugene McCarthy, Ed Muskie, Philip Hart, Jennings Randolph, and Howard Cannon. They joined Yarborough and William Proxmire of Wisconsin, who also had won a special election after Yarborough's victory. The thirteen Democratic senators elected that year averaged eighteen years of service in Congress. After 1958, Democrats kept control of the Senate until the resurgence of the Republican party under Ronald Reagan in the 1980's. Yarborough and his fellow senators confronted great foreign and domestic challenges in one of the most dramatic periods in the nation's history.[1]

The 1958 elections solidified Democratic control of the Senate and provided Yarborough a boost up the seniority ladder. Thanks to his 1957 victory, Yarborough had a leg up on his new Senate colleagues. The Senate was organized with sixteen standing committees and many more subcommittees. Yarborough remained on the Commerce Committee but rose ahead of four new members on the eleven-person committee. He gained three places on the Post Office and Civil Service Committee and took over chairmanship of the Civil Service Subcommittee, his first position as a chairman. He also gained seniority on the Labor and Public Welfare Committee and became chairman of the Veterans Affairs Subcommittee. He later served on the Education and the Health subcommittees. Yarborough's positions on committees which focused on domestic issues worked to his advantage. His assignments proved to be beneficial, especially given his longtime interests in education, the economy, and the environment.

While involved in the 1958 Democratic primary, Yarborough had launched the first of his major environmental initiatives that were to be one of the hallmarks of his Senate career, and he reintroduced his park plan in the new congressional session. Texas had only one national park at the time—Big Bend in Far West Texas. The Department of the Interior's 1955 survey rated Padre Island as the "highest priority" for public acquisition. "The golden sands of Padre Island and the white-capped blue waters of the Gulf of Mexico beckon Americans," Yarborough said, describing the long, narrow island that remained virtually untouched since the days of La Salle and the Karankawa Indians in the seventeenth century. Estimates of the cost to purchase the seashore from the private owners was $3.5 million. At a Washington, D.C., news conference in June 1958, Texas congressman Joe Kilgore, National Park director Conrad Wirth, and representatives from Senator Johnson's office joined a news conference with Yarborough calling for additional research for future legislation. Without consulting congressmen Kilgore or Wirth, Yarborough announced that his staff had already prepared a bill to authorize the Department of the Interior to purchase the island. Yarborough said it was time to preserve the "priceless heritage" and predicted the growing population of the American Southwest would overwhelm existing public parklands unless new areas were added. His unexpected move to purchase the site angered the very congressmen he would need to push the measure through the House. Although the legislation received favorable publicity, the bill languished in the Senate, entangled in the affairs of Texas and those in Washington.[2]

With his primary legislative effort stalled, Yarborough turned his attention to other fronts. He worked in favor of the National Aeronautics and Space Act of 1958, which created NASA. He fulfilled his campaign promises for tax relief when he pushed for a $200 increase for personal income tax exemptions and secured legislation to bring flood and drought relief to Texans. He coauthored the National Highway Act, which provided funds to begin construction of the new interstate highway system. He also worked to increase Social Security benefits and provide salary increases for postal workers and members of the armed services. With his committee assignments, he stayed close to the issues on which he felt the strongest—education and the national economy. He also successfully opposed a proposal by the Atomic Energy Commission to dump atomic waste in the Gulf of Mexico.[3]

YARBOROUGH TANGLES WITH JOHNSON

With a full six-year term in front of him, Yarborough felt more confident in acting independently of the Senate majority leader. Johnson was pleased with the resounding Democratic victory of 1958, which gave him a comfortable margin in the Senate. He also viewed the election as a plus for his own presidential ambitions. But as the Johnson train left the station, Yarborough refused to get on board. Yarborough's victory at the polls did little to heal the wounds of Democratic party activists who mistrusted Johnson. Yarborough, still upset by the reception he received from Johnson when he first arrived in Washington, had stated prior to that year's November general election that he would be neutral in the 1960 presidential race. Publicly, Yarborough explained that six senators wanted the party's nomination in 1960 and he was not going to choose one over the other. The junior Texas senator also tweaked Johnson at liberal Democratic gatherings. When Johnson accompanied President Eisenhower on a trip to Texas and to Mexico, Yarborough told one audience that the two were together to meet with friends of the "Republican wing of the Democratic Party." While his admonitions played well before the party faithful, such remarks inhibited a meaningful working relationship with Johnson. As long as LBJ served as Senate majority leader, he exerted tremendous influence over any legislation. Rayburn was one of Johnson's strongest supporters and unhappy with Yarborough's public statements. Yarborough understood as well as anyone in Congress the legislative control Johnson and Rayburn exercised. Nevertheless, he continued to tempt fate as he built a fence between himself and Johnson in the Capitol halls and in Texas. Yarborough's pronouncements set the stage for the 1960 presidential battle at the state and national level.[4]

Remarkably, in spite of Johnson's opposition, Yarborough achieved some legislative success with his G.I. education bill. The Senate passed his plan for a ten-year interest-free loan program for qualified veterans who entered the service after January 31, 1955. Yarborough and proponents argued that even though the nation was at peace, those serving in the military assumed a tremendous burden in the Cold War. Yarborough estimated four million veterans would become eligible under the bill. Objections to the legislation centered on the cost, which critics said would amount to $500 million annually. The Senate passed the bill by a 57-to-31 vote, with Johnson and Yarborough voting in favor of it. By this time, Johnson wanted legislation that also put him in a favorable light. Johnson knew that Rayburn would kill any bill in the House he actually did not want passed. Following Senate passage of the Cold War G.I. bill, Congressman Olin "Tiger" Teague (D-Texas), the chairman of the House Veterans Affairs Committee, predicted it could not pass the House and announced he had no plans for committee hearings. Teague also said that if the bill passed, President Eisenhower was certain to use his veto. Late in 1959, Johnson appeared with Yarborough during a televised session at the conclusion of the congressional session. During the broadcast, Johnson praised Yarborough's efforts on passing the Cold War G.I. bill. Yarborough described the year as "one of the hardest-working [congressional] sessions of record."[5]

Yarborough and Johnson voted together on a number of measures. Yarborough joined with the majority leader to cosponsor a proposal for a constitutional amendment to abolish the poll tax. By 1959, only five southern states retained the tax on voter registration: Texas, Alabama, Arkansas, Mississippi, and Virginia. Yarborough said the poll tax placed a "price tag on American democracy." He believed that many of the state's low-income residents never voted because of the tax. Those states that actually abolished the poll tax in the 1950's witnessed an increase in voter registration and participation. But in 1956 the Civil Rights Commission reported that only one of every four eligible African Americans in the South had registered to vote. The poll tax, a strong part of the Jim Crow laws in the South, relegated African Americans to a second-class citizenship. Prior to the 1960 Democratic party precinct meetings, Yarborough and Johnson both urged a primary referendum that outlawed the poll tax in federal elections. After withstanding fifty-three days of contentious debates, Yarborough also joined with Johnson on the Civil Rights Bill of 1960, which reaffirmed the authority of the Civil Rights Commission to investigate violations. The legislation had no real impact on segregation and the status quo, but Johnson and Yarborough were labeled "double-crossers" by many southern newspapers and Dixie Democrats as they witnessed the rising number of sit-ins and demonstrations across the South. Johnson cast his votes on these controversial issues with an eye on his presidential campaign. By contrast, Yarborough voted out of personal conviction based on what he perceived to be necessary to significantly change life in Texas and the rest of the American South.[6]

In late September 1959 Yarborough suffered a personal loss, the death of his political mentor, former Texas governor James Allred. Allred, sixty at the time of his demise, was serving as a federal judge in South Texas when he unexpectedly passed away in Laredo. Yarborough praised Allred as the greatest governor since Jim Hogg. The Yarborough family joined other state dignitaries in honoring the New Deal governor at his funeral services in Texas. As a memorial to his political mentor, Yarborough praised the accomplishments of Allred as attorney general and governor:

> **Not often through the mists of Texas time has a man risen from the masses who at once had a heartfelt and soulful concern for life's "have-**

nots" and possessed with that concern the iron and fire to fight unjust economic and political power whenever he found it. James V. Allred, one-time
shoeshine boy, sailor, lawyer, attorney general of Texas, twice Governor of
Texas, and a U.S. District Judge, was such a man.

Nothing I could say here could begin adequately to eulogize this great
Texan and great American who is justly mentioned in the same breath with
Sam Houston and Jim Hogg. He had the most sincere concern for the
rights and welfare of the individual of any man I have ever known. During his years as attorney general and in his administration as Governor,
the depression years of 1935–1939, all the people of Texas had fair, able and
impartial representation.

He was sharp in his wit, gentle with his employees, tireless in his work,
loving of mankind, and he believed in a God of mercy and justice and
charity.[7]

The eulogy revealed Yarborough's own philosophy. As he recognized the influence Allred exerted on his own career and beliefs, Yarborough also could
have been describing his own personal and political career. A person who rose
from humble beginnings to assume high public office was commonplace in
America. He believed the outstanding differences which set Allred on the
level with Sam Houston and Jim Hogg were his unflinching passion and commitment to improve the quality of life for those who were less fortunate. Allred was also outspoken and unafraid to confront those who abused the public
trust. He dedicated his public career to the benefit of all people, not just the
privileged few. Yarborough believed this was the measure of true greatness in
a leader.

YARBOROUGH REJECTS JOHNSON FOR PRESIDENT IN 1960

Returning home after the 1959 congressional session, Yarborough toured
the state making speeches before friendly audiences and organizations.
Within a few weeks, he addressed a convocation of Mary Hardin Baylor
College, an annual dinner of the American Jewish Committee in Houston,
a Farmers Union barbecue in Friona, the Texas Independent Auto Dealers
convention in San Antonio, and a Democratic rally in Dallas. The VFW presented him with one of their highest awards, the Silver Citizenship Award
for 1959. He spoke against prejudice and segregation on almost every occasion as he carried his moral convictions to the people. Concerning the 1960

campaign for the White House, Yarborough said the next president had to be a leader who represented the "rights of all Americans of every race, color, and creed." At a Dallas gathering, he appeared onstage with Johnson, who was busy shoring up his Texas support for the Democratic presidential nomination. Yarborough envisioned the approaching decade as a time of opportunity for the nation and its people. "The sixties call for men in public life who will be leaders of great causes, not the brokers of little ones," he proclaimed. He appeared alongside Johnson but still refused to endorse him.[8]

Yarborough was definitely in hot water with Johnson and Rayburn as the 1960 congressional session opened. With Rayburn's firm backing, Johnson's presidential campaign strategy centered on locking up the support of Democratic House and Senate members. He avoided states holding presidential primaries where delegates were selected by popular vote. Meanwhile, little-known Senator John Kennedy of Massachusetts was busy working all of these primary states. Johnson's Washington strategy soon unraveled. In early January, a handful of Senate liberals challenged Johnson in a Senate caucus over the selection of members to the Democratic policy committee. Traditionally, the Senate majority leader appointed these members. However, Senator Albert Gore (D-Tennessee) proposed that the Democratic members elect the committee members. The procedural matter was a direct challenge to Johnson's authority. In a showdown vote, Yarborough joined ten other senators in a losing effort. Johnson easily won the vote, but it was a costly victory. Many national political observers noted the disenchantment of his fellow Democrats and predicted Johnson would have a difficult time obtaining the nomination at the party's national convention in Los Angeles.

In Texas, many newspapers featured the confrontation on the front page, seeing it as a threat to Johnson and a blow to the Texan's chance to obtain the Democratic nomination. Yarborough said he voted his convictions as a "firm believer in sound and firm principles of government" and "basic democratic procedure." Speaker Rayburn saw Yarborough's vote in another light. The Speaker was furious at him for joining Senate liberals in their public rebuke of Johnson. "I couldn't be more disappointed in a man than I was in what he did. And that is on the record," Rayburn said in a rare public criticism of another elected official. Other colleagues joined the Speaker in issuing harsh statements. Congressman Teague, who held Yarborough's G.I. bill in his committee, was brief and terse. He condemned Yarborough's action as "unfortunate" when all other members of the Texas delegation in Washington felt Johnson had a realistic chance to be the Democratic candidate for president. Texas newspapers had a field day with the open break between the two Texas senators while ignoring the fact of their similar voting records in 1959. Every major daily newspaper carried stories on Yarborough's vote against Johnson. The *Fort Worth Star Telegram* ran a cartoon showing Johnson and Rayburn sitting behind Bless Our United Front signs, Yarborough behind them sticking out his tongue. Yarborough told radio listeners that he received more telegrams approving his anti-Johnson stand than all the messages on his other votes since entering the Senate. Yarborough may have satisfied his own conscience and impressed some liberals when he challenged Johnson and Rayburn on their number one issue—getting LBJ to the White House. Yarborough took pride in his controversial stands, especially when he chose principle over politics, but in this case he alienated the two individuals who had life and death power over his own legislation and tremendous influence in Texas. Yarborough said that every day at 5 p.m. during the regular congressional sessions, Johnson turned the Senate gavel over to the majority whip and crossed the Rotunda to attend Rayburn's "Board of Education" and have drinks with the Speaker. If Johnson asked Rayburn to block the bills of those who "wouldn't go along with him," Rayburn would instruct his committee chairs to hold the legislation. "I didn't gee-haw with that," Yarborough confessed, which meant that his bills "got pretty well stymied in the committees." His opposition also severely damaged his relationship with Johnson and Rayburn at a time he might have taken advantage of the opportunity to gain legislative and other political concessions. But once Yarborough made up his mind, he seldom changed course.[9]

In February, the liberal Democrats of Texas met in Houston to discuss their 1960 election-year strategy in advance of the May precinct meetings. Yarborough stayed in Washington but sent a telegram advising the liberals to "beware those Judas goats who led us to slaughter in 1952 and 1956." Maverick U.S. senator Wayne Morse (D-Oregon) predicted that if Johnson were the party's nominee, he would lose to Richard Nixon. During his speech to the Texas liberals, Morse said, "if I were a Texan, my favorite-son candidate would be Ralph Yarborough." Some members of the convention wanted to pass a resolution warning that a Johnson presidential nomination would be "an historic calamity." They believed Johnson failed on the five critical liberal issues of the day: civil rights, public control of monopolies, expansion of the labor movement, an end to government corruption, and active U.S. leadership in assisting oppressed nations and peoples. Yarborough publicly advocated all of these positions. Convention delegates tabled an official condemnation of Johnson, but they clearly exhibited their low opinion of the majority leader. Ever since Johnson and Rayburn's agreement to oust Shivers supporters in 1956, Texas liberals were upset with Johnson's reversal and "theft" of party positions. Creekmore Fath, one of the most outspoken members of the Democrats of Texas and a close advisor to Yarborough, asserted that much of Johnson's support came from Republicans. Fath predicted difficult times to come when "Johnson grass is dead" and people would be "cultivating Nixon weed." Yarborough denied having membership in the Democrats of Texas, but Johnson and others clearly associated him with the fractious liberals.[10]

At the same time that a solid group of Texas Democrats was castigating Johnson, his chances for winning the presidential nomination were disappearing faster than Yarborough's legislation. Kennedy was the acknowledged leader by early spring thanks to his active work in key primary states. Johnson still had not officially declared his candidacy. Nevertheless, the Texan expanded his efforts and began attacking Kennedy in speeches around the nation. Longtime Johnson aide John Connally prepared to open a national campaign headquarters in Washington, D.C. On July 5, only a week before the Democratic convention, Johnson finally announced his candidacy in the hope that Kennedy's popularity had peaked too soon. Behind the scenes, Yarborough was already on the Kennedy train—he believed that Kennedy was better suited to lead the nation than Johnson. When Yarborough attended the Texas Democratic convention in June, the Johnson forces controlled the delegate selection and they excluded Yarborough from the list of national delegates chosen. In a press interview, Yarborough said he could have been a delegate if he had voted for Johnson, "but I wasn't selected. So the question is moot." He added that he would campaign hard for Johnson or any party nominee in the 1960 election. Kennedy easily won the nomination and persuaded Johnson to accept the vice presidential place on the ticket. A Democratic victory would bode well for Yarborough, with his friend Kennedy in the White House and his nemesis Johnson departed from the Senate and ostensibly out of the way.[11]

THE 1960 PRESIDENTIAL CAMPAIGN: YARBOROUGH AS SENIOR SENATOR

The Republican and Democrat parties viewed Texas as a pivotal state in 1960. Both presidential candidates came to the state as the tension mounted in the close election. Yarborough enthusiastically campaigned for the Kennedy-Johnson ticket, managing to inject his own personality into the race. During an appearance in Dallas as part of a statewide swing for

Texas played a vital role in the 1960 presidential election. During a campaign stop at the Dallas airport on September 13, 1960, the crowd heard remarks from (left to right) Ralph Yarborough, John Kennedy, Lyndon Johnson, and Sam Rayburn. Courtesy Center for American History, Yarborough Papers (3Y436).

the ticket, he managed to throw barbs at his old nemesis Allan Shivers. Yarborough challenged Shivers, the head of the Democrats for Nixon effort in Texas, to defend the Eisenhower administration's "abandonment" of farmers and oil producers. Yarborough then fired up the rally by bragging that Kennedy soundly defeated Nixon in their nationally televised debate. Nixon was supposed to appear older and more experienced, but Yarborough said he just looked "old and tired." Before the campaign, Yarborough had conducted Senate hearings and authored legislation which established the first televised presidential debates.[12]

In Houston, Yarborough campaigned from "dawn to dark" as he worked many neighborhoods and suburban areas of the state's largest city just as if he were the candidate. He later accompanied a caravan of Democratic officials and supporters to woo voters in rural communities in the critical state. He also appeared on television, where he complained that the Soviet Union had passed the United States in world prestige under Eisenhower. Yarborough was exceedingly expressive in his praise of Kennedy, "the fighting Irishman," especially when compared to his earlier lack of cooperation with Rayburn and Johnson in the majority leader's ill-fated presidential campaign. The election was exceedingly close in Texas because of concern over civil rights issues and Kennedy's Catholicism.[13]

A record number of voters in the 1960 presidential election chose Kennedy-Johnson in one of the closest contests in American history. Over

The Alamo, famous Texas shrine in San Antonio, was the scene of a visit in September 1960 by Democratic presidential and vice presidential candidates John F. Kennedy and Lyndon Johnson, joined by Senator Yarborough. Courtesy Opal Yarborough.

2.3 million Texans voted, giving the Democrat nominees a narrow 46,000 vote margin over the Nixon-Lodge ticket. The close win returned Texas to the Democratic column for the first time since 1948. The Democratic victory changed the political scene in both Washington and Texas. With Johnson as vice president, Yarborough became the senior senator from Texas. Johnson's replacement had to be selected in a special election. Yarborough's sudden ascent to senior senator gave rise to speculation about his tempestuous relationship with some Texas congressmen. Yarborough's refusal to support Johnson's presidential ambitions still rubbed many senators, congressmen, other Johnson supporters, and the vice president himself the wrong way. Members also expressed concerns about patronage—the selection of individuals for federal appointments. Some House members feared that Yarborough, given his allegiance to Texas liberals and his independent nature, would not accept the time-honored tradition of selecting the nominees recommended by congressmen for postmasterships and other federal appointments. After eight years of a Republican chief executive, all Democrats were anxious for the return of federal patronage positions. Yarborough's office was literally overwhelmed with a mountain of mail when he returned to Washington after the election. Most of the letters contained a simple message: "Get me a job." Yarborough said he believed that many qualified people wanted to be given a position by the Kennedy administration. He expressed to his supporters and the press his hope that "our political view can prevail for a change."[14]

Yarborough's new role as senior Texas senator initially turned out to be a hollow victory in terms of patronage. The united political front displayed for the November election quickly gave way to new realities. Vice President Johnson and Speaker Rayburn remained in command when it came to approving most appointments. When Johnson accepted the vice presidency offer from Kennedy, they secretly agreed Johnson would retain veto power over nearly all appointments the administration made in Texas. Also, Rayburn maintained his masterful control over the House of Representatives, so the Kennedy administration was more than willing to bow to the Speaker's wishes in this arena. Within a few weeks of his nomination, word leaked out that Yarborough was the senior senator in name only. Any Texan wanting an appointment, from rural postmaster to a cabinet-level position, had to have Johnson and Rayburn's blessing. For months no one from Texas obtained an appointment unless approved by Johnson. The vice president had John Connally, one of his key advisors, appointed secretary of the navy. Yarborough protested to the Kennedy administration.[15]

Finally, after Yarborough's confrontation with Johnson over judicial appointments, the entire selection system for Texas broke down. Woodrow Seals wanted an appointment as U.S. attorney for the Southern District and had Yarborough's strong support. Johnson objected even though Seals had supported LBJ in his elections. Yarborough exercised his senatorial powers to block sixteen judicial appointments in the state because they were "personally obnoxious to him." Included in the list were Sarah Hughes of Dallas (who as district judge swore in Johnson as president after Kennedy's assassination) and Ben Connally, son of former U.S. senator Tom Connally. At this stage the impasse forced the Kennedy administration to intervene. After a meeting with Yarborough and Johnson, Attorney General Robert Kennedy approved the Seals nomination. According to Johnson aide Bobby Baker, Yarborough said, "Have Lyndon withdraw eight of his nominees and I'll clear the other eight. And it's got to be fifty-fifty from this day forward." Johnson believed that Yarborough conspired with Bobby Kennedy to "double cross" him and "reduce him to cut-dog impotency in Texas and to drive him from the national ticket." After this episode, Johnson even "toyed with the idea of resigning from the vice-presidency and returning [to Texas] to run against Senator Yarborough in 1964," Baker claimed. Yarborough thwarted Johnson's appointments monopoly and Robert Kennedy ended up taking the full brunt of the vice president's wrath. When the smoke cleared, neither Yarborough nor Johnson was satisfied. But Yarborough had forged a stronger relationship with Robert Kennedy, which would prove beneficial as events unfolded.[16]

A second political blow aimed at Yarborough was the selection of the interim senator to replace Johnson. To fill Johnson's vacant Senate seat, Governor Daniel nominated William Blakley, the candidate Yarborough defeated in the 1958 Democratic primary and the close friend of Shivers. Johnson's vacant senate position attracted great attention in early 1961, so Blakley's announcement that he planned to run in the special election did not prevent a number of Democratic challengers from announcing. Congressman Jim Wright, State Senator Henry B. Gonzalez, former congressman Maury Maverick Jr., Attorney General Will Wilson, and Blakley were the leading Democratic contenders for the April 4, 1960, election. Midwestern University professor John Tower, defeated by Johnson in the 1960 Senate general election, returned for another attempt as the sole Republican in the crowded field. Both Yarborough and Johnson remained silent as to their choice for the open seat, making matters difficult for Democrats of all political persuasions.

With the large field of candidates, Texas voters probably thought they were looking at the telephone directory instead of a ballot. A total of seventy-one names appeared on the ballot. When the votes were counted, Tower and Blakley received the largest number and headed for a runoff. With Texas Democrats splitting their votes among the many candidates, Tower emerged as the front-runner by a wide margin, winning 30 percent of the vote.[17]

Kennedy and Johnson endorsed Blakley in the runoff, but leaders of the Texas liberals refused to choose either candidate. Many liberals believed that by electing Tower many Shivers Democrats would leave the party and become Republicans, thus making Texas a true two-party state. Many Democratic loyalists felt that Yarborough, when he came up for reelection in 1964, would be the distinct winner if many conservatives left the party for the Republican fold. Removal of the Dixiecrat conservatives to the GOP would push the party into becoming a legitimate second party whose nominees could begin to draw on a larger conservative base and make the Republicans valid contenders in many areas of the state. While the liberal *Texas Observer* called for Tower's election, the conservative *Dallas Morning News* declared its support for Blakley. Both candidates were conservative, but the *News* endorsed Blakley primarily because he would cancel Yarborough's input on patronage issues. Yarborough never endorsed Blakley, and some of the senator's campaign workers joined Tower's campaign. Texas politics was always unusual, but the 1961 election appeared strange indeed. With many liberal Democrats "gone fishin'" or voting Republican, Tower eked out a narrow 10,000-vote victory over Blakley in a low turnout. Tower thus became the first Republican since Reconstruction to win a statewide office. Breaking his silence, Yarborough said that the election was not a repudiation of Kennedy or Democrats. "There was nothing in the race to call out the voters," Yarborough surmised. At least one newspaper noted the irony of Tower's election. The *Fort Worth Star Telegram* editorialized that Johnson's maneuver to run for two offices in November set the stage for Tower's victory the following May: "Had this not been done, the successor to Johnson's seat would have been nominated in last year's Democratic Primary and would undoubtedly have ridden with the party to victory in November." Vice President Johnson refused comment but he understood the outcome.[18]

Texas and the nation suffered a great blow with the death of Speaker Sam Rayburn in November 1961. Rayburn, 79, died only a few months following a diagnosis of cancer. People across the country mourned the loss of "Mr. Sam," whose legislative career and reputation as Speaker may never be equaled. Yarborough greatly admired and respected Rayburn for his mastery of Congress and his unabashed loyalty to the nation and the Democratic party. Yarborough paid tribute to Rayburn on the Senate floor in early 1962. He described the Speaker as the ideal public servant and the equal of Henry Clay. Rayburn was the epitome of a man who devoted his life to public service at the expense of his own personal gain, a course Yarborough, too, followed. Yarborough and Rayburn differed primarily in their allegiance to Johnson. Ironically, Yarborough came closer to fitting the Rayburn mold of public service and commitment than did the Speaker's own protégé.[19]

With Rayburn's death, the Johnson-Yarborough rivalry continued throughout the years of the Kennedy administration. John Connally, the Johnson aide who became Kennedy's secretary of the navy, decided to return to Texas and run for governor. During the 1961 Christmas holidays, Yarborough met with supporters in Houston to discuss the possibility of running again for governor while holding the Senate seat. Yarborough believed he had a strong organization and that the conservative faction of the party had weakened as a result of further defections to the Republican party in 1960. Many liberals saw Yarborough as the only viable opponent to Connally and the Johnson forces. Also, Governor Daniel declared for a third term, thus the conservative and moderate vote could conceivably divide between the incumbent and Connally. Liberal leaders perceived that a further purge of the conservative elements of the party combined with an increased number of African American and Mexican American voters would accomplish two major goals. First, Texas would finally become a two-party state with clear philosophical division between the two major parties. Second, the newly aligned Democratic party would be a clear break from the conservative southern Democrats and more closely reflect the national organization. However, Connally's emergence as a new statewide leader would reassert Johnson's control over Texas Democrats and marginalize efforts to restructure the party. A Yarborough gubernatorial effort appeared to be the best solution for the liberals. He was popular enough to motivate new minority voters and to attract moderates in the party. But Yarborough's vote was especially important to national Democrats and the Kennedy administration. He stood alongside a mere handful of southerners willing to consistently side with Kennedy on controversial domestic and foreign issues, and the president knew Yarborough would back civil rights legislation and repeal of the poll tax.[20]

Yarborough soon resolved what was described as one of the "great mysteries" of the political year when he announced he would not run for governor in 1962. He met with other supporters, his staff, and finally with President Kennedy on the matter. He officially declared in late January that in spite of encouragement from people in Texas, he declined to enter the governor's campaign. He indicated that the president expressed concerns about his leaving the Senate seat, making John Tower the senior senator from Texas. Furthermore, liberals had a qualified candidate to enter the governor's race —Don Yarborough. Although they had the same last name, the two Yarboroughs were not related. Don, a young Houston attorney, bore a striking physical resemblance to a younger Ralph Yarborough and they held similar political philosophies. A Marine veteran, University of Texas graduate, and political unknown until 1960 when he ran for lieutenant governor against the incumbent Ben Ramsey, Don Yarborough surprised many in the race by gaining over 650,000 votes against Ramsey, undoubtedly because of his well-known name. (Don Yarborough was the first of many candidates with the Yarborough surname to enter Texas politics after 1960.) In the May 1962 primary, Connally and Don Yarborough finished first and second respectively, eliminating incumbent governor Daniel. Connally subsequently defeated Don Yarborough in the summer runoff election, which made Johnson's former aide the heir to the conservative legacy in the governor's office and put him in a position to make Yarborough's tenure in the Senate more difficult.[21]

Once Connally became the Democratic nominee, Johnson and the leaders of the Texas congressional delegation attempted to obtain a unanimous endorsement from all the state's congressional Democrats. Meeting at their traditional midweek lunch at the capitol, Congressman Jack Brooks prepared a resolution endorsing Connally in the general election. With all the members of the delegation and Vice President Johnson in attendance, Yarborough refused to sign the endorsement. He requested a number of revisions and finally submitted a resolution of his own. He wanted the members to sign a resolution praising his work and endorsing his own reelection to the Senate in 1964. After a few uncomfortable moments, the session ended with Yarborough the only member from Texas to deny Connally's endorsement. House members also declined to sign Yarborough's petition. The awkward incident did nothing to improve Yarborough's relationships with leaders of the state's Democratic delegation. Still smarting from the patronage dispute, Yarborough mistrusted Johnson and Connally. He suspected a coordinated effort to discredit him in advance of the 1964 election. Even after he heard assurances that the vice president and the governor were not trying to recruit a primary opponent, Yarborough, now a battle-tested veteran, maintained his steady vigilance over the political scene.[22]

PADRE ISLAND NATIONAL SEASHORE ACT

Yarborough's decision to forego the 1962 governor's race aided his legislative efforts. In recognition of Yarborough's loyalty, President Kennedy endorsed the Padre Island National Seashore bill. Following the recommendation of a Department of Interior study on the island, Yarborough reduced the size of the proposed site to encompass slightly more than eighty-eight miles. South Texas Congressmen Joe Kilgore and John Young, the two Democratic House members who opposed the legislation as originally introduced by Yarborough, came forward with their own measure, which called for a small, sixty-five-mile-long preserve. Their change of heart occurred as a result of popular support for a Padre Island park. In the early 1960's, several major Texas daily newspapers which at one time promoted the remote area as the next "Miami Beach" now endorsed a national park. The *New York Times* declared that the islands represented one of the finest undeveloped shorelines in the nation and labeled the site "a place of superlatives."[23]

As the park proposal advanced in 1962, George Sandlin, former Democratic state chairman and Allan Shivers' friend, suddenly appeared. Sandlin's corporation purchased a prime area of the proposed park—24,000 acres on the south end of the island—for $5 million. Also, opponents to the park proposal argued for construction of a paved road to run the entire eighty-eight-mile length of the unspoiled island under consideration for federal acquisition. Texas Land Commissioner Jerry Sadler added to the storm when newspapers published his remarks that the proposed park represented a federal land grab that threatened Texans. Sadler compared the issue to the battle between the state and federal government over control of the oil-rich offshore lands known as the Tidelands. "Did we fight and win the tidelands only to hand them back piecemeal?" Sadler asked.[24]

In spite of these obstacles, difficulties with Congress, and Vice President Johnson's quiet opposition, Yarborough sensed victory at hand and redoubled his efforts to line up support. During the previous summer, Vice President Johnson traveled to South Texas with Yarborough, Interior Secretary Stewart Udall, and National Park director Conrad Wirth. During a well-attended meeting at the Corpus Christi municipal auditorium, the crowd cheered Yarborough when he declared he would not back down from an eighty-eight-mile park. Vice President Johnson, who followed Yarborough, said he hoped that the "minor differences" between the Senate and House bills could be put aside "so future generation can enjoy what we have enjoyed." In making his first public speech in favor of the park, Johnson refused to make a specific recommendation. Congressmen Kilgore and Young were not at the meeting, though Johnson still relied upon them for support. But his trip with Yarborough acknowledged the growing popularity of the Padre Island bill. The visiting delegation from Washington left Corpus Christi for a fish fry and a flight over the island. After their return to D.C., Yarborough gained passage of the measure in the Senate in 1961 but once again it failed to move out of the House. The bill remained lost like a sunken treasure galleon in the murky waters of the House Interior and Insular Affairs Committee.[25]

When President Kennedy added his authority to Yarborough's Padre Island bill, Yarborough declared that the president knew "the need to save America's fast vanishing shoreline." Kennedy also compared the proposal with two other popular coastal initiatives before Congress, Cape Cod in Massachusetts and Point Reyes in California. Yarborough enlisted support from two influential political figures in Congressman Kilgore's South Texas district: Cameron County judge Oscar Dancy and Cameron County Democratic chairman Jack Scaggs. Judge Dancy flew to Washington to help break the impasse. The combined pressures appeared to work as an agreement neared between Yarborough and the two South Texas congressmen. Suddenly, Senator John Tower, who had heretofore been uninvolved in the dispute, entered the scene. Tower announced his opposition to a park on Padre Island and stated that he envisioned more private, commercial development that revived the "Miami-type resort" plan from the past.[26]

When Yarborough brought the Padre Island bill to the Senate for consideration on April 10, 1962, he and Tower faced off in their first public confrontation in the historic chamber. Tower told senators that the bill should be returned to the Committee on Interior and Insular Affairs based on what he termed "considerable opposition" in Texas. Tower referred to Land Commissioner Sadler's statements and questions over land titles and mineral ownership. The junior senator also said that the Corpus Christi Naval Station would lose its target range on the island if it became a federally designated national seashore. The only suitable site left for the navy would be "in the middle of the King Ranch," Tower remarked, "and I tremble to think what might happen if we tried to take over a portion of the King Ranch."[27]

Senator Pete Anderson (D-New Mexico), chairman of the Senate committee that favorably reported the bill, replied. Anderson said that his committee had paid "great attention" to all of Tower's concerns. He noted that Land Commissioner Sadler failed to appear on three occasions to testify. The New Mexico senator said that state mineral ownership frequently occurred in these types of federal acquisitions and "is not an unusual situation in the public land states of the west." After years of work on the proposal, Anderson declared the time had come for the Senate to act on the committee's recommendation. In addition to the merits of the case, Anderson said that Yarborough's "dogged insistence" on the legislation made it a necessity. Yarborough was "about as persistent a pleader as I have ever encountered," Anderson said. "Day after day he would stop me in the hall and say, 'When is my bill going to be considered?' I do not want him back again. I want to be footloose from him," Anderson quipped to his amused fellow Senators.[28]

In response, Yarborough added that Anderson's committee had more than adequately reviewed all of Tower's concerns. Yarborough, the former assistant attorney general who once defended the state's oil reserves for the public schools and universities, declared that Texas would not lose any of its mineral interests after the island became a national seashore. "The oil will be owned as before," he declared. Yarborough noted the endorsement of the Texas Parks Board and ruled out any possibility of a state-operated seashore when he candidly stated, "The people down there do not have enough money with which to set it up." In his final argument, Yarborough asked for approval because "no other problem has aroused such public interest as this one has in the five years I have been in the Senate." He talked about the island's unspoiled beauty and its history of lost Spanish ships and long-departed Indians. Yarborough defeated Tower's move to refer the bill back to committee by a 45-to-39 record vote. The fate of Padre Island once again passed to the other side of the Capitol, into the House of Representatives.[29]

As the summer wore on, debate continued over the size of the park, but final action seemed imminent. As negotiations went on behind the scenes, Yarborough wrote his friend Walter Hall about the changes. Even after the legislation went through another round of changes with House members, Yarborough said it was "still with the hope that it will pass this session." When Yarborough and House members finally compromised on an eighty-one-mile distance, the measure sailed through with overwhelming majorities in both houses. In a bill-signing ceremony at the White House on September 23, 1962, President Kennedy turned to hand a commemorative pen to a beaming Senator Yarborough. The president again lauded Padre Island, now joined with Cape Cod on the Atlantic and Point Reyes on the Pacific, as part of a triple crown for coastal preservation, "three exceptional sites which have been preserved for the people of the United States." After five years of work for an area described by the National Park Service as the "highest priority" and on a bill that in Yarborough's own words "died many deaths," Texas and the nation finally gained an invaluable, unique natural preserve.[30]

*Stewart Udall, President Kennedy's secretary of the interior, observes a map of the
Padre Island National Seashore with Senator Yarborough. Signed into law in
1962, the Seashore became the first major national park sponsored by Yarborough.
Courtesy Center for American History, Yarborough Papers (3Y434).*

Throughout the fight and for many years after the bill passed, Yarborough
maintained that Vice President Johnson fought his proposal tooth and nail.
The bill finally passed in Congress while Johnson was away on an overseas
mission to Southeast Asia for President Kennedy. Richard Yarborough, the
senator's aide, recognized the opportunity to act. He told his father that
Johnson would be gone for three weeks, giving Yarborough a window of opportunity. "This is your chance to pass it and probably your last chance,"
the young Yarborough insisted. The senator actually canceled a number of
speeches and public appearances. He then called key committee members,
urging them to pass the agreed-upon bill. When the vice president returned
from his trip, Yarborough laughed and said, "That Padre Island bill was lying
on Kennedy's desk to be signed." Johnson made no public comments about
the bill's passage that created the Padre Island National Seashore. The National Park Service took five years to complete purchases and finalize plans
for the park. The original estimate of $5 million eventually totaled $23 million due to litigation and higher prices for land. When the protected area was

formally dedicated during the Johnson administration in 1968, Yarborough appeared alongside Lady Bird Johnson, an enthusiastic supporter of the modern treasure that is now Padre Island National Seashore.[31]

The Padre Island legislation concluded Yarborough's five-year effort to protect the unspoiled beaches and dunes on the nation's longest seashore from commercial development. The bill represented his first major victory in natural resource protection. His accomplishment, when added to the seashores protected in California and Massachusetts, provided a positive statement for the Kennedy administration, whose environmental record has been labeled by some historians as "anemic." Congressional authorization of the Padre Island National Seashore occurred during a period described as the dawn of the new environmental age. Saving a pristine Padre Island served as a commitment to the traditional conservation goal of protecting unique, natural sites. But the act also set the stage for creation of protected areas for reasons beyond traditional conservation and for using the power and money of the federal government to do so. The desire to keep Padre Island as an undeveloped, largely inaccessible preserve marked the dawn of the new environmental age that began in the 1960's. Wilderness areas, seashores, historic trails, scenic rivers, and many other diverse sites would soon rise to the forefront of the national agenda. Yarborough's victory enabled him to gain recognition as a national leader in the new environmental movement. It also gave him the confidence to use federal authority for other environmental initiatives in his Senate career.[32]

THE BILLIE SOL ESTES AFFAIR

Johnson and Connally were Yarborough's main antagonists, but Yarborough suddenly had other political problems in 1962. State and federal investigators looking into the affairs of Texas businessman and Democratic contributor Billie Sol Estes made some startling discoveries. Estes and three other men were charged with a multimillion dollar case of fraud and theft by a federal grand jury in March 1962 following an extensive FBI investigation. Estes' dealings in phantom storage tanks and phony mortgages and other shenanigans also led to the dismissal of Department of Agriculture officials, and one investigator in the department died, which made the case even more volatile. More than a dozen companies claimed that they had loaned $22 million against ammonia fertilizer tanks owned by Estes and others. Many Texas political leaders, including Johnson and Yarborough, were beneficiaries of Estes' campaign donations. Estes had first supported Yarborough in his 1954 campaign against Shivers. His last donation before his indictment was in December 1961, when he contributed to production costs for Yarborough's radio broadcasts. According to news reports, Yarborough received as much as $200,000 in campaign contributions from Estes. Yarborough denied the amount but acknowledged receiving $1,700 from him. Vice President Johnson immediately separated himself from the growing scandal, claiming that he had turned down requests by Estes. Johnson said the West Texas businessman was a member of the "ultra liberal group, the Democrats of Texas" with whom Johnson had political differences.[33]

Revelations of Yarborough accepting what appeared to be tainted money shocked many Texans. Following Estes' arrest, Yarborough received dozens of letters on the affair. Many were critical of the senator for his acceptance of campaign contributions from Estes. One constituent said, "I am surprised that any man whom we have considered smart enough to be elected to the high office of Senator is so naive to think that he can accept money from anybody without the expectation on the part of the giver, that it will in some way be reciprocated." He compared the affair to that of former U.S. senator Joe Bailey, who wasn't "smart enough to refuse to accept money from a Corporation, and that not only wrecked his career, but really wrecked his life." Yarborough expressed his concern over the "wild charges" and maintained that he had not accumulated any fortune or property after entering the Senate in 1957.[34]

Yarborough's friends rose to his support. Roy Selman stated that he did not care "if you got $1,700 or took $10,000 from Estes or Billy the Kid or Jesse James. Nothing, but nothing, will ever make me doubt your sincerity of purpose or intellectual honesty." They believed the attacks originated with political adversaries and editorial boards who consistently opposed the senator. Several warned of a "whisper campaign" linking Yarborough directly with the Estes scandal "in an effort to destroy you politically and protect the culprits who may be guilty." Detractors included the *Dallas Morning News*, or "the irresponsible Newsance," as Bonner Frizell put it. One officeholder accused of spreading derogatory information was Texas land commissioner Jerry Sadler. Sadler was trying to undermine Yarborough's Padre Island park initiative and viewed the news as an opportunity to kill federal efforts to acquire the natural area.[35]

Tom Pollard, a Tyler attorney and longtime Yarborough friend, said that people were aware of the "malicious smear tactics of our supposedly independent and impartial newspapers." While it was regrettable that Yarborough took money from Billie Sol Estes, "it is common knowledge in Texas that if there is any money around to be had from politics that our honorable Vice-President always gets there first for the most." Even people in the business community noted that questions arising over Yarborough's integrity seemed out of line. "I resent the charge that is being made and the implications that are being advanced of your integrity," wrote Imperial Sugar Company board chairman I. H. Kempner. "I regret that such an unwarranted assault should be made and publicized on a man who occupies such a high position and the implications asserted and circulated on such a low level." [36]

The Billie Sol Estes affair made national news because of his ties to Johnson and Yarborough. The *Washington Post* was particularly critical of those linked to the scandal and singled out Yarborough in an editorial on May 21, 1962. The editorial inferred that when Yarborough accepted $1,000 from Billie Sol Estes for tickets to the Democratic National Committee celebration of President Kennedy's birthday, he had "opened the door to corruption." The Texas senator defended his position in a letter to the *Post*, which he quoted in his letters and reprinted in his June 5, 1962, *Washington Report* newsletter. Yarborough acknowledged that when fund-raising appeals were made, "one always runs a danger of finding some contributor who does not turn out well later on. Neither I nor the Democratic Party has found it possible to screen contributors with a lie detector, or look in a crystal ball to see how they will turn out in the future." He stated that his votes for the previous five years in the Senate were proof of his independence from any contributor. "You, or anybody else, who hints that I improperly used one bit of power of my office for Mr. Estes, lies. With your innuendo of guilt by association, go burn your incense before Joe McCarthy's image," Yarborough indignantly advised. Recognizing the significance of the issue, Senate Democratic leader Mike Mansfield (D-Montana) and Republican senator Barry Goldwater (R-Arizona) publicly defended Yarborough in a rare show of bipartisan support. Mansfield stated in a Senate floor speech that "Yarborough had laid his cards on the table" and was innocent of any wrongdoing. Goldwater, already a leading candidate for his party's 1964 presidential nomination, said he saw "nothing wrong with acceptance by the Senator from Texas of money from Mr. Estes long before there was any indication or inkling that Mr. Estes was engaged in wrongful practice." [37]

The Estes contributions raised another issue for Yarborough and Washington officials. The *Washington Post* noted that many congressmen and senators distributed radio and television tapes recorded at House and Senate studios at prices below commercial rates. Each elected official paid for the distribution of the tapes and any charges levied by radio or television stations. But as a matter of practice many media outlets at this time ran the productions as a public service announcement or utilized the tapes for news stories. Over one hundred stations in large and small markets broadcast Yarborough's reports.

Yarborough revealed that Estes contributed $1,700 to help finance his weekly five-minute public radio programs in Texas. Yarborough said that the total costs of the programs were $24,400. The cost was paid for by contributions from individuals and included the Estes contribution. Texas' other senator, John Tower, also had a privately funded radio program at this time, paid for by the Republican Senatorial Committee. Of all the U.S. senators of this period, nearly three out of every four had their own radio or television program paid for by contributions from supporters or party committees. During the 1950's when he was a senator, Lyndon Johnson also had his own radio program supported by contributions. At the time the controversy arose, Yarborough's tapes were carried on about 100 radio stations weekly at a cost of approximately $150 per week. The widespread use of radio programs by senators of both parties also contributed to the response from Mansfield and Goldwater.[38]

Immediately after the Estes scandal appeared in the *Dallas Morning News*, Yarborough called on the Kennedy administration for assistance. His early support for Kennedy's presidential campaign was not forgotten. Yarborough received immediate aid from Attorney General Robert Kennedy. Yarborough complained that the newspaper stories implicated him in a federal crime and requested to have the FBI investigate and clear his name. Within a week, the Dallas FBI office provided information that substantiated Yarborough's position that he received only airplane trips and several thousand dollars from Estes. Yarborough received his absolution, but the experience of having his name associated with a serious political scandal unnerved him. Given the strife in Texas politics, Yarborough knew that future opponents would again raise the issue. The attacks also reconfirmed his long-standing antipathy towards the *Dallas Morning News* and added to his mistrust of the news media. His difficulties with Texas newspapers and reporters plagued him continuously throughout his Senate years.[39]

10 *The Rancid Smell of Gunpowder*

"One of the brightest and widest smiles in Washington adorns the leathery face of Texas' senior Sen. Ralph Webster Yarborough" the editor of the *Lewisville Leader* wrote in 1963. As he approached the end of his first full term in the Senate, Yarborough had reason to be optimistic. His star was rising in Washington as a loyal supporter of President Kennedy. Yarborough had ceremonial presidential pens from dozens of bill signings on programs ranging from education to his Padre Island bill. His stalled legislation showed new life and his ongoing fight for the Cold War G.I. Bill appeared to gain support. Yarborough's popularity in Texas grew as he kept up his frequent visits, making speeches as often as he could fly back to his home state. Organized labor, farmers, educators, senior citizens, veterans, and even many business people now called themselves Yarborough fans. Increasingly larger crowds came to hear him speak. Whether addressing a high school commencement or a statewide veterans' meeting, many Texans exhibited a growing desire to hear about events in Washington and enjoyed Yarborough's enthusiastic, hand-waving and fact-filled performances.

Newspapers began to give him more coverage as he began to provide more one-on-one interviews on legislative issues and national policy. Opal Yarborough's popularity soared as well. Opal, who was always behind her husband's political efforts, also made more public appearances and gave more interviews about her life in Washington and Texas. The family maintained their home in West Austin and a Washington, D.C., apartment, but Opal found herself on the road traveling and making public appearances nearly as often as her husband. At least once a month they returned to Texas, where Yarborough made appearances and gave speeches in nearly every area of the state. Diverse groups, which included the postal workers in South Texas, military veterans in Lubbock, and NASA employees in Houston, heard Yarborough during his whirlwind trips. During the summer of 1963, the editor of a small city newspaper praised the senator who "has something on the ball regardless of how many of us may differ with his political views." The *Lewisville Leader* editor who experienced Yarborough for the first time praised his knowledge, energy, and drive. At a speech at a local festival, Yarborough never broke a sweat as others sweltered beneath the summer sun. "Without benefit of notes, he began unreeling pertinent information about the Lewisville area that few, if any, residents knew." As he maintained his whirlwind schedule, he even managed to return to Austin in November to cast his vote to repeal the state's poll tax and attend his first University of Texas football game in years.[1]

Yarborough made headway on his legislative initiatives, but Congress still held up President Kennedy's major bills. The primary opposition came from the administration's increased commitment to civil rights legislation. The president's Civil Rights bill was particularly controversial, but Martin Luther King's presence and his famous "I Have a Dream" speech in Washington during August provided support for Kennedy's civil rights program. Yarborough and many Texans sensed the old barriers enforcing racial segregation faced a severe test. Most public schools and businesses in Texas still barred African Americans in 1963, but for a variety of reasons more and more people began to support changes to strike down the most blatant signs of discrimination. From small towns to urban Texas, white and colored signs still stood affixed to many structures and facilities, but some communities began integrating schools, parks, restaurants, and other public facilities without incident. In the meantime, Americans witnessed an ongoing televised spectacle on the evening news that featured images of white police officers and hostile crowds beating civil rights activists in communities of the Deep South.

The civil rights issue generated the largest numbers of constituent letters to the senator's office. Brief handwritten notes, telegrams, and long typed letters poured into the Capitol office. Many of those supporting civil rights referred to biblical quotations and the moral responsibility of southerners to end segregation. A number of the writers knew the senator and reminded him of his pledges for honesty and commitment to justice he displayed as a district judge and later as a candidate. Others believed segregation harmed Texas business and endangered the nation's reputation in world affairs. Typical of the thousands of letters supporting civil rights was one that came from Elaine Anderson of Austin, who said "we must realize that deprivation of the rights of some citizens of this country cripples and removes the rights of all of us." She added that Yarborough's support for civil rights would demonstrate that "the South does have some intelligent statesmen." Critics of the legislation were just as numerous and vocal. Arguments against federal legislation centered on racist and economic arguments. Opponents feared their property would be confiscated and their homes and businesses would lose value if integration occurred. Some feared the civil rights movement was part of a communist conspiracy to undermine the national government. Others believed the bill would create a federal police state and infringe on the rights of whites and blacks while trampling on states' rights. The Texas Junior Chamber of Commerce said the legislation was unneeded and misguided. The proposed act was "anathema to the free enterprise system, private property rights and the individual freedom of association." Some were even more direct in their opposition. "I will not associate or fraternize with negroes and will not permit my children to go in any dance hall, theater or swimming pool which is integrated." Public sentiment was shifting in Texas, but hostilities and uncertainties remained as no consensus plan emerged during the torrid summer of 1963 and Congress continued to hold up Kennedy's legislation.[2]

As the stalemate over civil rights continued in Washington, supporters organized a special "Salute to Senator Ralph Yarborough" dinner in preparation for his 1964 reelection campaign. Over three thousand enthusiastic Yarborough supporters packed Austin Municipal Auditorium on October 19, 1963, in his largest fund-raising reception to date. The Yarborough faithful viewed a filmed tribute from President Kennedy who stated, "Yarborough speaks for Texas in the U.S. Senate" and he "speaks for progress for our people." Kennedy pointed to Yarborough's work in education, veterans' benefits, support for the nuclear test ban treaty, and the passage of the law that established the Padre Island National Seashore. Additional praise came from newly appointed Postmaster General John Gronouski and Yarborough's longtime friend J. Frank Dobie. Gronouski praised Yarborough as a steadfast supporter of President Kennedy and one of the most vigorous fighters for progressive legislation. He said the radical right and their "fraudulent patriotism" wanted Yarborough defeated and warned against their emotional and sometimes violent actions. Finally, J. Frank Dobie provided an eloquent description of his friend as the "best read man that Texas has ever sent to Washington." The Texas writer said Yarborough worked only for the public good and not his own personal gain. "He does not try to milk the public for private profit. He seeks the good of people." Dobie concluded, "when values of life—values beyond money, values that express civilization, enlightenment, and justice for the human race come up, we can count on Senator Ralph Yarborough to stand for those values." Notably, no statewide officeholder and no Texas daily newspaper covered the event. But Yarborough bragged to Walter Hall that members of the capitol press corps said the dinner was the "largest political dinner ever held in Austin, bigger than Price Daniel's or John Connally's." Sponsors never extended an invitation to Governor Connally. Vice President Johnson, who was invited, was at another event in New England. Only Texas congressmen Jack Brooks and Henry B. Gonzalez attended. Others supplied congratulatory telegrams and letters. Many elected officials in Washington and Austin still opposed Yarborough and yearned for a more conservative replacement in 1964.[3]

KENNEDY'S REELECTION AND THE TRIP TO TEXAS

Like Yarborough, Kennedy expected a tough reelection battle. As the Kennedy administration pushed its national agenda with its focus on civil rights, keeping Texas in the Democratic fold in 1964 appeared difficult. Kennedy and Johnson narrowly defeated Nixon in the state in 1960, reversing the trend of Republican presidential victories since 1952. Yarborough urged Kennedy to come to Texas to demonstrate that the president was sincere in wanting white southerners to recognize the need for change in their relationships with African Americans. Johnson on the other hand feared that Kennedy's support for civil rights and the president's alignment with Yarborough and Texas liberals undercut his own popularity in his home state. By the fall of 1963, Governor Connally publicly criticized the administration's attention to the civil rights issues and did not want Kennedy cutting into his fundraising. The governor and other conservatives believed the presidential ticket and Yarborough were vulnerable in 1964. A published poll of Texas voters in September 1963 revealed Kennedy and Johnson were trailing Connally in approval ratings. The Democratic president had a 50 percent approval rating compared to the governor's 61 percent positive rating. However, 42 percent disapproved of the president's performance whereas only 13 percent registered a negative vote for the governor. But private polls given to Yarborough indicated both he and the president were in better shape with the Texas electorate than some wanted them to believe. A job-performance poll conducted by the Kaplan-Chamberlain firm in Houston revealed that as of September, Kennedy, Johnson, and Yarborough all had positive ratings in the largest city in the state. Kennedy had 65 percent of the respondents rating him as "excellent" or "pretty good." Johnson received a rating of 57 percent and Yarborough 54 percent in the same poll. On the negative side, 28 percent perceived Kennedy as "not so good" or "poor" while Johnson totaled a 31 percent negative score. Yarborough's negative numbers were the lowest of the three with only 19 percent dissatisfied. Houston was a good indicator of the rest of the state, and the Democrats appeared to be in better shape than many political observers believed.[4]

Kennedy and his advisors had no desire to see the state slip away from them in 1964. Although many historical accounts examining the Kennedy assassination stated that the president came to Texas to personally quell the dispute between Yarborough and Connally and the liberal and conservative factions, the trip focused on enhancing the president's image in Texas and opening up the checkbooks of wealthy contributors in a pivotal electoral state. As the once-solid Democratic South seemed less and less certain for Kennedy in 1964, the twenty-five electoral votes from Texas magnified in importance. After an October meeting in Washington, Kennedy calmed some of Governor Connally's concerns by agreeing to host a fund-raiser in Austin with proceeds going to the state party. Connally succeeded in reducing Kennedy's campaign fundraising events, but the president's itinerary revealed his intention to spend most of his time with influential businessmen in Houston, Fort Worth, Dallas, and Austin. Kennedy met with very few political organizers and party activists. He was fully aware of the breach between the Johnson-Connally Democrats and the Yarborough enthusiasts, but he knew he needed both organizations to win the state in 1964. Kennedy's irritation with Johnson stemmed from his conduct as vice president and his lack of desire to resolve the political problems in Texas. Johnson was sullen and despondent in the number two position as speculation arose prior to the Texas trip that Kennedy might replace him as his running mate in 1964. Public speculation on Johnson's removal only reinforced the importance of the Texas trip to Kennedy. As a result of the president's assassination, the story that his visit was mainly to quell the stormy political waters in Texas gained wider circulation than Kennedy's own electoral concerns. Even as Texas Democrats united after the great tragedy, the personal sniping between Connally and Yarborough continued.

The disputes between the senator and the first-term governor began well in advance of the trip. Connally, long a Johnson operative, never supported Yarborough in his gubernatorial elections and his Senate race. He also disliked Yarborough's style and personality. Once he became governor, Connally openly criticized both Yarborough and Kennedy on the civil rights issue. The governor called for "voluntary integration" and claimed the administration tried to "go too far and too fast." In a statewide telecast, Connally complained that the public accommodations section of the proposed Civil Rights Bill would "destroy personal property rights." The governor believed that if the law were enacted private businesses could not refuse service to individuals and the U.S. attorney general would have too much power to intervene in local affairs. Connally determined to keep his distance from the Kennedy administration, which by 1963 demonstrated a stronger commitment to civil rights. The governor also believed that Kennedy favored Yarborough as he isolated Vice President Johnson. In the weeks before Kennedy's visit, many of the state's newspapers prominently displayed the rift between Yarborough and Connally. Siding with Yarborough, Congressman Henry B. Gonzalez of San Antonio complained that the split could only aid Republicans. Gonzalez specifically complained about the "cold shoulder" Yarborough received from the governor and other state Democratic leaders and contributors.[5]

President Kennedy and his advisors were only too aware of the political disagreements and the patronage fights between Johnson and Yarborough. They read the papers and heard from Texans. Franklin Jones Sr., a Marshall attorney and a Yarborough supporter, asked Attorney General Robert Kennedy to help "correct the snubs directed toward the Senator." Jones explained that "many a political realist believes LBJ and his cohorts are moving heaven and earth to get a conservative opponent to Sen. Yarborough." Jones and many others expected a tough reelection campaign in 1964 for both the senator and the Kennedy-Johnson ticket.[6]

When decision time arrived for the Texas trip, President Kennedy's advance team assigned the responsibility to Governor Connally. The Kennedy forces knew Yarborough provided important political support and volunteers but that Johnson and Connally held the keys that would open the doors to wealthy Texas contributors. (In fact, Kennedy's private Lou Harris poll showed Yarborough with a rating ten percent better than Kennedy-Johnson, and the story leaked to Texas newspapers.) The governor's office, working closely with Vice President Johnson's staff, scheduled all of the public events, individual meetings, and fund-raising appearances. Yarborough, who believed he was the foremost supporter of the president in Texas, chafed at what he believed was a personal as well as a political slight to him. He was already upset with Johnson over the patronage fights and his suspicion that the vice president kept him off the powerful Senate Appropriations Committee. Now, the Kennedy operatives joined with the Governor's office. They left Yarborough and his staff completely out of the planning process. Nevertheless, Yarborough agreed to participate in events in Texas as a political necessity and because of his loyalty to the president.

Kennedy wanted all of the state's leading Democrats to appear with him during the swing through Texas on the "nonpolitical trip." In a letter to the senator, Connally requested Yarborough's "active help," saying "we need for you to come down and join us in traveling through Texas with the President and Vice President." The governor concluded, "I am looking forward to being with you down here in Texas on November 21st and 22nd. Meanwhile, let's lend every effort toward making our Texas Welcome Dinner a success." Connally's letter included 250 tickets for the November 22 dinner for Yarborough to sell. The money from the final Kennedy appearance in Austin would be used "to help elect Democrats and defeat Republicans in the 1964 general election." Eugene Locke, the chairman of the State Democratic Executive Committee, and Frank Erwin Jr., secretary of the SDEC, chaired the event, the only scheduled fund raising program for the state Democratic party. Both Locke and Erwin were staunch Connally supporters and controlled the SDEC. In a separate invitation from Locke and Erwin to party officials, Governor Connally provided the introduction to the president and vice president, the only featured speakers. Senator Yarborough's name appeared neither in the solicitation nor in connection with any other event that involved the presidential entourage. Protocol required an invitation, but Connally and the state party had no intention of letting Yarborough share the limelight. Knowing he would play second fiddle on this orchestrated tour, Yarborough agreed to participate and sing his own tune. His staff and friends sold over $11,000 in tickets to the $100 per plate dinner. In a series of letters to Kennedy and the state party, Yarborough also urged the inclusion of "people to represent the Loyal Democrats of Texas" in the dinner and scheduled events. Several of these activists were added to the official functions at the last minute.[7]

On November 21, 1963, Yarborough rode on the plane from Washington to Texas with Kennedy and the president's party. They met Vice President Johnson in San Antonio for the dedication of the United States Air Force School of Aerospace Medicine. Plans called for Yarborough to ride in the parade with Vice President and Lady Bird Johnson but at the last minute he opted to ride in the convertible with popular Congressman Henry B. Gonzalez of San Antonio. Upon arriving in San Antonio, Yarborough learned more details of the Texas tour. Maury Maverick Jr., the liberal state Democratic committeeman, said the Connally staff prevented him and other Yarborough supporters from attending the airport arrival and the planned festivities. Connally intended to move the senator from the head table to the floor at the president's Austin dinner and deleted Yarborough's name from all official press releases. He also omitted Yarborough from a reception at the governor's mansion. To express his displeasure, Yarborough decided to join

President Kennedy greets well-wishers outside Fort Worth's Texas Hotel only hours before his assassination. Behind him are Senator Yarborough (left) and Governor Connally (center), whose political feud boiled during the November 1963 trip to Texas. Fort Worth Star Telegram *photo. Courtesy Special Collections, University of Texas at Arlington.*

his congressional colleagues and avoid Johnson. At the next appearance in Houston, Yarborough got into the car with Congressman Albert Thomas, who was honored at a dinner that night. Following the dinner, Yarborough accompanied the presidential entourage as everyone flew to Fort Worth to spend the night. Opal remained in Austin in preparation for Kennedy's expected arrival on the afternoon of November 22.[8]

After an early morning breakfast with Fort Worth business representatives, the group departed for Dallas where Kennedy was to speak at a luncheon at the Dallas Trade Mart. The presidential motorcade slowly moved through downtown Dallas and, at the president's request, without the bubble-top on the limousine. Unlike the previous day, Yarborough rode with Vice President Johnson, Lady Bird Johnson, who sat between the two men in the back seat, and Secret Service agent Rufus Youngblood. Their Lincoln convertible was the fourth car in the parade. President Kennedy and his wife, Jacqueline, accompanied by Governor Connally and his wife, Nellie, rode in the second car. The car between Johnson and Yarborough's vehicle and the president's convertible contained Secret Service agents and two Kennedy aides. The motorcade departed Love Field in Dallas at noon for downtown. Forty minutes later President Kennedy was mortally wounded and Governor Connally suffered serious wounds. Secret Service agent Rufus Youngblood forced the Johnsons and Yarborough to the limousine's floor at the sound of the first shot. As the presidential limousine sped to nearby Parkland Hospital, Yarborough and the Johnsons followed. At the tumultuous scene at Parkland Hospital, Yarborough arrived in time to see the president and the governor taken into the emergency room. Reporters following the cars in the presidential motorcade began to arrive shortly thereafter. Ronnie Dugger, the publisher of the *Texas Observer* and a close acquaintance of Yarborough, was the first reporter to question him at the hospital. Yarborough barely responded. "It is too horrible to describe. They were seriously hurt," he whispered. Yarborough remarked that after the two victims were inside the emergency room, he watched Mrs. Kennedy enter. When asked where the president was shot, Yarborough replied, "I can't tell you where." If he saw Kennedy after the president was shot he undoubtedly knew the shots were fatal. As the motorcade approached the underpass on Elm Street, Yarborough told Dugger he heard three shots and "knew something was wrong." He said after the final shot, one of the Secret Service agents climbed on the car and was violently beating his fists on the hood. "This is a deed of horror. This is indescribable," he said as he and others stood in shock outside the hospital in the anxious minutes after the shooting. Doctors pronounced President Kennedy dead at 1 p.m. Published photographs taken outside the hospital emergency room immediately after Kennedy died showed a visibly shaken Yarborough with tears running from his eyes.[9]

"It was my honor and privilege to travel to Texas with the President and Mrs. Kennedy on the Presidential Jet on November 21 and 22," Yarborough wrote as he described his version of events on the fateful trip. Yarborough's unpublished, hand-written account of the Kennedy trip to Dallas covered seven legal pages. The text was part of a speech set for delivery on the Senate floor following the assassination to recount the senator's view of the trip to Texas and in defense of the people of Texas. Yarborough said that everywhere the president spoke, from scheduled events to spontaneous ones such as his speech on the open square in front of the Texas Hotel in Fort Worth, thousands of Texans appeared in appreciation. The great reception buoyed Yarborough's spirits and confidence. In San Antonio, Yarborough said that President Kennedy was "seen by more people than ever came to any parade in

San Antonio." Thousands more witnessed the motorcade in Houston, Fort Worth, and Dallas. Alongside the roads leading to the cities, people lined the streets for miles just to catch a glimpse of the president and his motorcade. Yarborough estimated that "more than a million Texans, more than 10% of the entire population of the state," saw President and Mrs. Kennedy. Everywhere, people were "exulting, cheering, waving, calling to the beloved and esteemed President." The overwhelming response convinced Yarborough that Kennedy was stronger than ever in Texas prior to his death. Yarborough tried to put the best light possible on Dallas in view of the animosity expressed toward that city after the assassination. In the days preceding Kennedy's arrival, right-wing militants flooded the city with hate-filled literature and the "American-Thinking Citizens of Dallas" took out a full page ad in the *Dallas Morning News* vilifying the president the day he was killed. Yarborough contradicted this image and stated "hundreds of thousands of friendly people massed in dense throngs on every street to show their love and affection for the President and Mrs. Kennedy." As they passed through the downtown streets of Dallas and neared the end of the parade route on Elm Street, Yarborough clearly heard the gunshots from above. President Kennedy was "cut down from behind by rifle fire by an assassin lurking in a dark corner of the fifth floor of that last building." Yarborough wrote they were only four minutes away from the scheduled speech at the Dallas Trade Mart when the "assassin's bullets snuffed out the President's life." He carefully deleted in red a remark which stated "when the President was murdered."[10]

In a private letter to his wife shortly after the assassination, Yarborough described his reactions after viewing the December 14, 1963, issue of the *Saturday Evening Post* that printed pictures of the president's final moments. He said he had an impression that after the first shot rang out, "the lead cars in the caravan either slowed down or came to a virtual stop." Whether or not the procession had come to a complete standstill, Yarborough was certain that he smelled gunpowder after hearing the three shots. "The rifle would have been up in the window on the fifth floor behind us, and the burnt powder was falling out into our car, as the assassin shot at an angle down into the back seet [sic] of the first car." Yarborough began hunting at an early age and was quite familiar with the sounds of rifle fire and the smell of gunpowder. He stated with absolute certainty that the shots and the gunpowder in the air came from overhead as the car continued along the path followed by the president's limousine.[11]

An interview with a foreign correspondent a few months after the assassination provided additional insights into Yarborough's memories of the event and its impact. The writer, an Irish correspondent who appeared with Yarborough at an awards banquet shortly before the Kennedy assassination, noted a tremendous change in the senator's appearance. "I was shaken by the change in him in the few weeks since we had last met. He looked older and greyer and his face had the unmistakable signs of one who is striving to live with great grief." Yarborough again described the events of November 22 in Dallas. At the moment shots rang out in the motorcade, Yarborough said his view was partially obscured by the Secret Service car behind the president and he could not tell who had been shot. But he again said that he clearly recognized the sounds as rifle shots. Once the lead car accelerated, Yarborough said they knew something was wrong. The car with Johnson and Yarborough followed Kennedy's to the hospital. Yarborough said that it was "a stupid, senseless waste of a wonderful life." He asked, "Why did it have to happen?" The reporter noted that Yarborough wept openly during this portion of the interview. Throughout this and other descriptions of the event, Yarborough never mentioned any conversation that took place with Vice President Johnson during the five minutes they sped to Parkland Hospital.[12]

Suspicions about a conspiracy involving foreign powers and even President Johnson himself circulated throughout the country within hours after the assassination. On November 29, President Johnson reacted to these stories and appointed Chief Justice Earl Warren to head a bipartisan panel to investigate the assassination and resolve the unanswered questions arising from the president's murder. As an eyewitness and a participant in the presidential motorcade, the Warren Commission requested information from Yarborough shortly after the assassination. In a letter to Chief Justice Warren, Yarborough stated that he did not believe the Secret Service responded quickly enough after the first shot was heard. After the second shot, he said, "I could smell gunpowder very strongly and the rancid smell of gunpowder stayed in our nostrils for minutes as we raced toward Parkland Hospital." Yarborough mentioned to Justice Warren that he was an experienced hunter and also served in the infantry during World War II. He said he presumed that the powder he smelled must have come "from behind the third car in which we were riding, and over our heads and over the heads of those in the second car, the Secret Service car, into President Kennedy." He stated that he could not be sure at the time what had happened to the president, but it was still "a horrible experience, to hear, to partially see . . . to smell the gunpowder from the assassin's murder weapon." Although he was an eyewitness to the event, riding only a few feet behind the president, the Warren Commission never called on Yarborough to testify during its ten-month investigation. Yarborough never discussed whether or not Lee Harvey Oswald was part of a larger conspiracy. But he definitely believed Lee Harvey Oswald was the lone gunman who shot President Kennedy in Dallas. His observations and statements supported the lone assassin theory based on his memory of the scene that day in Dallas as the motorcade passed below the Texas Schoolbook Depository Building. Yarborough also thought the fallen president was better served by deeds and words rather than to continuously speculate and dwell on the circumstances of the assassination. Despite their many disagreements, this was one point on which Yarborough and Lyndon Johnson now both agreed.[13]

In spite of animosity toward John Connally, Yarborough immediately sent a letter to the Texas governor as he recuperated from his wounds. "Opal and I send our heartfelt sympathy in the tragedy." He said that he prayed for a full and complete recovery and "a full life rich in years and in service." Yarborough also forwarded a message to the new president. "Under the great burdens and duties you bear as leader of America and the free world, I pledge my support in Texas and the nation." In the immediate aftermath Yarborough quickly forgot the turmoil and ill will created between the Texas officials prior to the Kennedy trip. He realized that Texans and the rest of America had a difficult task absorbing the death of the young president, especially in the circumstances in which the crime occurred. Television now played an integral role in communicating the news. The extensive coverage about the assassination placed all other local political concerns in the background. Yarborough recognized that Johnson needed immediate support in the task of holding the nation together. Likewise, the new president wanted encouragement and cooperation from his former adversaries, especially those like Yarborough and other liberals who were closely linked with Kennedy. Yarborough recognized that with Kennedy gone and Johnson in the Oval Office, uncertainties confronted nearly everyone in the nation as to how Lyndon Johnson would perform as president. As Yarborough knew only too well, Johnson had the image of a Texas "wheeler-dealer" who would stop at nothing to obtain his political objectives. But Yarborough also knew an earlier Johnson who touted the New Deal and worked for civil rights and better opportunities for the less fortunate. Yarborough had to be encouraged when he learned the president announced he intended to carry on the Kennedy ideas and legacy of a better America and world peace.[14]

Hundreds of letters, cards, and notes poured into Yarborough's office following the assassination. All of them expressed shock and sympathy and reflected the sorrow and anguish many Texans felt. The correspondence came from many of Yarborough's longtime friends and supporters. Local officials, party leaders, businessmen, and school children sent letters and suggestions of ways to honor the fallen president. Many of these individuals, who were sympathetic and embarrassed that the assassination took place in Dallas, suggested that some type of memorial be constructed. One recommendation included five thousand yellow roses, others suggested a simple cross, preservation of the presidential limousine at the Smithsonian, and even simple poems. Out of respect for Kennedy and because of his deep feelings for the nation, Yarborough shelved his political attacks on Connally and Johnson. He realized that recovery from the shocking event would take a considerable amount of time. But events in Texas quickly returned him to the reality of politics and the unsettled affairs at home.[15]

Only a few weeks after the assassination, Yarborough's actions became a point of controversy. Published accounts about Kennedy's trip rekindled internal political fires even as state leaders defended their state in the national media. In a December article by Leslie Carpenter published in several of the state's newspapers, Yarborough's behavior in San Antonio and Houston came under attack. Also, Congressman Jim Wright's name again surfaced as a potential challenger to Yarborough in the 1964 Democratic primary. Unidentified sources stated that Yarborough's refusal to ride in the parade car with Vice President Johnson in both San Antonio and Houston embarrassed the late president. While they were in Fort Worth, President Kennedy supposedly "spoke firmly and in tough language" to Yarborough. The president allegedly said, "you will either ride in the same car with Lyndon Johnson in Dallas or you will walk." Also, on that same morning, after a Kennedy aide secured a pledge from Yarborough that he would use the speech to call for unity in the Democratic party in Texas, Yarborough was added to the speaker's list at the scheduled Austin dinner. Only then did Yarborough bow to the "pressure of President Kennedy's envoy." What went unreported was Kennedy's conversation with Yarborough and his remarks to Johnson on the plane trip to Fort Worth. Instead of lecturing Yarborough, Kennedy apparently unloaded on Johnson about Connally's treatment of Yarborough during the first day. Neither Kennedy nor Johnson would benefit from any news stories that pictured divisions within the party or a snub of the Democratic senator from Texas. As they posed for photos the next morning in Fort Worth, Yarborough was the only man smiling behind the president; both Johnson and Connally appeared glum. With his complaints about his place in the Austin celebration apparently resolved, Yarborough enthusiastically jumped into the back seat of the convertible with Johnson and Lady Bird, the fourth car in the Dallas motorcade.[16]

Yarborough quietly responded to both the political and the personal attacks. He and his staff launched a series of letters urging Jim Wright to defer any decision to run against Yarborough in the 1964 primary. With even more vigor, Yarborough responded to what he called "an infamous lie, written solely for the purpose of slandering me." He believed the story of his resistance was planted because the "martyred President was dead and not here to refute it in person." Yarborough claimed it was part of an ongoing campaign launched by Connally and the governor's friends who were still trying to recruit a primary opponent for the 1964 Senate race. Yarborough believed that Governor Connally asked for President Kennedy's assistance in removing him from the Senate. "Of course, President Kennedy had no part in this," the senator said. In addition, Yarborough maintained that in earlier meetings "Connally tried to persuade President Kennedy to leave me off the president's plane, and not invite me to Texas." Yarborough insisted the president and his staff contacted him on three occasions urging him to be on the plane to Texas and on the return flight to Washington, D.C. In another letter, Yarborough described his concerns with the press attacks. Yarborough said he considered the president a friend and an ally since serving with Kennedy on the Labor Committee. On the flight to Texas from Washington, Yarborough said that Kennedy told him twice—"Ralph, we are friends." But he thought the president's remarks seemed "very strange" for "Presidents generally and President Kennedy in particular are not demonstrative men and say little about personal friendships." On an earlier trip to Arlington National Cemetery in the summer of 1963, Yarborough said he remembered President Kennedy looking at Lee's Mansion and saying, "I could stay here forever." Looking back on the two events, Yarborough wondered whether from "all the hate campaigns against him over the country he had a latent thought that he might be cut down before his time."[17]

Yarborough never made any of his complaints on the matter public. Within a short time after the assassination, he and Lyndon Johnson had reached a political accommodation. The latest attempt to discredit him did little damage for most Texans still mourned the president and looked on these political spats as meaningless. Yarborough admitted in a subsequent letter that he wanted to publicly respond to the story, but friends and staff persuaded him to wait. His patience seemed to be rewarded, because after several days "others had answered in a so much more effective manner than I could have personally, that any answer by me was unnecessary." Yarborough believed the story was planted by his political enemies in the Connally camp and the Johnson White House "as part of a clique plan to try to push Jim Wright into the race. Now they say Jim Wright put the story in the paper. I think all of them had some hand in it." Newspaper stories soon appeared that Congressman Wright held no interest in the race.[18]

Years after the assassination, Connally insisted that Yarborough instigated all of the problems during the presidential trip to Texas. Connally stated that President Kennedy believed that Yarborough refused an offer to ride with Vice President Johnson in the parade. Before the November 22 Fort Worth breakfast, President Kennedy asked Connally, "Did you know that Yarborough refused to ride with Lyndon yesterday?" Connally said the president then remarked, "What's the matter with that fellow?" and that "He'll ride with him today or he'll walk." After President Kennedy had an "earnest conversation" with Yarborough, the senator rode in the car with Johnson. "I'm fairly sure you could have fit into a thimble the number of words they exchanged," Connally commented. Connally said that after the assassination "there is no doubt that this fed the gradual growth of a public impression that the President went to Texas to settle a feud." But aside from telling Yarborough to ride in the car with Johnson, "there was no more to it than that. It was a case of bad manners, not bad politics. Kennedy was astute enough to know that one can lead to the other."[19]

Yarborough denied that such an exchange ever occurred. To the contrary, the president may have expressed strong words to Johnson and possibly to Connally over their feuds with Yarborough. Some Yarborough supporters stated that the senator told them that he chose to ride with Congressman Gonzalez in San Antonio and Congressman Albert Thomas in Houston primarily because they were extremely popular in their respective communities. (In Houston, Yarborough was originally scheduled to ride with Mayor Lewis Cutrer.) Yarborough staff members worked to alert Kennedy's aides to the tensions stemming from the seating assignments and Yarborough's exclusion from planned events, as well as those originating in the long-standing feud. When the presidential party reached Fort Worth on the evening of November 21, the Kennedy staff took charge and made parade-car seating assignments for the following day in Dallas and Austin.[20]

The exchanges in the aftermath of the assassination illustrate the depths to which personal malice and rancor drove the political process in Texas. In the difficult days after Kennedy's death, a temporary peace briefly ended hostilities out of respect for the fallen president and in recognition of the difficult job President Johnson faced. The period of cooperation ended quickly as Yarborough and Connally supporters realized that both men faced campaigns in 1964. Lyndon Johnson was now president and a unifying force for the nation. But his ascension to the office only temporarily quelled the battle between the liberal and conservative forces for control of the Texas Democratic party and the future direction of the state.

11 The Struggle for the Soul of the Nation

The contentious struggle between Yarborough supporters and Johnson-Connally backers subsided in 1964 but never entirely disappeared. All three of the state leaders in the Kennedy entourage that fateful November day became the beneficiaries of the widespread sympathy. As president, Johnson solidified public support with his leadership skills and calming influence in the uncertain aftermath of the assassination. Johnson carried forward many Kennedy administration initiatives and expanded them into what became known as the Great Society. Yarborough, because of his close philosophical identification with Kennedy, gained wider public support in Texas. Connally, the wounded governor, also became more popular with people across the state. All three of these leaders approached the 1964 election year with a similar agenda—appeal to a broader group of Democrats and win a convincing victory at the polls. Yarborough and Connally remained committed to Johnson, but both leaders hoped to assume the leadership of Texas Democrats and become the heir apparent to LBJ. Neither Yarborough nor Connally were willing to risk an open break with the president during 1964 for practical as well as sentimental reasons. Like Johnson, these two political rivals wanted their own popular mandates for future political battles. However, their mutual dislike and distrust continued to boil like water in a hot kettle.

Yarborough, frequently at odds with LBJ for the past decade, began his public rapprochement with President Johnson in the first few weeks of the new president's administration. A few days after Johnson took office, Yarborough publicly praised him as a man of "boldness, action and courage." Yarborough noted the difference in style between Kennedy the "Harvard man" and Johnson the "Texas man," but they were similar in ambition and ability. Because Yarborough held Kennedy in such high esteem, lauding Johnson and placing him on the same level with the fallen president was high praise from the Texas senator. When Yarborough also sent personal letters to President Johnson to convey his support and cooperation, Johnson recipro-

*Ralph and Opal Yarborough greet President and Lady Bird Johnson on their
arrival at a December 1963 reception given in their honor at the Senator's Austin
home. Johnson and Yarborough set aside their differences immediately following
the Kennedy assassination. United Press International Photo.*

cated and invited Yarborough as the only guest to one of his infamous, late
night dips at the White House pool. During a holiday trip to Central Texas in
December 1963, President Johnson and Lady Bird stopped at the Yarborough
home in Austin. Ralph and Opal scheduled a reception for the new president
and invited a number of liberal leaders. Yarborough described the event as
symbolic of how tragedy and national purpose reinstated the close relationship between the two Texans. Yarborough was still deeply shaken by the assassination and understood the trauma Johnson and people across the nation
suffered. As a student of American history, Yarborough frequently equated
the loss with the loss of President Lincoln nearly a century before. He realized that President Johnson and the country faced an uncertain future as they
entered the contemplated second Reconstruction for Texas and the rest of the
Old South. Yarborough made many efforts to commend Johnson through the
early months of 1964 and praised the president as the "architect of the safe
transition." The sudden change in the political order transcended the divi-

sion between Yarborough and Johnson and the rapprochement soon would be tested.[1]

Prior to Kennedy's assassination in late 1963, a number of prominent Democrats considered challenging Yarborough. Former Governor Allan Shivers, Yarborough's longtime foe from the 1950's, seriously contemplated a race to unseat Texas' senior senator. Shivers still maintained his old animosity toward Yarborough and believed he could defeat the incumbent in the May 1964 primary. Other possible opponents included John Van Cronkhite, the Austin public relations executive and Shivers' team member who worked against Yarborough in the 1950's. Also, Congressmen Joe Kilgore of McAllen, Jim Wright of Fort Worth, and former congressman Lloyd Bentsen Jr. evaluated their chances at unseating Yarborough. Kilgore, Bentsen, and Wright each counted on the behind-the-scenes support of Vice President Johnson, but the assassination had changed the political temperature faster than a Texas blue norther. With the exception of Shivers, the potential rivals no longer contemplated the race because Johnson considered Yarborough's reelection a part of his own presidential strategy. LBJ's visit to the Yarborough home in January symbolized more than a restoration of their working relationship—it was also a message to Democrats in Texas that Johnson wanted no disagreements now that he had the responsibility for leading the grief-stricken nation.

The new president had a different perspective on Texas politics and his relationship with Senator Yarborough. Johnson realized that his new domestic agenda wrapped in the Kennedy legacy appealed to Yarborough and liberals across the nation. Because Republican John Tower held the other Senate seat from Texas, Johnson needed a friend who would work with his administration and not create additional problems back home. Johnson also knew Yarborough had the strong support of organized labor, national liberals, and minorities. Johnson had a mixed record with the unions as a senator, and labor leaders played a pivotal role in national Democratic politics. Now that he had a national agenda to consider, Johnson realized that undermining Yarborough in Texas would make his own political situation more difficult with liberals and labor at the national level. Johnson understood that many of the national Democratic leaders who supported Kennedy were suspicious of his commitment to civil rights and other items crucial to the liberal agenda. Johnson needed to unite all the Democratic factions as he faced his own party's nomination process in 1964. He then had to compete as the first southern presidential nominee since the Civil War against an unknown Republican nominee. In reality, Johnson knew he had little to gain and much to lose in challenging Yarborough. Johnson finally realized his goal of gaining the presidency, a role played before a national audience—not just before the folks on the stage back home. Also, Johnson had a personal interest in controlling conservative Democrats in Texas. He had no desire to see the dirty laundry from the back alley fights between Texas liberals and conservatives being aired before the nation on the evening news or on the front page of the *New York Times*.

Yarborough had other advantages working for him in 1964. He enjoyed seven years of Senate experience led by a veteran staff in Washington and in Texas. Throughout much of his first term as senator, Yarborough's only son, Richard, toiled as the main cog in the Washington office that kept the legislative and political wheels turning. Dick, as his friends and coworkers called the young Yarborough, was as reserved as his father was outgoing. He also suffered from arthritis, which plagued him much of his life. But Dick knew how to keep the political bridges maintained between Yarborough and other public officials and constituents. Senator Yarborough composed most of his own speeches and committee schedule but was never adept at managing a large organization. The Senate staff relied on Dick as the central figure in resolving the everyday problems and keeping the office running as smoothly as possible. He became the calming force in the center of the frequent political and legislative storms. Dick passed judgment on letters, made critical scheduling assignments, and provided timely rulings on legislation for his father. Aides frequently ran ideas and proposals in front of Dick to enlist his support before approaching the senator. The staff viewed him as the "court of last resort" in the office, especially when one of the aides ran afoul of the senator when they had made a mistake or fallen behind in their job. Having the senator's son on your side proved to be a valuable asset should a confrontation arise.[2]

Ralph Yarborough's enthusiasm grew, for he truly believed in the many causes that steered his legislative efforts. Although he sometimes opposed his fellow southern senators on domestic issues, he established working relationships with most of them. His best friend remained Tennessee senator Albert Gore Sr. The Gores and the Yarboroughs lived in the Methodist Building apartments only a block away from the Senate offices. Gore and Yarborough were close philosophically and the two couples often attended social affairs and dinners together. Not one to frequent the social scene, Yarborough spent most of his waking hours at his capital office. He carried small black notebooks which contained typewritten lists of Senate bills with their descriptions and the committees to which they were assigned. He kept his own bills separate from other current legislation. Any bill with his name on it meant "he was enthusiastically for it," legislative aide Charles Caldwell recalled. When working with other senators and congressional members on his legislation, Yarborough exercised a degree of intensity rare in even the most dedicated public servants. Yarborough demanded a lot of himself and he likewise expected the same degree of commitment from his staff. He hired supporters from Texas and veterans from Washington. Early in his Senate term he had broken the color barrier when he hired the first Mexican Americans, Sandra Padilla and Carlos Rivera. In early 1963, Marian Robinson became the first African American in the Texas senator's Washington office and the first black woman to work for a senator from the South.

Many staff members recall being chastised by the senator for their lack of compassion when they failed to deliver timely information on an assignment. Yarborough worked nearly every hour he was not asleep, and he expected the same commitment from others. Yarborough cajoled and pushed his staff members to excel and outwork the competition—especially since they worked to change the course of history. When one young aide complained that they could not complete all of their work, the senator's reply was "don't ever say you can't do something." In addition to adopting Yarborough's work ethic, each employee subscribed to his political philosophy. According to Caldwell, everyone who worked there even for a day knew the enemy: "Dixiecrats and John Connally."[3]

Yarborough's work habits and dedication were legendary, but he was often his own worst enemy because of his attention to detail and lack of organization. His desk was probably the most cluttered and disorganized of any senator's in Washington. He insisted on personally responding to all mail from his family members and had each relative's letter marked with a special YARBOROUGH FAMILY MAIL sticker. Selected supporters obtained other unique markings. With many relatives and close friends, the mail quickly piled up on his desk. Mounds of yellow legal pads with the senator's handwritten notes added to the congestion. Aide Jim Boren recalled that the staff had to move in extra tables just to accommodate the letters awaiting his signature. "It was like he was still on the bench way back in Austin, Texas, rather than dealing with the fact that he was now a U.S. Senator," Caldwell observed. Earlier in his career, Yarborough grew accustomed to doing much of his own legal and campaign work without funds and little staff. As the senior senator from Texas, some of his old habits and personal quirks interfered with the efficient operation of his office. This worrisome trait caused headaches for his staff and often contributed to strained relationships with constituents and other lawmakers. But as he approached reelection in 1964, these were only minor problems for Yarborough as he neared the peak of his popularity.

JOHNSON AND YARBOROUGH COMBINE FORCES

Many Texas Democrats were willing to lay aside their ongoing internal struggles for the sake of unity in 1964. However, Allan Shivers had no qualms about breaking the unwritten peace by challenging Yarborough and crossing President Johnson. In January 1964, Shivers secretly commissioned a poll assessing his political prospects and Yarborough's popularity. Shivers was no doubt surprised with the results. Yarborough tallied nearly 50 percent of the poll in a four-way race defeating Shivers, Wright, and Van Cronkhite. Furthermore, when Texas voters were asked whom they would most like to see defeated in a race, Shivers led with 29 percent compared to 20 percent for Yarborough. Finally, the poll showed that in a one-on-one campaign between Yarborough and Shivers, the incumbent would win handily by a nearly two-to-one margin. Shivers' only hope for defeating Yarborough would be with Connally's active support "with both hammering hard to deflate the incumbent Senator's popularity." As much as Connally wanted to help, his first allegiance was to Lyndon Johnson. Recognizing Yarborough's strong popularity coupled with Johnson's support, Shivers realized the 1964 race was a losing proposition. Shivers had faced similar circumstances in 1956 when, challenging Johnson and a united front, he lost control of the Texas Democratic party. He backed out of the Senate race but remained one of Yarborough's staunchest critics.[4]

At the White House, the new president angered some of his old friends by his alliance with Yarborough. Johnson told his close friend and *Austin American* publisher Houston Harte that Connally became infuriated when he learned that the president wanted Yarborough to run unopposed in the primary. Connally and others wanted Shivers to run. The president complained to SDEC Chairman Frank Erwin about Connally's activities. "We're going to have to have a knock-down dragout in Texas at the convention and I'll just have to pay all my attention," Johnson lectured Erwin. "Now the truth on this is Yarborough votes with me more than anybody in the Texas delegation," the president revealed. He said Yarborough was not his first choice for the office "but I damned sure don't want two Republicans up here voting against me and I have enough trouble with just one." He concluded, "Yarborough has been as meek as a lamb ever since I became President." Johnson stayed very close to the Texas political situation. He became even angrier with Connally when the governor continued to seek an opponent for Yarborough. He said he had called to Texas fifteen times to speak with the governor, but Connally had never called him. Johnson complained about his former aide's lack of understanding about the larger political scene and his betrayal by associating with Allan Shivers. He warned Erwin that he was spending too much time worrying about Connally and the politics back in Texas instead of pressing national concerns in Washington. "If he hates so bitter, and is so vindictive, that he's just got to have a man up here to pull out this fellow that's voting with me, then I can't help it," Johnson stated in frustration. Erwin complained that the president had "run off with his life long enemy" but pledged his support for Johnson's position. The president's persistence finally paid off. Shivers dropped out and South Texas congressman Joe Kilgore announced he would not challenge Yarborough in the Democratic primary. Congressman Jim Wright's last-minute flirtation candidacy never materialized into anything more, which left Yarborough with no experienced political opponent.[5]

Yarborough believed he held a commanding position in 1964 even without the president's behind the scenes efforts. Chuck Caldwell, one of the Senate aides still active in Texas politics, raised the issue of running without an opponent. Yarborough indulged in a rare moment of cursing (which very few people recall). Caldwell said as he drove the senator in a car, Yarborough pounded his fist on the dashboard in a fury. The senator suddenly exclaimed, "I want those sons of bitches to run somebody against me because I want to beat the hell out of them." Yarborough loved the political fray and was most energetic and persuasive while on the campaign trail. He could not wait to return to Texas for his round-the-clock tours of the state. Yarborough chastised Caldwell and others who even mentioned the possibility of a walk. Yarborough preached Democratic unity but he wanted a convincing victory to reinforce his position for future battles with John Connally.[6]

One major challenger who was clearly not under Johnson's influence entered the Senate race at the last minute. Gordon McLendon, a Dallas conservative businessman and a popular Texas radio personality, joined the race on the final day before the filing deadline. Known best as "the Old Scotsman," McLendon was recognized throughout Texas and much of the nation. His radio "Game of the Day" baseball broadcasts, which were merely descriptions of games with sound effects in the background, were very popular until they went off the air. The Liberty Broadcasting System, owned by McLendon and his father, became the second-largest radio network in the nation by 1952 but dissolved after a court battle with baseball owners over McLendon's simulated game coverage. He later became a pioneer in radio station formatting in the 1950's and owned stations throughout Texas and the nation. By the early 1960's, he was a millionaire and had created a strong radio network in the state. McLendon frequently provided political commentary on his shows but had never run for political office before filing in the 1964 Democratic Primary. He intended to be the next W. Lee "Pappy" O'Daniel and rise from political obscurity through entertainment and his access to the radio stations.[7]

NEW CHARGES FROM BILLIE SOL ESTES

After McLendon officially filed to run against Yarborough, the challenger and the incumbent launched attacks. McLendon made a dash around the state, often appearing with Hollywood actors John Wayne and Chill Wills, two personal friends with similar conservative political views. The incumbent wasted no time, immediately characterizing McLendon as a "Republican stalking horse." The fact that McLendon's Liberty Broadcasting System declared bankruptcy in 1952 with $750,000 in debts led Yarborough to charge McLendon with financially irresponsibility. McLendon, in turn, attacked Yarborough's Senate voting record. The race attracted attention in the early weeks, but the relative quiet abruptly changed following publication of an interview by the *Dallas Morning News* on April 12, 1964. Estes, convicted and serving time in federal prison, claimed that he gave Yarborough $50,000 in cash in 1960, when federal law limited annual donations to office holders to $5,000. McLendon held a statewide television broadcast on April 25 in which he produced two witnesses who claimed they saw Estes personally give Yarborough the envelope with the cash. These new developments resurrected the 1962 stories of Estes' contributions to Democratic officeholders, including Lyndon Johnson and John Kennedy. The alleged Yarborough $50,000 cash contribution drew headlines. Yarborough immediately labeled the event "an infamous lie," but the damage was done. McLendon made the affair the centerpiece of his primary campaign against Yarborough in the weeks before the May 2 primary, frequently airing the charges on news casts at his radio stations.[8]

Yarborough, who weathered the Estes scandal in 1962, realized that future opponents would drag it up again. However, the newest charge of a $50,000 cash delivery added a new, more dangerous element. Yarborough and his closest advisors considered the story the silver bullet that could kill his reelection. The senator and his campaign quickly responded. Yarborough viewed McLendon's charges as a personal attack on his integrity, an asset he prized higher than all others. First, Yarborough called on Attorney General Robert Kennedy to request an FBI investigation. These findings would substantiate his innocence and embarrass both McLendon and the *Dallas Morning News*. The Yarborough campaign and Walter Hall complained to the Federal Communications Commission (FCC) about the McLendon radio stations carrying the "news" story. A few days later, U.S. Attorney Jack Miller released information stating that one of McLendon's witnesses in his broadcast had recanted his story. Yarborough was on his way to his final campaign telecast when a highway patrolman intercepted his car between Dallas and Fort Worth, telling him to contact his Washington office on the Miller announcement. Yarborough then responded with his own statewide television broadcast. He denied any transaction with Estes and provided his own witnesses who said they never saw the senator accept any money from the convicted swindler. Yarborough's counterattack the day before the primary reversed any momentum McLendon gained from the Estes story.[9]

On election day, Yarborough easily defeated McLendon with 905,000 votes to 672,000 as he carried 213 counties. For the first time, Yarborough outspent his opponent, thanks to the fundraising efforts of J. R. Parten, Walter Hall, and many Johnson Democrats who united behind his candidacy. The FBI investigation coupled with Yarborough's reputation for honesty thwarted yet another potentially career-ending affair that involved Billie Sol Estes. The political peace between Yarborough and the Johnson-Connally faction of the Democratic party survived its first hurdle of the year. But the Estes story would never go away as long as Yarborough held office.[10]

CIVIL RIGHTS AND THE THURMOND-YARBOROUGH MATCH

At the Texas Democratic party's first convention in May 1964, the delegates remained committed to presenting a united front instead of engaging in their traditional squabbles. Connally and Yarborough both won convincing victories in the primary elections. Their supporters waged a few behind-the-scenes battles over delegates, but the Houston convention was a far cry from the earlier donnybrooks between Texas Democrats. The relatively brief five-hour convention on June 16 was, according to newspaper accounts, "conducted in an atmosphere of relative harmony by Texas Democratic Standards." Delegates chose Governor Connally to head the ninety-nine-member delegation to the Los Angeles national convention. The Texas group contained representatives from both the conservative and liberal factions and was instructed to put forth every effort to secure Johnson's nomination and victory. Working behind the scenes, President Johnson "helped tie a number of loose strings of discord to keep Texas Democrats from airing their bitter liberal-conservative fight before the national eye." While Johnson received credit in the press for his work, Yarborough also counseled his supporters to maintain a civil front. Yarborough knew that thanks to his own initiatives and with the president's cooperation, he now had the backing of many of the conservative and moderate Democrats who opposed him in the past. The mutual political interests of both the president and the senator provided the oil for calming the once-turbulent Texas political seas in 1964.[11]

The summer of 1964 burst forth as one of the most intense, historic periods in the nation's history. The Johnson administration risked its prestige and honor to secure passage of the Civil Rights Act of 1964. In what many historians have referred to as the "Second Reconstruction," the House of Representatives passed the measure by a two-to-one margin in the spring. Proponents called the bill a "struggle for the soul of the nation." However, Senate passage appeared uncertain even with Johnson's full, public support. Senators Richard Russell (D-Georgia), Allen J. Ellender (D-Louisiana), John Stennis (D-Mississippi), and Lister Hill (D-Alabama) teamed together to pick apart the bill piece by piece. Senator Russell captured the essence of southern opposition when he stated the legislation would "turn our social order upside down." The debate ranged for months in the Senate until early June. Yarborough spoke in favor of amendments to preserve trial by jury and for the cloture vote to end debate on the bill. This marked the first time the Senate invoked cloture on a southern filibuster against a civil rights measure. Yarborough withheld a public commitment on the measure but never joined the other southern Democrats who filibustered on the Senate floor. Tower, the only Republican senator from the south, joined with the eighteen Senate Democrats opposing the bill. In Texas, Yarborough assured supporters, especially African Americans, that a bill would pass. Yarborough, the grandson of Confederate veterans, had voted for all civil rights legislation during the previous two presidential administrations and maintained his record in the Johnson administration. He correctly perceived that he could withstand any political damage from the vote in the 1964 election. He also realized that events in Washington and the rest of the south were dramatically beginning to transform the region. In other circumstances, Yarborough enjoyed playing the antagonist simply to distinguish himself from other southern Democrats. In this case, he expressed his beliefs and convictions and became part of history. He and Senator Al Gore Sr. of Tennessee were the only southern senators to favor the 1964 Civil Rights Act when the Senate passed the bill in June.[12]

Yarborough chose June 19, or "Juneteenth," as their day of liberation is known to African Americans in Texas, for a public statement. He said he voted in favor of the Civil Rights Act because it represented the "consensus of American thought" which would end what Yarborough termed as the "greatest internal danger" the nation faced. Privately, legislative aide Alex Dickie recalled Yarborough telling him that the vote could spell defeat in the upcoming election. Yarborough predicted a Republican opponent would use his stands on behalf of civil rights as a weapon against him in East Texas. "But if I had it to do over I would vote the same," Yarborough maintained.[13]

Civil rights legislation became a centerpiece of Lyndon Johnson's administration. Yarborough held the distinction of being the only southern senator to support every significant modern civil rights bills from 1957 to 1970. The historic vote in 1964 led to the Voting Rights Act of 1965. Yarborough worked for passage of this bill to break the wall of legal barriers erected by Texas and other southern states to restrict minority voter registration and participation. In doing so, Yarborough put himself ahead of public opinion in Texas. He joined President Johnson as both men seized the opportunity to break away from their traditions and southern political culture. LBJ needed the assistance of a handful of southerners for his initiatives. Throughout Johnson's term as president, congressional and senate Republicans united with most southern Democrats in opposition to federal civil rights legislation. Yarborough distinguished himself as the president's staunchest supporter from the former Confederate states. The former Johnson adversary became an energetic advocate and sponsor of many of the administration's bills on civil rights, housing, and education.

In doing so, Yarborough defied conventional political wisdom and followed his own path. He first chartered his course when he entered the Senate in 1957 and supported the Civil Rights bill while simultaneously opposing most other Dixie Democrats in his refusal to sign the Southern Manifesto. Yarborough's Senate office received thousands of letters on civil rights issues throughout his term of office, the most of any subject matter. According to staff members, the overwhelming majority of the correspondence opposed civil rights legislation. Staff members had an easy task convincing Yarborough that opposition letters were not representative of the majority of Texans since many organizations sponsored letter drives on controversial issues like civil rights. These mass mailings had little influence on Yarborough's vote because he generally voted his convictions, even during the months leading up to reelection.[14]

Of the many letters he received on the civil rights issue, Yarborough received one that made a solid impression. A motel owner in the small community of Wharton sent a plea to Yarborough asking him to support the Civil Rights bill of 1964. The author explained he favored the landmark legislation not on principle or ideals, but because "it's simply good business." The letter explained how the lodging owner turned down many customers because "they just happened to be Negroes." If he had let them register and stay, there would have been "hell to pay" from other business owners in the community. The letter's originator explained that he knew Yarborough's vote would be difficult, but passage of the bill would take "this heavy load off people like me." From a practical economic standpoint, one representative small-business owner knew that federal action, cloaked in dollars and cents, could overcome local officials and long-standing custom. Yarborough made numerous copies of the letter and distributed them to friends and other senators before the historic vote. The statement provided the significant point that there were those who quietly hoped for change as well as the more vocal opponents who bombarded officials and the news media.[15]

Yarborough appeared uncharacteristically reserved during floor debate on the Civil Rights bill. But his confrontational style brought him national headlines and led to some scathing criticism from his detractors in Texas. In what began as a "joke" and a friendly tug of war, Yarborough and Senator Strom Thurmond (D-South Carolina) ended up in a ten-minute wrestling match outside a Senate hearing room in the summer of 1964. The Washington, D.C., heat coupled with contentious civil rights debates often resulted in fiery exchanges between senators. But Yarborough and Thurmond took their differences one step further in what turned out to be a nationally publicized incident. The confrontation exhibited the lengths to which Yarborough went to express his views on civil rights and issues of morality. Thurmond in particular was very bitter over the 1964 Civil Rights Act and eventually deserted Democrats for the Republicans after the vote.

The confrontation began during a Senate Commerce Committee meeting to approve the nomination of Leroy Collins as the civil rights mediation chief a few weeks after passage of the Civil Rights Act. The Senate Commerce Committee convened unsuccessfully several times in an attempt to approve the nomination. Thurmond, who opposed the Collins nomination, skipped the committee meetings in an effort to deny the candidate the position. As reported by the newspapers around the nation, on July 8 Yarborough was standing in the doorway to the committee room and noticed Thurmond passing by. Yarborough attempted to pull him into the meeting, but Thurmond pulled Yarborough into the hall. "I'll make an agreement with you, Ralph," Thurmond challenged. "If I can keep you out, you won't go in, and if you can drag me in, I'll stay there." Both men took off their jackets and began wrestling on the floor until the lighter Thurmond pinned Yarborough on the floor, where he remained for several minutes vainly struggling to escape. Senator Frank Lausche (D-Ohio) arrived and warned both men that they were risking heart attacks. Senator Warren Magnuson (D-Washington), the committee chair, also arrived and told the men to "break this up." At that point, both red-faced senators got up off the floor and went into the hearing room. Later, after the committee meeting concluded, Thurmond and Yarborough appeared together smiling in the hall. Yarborough stated it was merely a "friendly wrestling match. I had the weight advantage, but he has taken secret guerrilla training and knows the holds." Thurmond stated that it was "all in jest." The two sixty-one-year-old senators later held a brief news conference to demonstrate their congeniality. The committee finally voted on the Collins nomination. He was approved on a 16-to-1 vote with the only dissent coming from Senator Thurmond. Yarborough lost the match but won the vote.[16]

After the story made the newspapers, Yarborough received correspondence about the incident criticizing his behavior in the "wrestling match" with Senator Thurmond. "I have never witnessed a 'live' wrestling match, but it would indeed be a treat to witness any match in which you would participate," one critical constituent wrote. He suggested that after the 1964 election, Yarborough should contact a local wrestling promoter in Lubbock for a job. Another critic expressed dismay at the senator's activities and attacked him for his votes favoring civil rights. "You see, we Texans are beginning to realize that out of 11 former Confederate States, and its 22 Senators, ONLY Mr. Ralph Yarborough was a stanch and dedicated supporter of the Civil Rights Bill." Not surprisingly, most Texas newspaper editorials roundly condemned Yarborough for the episode. The *Dallas Morning News* editors, long opponents of the senator, caustically wrote, "we always figured Yarborough was the 100th smartest man in the U.S. Senate but now it's doubtful he could make it with the slow-moving group in the gym class either."[17]

Not everyone was critical. Some encouraged Yarborough and congratulated him on his actions. "If you must duel with a physical culture faddist, insist on choice of weapons, say grammar or rationality at ten paces," Texas judge Franklin Jones wrote. Others congratulated him on his readiness to fight while another stated "us Texans like vinegar with our greens." A short note from one admirer said they were concerned with his well-being and enclosed a newspaper ad for karate lessons. The incident may have cost Yarborough some support, but he certainly gained publicity that he seldom received in the Texas daily newspapers. Many Texans appreciated Yarborough for his tenacity and willingness to take public stands on unpopular positions. Although he was the technical loser in the actual match, the embarrassment probably turned in his favor once the initial story passed. He enhanced his reputation by living up to the Texan image of fighting for one's independence, even if it meant going to the mat at the U.S. Capitol. In a larger perspective, the wrestling match illustrated the tensions among southerners over civil rights. The struggle was indicative of the resistance to integration by most elected officials in the former Confederate states. Yarborough's media critics believed the incident would harm his reelection efforts, but the apparent loss became a gain. As events unfolded, 1964 turned out to be a Democratic year—especially in Texas.[18]

BUSH VERSUS YARBOROUGH IN 1964

To challenge Yarborough in 1964, Texas Republicans nominated a wealthy young man who moved to Texas from Connecticut. George Bush was a decorated World War II pilot, Yale graduate, and a millionaire, based on his ownership of the Zapata Offshore Oil Company. Bush posed a serious threat to Yarborough and the Democrats in the November general election. The young Republican moved his business and family from Midland to Houston in 1958. He became a GOP candidate for Senate in 1964 when he defeated Jack Cox, the 1962 Republican gubernatorial candidate who nearly upset Connally in the general election. Bush attended the 1964 Republican National Convention as a Goldwater delegate. He opposed the Civil Rights Act of 1964 and announced his opposition to other domestic efforts originating from Washington. He aligned himself with other conservative causes dear to the Republican right, which included arming a Cuban government in exile, opposition to foreign aid, and a call for the United States to withdraw from the United Nations if the People's Republic of China gained admittance to the world organization. Bush's stands made him popular with the extremists dominating the Texas Republican party that year, but he left himself wide open to attacks from Yarborough and the Democrats.[19]

Yarborough, the unlucky candidate in many previous elections, appeared fortunate in 1964. He benefited from his resurrected friendship with LBJ, the president's unprecedented popularity in Texas, and Barry Goldwater's perceived extremism. In spite of his ongoing differences with Governor Connally, the state party organization outwardly presented a united effort for all its nominees. Johnson wanted a clean sweep in his home state to add to his national mandate for his administration. For his part, Yarborough was also primed and ready for the general election. Democrats preached unity but Yarborough ran his own separate program as before. His Senate office staff and campaign organization were coordinated. Organizers worked in the urban minority communities as part of VOTE, a program funded by organized labor and eastern foundations to eliminate the poll tax and register minority voters. Workers in the VOTE program prepared to mobilize thousands of these new voters. He also had unprecedented financial assistance and the seemingly unlimited support of the Johnson-Humphrey campaign. The pall of the Kennedy assassination still haunted the minds of Americans. Most Texans knew of Yarborough's participation in Kennedy's final days and were aware of his close association with the martyred president. Yarborough and many other Democrats had the added benefit of the Republican presidential nominee, conservative Arizona senator Barry Goldwater. The GOP nominee proved to be a continuing drag and embarrassment to other Republicans as the 1964 elections approached. Goldwater opposed civil rights and most of the federal antipoverty measures launched by the Johnson administration. His declaration that "extremism in the defense of liberty is no vice" pleased the archconservatives in the GOP, but most Americans viewed Goldwater as a dangerous extremist.[20]

Along with the presidential contest, the Senate race was the key election in Texas. The GOP hoped to expand its base in the state and develop a legitimate second-party organization. The Senate seat appeared to be the easiest target, and Bush wasted no time in attacking Yarborough. Bush charged that the incumbent demonstrated fiscal irresponsibility because of his "excessive concern with the welfare of pressure groups." According to the Republican challenger, Yarborough placed "national partisan politics above the opinions and interests of the people he was elected to represent. Clearly he feels obligated to listen to voices other than those of a majority of Texans." Referring to the well-publicized match with Senator Thurmond, Bush stated that never before had a senator from Texas "shown such disregard for the dignity of his office by rolling around on the floor in a schoolboy wrestling match while colleagues and reporters watched in undisguised amazement." Bush attempted to expand his appeal to conservative and moderate Democrats as he tried to portray Yarborough as out of step with ordinary Texans. "Although I am a lifelong Republican, I respect all Democrats of conviction and integrity," Bush remarked.[21]

The Bush campaign attempted to score points against Yarborough because of his support for the 1964 Civil Rights Act and his endorsement of the amendment to abolish poll taxes. One example of this effort was an editorial by Jack Howerton of the *Cuero Record* reprinted in Bush's campaign mailouts. The article criticized Yarborough for leaving a Texas Press Association convention to return to Washington for a vote on the "so-called civil rights bill," which critics stated "takes away more rights from Texas citizens than it bestows." The editorial chided Yarborough for being a yes man to the "big national labor bosses." According to Howerton, most publishers agreed that Yarborough would not be the Democratic senatorial nominee if Lee Harvey Oswald's shot from a state book depository window had not killed President Kennedy. He also stated that Johnson still disliked Yarborough and would have difficulty carrying his home state against Goldwater with the "albatross" senator on the ticket. Bush's television ads depicted Yarborough as an "extremist" and a "left wing demagogue." He tried to offset Yarborough's presidential support with an endorsement ad from former President Eisenhower. He also criticized Yarborough for employing his son as part of his Senate office staff. Most Texas daily newspapers endorsed Bush while they announced their support for President Johnson.[22]

Yarborough made the most of his links to the president and his ties to Kennedy. He utilized personal appearances and television in his largest and best-coordinated campaign effort. His campaign ads carried glowing statements from Presidents Kennedy and Johnson. LBJ made several public statements praising Yarborough. "No Senator in our land is more dedicated to the cause of the people than you," Johnson wrote as he expressed confidence in Yarborough's reelection. A "Women for Yarborough" organization formed, headed by Lady Bird Johnson and other well-known Democratic women. At every appearance, Yarborough urged Texans to vote a straight party ticket in November. He also constantly reminded voters he was the only Democratic senator from Texas. Opal and other Yarborough family members fanned out across Texas in the final month of the campaign, making personal appearances and shaking the hands of donors. In local communities, Yarborough focused on his role in providing millions of federal dollars spent in the state on construction projects, new programs, and payrolls. Yarborough scored points against Bush by citing his opponent's opposition to the nuclear test ban treaty,

Feuding Texas Democratic leaders appeared to be united in November 1964 to support the Johnson-Humphrey team. Leaving Air Force One in Austin for a campaign appearance were President Johnson and Lady Bird followed by Muriel and Hubert Humphrey, Nellie and John Connally, and Ralph and Opal Yarborough. Courtesy Center for American History, Russell Lee Collection (3Y169).

farm programs, and aid to education. Yarborough claimed Bush was to the right of Goldwater and chided his opponent for refusing to publicly disavow the extremist John Birch Society. He called Bush a "carpetbagger" and said the Bush family was trying to buy the Senate seat "just as they would buy a seat on the New York Stock Exchange." Yarborough made every effort to paint Bush as an outsider and right-wing extremist in the mold of Goldwater. In doing so, he essentially followed the same techniques the Johnson presidential campaign used with great success in 1964. The Johnson campaign labeled Goldwater reckless, unstable, trigger-happy, and scary and simultaneously aligned other Republicans with him.[23]

Shortly before the election, Yarborough suffered a personal loss when his father passed away. The senator visited his hometown of Chandler on October 13 to celebrate C. R.'s one-hundredth birthday. The nine surviving Yarborough children attended the event in the family home where Ralph was born. Eleven days later, Yarborough suspended his campaign as he and his family returned to their East Texas home to bury the family patriarch. At the time of his death, C. R. had three sons and six daughters, twenty-five grandchildren, forty-five great-grandchildren, and seven great-great-grandchildren. Yarborough credited his mother and father for the energy, drive, and ambition they gave each of their children. Both parents emphasized education, hard work, honor, and integrity. Yarborough said, "Above all I cherish his memory for the values of life he gave me." Tributes from President Johnson and many other Texas political leaders poured into Chandler. C. R. was buried beside his wife in the family cemetery in Chandler only a short distance from their home. On his return to Washington, Yarborough prepared a memorial booklet containing the many news stories and a short history of his father's life.[24]

Yarborough believed that even with Lyndon Johnson's dictates for a solid front, Connally and others worked behind the scenes for Bush. His suspicions were correct. The Texas Democratic party, controlled by Connally and Erwin, conducted a number of private polls prior to the 1964 general election. Connally received the results but they were never given to the Yarborough campaign. In October 1964, surveys indicated that Johnson maintained a two-to-one lead over Goldwater in Texas and Connally had an even larger lead over his Republican opponent, Jack Crichton. The report's authors warned that Johnson's association with Yarborough tarnished the president's image. Also, the senator's campaign was faltering "in the face of a well-organized attack by the Bush-for-Senator forces." Yarborough was seen as an "ultra-liberal" whose association with Billie Sol Estes harmed his reelection chances and reflected on the president. Yarborough and Bush were tied in the October poll as the incumbent's lead dropped with the approach of the election. Bush, who saw the Democratic party polls during his campaign, believed the numbers and thought he had a chance for the upset. However, neither Bush nor the pollsters counted on the large minority voter turnout for the Democratic nominees. The VOTE campaign produced thousands of African Americans and Mexican Americans who voted overwhelmingly Democratic. Pollsters contacted very few of these households and were largely unaware of their existence. Yarborough knew his archrival Connally publicly urged a straight-ticket vote but aided Bush behind the scenes. When Connally and Yarborough appeared together at a campaign stop, a reporter asked the senator how the two were getting along. Yarborough wryly stated that he and Connally were "just as close together as we've ever been."[25]

Making his best effort, Yarborough campaigned as an incumbent office-holder rather than a challenger seeking office. Yarborough's Senate experience and his teamwork with the president increased his viability. Bush had the Republicans and some conservative Democrats in his corner, but the majority of everyday people in Texas supported Yarborough and the other Democratic candidates. During a Bush appearance at the General Dynamics plant in Fort Worth, Ralph's brother Harvey described the challenger "as impressive as a last year's burro." People hardly noticed Bush and were uninterested when told he was the Republican Senate candidate.[26]

As much as he tried, Bush could not paddle fast enough to defeat the current generated by Yarborough and the Democrats. Yarborough's charge that Bush was a "carpetbagger" and supported by the right-wing John Birch Society also stung the candidate. The challenger believed that his sixteen years in Texas and the oil business gave him credentials to call himself a bona fide Texan. But Bush's eastern ties, his Goldwater affiliations, and the popularity of Democrats made his hope of an upset an illusion. Bush confronted a seasoned campaigner and came face to face with the hard realities of running a statewide race in Texas. In his concession speech on election night, Bush said that Yarborough beat him "fair and square." Bush gained over a million votes and ran well ahead of Goldwater in Texas, finishing with 43 percent of the popular vote, a strong-enough showing to allow him to remain one of the best hopes for Texas Republicans. Yarborough 's impressive win defeated the strongest Republican nominee on the ballot and the premier GOP rising star. His solid victory gave him all but thirty-four Texas counties. Bush carried only a group of traditionally Republican counties in the Panhandle, the Hill Country, and Dallas. Yarborough and the Democratic ticketed also benefited from strong local efforts, especially in Harris County and other well-organized urban and rural counties. Mass mailings to new minority voters, block walks, precinct meetings, and a well-coordinated election day effort swelled election day turnout. Yarborough's win stands out because the race truly appeared to be much closer than the final results indicated. Many had predicted his defeat and hardly any of the political observers believed he would gain so many votes, but Yarborough surprised them all.[27]

After the 1964 election, Yarborough publicly accused the governor and the state party of working for Bush. Yarborough said party leaders conducted special schools in select locations to show Democrats how to vote a split ticket— in favor of Democrats Johnson and Connally and for George Bush. Connally frequently mentioned his larger majority compared to Yarborough's and claimed the Democratic sweep in 1964 "even carried Senator Yarborough into office." All pretenses of cooperation and friendship ended after the general election, even with Lyndon Johnson in the White House. Some conservative Democrats obviously defected to Bush in the Senate race, and the state party's activities may have influenced a handful of these voters. Yarborough, the loyal Democrat, viewed these transgressions as political desertion. Yarborough still harbored ideas of returning to Texas one day to run for governor. He believed his leadership and accomplishments would lead the liberals in Texas to wrest control of the Democratic party, thereby forcing conservatives to choose between the two political parties. Yarborough believed the president's national popularity and the optimistic mood of the country presented the opportunity to challenge the status quo in Texas. But in order to accomplish his goal in Texas, he had to juggle his busy legislative agenda while contesting the popular governor at home.[28]

THE YARBOROUGH-CONNALLY FEUD BOILS OVER

John Connally was Lyndon Johnson's protégé. He had played an integral role in "Landslide Lyndon's" controversial 87-vote victory over Coke Stevenson in the 1948 Senate election and served as a political operative in Texas who looked after Johnson's interests during the intraparty fights of the 1950's. In 1960 Connally coordinated Johnson's unsuccessful bid for the Democratic presidential nomination. At Johnson's urging, President Kennedy appointed Connally secretary of the navy. With Johnson's assistance, Connally returned to Texas to unseat Governor Price Daniel and then defeat Don Yarborough in a runoff. If anyone was ever cut from the same cloth as Johnson, it was

John Connally. One observer noted "you could take either one of their egos, slice it up, and have healthy portions for any six ordinary men." As governor, Connally maintained a close relationship with President Johnson. Although they differed on domestic policies, Connally remained loyal to Johnson to the end of his presidency. Connally, described as the "most anti–Robert Kennedy man in Lyndon Johnson's circle," united with Johnson to try to deprive the younger Kennedy of the Democratic nomination in 1968. Connally became one of the most vocal Yarborough critics and the latest state Democratic leader to clash with the senator over the future direction of the state.[29]

Surprisingly, for two men who intensely disliked one another, Connally and Yarborough had similar backgrounds and personalities. Both men lived through the Great Depression and were World War II veterans. Both were attorneys and graduates of the University of Texas. They also had great personal and political ambition combined with exceptional oratorical skills. During the postwar era, the common bonds that bound people together during the depression quickly unraveled. Politics and business provided the separation. As Lyndon Johnson rose to power in the Senate, Connally joined his inner circle and also took control of the conservative and moderate wing of the party from Shivers in 1956. Connally became wealthy as the administrative assistant and later the executor for wealthy Texas oilman Sid Richardson. Connally courted businessmen in executive offices and country clubs as easily as Yarborough rubbed shoulders with working people in the refineries and local cafes. Connally remained in the thick of the Johnson-Yarborough feud as it continued through the early 1960's. Connally and Yarborough enjoyed the political limelight and feasted on political controversy. Both state leaders realized they occupied positions of leadership not just in Texas but in the nation. Their battles gained importance based on the attention garnered from the Kennedy assassination followed by Johnson's rise to the presidency.

Texas and the rest of the Old South were now the focal point of the Johnson administration's thrust to improve civil rights and the plight of the poor. How individual leaders within each southern state accepted or fought these changes determined the course of events for years to come. The civil rights issue provided the best indicator of the differences between Yarborough and Connally. The *Dallas Morning News* indicated that of the 325,000 black students in Texas public schools, only 20,000 attended classes with white students by 1964. A decade after the Supreme Court's 1954 decision outlawing segregation, Texas' local elected officials still effectively resisted integration of public schools. Arguments and lawsuits over the process and speed of allowing minority students to attend formerly all-white campuses extended

throughout the state. As governor, Connally worked to enhance public education by advocating teacher pay raises and made token minority appointments to state agencies. The governor took a "go slow" approach as he criticized federal action while he encouraged local officials to continue their
opposition and delaying tactics. Yarborough's strong advocacy for civil rights
and federal funding for education was in stark contrast to the governor's
"moderate" positions. After the nationwide coverage of the bloody beatings
of civil rights workers during a march in Selma, Alabama, in March 1965,
Yarborough took the floor in the Senate to blast Alabama governor George
Wallace. "Shame on you, George Wallace, for the wet ropes that bruised the
muscles, for the bullwhips which cut the flesh, for the clubs that broke the
bones, for the tear gas that blinded, burned and choked into insensibility,"
Yarborough cried. Connally never condemned these atrocities as harshly as
Yarborough, though he never used extreme measures such as those of Governor Shivers, who called on Texas Rangers to prevent integration at Mansfield High School in 1956. In any case, Connally failed to provide meaningful
leadership for other state and local officials who stood on the front lines and
held the responsibility for the implementation of integration. He opposed
the one-man-one-vote principle. In 1968, Connally shocked many when, on
learning of Martin Luther King's assassination, he said, "Those who live by
the sword die by the sword." Texas never experienced violent confrontations
between white segregationists and civil rights advocates like those in Alabama and Mississippi, but the state and many of its leaders were still closely
tied to the gray ghosts of the past.[30]

Yarborough and Connally differed on nearly every issue, from major policies to small affairs. Once the 1964 election returns were filed away, the fighting between the governor and the senator became as predictable as the Texas
summer heat. Occasionally, even a minor flare-up blew up into a major fire-
storm. An August 1965 *Dallas Morning News* article revealed that a member
of Yarborough's staff had provided information to a national magazine for
an attack on the governor: Yarborough aide Chuck Caldwell supplied several
unflattering stories about the governor to a reporter for *The Nation*. Reporter
Sam Wood's article, "Yarborough Plot to Smear Connally Revealed," described an elaborate plot to discredit the incumbent governor, an effort that
was part of a Yarborough plan to run for governor in 1966. The story circulated throughout Texas and appeared in many national newspapers. Caldwell
later admitted to providing information to the *Nation* reporter without the
senator's knowledge. Yarborough, who knew nothing of the plan, was livid
with Caldwell and eagerly consented to giving his young aide a leave of ab-

sence from his Senate job. In the meantime, SDEC Chairman Frank Erwin, Connally's close ally, responded with an attack on the senator. Erwin reminded Texans that Yarborough "refused" to ride in the car with Vice President Johnson on the day before President Kennedy's assassination. The state Democratic leader labeled Yarborough as "divisive and destructive" while he praised Connally for his "progressive leadership." The incident confirmed the suspicions of many Connally supporters and fueled their animosity toward Yarborough. They believed that Yarborough would never stop his attacks on Connally. The senator's adherents despised the governor and the state party's leadership just as strongly.[31]

The Yarborough-Connally feud continued throughout the terms of both elected officials. They disagreed over almost every conceivable issue and program, jabbing at one another on voter rights, antipoverty programs, federal disaster aid, and a host of other matters. Both vied for public attention and fought for recognition. Yarborough enjoyed being mentioned as a potential candidate against Connally but had no real intention of running for governor that year. However, his attacks clearly conveyed the message that he wanted a serious challenger to go up against Connally.

Yarborough purposely singled out Connally's opposition to domestic legislation favored by the Johnson administration. Connally's unwavering support for Johnson diminished when federal programs brought in new administrators and dollars over which state officials had no oversight. Connally wanted control over the program content as well as the people who worked in these offices. Yarborough was more interested in expanding the federal presence at Connally's expense. He criticized Connally's opposition, characterizing it as an abuse of power. Connally's vetoes or threatened vetoes of federal programs added more fuel to the political fire between the senator and the governor. Behind all of Yarborough's attacks was a calculated effort to discredit the governor, increase his own stature, and ultimately capture control of the Democratic party. Walter Hall praised Yarborough and observed, "there is no question but that you are getting under John's skin and the skin of many of his friends." Connally was not about to stand still and make himself a target—he launched his own stinging criticisms of federal bureaucrats and Yarborough. The squabble continued like a soap opera, keeping individuals across the political wavelength tuned in to the Democrats' struggles.[32]

During a speech in December 1965 on the Senate floor, Yarborough accused Connally of deliberately undermining antipoverty legislation by using his veto power to cut wages on federally sponsored local programs which included the first rural program in six South Texas counties. Yarborough

ALWAYS SOMETHING

The Yarborough-Connally rivalry provided ample fuel for Texas newspaper columnists and cartoonists, as illustrated by this example from the Dallas Morning News *of August 10, 1965. Reprinted with permission of the* Dallas Morning News.

charged the governor with stalling programs that paid $1.25 per hour while encouraging those that paid $1 per hour as part of an effort to placate conservative businessmen. Ironically, GOP Senator Tower came to Connally's defense and provided data showing how the governor bested President Johnson and Senator Yarborough in terms of popular votes. A number of close Senate votes followed as Yarborough successfully pushed for federal legislation that prevented a governor's veto of community antipoverty projects.[33]

In the same year, Yarborough actively opposed Connally's state legislation changing the terms of office from two years to four years for statewide elected officials. When Texas voters defeated the constitutional amendment, Yarborough claimed the governor was frustrated because people rejected his "grab for a four year term." Connally responded that the charge was another of Yarborough's "wild and irresponsible" statements. Even with these victories in Washington and at the polls, at the state convention in 1966 Yarborough and liberal Democrats were not able to successfully challenge Connally's control of the Democratic party. After the meeting, Yarborough called Connally, Attorney General Waggoner Carr, and Senator John Tower "identical political triplets."

When Democratic congressman Jim Wright, who Yarborough hoped would challenge Republican John Tower, dropped out before the primary, Carr easily won the May election to become the Democratic nominee in 1966 against Tower. Many Texas liberals withheld their support from Carr and once again defected to the Republican candidate in the Senate race. With the Democratic party so divided, Tower won a surprise victory. As Yarborough explained to Frankie Randolph, Carr ran his election "denouncing me for the Democratic votes that I've cast."

Connally attacked Yarborough for the senator's support of federal voting rights legislation which outlawed the poll tax in state elections, charging that Yarborough wanted a "police state activity designed to humiliate his own people" and that he worked to discredit Carr. Yarborough countered by again questioning why public officials wanted to prevent people from voting. The nation was watching, Yarborough warned, and state leaders were an embarrassment because of their reluctance to "bring Texas into the twentieth century." Neither Connally nor Yarborough seemed to gain the upper hand for an extended period of time. The only winners were the state's newspapers whose circulations climbed as they covered the running battle.[34]

Even a devastating Texas hurricane could not prevent Yarborough and Connally from criticizing the other. In September 1967, Hurricane Beulah slammed into the Texas coast resulting in an estimated $1 billion in damage to structures from the high winds and flooding. Immediately after the storm subsided, Yarborough accompanied federal officials for a firsthand view of the damage. He urged the Office of Emergency Planning to declare the South Texas region a federal disaster area so residents and businesses could qualify for assistance and loans. Officially, the governor of the state first had to solicit a presidential declaration. Connally's request was not submitted until a week after the storm. Yarborough said Connally failed to contact the Johnson administration because he, Yarborough, was on-site with investigators before the governor visited the scene. Connally, stung by the accusation, replied that Yarborough had a "complete disregard for the truth" and branded the senator as a "very despicable demagogue." This argument also made newspapers and television broadcasts around the state. Yarborough complained the Texas press sided with Connally in order to make a "personal attack" and distract attention from the governor's "obvious and negligent failure."[35]

The ongoing battle between the two continued even after Connally announced he would not run for a fourth term for governor in 1968. Yarborough was obviously pleased to see his foremost critic withdraw. In a nationally televised interview with columnist Rowland Evans, Yarborough surmised that Connally decided not to run for another term because he sensed the decline of his popularity and approval ratings. Yarborough charged that the "mantle of martyrdom" Connally acquired as a result of the Kennedy assassination had faded in the minds of Texans. Yarborough discounted Washington rumors that President Johnson would bring his longtime friend into his cabinet as secretary of defense to succeed Robert McNamara. Connally actually entertained the idea of the post and received support from many prominent Democrats in Texas. Yarborough maintained his rival was "just not qualified" and did not have the temperament for such a difficult job. Connally's name also surfaced as a potential vice president should Robert Kennedy receive the Democratic nomination. Yarborough bristled at the idea. As governor, Connally attacked the Kennedys continuously, Yarborough charged, and he pledged to fight any attempt by the Texas governor to gain the number two position. After Robert Kennedy's assassination in 1968, Yarborough endorsed Senator Eugene McCarthy while Connally supported Vice President Hubert Humphrey. Few people expected Yarborough or Connally to agree on any issue or candidate, especially given the long-standing, bitter rivalry.[36]

The irony was not lost on Lyndon Johnson—his protégé opposed him more often than his former liberal critic. On a larger scale, the ongoing battle between Yarborough and Connally centered on control of the Democratic party and its future in a two-party state. Republican strength began to increase in major urban areas primarily because of opposition to Lyndon Johnson and his advocacy of civil rights and Great Society programs. Also, Connally, as the leader of the conservative-moderate Democrats, began to openly criticize Johnson's policies on repeal of state right-to-work laws, state control of antipoverty programs, and federal monitoring of the state's voter registration program. At the same time, Connally remained one of the president's staunchest defenders on Vietnam. In Washington, Yarborough emerged as one of the president's most enthusiastic supporters just as Connally began to put distance between himself and Johnson. The only major exception for Yarborough was the Vietnam policy. Yarborough believed the Great Society was the key to unlocking the active support of vast numbers of people in Texas who would welcome a liberal agenda. Yarborough was ecstatic when the first voter registration drive without a poll tax held in 1966 brought in more than 500,000 new voters in the state. In spite of the growth of the Republican party in the major cities, Yarborough and other Texas liberals felt that they could widen their base of support in the cities and in rural Texas at the expense of the conservative faction of the Democratic party led by Connally. In some local areas, this strategy was successful in the late 1960's. But other national events in the turbulent era offset what otherwise might have been a sound game plan. Both state leaders still professed their loyalty to the Johnson administration, but both men had their own agendas to advance. In his fights with Connally, Yarborough sometimes needlessly antagonized Connally and aggravated potential supporters and alienated some large contributors who played all corners of the political game.

The Yarborough-Connally battle reflected the continuing struggle among Texas Democrats in a state still dominated by one-party politics. The personalities of both leaders actually stalled the movement toward a two-party state. Conservatives who might otherwise have left for the Republican party in the 1960's were attracted by Connally's popularity and their dislike of Yarborough. The middle-of-the-road Democrats who supported both leaders were tossed back and forth like a ship between the waves created by the two leaders. Rank and file Democrats in the state during Johnson's term of office seemed to be satisfied with both men. Connally received better media coverage and was held in higher regard by the editorial boards of the state's largest newspapers. He also earned credit for holding conservatives in the Democratic party and so maintaining its dominance. Undoubtedly many conservatives remained in Connally's corner in the hope that they could still somehow knock out Yarborough in a scheduled event. However, many new voters, especially African Americans and Mexican Americans, supported Yarborough. Both Connally and Yarborough maintained a high degree of visibility and leadership late in the era of one-party politics. Yet both had difficulty in transferring their individual popularity to other candidates, which reflected internal weaknesses in the organization of both conservatives and liberals. Ralph Yarborough's support could not enable Don Yarborough to overcome Connally's popularity. Waggoner Carr, with Connally's public endorsement, could not unseat John Tower in 1966 as Democratic liberals joined an unlikely union with state Republicans to defeat their own nominee.

When Connally announced he would not run for reelection in 1968, Yarborough's name surfaced again for the governor's office. At a joint appearance with the Texas governor at a Mexican American conference in El Paso, crowds cheered Yarborough and booed Connally—all in front of President Johnson. Yarborough critics hoped he would file for governor in the belief that a well-financed, popular conservative could defeat him, which would demonstrate his vulnerability in the next Senate election. The *Dallas Morning News* reported in late November 1967 that Yarborough told some of his closest friends of his decision to run for governor. However, as J. R. Parten remarked to Walter Hall, Yarborough, who could run for governor while holding his Senate seat, rendered "a much more important service in the Senate." On January 13, 1968, after weeks of speculation, the senior senator announced his decision to pass on the governor's race and remain in Washington. Yarborough understood the importance of his role in the Senate, but he retained his fascination with the governor's office. As he explained to Fagan Dickson, "the main pull to my running was my desire to bring the Government of Texas into the 20th century."[37]

With Yarborough out of the race, Lieutenant Governor Preston Smith and liberal candidate Don Yarborough emerged from a crowded primary field. Senator Yarborough endorsed Don Yarborough in the runoff election, but the more conservative Smith prevailed in the runoff by over 100,000 votes. This marked the best effort by Don Yarborough and Texas liberals to win the governor's office. However, Smith made headway attacking Don Yarborough as a radical supported by eastern labor bosses. Smith also criticized liberal giveaway programs sought by "those who tell the government to pay them or they will burn down another neighborhood." The tenor of Smith's televised spots were similar to those of Richard Nixon in the 1968 presidential election. The ads depicted burning cities, street crime, and violent demonstrations in vivid scenes purposely designed to alienate traditional white Democratic voters from their candidates. These inflammatory, yet clearly effective ads set the precedent for the tack the opposition would take in the 1970 election when Ralph Yarborough would be seeking reelection to the U.S. Senate.[38]

12 Acts of Congress and Acts of Madness

Throughout Lyndon Johnson's presidency, Yarborough remained one of the strongest supporters of the Great Society. Yarborough believed that extensive federal commitment was the best solution to the nation's poverty and racism problems. Just as the New Deal promised hope for Americans in the years of the Great Depression, Yarborough felt that now the nation could achieve the unrealized goals of educational and economic opportunity for all of its citizens. The federal government was the only agency that could take the initiative and set the standards for local government and private business. As a student of history, Yarborough recognized this was a rare opportunity to achieve meaningful social and economic reform. He had customarily worked at a rapid pace his entire professional and political career, and the tensions of the time coupled with the necessity for accomplishing his goals drove him at a fever pitch. He became one of President Johnson's most consistent allies in the Senate, supporting the administration's domestic initiatives while pressing many of his own. Even so, the rivalry between the two men still produced occasional sparks when he and the President tangled over legislation. Yarborough's penchant for taking on numerous assignments increased during the heyday of the Great Society as he pushed himself and his weary staff in many directions. He also promoted his own agenda to expand national programs and services which sometimes ran contrary to even the most ambitious designs of the Johnson administration.

A cornerstone of the Great Society was the emphasis on public education, an area reserved almost exclusively to the states and local governments. Education occupied a major position in Yarborough's agenda as well. When they had served together in the Senate, Johnson acknowledged Yarborough's expertise in public education. Both Johnson and Yarborough relished teaching in small, rural schools in Texas in the formative years of their careers and used anecdotes from their individual experiences in public statements. Yarborough consistently touted education as a gateway to individual accomplish-

ment and a better, more equal society. He firmly believed education benefited all Americans regardless of one's heritage and background. It provided
the upward mobility which would break the cycle of poverty and expand
America's middle class. High rates of crime and unemployment were linked
to poor education. Thus by 1965 many Americans believed the time had come
for the federal government to break tradition and begin supporting local educational efforts. But concerns still existed over the propriety of the federal
government entering this new arena. But school officials, community leaders,
and vocal parents drowned the opposition with cries for more financial assistance — and Washington was ready to respond. Furthermore, federal aid
to education was more palatable than other proposals that directly addressed
poverty. Other controversial programs such as a guaranteed national income
and extensive unionization of workers never made it onto the Great Society's
agenda.

In the early years of the Johnson administration, Yarborough worked on
nearly every single piece of education legislation that wound its way through
the Congressional maze. "Nothing matters more to the future of our country," declared President Johnson as he vowed that education was his number
one priority. Yarborough proclaimed that America could avoid a future crisis
through better education. He then cosponsored the Elementary and Secondary Education Act of 1965, the president's initial major legislative victory and
the first general education measure ever to pass Congress. The $1.3 billion
bill provided funds for textbooks, libraries, education centers, special training, and other educational needs of school children in districts throughout
the nation. Yarborough played a critical role throughout passage of the bill,
especially with his vote to break a deadlock on the House-Senate Conference
Committee. The legislation played a critical role in breaking the final resistance to integration of public schools. Federal dollars, not bayonets, broke
down the Jim Crow barriers and de facto segregation in Texas and the rest of
the South, for the strings attached to Washington's dollars for public schools
required elimination of segregated facilities. Together with the civil rights
acts, federal education initiatives finally brought about the "Reconstruction
of Southern Education" that slowly wore down official resistance. However,
public resistance at the local level remained strong in many areas of the nation
as integration proceeded through the 1960's. Local school officials and citizens wanted the money from Washington but continued to drag their feet
on integration.[1]

Yarborough authored or played a major role in passage of many popular educational programs during his Senate career: the Higher Education

Act, the Vocational Education Act, the Educational Television program, the National Science Foundation, the College Classroom Construction Program, the Library Services Act, the National Teacher Corps, the Adult Basic Education Program, Headstart, Job Corps, VISTA, and many others. Most of these programs became immediate successes and are now permanent fixtures in public education. Before Yarborough left the Senate in 1971, nearly four out of every five students attending college benefited from loans or scholarships provided by the Higher Education Act. The foundation laid by these programs forever changed the complexion of public education in the United States. Poor students and poverty-ridden school districts now had access to new funds to help level the playing field for students and compete with those from wealthier areas. Senator Wayne Morse (D-Oregon) named Yarborough "Mr. Education of the U.S. Senate" for his dedication and work. In addition to these landmark initiatives, two of Yarborough's most significant measures earned him a place in the annals of innovative educational efforts: the Cold War G.I. bill and the Bilingual Education Act.[2]

THE COLD WAR G.I. BILL

Passage of the Cold War G.I. bill was a perpetual frustration for Yarborough prior to 1966. When he first entered the Senate in 1957 during the Eisenhower administration, Yarborough tried to pass the measure that provided educational loans and benefits to anyone who had served in the U.S. military after World War II or after the Korean War. The Senate passed his bill in 1959, but opposition in the House and by the Republican administration killed the measure. Yarborough suffered the same problems during the Kennedy administration, when concerns over the costs of the expanded benefits program coupled with opposition from the Department of Defense prevented passage. Finally, Yarborough hoped the Johnson administration would accept his proposal as an extension of its widened education efforts. Yarborough also believed chances for passage improved with the widening of the war in Vietnam. This was now a shooting war as opposed to the earlier, combat-free days of the Cold War. Soldiers in Vietnam faced more hazards and the public became more supportive of additional benefits for veterans. However, the Johnson administration continued to oppose the initiative.

In a letter to the president in May 1965, Yarborough argued that the expanded G.I. bill would aid an estimated two million men and women in the armed services. Also, he noted that the added benefits would offset costs for other Great Society training and education programs. Politically, Yarborough argued that Democrats and the administration could upstage the opposition, pointing out that "The Republicans are trying to create an issue of being the Party concerned with helping the fighting men," a claim the G.I. bill would help deflate. Yarborough's letter set off a flurry of memos and meetings in the Johnson administration. Johnson's aides recommended delay and continued opposition or a search for an alternative to the bill. Many were concerned that the public would begin associating the Vietnam "conflict" with the Korean Conflict, which ended in a stalemate after years of warfare. The Veterans Administration finally came out in favor of Yarborough's bill after the Senate Committee on Labor and Public Welfare passed it on June 1. But the Johnson administration remained opposed. Behind the scenes, it convinced House chairman "Tiger" Teague to hold up the legislation in his Veterans' Affairs Committee. However, Yarborough sensed the timing was right and refused to weaken the legislation. Teague's committee finally passed the measure on to the full House. The full House passed the measure in February and the White House scheduled a special Rose Garden signing ceremony on March 3, 1966. After eight years of effort, Yarborough jubilantly celebrated the passage of the Cold War G.I. bill. "I never felt so happy as when I stood at our President's elbow as he signed that bill," Yarborough remarked as he accepted the signing pen. President Johnson complained that the legislation "busted" his budget but praised the program as a great accomplishment for veterans. The new law immediately expanded educational opportunities to more than five million veterans who entered the armed forces after January 31, 1955. They had a variety of opportunities from which to choose: on-the-job training, farm training, flight school, business school, or trade school in addition to high school or college. As a result of the bill's passage, millions of veterans attended college or vocational schools thanks to Yarborough's persistence and vision. His unwillingness to compromise on this issue provided big dividends for veterans and the nation.[3]

BILINGUAL EDUCATION

On his tenth anniversary in the U.S. Senate in 1967, Yarborough addressed the Mexican-American Joint Conference organized by Dr. George Sanchez in Austin. The nationally recognized scholar earlier had convinced Yarborough that public schools were "atrociously negligent" in teaching Spanish and other foreign languages. Yarborough's appearance at the conference previewed a series of South Texas public meetings scheduled by his Senate Labor Committee to promote bilingual education. These marked the first-ever congressional hearings on the problems confronting bilingual education. Yarborough delivered a wide-ranging criticism of social conditions in Texas that reminded many in the audience of his speeches during his gubernatorial campaigns. After praising Sanchez' contributions to education, Yarborough complained about the low wages paid to minorities and farm workers. He then called for a minimum wage law in Texas and for free college tuition for state residents. Many antipoverty programs were established to address these problems, but they were underfunded and controlled by city halls and politicians who opposed the federal efforts. "Sometimes victories are defeats themselves. People get satisfied with half-way victories and they stop," Yarborough observed. As was his custom, he frequently launched into long soliloquies beyond the immediate subject area to address other social ills and injustices. Politically, he used the conference to increase his exposure in South Texas and as a forum to indirectly criticize Governor Connally. The hearings also demonstrated Yarborough's appreciation for the expanding numbers and potential political power of Hispanics in Texas and the American Southwest.[4]

The Spanish language and culture were established in the American Southwest several centuries before the settlement of English-speaking citizens there. But from the earliest days of the Republic of Texas, the white majority practiced discrimination and sometimes directed violence at Mexican Americans. These practices carried into twentieth-century Texas. Mexican Americans in Texas lived with inferior, segregated facilities and discriminatory practices similar to those endured by African Americans in the Jim Crow era. During the Senate hearings in 1967, Yarborough heard the catalog of frustrations handed down by generations of Mexican Americans. In Corpus Christi, vivid stories from Mexican American witnesses detailed the poor treatment they received in the state's public schools. Carlos Truan, a director of the League of United Latin American Citizens (LULAC) who would eventually win election to the Texas Senate, described his experience as a child entering public school, where he was physically whipped when he spoke Spanish instead of English. "I was placed in the so-called 'beginners grade' and not the first grade because of the language," Truan recalled. Others complained that some children had difficulties learning English because they had no exposure to the language prior to enrolling in school. Nearly all the participants supported Yarborough's bilingual education proposal, which some termed a "radical suggestion." Dr. Hector Garcia, the founder of the American GI Forum, said, "true American democracy will be possible when the majority becomes bilingual in the Southwest." Yarborough wanted $100 million in federal funds to plan and develop a bilingual education program for public schools. (Yarborough himself was bilingual, having learned German during his post–World War I trip to Europe as a young man. He spoke some Spanish but was not fluent.)[5]

The primary debate over the legislation involved instruction in both English and Spanish in the same classroom. Some members of the Johnson administration opposed the emphasis on Spanish language instruction alongside English. Armando Rodriguez of the Office of Education argued, "We didn't want students to be prohibited from using their language and then having [to] come back ten years later and have to learn their language through a language course." President Johnson gave the measure his initial blessing but his staff never fully pushed for passage. White House legal advisor Barefoot Sanders questioned whether the administration should drag their feet on bilingual education "after we came out so badly on the Cold War G.I. bill." A year after introducing the legislation, Congress passed Yarborough's bill as part of the Southwest Development Act. Yarborough's legislative skills came into play as he outworked those in the administration and Congress attempting to hold up the legislation. Proponents credited Yarborough as the moving force behind the bilingual education effort and publicly chided Johnson administration officials for their lack of support. The Bilingual Education bill provided federal funds for an estimated two million non-English-speaking children to increase fluency in English. News accounts recognized the bill as a "Yarborough achievement" and the senator highlighted the act as one of his major accomplishments. Mexican American leaders expressed their appreciation and collectively remained among his strongest supporters. Yarborough was fortunate to complete his work within a year, for the war in Vietnam and civil unrest in the nation put the brakes on any new major education initiatives.[6]

The American Medical Association called the 89th Congress "the most health-oriented Congress in the world" in recognition of its steady flow of legislation from 1965 to 1966. The final victory for the Medical Care Act of 1965, popularly known as Medicare, came in July 1965 and served as the standard for the Great Society's victory in the health field. Yarborough cosponsored the bill and praised the legislation in his constituent newsletters and press release that year. Since 1958 Yarborough had continuously served on the Health Subcommittee of the Senate Labor and Public Welfare Committee. With his passion for finding federal solutions to health-related problems, he sponsored and participated in many of the bills that expanded the federal government's role in health care. In 1965 the committee passed bills, signed by President Johnson, that expanded federal grants for doctors, nurses, and other health professionals. Other bills authorized construction funds for medical libraries and rehabilitation centers. The Older Americans Act of 1965 created a new federal office that focused on programs for needy senior citizens. Additional bills covered child nutrition, neighborhood health centers, veterinary medicine, and treatment for drug abuse. Yarborough sponsored or co-sponsored and actively worked on all of this legislation. On the Senate floor, Majority Leader Mike Mansfield praised committee chairman Lister Hill of Alabama and his Senate committee for establishing "a new record in the field of health legislation."[7]

THE GUADALUPE MOUNTAINS NATIONAL PARK AND THE ENVIRONMENT

Yarborough established himself as a staunch advocate for the environment with his passage of the Padre Island National Seashore legislation in September 1962. He demonstrated his maturity as a senator with his work on his next proposal—protection for the remote Guadalupe Mountains in Far West Texas. Almost immediately after President Kennedy signed the Padre Island legislation, the Texas senator filed legislation to create the Guadalupe Mountains National Park. The proposed area stood in direct contrast to the flat, open Gulf beaches on the Texas coast. The remote, arid region and rough terrain inhibited development, and the area remained largely uninhabited well into the twentieth century. The Guadalupe Mountains in the Trans-Pecos area were the remains of limestone reefs formed millions of years ago that are the highest elevations in the state of Texas. Although located in the Chihuahuan Desert environment, the mountains supported a wider array of plant and animal life due to the high elevation. Early Indian inhabitants came as early as 12,000 years ago. They were followed by the Mescalero Apaches, who inhabited the mountain region through the 1800's. Spanish conquistadors, Texas Rangers, and travelers on the Butterfield Stage all remarked on the stark beauty of the Guadalupe Mountains, especially the southernmost peak, which seems to rise suddenly over the desert floor. This dramatic 8,076-foot elevation became known as El Capitan. Nearby Guadalupe Peak is 8,751 feet, the highest point in Texas. Grizzly bear, bighorn sheep, clear springs, majestic canyons, golden eagles, and abundant varieties of birds were recorded during many early expeditions in the mid-1800's. Visitors who recorded some of the earliest wildlife sightings noted that in the clear desert air they could see the mountains a week before they reached the site. The earliest American settlers did not come into the area until the 1870's, when the threat from the Mescalero Apaches subsided.[8]

Yarborough's Guadalupe Mountain parks bill received a much friendlier reception in Congress in 1965 than the Padre Island National Seashore legislation had when it was proposed. He recalled that he first saw El Capitan in 1927 while working as a young attorney in El Paso. He described the area as "splendidly isolated and majestically beautiful." Most of the 70,000 acres in the proposed park were owned by J. C. Hunter Jr., a rancher whose family had purchased the site in 1924. Hunter supported the national park proposal and, working with his friend Glenn Biggs, he invited writers, elected officials, and conservationists to the ranch to get a firsthand view of the mountains. Yarborough publicly commended Hunter for his land stewardship and his efforts to preserve the holdings without commercial development. Estimates for acquisition of the property were $1.5 million, less than 1 percent of the $150 million requested by the Johnson administration for purchase of a dozen target parklands. The federal government already held title to 5,600 acres following a donation by Wallace Pratt, a Humble Oil Company geologist and a longtime proponent for creation of a park. The National Parks Advisory Board recommended purchase of the site in 1963 and the Guadalupes were among twelve areas supported by the Johnson administration for inclusion in the national system. Yarborough lined up endorsements from the Texas Legislature, the chambers of commerce of many West Texas communities, and wildlife and conservation groups, along with many oil and gas companies with holdings in the region. Notably, Congressman Richard White, in whose district the proposed park was located, publicly favored the legislation and authored the companion bill in the House. Senator Joseph Montoya of New Mexico also favored the bill. The proposed park was only a few miles from the New Mexico state line and close to Carlsbad Caverns in southern New Mexico. Even some of Yarborough's staunchest critics supported the bill. Senator Tower, Governor Connally, Land Commissioner Sadler, and a host of other state officials who normally opposed Yarborough gave their support. Finally, the state's largest daily newspapers called for the creation of the park. Most editorials spoke of its unique, pristine condition and proximity to Big Bend National Park and Carlsbad Caverns. Enactment would "complete a group of three great national parks in the same area."[9]

Following Yarborough's introduction of the first bill in November 1963, support for the park rapidly increased prior to the Senate hearings in 1965. The scenic beauty and unique features of the Guadalupes undoubtedly attracted much enthusiasm. In West Texas, the economic arguments favoring the Guadalupe Mountains National Park also carried weight. Many West Texans believed that the area was often slighted when it came to government services and expenditures. Thus many viewed the park as a mechanism to draw more people to the area. Tourists brought dollars that otherwise would go elsewhere. Furthermore, because Yarborough had the support of landowners and local business people, the proposal gained much broader support than his earlier Padre Island legislation. He had alienated local congressmen by announcing the Padre Island proposal without their knowledge. With the Guadalupes, Yarborough and his staff secured the support of Congressman White and local officials well beforehand and had his sponsorship for the House version of the bill. By 1965 domestic initiatives by the Johnson administration received wide support in Congress and throughout the nation. Environmental legislation and park acquisitions were sometimes viewed as an extension of Johnson's Great Society programs. The legislation moved forward as the new environmental movement blossomed nationwide. Yarborough's groundwork for the legislation and the favorable political atmosphere in Washington made his second parks proposal a much easier task when compared to the bill the House passed by a voice vote in June 1966. The Senate passed the legislation in October. On the 15th, President Johnson signed the bill into law, creating the Guadalupe Mountains National Park. Land acquisition began the following year and continued for several years. The requested $1.4 million funding was reduced to $200,000 as part of an overall congressional cost-cutting program. Yarborough worked two more years for federal funds to complete the entire acquisition while preserving the scenic canyons and fragile areas. Yarborough, who objected to putting roads into the heart of the Guadalupes that would threaten the sensitive plant and animal life, finally secured more than $1 million to allow the Park Service to complete the acquisition for the park. The park was finally dedicated in September 1972, two years after Yarborough left the Senate.[10]

Yarborough, who hailed from a state consistently ranked at the bottom in natural resource protection, broke new ground and brought Texas into the modern environmental movement. He accurately foresaw America's new desire to preserve its heritage and expand the federal government's role and vision with a wide array of historic and natural areas. In addition to the passage of Padre Island National Seashore and the Guadalupe Mountains Na-

Yarborough loved grass-roots campaigning and was known for his knowledge and compassion. Yarborough often talked with Texas farmers about soil conservation, water projects, and farm programs that he sponsored in the Senate. Courtesy Center for American History, Yarborough Papers (3S387).

tional Park legislation, Yarborough authored bills that established Fort Davis Historical Site in West Texas and the Alibates Flint Quarries National Monument in the Panhandle. He sponsored the Golden Eagle Protection law, the 1966 and 1969 Endangered Species Act, and the Landmark Water Quality Improvement Act. Yarborough cosponsored every major water, air, and solid-waste pollution measure passed by Congress from 1961 to 1970. At the urging of proponents in his native East Texas, Yarborough passed a Big Thicket National Park bill in the Senate but failed to see its final passage before he left office in January 1971. Motivated to save the pristine area where he sometimes explored and hunted in his youth, Yarborough fought to preserve several hundred thousand acres of forest from timber and oil companies. After leaving office, Yarborough continued to fight for, and eventually saw in 1974, the creation of the Big Thicket National Preserve. By the time he left the Senate, Yarborough had established a national reputation as one of the leading environmental lawmakers of his era. No U.S. senator from Texas has ever matched his record.[11]

VIETNAM

Yarborough supported the president's Vietnam buildup in 1964. He and many other Cold War liberals vocally opposed communist aggression and supported national defense expenditures. He publicly described the Vietnamese conflict as a test between communism and the free nations of the world. Yarborough wanted to see South Vietnam join the world's other democracies in order to protect the strategic interests of the United States. The Texas senator voted for a larger commitment in the election year of 1964. Yarborough defended Johnson's position to retaliate against North Vietnam. After the Tonkin Gulf incident, Yarborough stated that when U.S. forces were attacked, they should return fire. He declared that the "wanton attacks on our ships" by Vietnam would be met. The nation firmly united behind the president, and Yarborough joined the great majority who approved the increased buildup in Vietnam "in defense of freedom."[12]

By the summer of 1965, Yarborough began privately to question the wisdom of extending U.S. involvement in Vietnam by sending additional troops. In July 1965 President Johnson addressed the nation, calling for a united front and an expanded effort by the nation to win the war in Vietnam. Faced with the prospect that the South Vietnamese government was near collapse, Johnson and his administration believed that an increased commitment was necessary to convince North Vietnam and the rest of the world that the United States would meet its commitments. Yarborough took the opportunity to call for enactment of the Cold War G.I. bill as more and more enlistments expanded the number of deserving veterans. Likewise, in his November 1965 Veterans' Day statement, Yarborough mentioned the benefits of the Cold War bill only. While Yarborough noticeably refrained from making public statements pro or con on the war itself, other Texas elected officials made every effort to show their support. Governor Connally and Senator Tower strongly supported the war and began accusing early opponents of the conflict of being communist sympathizers. At a 1965 Veterans' Day rally in San Angelo, Connally and Tower made a joint appearance, where the governor stated that a "vocal minority of beatniks, peaceniks and draftniks" were disregarding the nation's interests in opposing communism. In 1965 few people in Texas spoke out against the war. Most Texans believed President Johnson made the correct decision in expanding the nation's commitment, and they supported the war as an effort to contain communism.[13]

A little-publicized debate on the Senate floor on March 1, 1966, revealed Yarborough's early concerns with the war. By early 1966, the United States had over 200,000 troops in Vietnam and had extended bombing to North Vietnam. By this time, the conflict was clearly an American war. During a floor debate over extending appropriations for Vietnam, Yarborough questioned Senator William Fulbright (D-Arkansas) on a number of issues. Fulbright, the Senate Foreign Relations Committee chairman, was by this time an opponent of the war. Yarborough raised the issue of the appearance of U.S. bombers close to the Chinese border. "Are we tweaking the tiger's tail and trying to lure him into war," Yarborough asked, as he noted that bombs fell within a few miles and literally only seconds away from China's southern border with North Vietnam. In a second line of questioning Yarborough, quoting a February 21, 1966, *U.S. News and World Report* article, stated of the 12,000 villages and hamlets in Vietnam, the Vietcong held 11,000. He then asked Fulbright if the United States intended to attempt to recapture and pacify the settlements or "do we intend to burn these villages down and destroy them?" Fulbright's response noted the destruction of Vietnamese homes and their economy, making the U.S. action equivalent to that of the French, the former "colonial masters" of the embattled nation. Yarborough supported the legislation extending further funds for the war, but his line of questioning clearly indicated his growing concerns over the conduct and course of the war. Yarborough was not willing to publicly break with the administration and oppose a war which the vast majority of people in Texas and the rest of the nation still supported in 1966 but philosophically he was more aligned with Fulbright and other critics. By the summer of 1966 some liberals in Texas began to criticize the war and call for the withdrawal of U.S. troops. After the Fulbright exchange, *The Texas Observer* concluded that Yarborough had joined the camp of the Senate critics of Johnson's Vietnam policies. Yarborough quickly denied the comment and pointed out that he had voted for every appropriation for the war. He stated that he opposed immediate withdrawal because such a move represented an "abandonment of South Vietnam." However, he said, he favored an "honorable" negotiated settlement with North Vietnam. Quoting his former World War II commander in the Pacific, General Douglas MacArthur, he expressed concern about squandering men and resources in a major land war in Asia. Organized labor, many Texas Democrats loyal to Yarborough, and notably Walter Hall remained supportive of administration policies in Vietnam—all of which tempered Yarborough's public criticism of the war. Yarborough's caution indicated his departure from unquestioned support of Johnson's policies to a middle-of-the-road position. In his efforts to find an adequate solution, his consternation rivaled that of Johnson. The two Texans differed in that

Yarborough's commitment weakened with time as casualties increased with no discernible military progress.[14]

Yarborough's opposition to the policies in Southeast Asia solidified by 1967, when he concluded that the Vietnam War had replaced the Great Society as the number one priority on the Johnson administration's agenda. Economic reality squeezed the life out of Johnson's guns-and-butter budgets. Rising inflation coupled with the ever-increasing costs of the Vietnam War put the squeeze on funds for domestic programs. Also, throughout the nation public opinion shifted toward opposition to the extension of many civil rights and antipoverty programs. Beginning with the riots in Watts in the summer of 1965, death and destruction seemed to many Americans to be one of the outcomes of the civil rights movement. Many cities, mostly in the north, exploded the next three summers as Americans experienced the turmoil resulting from generations of poverty, frustration, discrimination, and the pent-up anger of African Americans. The smoke and fires from urban riots in the nation's cities appeared similar to the pictures of flaming villages in Vietnam. By 1967, the emphasis on anticrime bills as a response to racial violence signaled a dramatic change in the civil rights movement. The nation's battles on the inner-city streets seemed too much like the fighting in the jungles of South Vietnam. As Martin Luther King Jr. so succinctly analyzed the new situation, African Americans now had the right to eat hamburgers, but they had to somehow get the money to buy them.

Throughout 1967, Yarborough and other Senate liberals hoped to prevent any reductions in domestic spending in order to force the president to choose butter instead of guns. Yarborough continued voting for military appropriations but became increasingly frustrated as the administration backed further away from commitments to Great Society programs. Despite a stronger bombing campaign, more U.S. troops, and continued assurances from the Johnson administration that victory was somehow certain, Yarborough instead saw the 70,000 American casualties and the military stalemate. He concluded that for the nation there was no light at the end of the Vietnamese tunnel. As a decorated veteran and fervent supporter of the military, Yarborough's decision did not come easily. He struggled for many months as his loyalty and unswerving devotion to his country clashed with his concerns over the war's costs to the nation and its detrimental impact on the U.S. position as the world's advocate for democracy.

Many Texas congressmen also had doubts about the war, but no one expressed them publicly for fear of offending the president and stepping out too far in front of public opinion at home. But the president knew of Yarborough's disenchantment and expected that the outspoken senator would speak his mind and fight him in Congress. In the spring, President Johnson celebrated the 30th anniversary of his first election to Congress at a large outdoor rally in San Antonio. Yarborough, Connally, and many other dignitaries attended the well-publicized event. As the television cameras rolled, Johnson leaned over to say a few words to Yarborough and hand something to him. They both grinned. Only a few people were close enough to hear the President say, "Ralph, I'm going to give you this little pen knife. I hope you use it on my enemies as well as you do on me." Yarborough later drew the president's ire when he branded a proposed invasion of North Vietnam as "madness." Yarborough's comments were discussed in a critical August 1967 cabinet meeting on the administration's war policies. During that tense session, Johnson directed Secretary McNamara to convince the Texas senator that the administration had no plans to widen the war in this manner. Walter Hall, Yarborough's longtime financial supporter, warned him that Johnson's Vietnam policy could prove to be "his political death warrant." This episode marked the turning point in Yarborough's position on the war. Divisions over Vietnam, not the skirmishes over domestic legislation, broke the bond between Yarborough and Johnson.[15]

In 1968, Yarborough expanded his criticism and publicly expressed his concerns with the war. North Vietnam's Tet Offensive in January severely damaged the credibility of the administration and the military, whose optimistically forecasted end to the conflict proved elusive. In his April 19, 1968, newsletter, Yarborough described the American casualties in the war as "depressing." Billions of dollars disappeared into the Southeast Asia quagmire instead of being spent on American schools, housing, and other Great Society programs which helped Americans. No peace settlement appeared on the horizon to stabilize the region and reduce American involvement. The long and increasingly expensive conflict was wearing on Yarborough and the American people. Nonetheless, even as he raised his concerns, Yarborough hesitated to publicly confront the administration while Johnson was still president. Once Johnson announced he would not seek reelection, Yarborough and many others vainly hoped the president's withdrawal would lead to negotiations with Vietnam. The majority of Texans continued to support the war effort, but the dissenters were becoming more prominent even in the Lone Star State by 1968. Most Texas liberals by this time publicly denounced the war and privately encouraged Yarborough to make a stand calling for withdrawal of U.S. troops.[16]

With the continued escalation of the war, Yarborough pushed for lowering the voting age from twenty-one to eighteen. "I have advocated lowering the voting age to 18 since my first campaign for Governor of Texas in 1952," Yarborough announced before the Senate Judiciary Committee in the spring of 1968. Yarborough linked the voting-age initiative to earlier movements in the United States to expand the electorate and involve more people in the democratic process. He compared the initiative to abolition of property-ownership requirements, women's suffrage, and the Voting Rights Act of 1965. "The infusion of new segments of the population into the electorate has brought with it new ideas and new energies," he said. Yarborough noted that individuals who were eighteen could engage in many other adult activities—marriage, paying taxes, and working for the government. The measure was morally correct from Yarborough's standpoint as well as a practical political position. Foremost in the minds of most young men in their late teens was the military draft. Yarborough and other supporters realized millions of men and women would be newly enfranchised with the legislation. Yarborough believed that these new voters would flock to his banner in gratitude for his work. He also hoped that many draft-age voters would shift their support to antiwar candidates like himself.[17]

Lyndon Johnson shocked the nation on March 31, 1968, when he told the television audience he would not seek another term as president. The Vietnam War and Johnson's rapid decline in the polls as well as his personal health concerns spurred his decision. After his surprise statement, even the president's staunchest critics praised his decision as an act of patriotism and unselfishness. Yarborough's response to President Johnson's statement commended his domestic accomplishments and delineated their differences over Vietnam. Six million more Americans were at work, wages were higher, and corporate profits had increased since Johnson became president. Yarborough praised him for the "human results" during his years in office. Expanding educational opportunities and funding, Medicare, and the War on Poverty provided benefits for millions of Americans. "Unfortunately the tragedy and bloodshed of the war in Vietnam have overshadowed many of these outstanding victories," Yarborough stated. "I have opposed escalation to a bigger and bigger war. I have urged the President to seek a negotiated settlement and to end the war honorably." After Johnson announced in his speech that he would curtail bombing and pursue peace talks with North Vietnam, Yarborough said, "it would be an appropriate crowning touch for this administration if this peace effort succeeds." With his fellow Texan now out of the presidential picture, Yarborough openly moved to support his friend and philosophical ally Senator Robert Kennedy, much to the chagrin of Johnson and Connally.[18]

Yarborough often stayed in his cluttered Senate office until after midnight working on legislation and talking with friends and constituents. Courtesy Center for American History, Russell Lee Collection (3Y168).

Yarborough increased his public expressions of concern over the war in Vietnam following Johnson's withdrawal. He joined Senator Edward Long (D-Louisiana) to cosponsor legislation that allowed young men appearing before a local selective service board the right to counsel, which Selective Service regulations prohibited. Yarborough said the rule was a "shocking violation" of the Bill of Rights. He also took the opportunity to show his concern over the war that continued to escalate and claim more American lives. The week he introduced the bill, Yarborough said 562 Americans were killed in Vietnam, the highest weekly total of American deaths since the unfortunate war began. "In this context, the decision of the local draft board cannot be viewed merely as a matter of administrative classification; rather it must be considered for what it is: a very human matter involving the possibility of death." Yarborough believed that legal counsel was a fundamental right that even the Vietnam War should not override. Yarborough filed the legislation knowing that he was openly aligning himself with the most vocal critics of the war. He also realized that his own increased opposition to the Vietnam War would create problems back in Texas.[19]

MARTIN LUTHER KING JR. AND
ROBERT KENNEDY ASSASSINATIONS

Martin Luther King's assassination in Memphis created widespread turmoil and rioting throughout the nation. Yarborough, one of the few southerners to consistently support the civil rights movement, was the only prominent elected official from Texas to attend King's funeral. Ralph and Opal flew to Atlanta for the King services on April 9, 1968. "The senseless shooting in Memphis of the Rev. Dr. Martin Luther King Jr. was an act of madness, and the events that followed were just as irrational," the senator stated in his release to the media. Yarborough canceled a planned trip to Africa and a weekend visit to San Antonio for the opening of HemisFair so that he could attend the King memorial. When he returned to the capital, the outbreak of rioting in cities across the nation greatly disturbed Yarborough. The fires in Washington, D.C., came within a few blocks of the Capitol. Yarborough ascended to the roof of his Senate office building, where he could easily see the fires. The following day Yarborough joined police in an investigation of the riot-stricken areas. "It was one of the most shocking sights of my life," he remarked. The destruction reminded Yarborough of the Europe he witnessed after World War I and as a soldier in World War II. The chaos from the riots was just the opposite of what Yarborough and other Americans sought following the enactment of the civil rights laws. More unfolded with the assassination of another national leader—presidential aspirant Robert Kennedy.[20]

Yarborough described Robert Kennedy as a "voice of conscience" who "sought to arouse the nation, for the poor at home and for peace in the world." Yarborough delivered his memorial on the Senate floor and distributed his remarks to the press following the assassination on June 5, 1968, in Los Angeles. Yarborough had established a solid working relationship with the younger Kennedy when he served as attorney general for his brother John. Their relationship was a far cry from the enmity and distrust between Robert Kennedy and Lyndon Johnson. Kennedy often had sided with Yarborough in the patronage disputes with Johnson when Johnson was vice president and had helped Yarborough refute charges related to the Billie Sol Estes affair while LBJ and other Texas politicians sped from the scene faster than a jackrabbit before a grass fire. Following his election to the U.S. Senate in 1964, Yarborough also worked with Robert Kennedy on the Labor and Public Welfare Committee. In the three years on the committee the two men came to know one another quite well. "No other family in America has given more generously to the nation in this generation than the Kennedys," Yarborough said.

"Assassins have cut down two of America's most gifted sons of this generation, early in their brilliant careers." Yarborough's shock was genuine. He
was an eyewitness to the 1963 assassination of John Kennedy and grieved for
many months. Now he and the nation suffered the loss of the second member
of the family in less than five years. Ralph and Opal attended the services at
St. Patrick's Cathedral in New York City as the solitary high-ranking family
from Texas. The couple had expected to attend a family reunion in East Texas,
but once again a tragic event shattered the plans of Yarborough and thousands of other Americans. Yarborough rode on the Kennedy funeral train and
remarked that "America has experienced nothing like this since the funeral
train of Abraham Lincoln in 1865" as he noted the hundreds of thousands of
people who lined the tracks. Yarborough sent a telegram to Will Davis, the
chairman of the Texas SDEC, in an unsuccessful request for postponement
of the State Democratic Convention. The consistently upbeat Yarborough
became subdued and concerned for the nation's welfare in 1968. Vietnam, the
assassinations, and the social unrest throughout the nation tested the commitment and dedication of Americans of all political persuasions. Yarborough
mourned the loss of Kennedy and King but quickly emerged with his determination intact. Democrats still had to choose a nominee for the 1968 election as he looked forward to another election campaign in Texas. Following
Robert Kennedy's assassination, Yarborough openly broke with the administration when he endorsed Senator Eugene McCarthy for the Democratic
presidential nomination instead of Hubert Humphrey.[21]

1968 — "YEAR OF ANXIETY"

Yarborough recognized as well as anyone the difficulties facing the nation
in the traumatic time which he termed the "year of anxiety." In light of the
political and social upheaval in the nation, he accomplished a number of noteworthy achievements. These included additional funds for educational needs,
especially those addressed in his newly enacted Bilingual Education bill. He
also obtained federal funds for Padre Island and the Guadalupe Mountains
national areas in Texas. He anticipated action on his Big Thicket National
Park bill and introduced a Universal Education bill for tuition-free higher
education. He also filed legislation for Compensation to Innocent Victims
of Crime. However, he expressed his frustration when he talked about civil
rights and Vietnam and recognized the Democrats were losing the public's
confidence. "We in Congress can remove legal barriers, but we cannot legis-

The Yarborough family took pride in the selection of their Chandler home as a state historical landmark in December 1966. Flanking the historical marker are Harvey (left) and Donald (right), Ralph's two brothers who worked on all his campaigns, from district judge to U.S. Senate. Courtesy Opal Yarborough.

late personal lives," Yarborough observed in the context of the nation's on-going racial conflicts. He also said that Americans "must finally begin to ask the hard question about this war" and find a solution to the conflict. Race and the war were the focal points of 1968. Open conflict extended to the streets and hotels of Chicago during the turbulent Democratic National Convention. Tensions over integration and the rising tide of white resistance proved to be the determining factors even though the Vietnam War commanded more headlines.[22]

Not all was gloomy for Yarborough during 1968. On January 13 he had announced his decision to forego the race for Texas governor, although he confided to friends that he realized this represented his final opportunity to become the state's chief executive. The governor's $40,000 salary and $2 million executive budget exceeded his $30,000 annual Senate pay and $200,000 office account. As he had told Walter Hall and Fagan Dickson, he desired "to bring the Government of Texas into the 20th century." But another associate told him that while the governorship would have been better for both

Texas and Yarborough personally, "it is better for the nation as a whole for you to stay in the Senate." Yarborough ultimately concluded that his future remained in the Senate, where he could continue working on "progressive legislation in which I believe." Behind the scenes, both J. R. Parten and Walter Hall urged him to stay in the Senate. In addition, many national organizations affiliated with his legislative efforts and his fellow Democratic senators urged him to remain in the Senate in the critical election year.[23]

Returning to Texas on the last weekend in June, Yarborough attended the swearing-in ceremony for longtime friend William Wayne Justice and his nephew Richard Brooks Hardee. Justice, who had served for seven years as the U.S. district attorney for the Eastern District of Texas, was nominated and approved as federal judge for the Eastern District. Hardee had served as an assistant U.S. attorney under Justice and was appointed to take the office of district attorney vacated by Justice. Ardent political supporters of Yarborough, both men hailed from Yarborough's home county, Henderson, and had graduated from the University of Texas Law School. Justice and Hardee appeared at the announcement of Yarborough's first gubernatorial race in 1952 and recorded radio spots for him. Yarborough needed to broaden his support for difficult times that lay ahead. He and the liberal activists prepared to challenge the Connally delegation before the Credentials Committee of the 1968 Democratic National Convention. The state convention, controlled by the governor, ignored Yarborough and other liberals. In their places as delegates were "several Goldwater Republicans and Shivers supporters who are associates of John Connally, but unrepresentative of Democratic voters in this state."[24]

Before the Chicago convention, Yarborough appeared with Eugene McCarthy at a Houston press conference to recommend the senator from Minnesota. "I wholeheartedly and enthusiastically endorse his candidacy for the Presidency of the United States," Yarborough said in his prepared release. He also attacked the unit rule, which committed all Texas delegates to one candidate at the national convention. "It is incumbent on John Connally if he really believes in democracy to announce in the next 24 hours that he is abandoning the Unit Rule—and let this Texas delegation vote like they want to." Liberal Texas Democrats attempted to include fifty antiwar advocates among the 104 Texas delegates to the national convention in Chicago. But the governor's delegates prevailed as Yarborough and other McCarthy supporters remained excluded. Connally spoke at the national convention in defense of the Johnson administration's policies in South Vietnam and specifically criticized McCarthy. The Texas delegation remained nearly united as the

Democratic party endorsed the continuation of aggression in Vietnam and selected Hubert Humphrey as the presidential nominee along with Maine's Edmund Muskie as the vice presidential nominee. Many Texas delegates privately feared that because of the open warfare between the Yarborough and Connally Democrats that Richard Nixon would carry the state in November. Yarborough supporters were concerned because the senator had endorsed losing candidates in the 1968 Texas governor's race and might be doing the same in the presidential race. Their only victory in Chicago was securing a commitment to abolish the hated unit rule which conservative Democrats used to control the party. McCarthy left the country after the Chicago Democratic convention and never endorsed Humphrey. Yarborough and most Texas liberals came out for their party's nominee. Connally and Yarborough separately endorsed the Humphrey-Muskie ticket, but the divisions between the two remained as wide as the Grand Canyon.[25]

The 1968 election was a watershed in American politics. The bitterness and divisions created by racial tensions and the Vietnam War dwarfed other concerns. Democratic unity and vision that brought Yarborough and other Democrats to Washington disappeared in the turmoil of 1968. Richard Nixon, the Republican presidential nominee, rose like a political Lazarus after being written off as a footnote to history. Divided as the Democrats were, they attempted to patch up their tattered banners for the November election. Republicans on the other hand ran a united and well-financed campaign. Humphrey's beleaguered campaign began to gain momentum a month before the general election as prospects at the Paris peace talks between the United States and North Vietnam improved. The Humphrey-Muskie campaign temporarily united the warring factions of the Texas Democratic party. But the Democratic campaign became a two-headed monster as both conservatives and liberals pursued their separate programs. Connally remained loyal to Humphrey despite pressure from some conservative Democrats to stay away from the presidential campaign. Many conservative Democrats bolted to join former governor Allan Shivers and the Democrats for Nixon-Agnew campaign. However, only two Texas Democratic congressmen refused to endorse their party's candidates.

Yarborough and Jim Wright co-chaired the 1968 Texas campaign for Humphrey. Wright represented the Johnson wing of the party and Yarborough served as head of the party's liberal wing. Based on an agreement between Humphrey and his campaign, Yarborough believed that the money for the presidential campaign in Texas would be distributed equally. But he said "that part of the bargain was never lived up to by Humphrey's headquarters." Yarborough used his own staff and volunteers and appeared with Humphrey throughout the state in campaign appearances. Yarborough and Connally flew the flag of truce long enough to escort Humphrey to rallies in Fort Worth, Dallas, Waco, and Austin. The three leaders even sat next to one another on campaign stops and for photos. Yarborough told audiences that he and the governor were not at war, "we just had skirmish operations to test each other's flanks and borders." The senator said he and Connally agreed that a Humphrey victory was a necessity. He took great delight in noticing that he received more applause at the rallies than John Connally. After Connally was booed by students at a rally in Austin, the governor dropped off the campaign trail and left Humphrey to tour with Yarborough to South Texas and El Paso. With two weeks to go in the election, Yarborough boasted that Humphrey would carry Texas. President Johnson came to the final rally at the Astrodome in Houston and ended any speculation about his support for Humphrey when he declared that the Democratic nominee should be the next president.[26]

The last-minute efforts and the unity appeals worked for the Democrats in Texas. Humphrey narrowly edged out Nixon in Texas, 1,267,000 votes to 1,227,000 votes, while third-party candidate George Wallace finished an impressive third with nearly 582,000 votes. Humphrey finished with a majority of the minority precincts of the large cities and the counties in areas with strong Democratic votes: South Texas, Central Texas, and rural East Texas. However, Humphrey's victory in Texas was not enough; Richard Nixon won the presidential election with only 43 percent of the popular vote while winning thirty-two states and an electoral majority. Nixon's election changed the course of national politics, but the divisions in the country remained. The Vietnam War continued unabated and Nixon expanded the conflict into Cambodia in 1970 and extended the bombing campaign. In spite of reductions in ground troops and continued peace talks, the war continued to be as contentious and divisive as it was during the Johnson administration. In addition, discord continued over federal policies for ameliorating the discrimination and poverty endured by the nation's minority citizens. Racial politics entered a new phase as more white Americans turned their back on the egalitarian ideals of the early 1960's.[27]

More than a decade after the 1968 campaign, Yarborough expressed his feelings and described his motivations in a letter to Bernard Rapoport. Yarborough maintained his support for Johnson while he was planning to run for reelection but confessed he was "glad to see him withdraw." Thereafter, Yarborough first supported Robert Kennedy and then turned to Eugene Mc-

As often as he criticized Texas editors, Ralph remained an avid newspaper reader, as on this quiet morning with his wife, Opal. Courtesy Center for American History, Russell Lee Collection (3Y169).

Carthy following Kennedy's assassination. "It was the only time in my life that death, defeat and retreat eliminated three candidates and left me supporting a fourth for the Presidency," Yarborough wrote. McCarthy was justified in his refusal to support Humphrey, Yarborough believed, because of the brutality of the Chicago police against his supporters during the national convention. In Texas, the feud between Democratic conservatives and liberals was far from over. Texas remained Democratic in 1968 due to efforts made to preserve the state's Democratic tradition for Lyndon Johnson. The appearance of segregationist candidate George Wallace on the ballot likely took more votes away from Nixon than Humphrey in the state. Without Wallace, Nixon easily would have won the Lone Star State despite the temporary unity of the state's Democrats. The election results were an ill omen for Yarborough. The temporary peace between the Democratic factions ended as abruptly as an unhappy courtship.[28]

Within days after the November election, candidates began testing the waters for a run against Yarborough in the 1970 primary. Potential challengers mentioned were outgoing Governor Connally, Lieutenant Governor Ben Barnes, Attorney General Waggoner Carr, Congressman Jim Wright, and a host of other Democratic aspirants. Republican congressman George Bush

Two vital issues for Ralph Yarborough were family and the law. Ralph joins hands with his older brother Harvey Jackson (left) and his son, Richard (right), as he presents them for certification before the U.S. Supreme Court in 1967. Courtesy Center for American History, Yarborough Papers (3Y434).

of Houston quickly expressed his interest in a rematch with Yarborough. In addition, rumors circulated that Johnson would appoint Yarborough to a federal judge's position before he left office in 1969. If Johnson made the selection, Connally could then appoint himself as the interim senator. The scenario was similar to the one in 1957 when Yarborough won the special election to the Senate. Yarborough, who would be 68 years old during the next election, was still not one to duck a fight and quickly rejected the idea. He was also in line for the chairmanship of the Senate Labor and Public Welfare Committee and Democrats still held the majority in both the Senate and the House of Representatives. He believed his seniority position and membership on the Appropriations Committee were far more influential than a federal judge's seat. Furthermore, he saw himself as the undisputed leader of the Democratic party in the state. With Allan Shivers firmly in the Republican fold and Connally out of office, Yarborough believed he had one more opportunity to bring the state party and the majority of Texans to his banner. His efforts to sever the wealthy conservatives from the party and replace them with middle-class, working people representative of the state's population began to take hold after 1968. Many Yarborough supporters believed their efforts saved the state for Humphrey and other Democrats in 1968 and that they could repeat their performance in 1970.

Lyndon Johnson's final days in office closed the curtain on the long rivalry between the two unconventional Texas leaders whose relationship dated back to the Roosevelt administration. Throughout the 1950's and when Johnson served as Kennedy's vice president, the two seldom cooperated as they fought for domination of Texas politics. As they rode side by side behind President Kennedy's convertible in Dallas, events that one November afternoon changed the world for both Texas leaders. Once Johnson became president, they finally worked together for common goals and a national purpose. In spite of their improved relationship and the legislation Yarborough carried, he never considered himself part of the Johnson team. Yarborough resented the behind-the-scenes efforts by the president and his staff to stifle many of his favorite bills. As author of more Great Society legislation than any of his Senate colleagues, Yarborough bristled when Johnson received accolades for his accomplishments. Yarborough said that once Johnson became president, he still "tried to take credit for my work . . . He was a horse trader, the shrewdest politician I've ever seen operate." Yarborough recalled years later that before his death Johnson credited him with programs that comprised 80 percent of the Great Society. Lyndon Johnson had few equals and his legacy remains the subject of debate. Yarborough realized that he often toiled in the shadow of his fellow Texan, but that made him work harder in an effort to separate himself politically and philosophically from LBJ. Johnson's commitment to reform was tempered by the politics of the time and his wheeler-dealer image; Yarborough remained the straight arrow whose vision seldom strayed from the target of social and economic improvement for everyday working Americans.[29]

13 *Final Senate Years and Election Defeat*

Yarborough rejoined the Senate in 1969 with heightened prestige and influence. He became chair of the Senate Labor and Public Welfare Committee in the 91st Congress. He wanted the chairmanship because he felt that great strides had been made in education but comparable improvements in health care were lagging. He frequently expressed concerns over the high infant mortality rates in the nation, malnutrition among children, and the shortage of doctors and other medical personnel. He appeared more comfortable and less caustic in his remarks at hearings and on the Senate floor. Senate majority leader Mike Mansfield named him a trustee of the Kennedy Center for the Performing Arts. Many stories described him as relaxed, always busy, and happier than ever. He took particular pride in creation of a national committee to promote cancer research which launched a new "War on Cancer" by the federal government. His staff threw a surprise party for Ralph and Opal marking his twelfth year in the U.S. Senate. Senator Edward Kennedy, a potential presidential candidate and friend, attended the festivities along with Yarborough's fellow Texas congressmen. As he savored a slice of the Lone Star cake, Yarborough said he was not worried about the 1970 election. He had much work to do as the new committee chairman and the next election was "a long way off."[1]

An article in *Medical World News* provided a critical yet favorable view of Yarborough during his first year as committee chair. Yarborough had little patience with his critics in the Nixon administration. The journal described him as a "unique blend of Southern loquaciousness, Midwestern populism, and old-style liberalism." He was not a member of the Senate "club" but was considered more of a lone wolf. Yarborough still had one of the largest volumes of mail of all senators and still attempted to read and respond to as many letters as possible, much to the "despair of the staff." The heavy workload and Yarborough's drive for excellence resulted in high employee turnover and frazzled nerves. Rather than attend the frequent lobby receptions and cocktail parties, he regularly returned to his Senate office at night and worked until midnight. He still never used any language stronger than "darn" and, true to his Southern Baptist heritage, never drank alcohol. His son, Richard, the longtime manager of the office, accepted a position as an attorney with the Indian Claims Commission. Ralph and Opal maintained their Austin home and their Washington residence, filling both with books and antiques. (Hundreds of books lined the walls of the Yarboroughs' Washington apartment.) When he returned late at night, he frequently read until the early hours of the morning. "When a man reaches this stage in life, he is entitled to do as he pleases," Opal said in a Houston newspaper interview in early 1969. She said that she believed she shared her husband's views and work for "the betterment of the country."[2]

During Nixon's first year of office, Yarborough exerted his independence and influence. No longer restrained by a Democratic president, Yarborough made frequent use of his seniority and the press to pan the Republican administration. He remained especially critical of Nixon's Vietnam policies and contended that the military attempted to cover-up the murder of 200 civilians in what became known as the My Lai massacre. At a speech in San Antonio in 1969, Yarborough said the United States was "squandering" $3 billion monthly in Vietnam while hunger and poverty impacted 40 million Americans. He called for $5 billion in federal support for hospitals, expanded health care and cancer research, and a reduction in personal income taxes. He renewed his efforts for creation of a Big Thicket national park. A new biography by William Phillips entitled *Yarborough of Texas* touted his background and legislative accomplishments. The author praised Yarborough's independence, describing him as a courageous and progressive political leader who "can successfully challenge the most powerful forces of political and economic reaction." Anyone doubting that the senator was running for reelection only had to read the flattering biography. Yarborough eagerly anticipated his race for a third senate term.[3]

WHO IS LLOYD BENTSEN?

Yarborough relished his role as a political maverick. His affiliation with national liberal leaders and his voting record made headlines back home. The liberal Americans for Democratic Action gave Yarborough a 78 percent rating for the 1969 session. (Senator Tower's was zero.) Yarborough voted against other southern senators on two-thirds of the decisive roll calls in 1969,

Dickinson banker Walter Hall and his wife, Helen (left), were among the few wealthy Texans who provided financial support for Ralph and Opal (right) in every gubernatorial and senate campaign from 1952 to 1972. Courtesy Opal Yarborough.

more than any other senator from the former Confederate states. Texas newspapers labeled Yarborough as the "Least Southern" senator, and the *Dallas Morning News* mentioned that George Bush was still a potential Republican challenger in the 1970 Senate general election. President Nixon and Senator Tower were reported to be pressuring the Houston congressman to run again. In early January, the *News* mentioned that former South Texas congressman Lloyd M. Bentsen of Houston was a potential conservative Democratic challenger. Bentsen's announcement caught Yarborough off guard. Bentsen immediately drew the support of former governor Connally and employed John Mobley, Connally's executive assistant, as his campaign manager. Some Washington reports indicated that the primary battle would be a "political bloodbath." But most Texas political writers and liberal activists believed Yarborough could easily defeat Bentsen in the primary. The real test would come in November in a rematch with George Bush. Bentsen remained the only

Democratic challenger as the filing deadline passed. As the *Texas Observer* noted as late as February 1970, Bentsen would mount a solid challenge but "Yarborough should take him with votes to spare." The senator and his staff seemed more concerned with Bush and a multimillion-dollar media and advertising effort directed by the Nixon campaign team.[4]

Before his own announcement, Yarborough blasted Bentsen as a proxy for former governor Connally. The incumbent also referred to Bentsen's father. "His father's string of banks is putting pressure on people to support Mr. Bentsen," he charged, and were "turning the screws on down there" to have influential Democrats support his son. His untimely remarks made Yarborough appear more as a challenger than an experienced Senate incumbent. Yarborough formally announced for reelection on January 26 and expressed concern with the low voter registration numbers in a state that was now fourth in population. He also criticized President Nixon's veto of a $19.7 billion education and health appropriation bill. He blamed "runaway inflation" and high interest rates on the Nixon administration's monetary policies. He listed the Cold War G.I. bill, Padre Island National Seashore, the Bilingual Education Act, and "scores of other laws" in education, conservation, health, and veterans' rights as his primary Senate accomplishments. Yarborough declined to discuss Bentsen's charges that he was a "dove" on Vietnam.[5]

Yarborough paid his $1,000 filing fee a few days later, accompanied by his wife, Opal, former ambassador and longtime friend Ed Clark, and the widows of J. Frank Dobie and Walter Prescott Webb. Yarborough announced that Clark, long an associate of Lyndon Johnson, was his new state finance director. More than 5,000 Democrats attended the largest campaign dinner ever held for Yarborough at Houston's Albert Thomas Convention Center. Presidential aspirants Ed Muskie, Harold Hughes, and Alan Cranston attended the $5-a-plate turkey dinner. In a brief (by Yarborough standards) twenty-five-minute speech, Yarborough praised the efforts of national Democrats as he lambasted the Nixon administration's economic and Vietnam policies. When asked about his primary opponent, whom he appeared to ignore, the senator responded, "Who is Lloyd Bentsen?"[6]

Bentsen, forty-nine at the time of the election, was no stranger to Texas politics. His father, Lloyd M. Bentsen Sr., was a land developer and rancher in South Texas. The younger Bentsen served three terms in the U.S. Congress from 1949 to 1954, representing his home area of the Rio Grande Valley. He returned to Texas in 1955 to build his business interests. He became successful and with other family members owned a large corporation based in Houston with investments in insurance, banking, and savings and loans. Bentsen was part of the Connally inner circle during the 1960's. Connally called a meeting at his ranch in 1966 which included Bentsen and other close advisors. The governor at one point decided not to run for reelection and asked Bentsen to enter the governor's race with his support, but Bentsen and others persuaded Connally to run for one more term. After he decided not to run in 1968, Connally encouraged Bentsen to challenge Yarborough in the 1970 Democratic primary. Years before, Connally had urged Bentsen to challenge Yarborough in the 1964 primary. At that time, Bentsen's business interests plus Lyndon Johnson's overtures kept the former Texas congressman out of the race. At the beginning of the 1970 race, Bentsen said he visited with former governor Allan Shivers and President Johnson at his ranch in Johnson City. Neither offered much encouragement since they believed Yarborough could not be defeated in a primary. Johnson believed that Bush was a formidable candidate and the retired president did not want a primary battle that bloodied the Democratic nominee. Newspaper stories reported Johnson bluntly said that he would have no part of any effort to dump Yarborough. Bentsen, determined to make the race, stuck to his plan. He depicted the campaign against Yarborough as "relatively mild." He said he decided to take off the gloves when Yarborough attacked his father, Lloyd Bentsen Sr., who was involved with former Governor Shivers in the land exchange made famous in the 1954 governor's race. "In Texas we have a tendency of thinking of politics as a contact sport," Bentsen commented as he described his role during the race.[7]

The Texas that Yarborough knew from the 1950's was hardly recognizable in 1970. The old men who played dominoes and talked politics around the small-town courthouse squares were mostly gone. People no longer came to town on Saturdays to shop and watch movies or to hear campaign speeches. Most Texans now spent their Saturdays in shopping malls or in front of the television. By 1970, the state's population had increased to more than 11 million people. The cities and the suburbs expanded while rural Texas continued to lose its residents to urban centers. The largest metropolitan areas in the state, Houston and the Dallas/Fort Worth area, increased by more than 30 percent. Nearly 9 million people now lived in urban areas. Many white, middle-class city dwellers and suburbanites still harbored concerns over demands for economic equality by minority citizens. Republicans fanned the flames as part of Richard Nixon's southern strategy. White backlash grew in the face of increased intervention by the federal government in everyday life and court-ordered decisions requiring integration. Few objected to voting rights and access to public facilities, but resistance to any further moves that

Yarborough, a veteran of decades of Democratic political battles in Texas, lost the 1970 primary race to Lloyd Bentsen Jr. Photographer Shel Herschorn's picture shows an older, yet still vigorous Yarborough during the 1970 campaign. Courtesy Center for American History, Yarborough Papers (3S387).

addressed structural inequality increased among middle-class whites. School buses became the new symbol of "forced" integration. These Texans became the critical voters who determined the 1970 race.[8]

With only a month to go before the election, polls indicated Yarborough held a firm lead over Bentsen. His supporters believed the race was well in hand. But in early April Yarborough became concerned about spending most of his time in Washington involved in legislative and committee assignments. Yarborough began broadcasting radio ads in English and Spanish highlighting his health and education legislation. One series of promotions featured popular television series *Bonanza* star and Texan Dan Blocker. The Yarborough campaign issued press releases and the senator accused Bentsen of "pocketing war profits" because of his ownership and participation on the board of Lockheed Aircraft, a large national defense contractor. He also charged Bentsen with not paying his fair share of income taxes while taking advantage of federal subsidy programs. Yarborough was concerned when he learned that Bentsen planned to spend over $1 million for television ads in the closing weeks of the campaign. As the May 2 primary approached, the Senate was set to vote for confirmation of Judge G. Harrold Carswell of Florida, Nixon's controversial appointee to the Supreme Court. Yarborough opposed the nomination but hesitated to speak out against the nominee. Nixon selected Carswell, a conservative southern jurist, as his second nominee to the Supreme Court. Earlier, the Senate rejected Clement Haynsworth, another conservative judge from South Carolina whom Yarborough opposed. The Nixon administration charged that northern liberals would block any southern conservative on the nation's highest court, thus putting Yarborough in the position of voting for the second time against a neighboring judge and fellow southerner. After the Senate vote narrowly rejected Carswell, a terse Nixon appeared on national television to condemn the Senate and announced that the third nominee would not be from the South. Because of the regional politics in play and the widespread publicity on the nominations, the Supreme Court appointment decision played a large role in the electoral process. Once Yarborough cast his vote against Carswell, many political observers believed the vote alienated some of Yarborough's longtime Democratic supporters, especially among labor and in East Texas. Yarborough saw the choice as one of principle over politics, but Bentsen understood the volatility of white voters, many of whom now viewed the court as too friendly to minorities. Bentsen, who let it be known at a Houston Junior Bar Association meeting that he would have voted for Carswell, claimed Yarborough "should vote for Texas at least once in a while" and said it was a victory for the antisouthern- and ultra-liberals who viewed the Supreme Court as "a place to write laws rather than to interpret them."[9]

Bentsen's positions helped him receive the behind-the-scenes support of several Texas Democratic congressmen. Conservative congressmen Olin "Tiger" Teague, Bob Poague, and George Mahon worked on behalf of Bentsen and sent staff members to their home districts to work for the challenger. Bentsen aggressively denied all of the charges Yarborough leveled against him. He announced the family never received $100,000 in subsidies from the Department of Agriculture. The federal agency made a mistake as Bentsen said he only received several thousand dollars. He maintained that in 1948 his father allowed Mexican Americans access to a swimming pool when they were denied admission by the operators. Bentsen said he resigned his position on the Lockheed board and had no conflict of interest when voting on contracts to the defense firm. On the campaign trail, he characterized Yarborough as belonging to "another era" of horses and buggies while Texas was now in the "jet age." He also continued his criticism of Yarborough's opposition to the Vietnam War. Bentsen covered the state with billboards which appeared as frequently as Coca-Cola signs. But in late March, he still seemed mired far behind Yarborough in what one correspondent viewed as a potential "slaughter" and a runaway victory for the incumbent. In fact, Yarborough's team worried about a lack of funds as the intensity increased. Bernard Rapoport complained to Walter Hall that money "is coming very, very tight" and "the labor money has been very disappointing." The race was far from over as the Bentsen campaign had already prepared a series of devastating television ads for the final weeks of the campaign.[10]

Bentsen confirmed Yarborough's worst fears when the challenger's campaign unleashed a series of television commercials linking Yarborough to riots and violence and targeting his opposition to the Vietnam War. In the ads, Bentsen accused Yarborough and liberal Democrats of spawning crime, looting, and burning. Scenes of clashes between police and protesters from the Chicago Democratic Convention in 1968 and of police spraying tear gas on demonstrators in Washington flashed across the screen. Bentsen claimed Yarborough's support for McCarthy in 1968 and his endorsement of a Vietnam War moratorium in 1969 supported his accusations. Yarborough exploded when he saw the ads, calling them "slanderous, libelous and false." Former *Texas Observer* editor Ronnie Dugger suggested that the Yarborough campaign file a complaint with the National Fair Campaign Practices Committee and ask the Federal Communications Commission to stop the Bentsen spots. At a Dallas news conference a week before the primary, Yarborough said Bentsen "has caused people to think I marched with the demonstrators." He called the spots part of Bentsen's "Big Lie" and equated them with the 1954 "Port Arthur Story" used against him by the Allan Shivers campaign. Bentsen refused to withdraw the ads and told reporters during a campaign stop that Yarborough was "just a damned troublemaker." He also accused Yarborough of favoring forced busing to integrate schools while opposing voluntary prayer in public schools.[11]

By almost any standard, the final weeks of the race resembled a back alley fight more than a political campaign. Yarborough must have felt he had returned to the 1950's as he faced an aggressive, articulate, and well-financed candidate with a resolve to win at any cost. The final weeks featured charges and countercharges as the two men taunted one another around the state. Late polls still showed Yarborough with a slim lead over Bentsen, but projected turnout raised concerns. "I'm trying to get my troops onto the battlefield now, telling them not to wait for the fall. But it isn't that easy," he told a *New York Times* reporter a week before the May 2 primary election.[12]

On election day, Bentsen stunned Yarborough with an unexpected victory, winning by a vote of 812,000 to 721,000. At an Austin news conference on Monday after the election, Yarborough blamed his defeat on the "big lie technique" and Bentsen's irresponsible charges of spawning violence in the streets, opposing school prayer, and favoring busing. Maury Maverick Jr. was even more caustic when he said Bentsen's victory was "anti-nigger, anti-Mexican, anti-youth and sock-it-to-'em in Vietnam." Yarborough also attributed his defeat to his votes against Nixon's Supreme Court nominees Carswell and Haynsworth and to Republican voters who "crossed over" and voted for Bentsen in the Democratic primary. Yarborough surprised many when he announced his support for the party nominee against George Bush in November, but he refused to mention Bentsen by name. Political analysts also believed that many East Texans and labor union members who composed the bedrock of Yarborough's support stayed home on election day in protest of what they considered his antisouthern votes and his outspoken opposition to the Vietnam War. Minority turnout in Houston and other urban areas that heavily favored Yarborough were also below average. Also, many key supporters throughout the state were the same ones Yarborough had in the 1950's, an indication that his organization had stagnated in his later Senate years. Longtime supporter Creekmore Fath noted that as many as two hundred stalwart local organizers had died since Yarborough's last election in 1964. A year before the election, Fath said, "I talked to Ralph and said we have got to put somebody in Texas to organize now because the organization is flat dead and you don't have anything left. You've got to go out and find new people to take over the campaign managers jobs in these counties where you no longer have somebody." After he rejected Yarborough's offer to run the ill-fated reelection effort, Fath recalled his concerns over the lack of preparation. "Ralph wouldn't listen. He wouldn't do a blamed thing about it," he said.[13]

Yarborough stayed in Washington, returning to Texas with less than three weeks before the primary election. His tardiness was partially due to friends in Texas who failed to ring the alarm. He realized Bentsen would outspend him, but he seemed unprepared for the final media blitz by the challenger. Yarborough spent $311,000, half of which came in donations and the other half he borrowed. He had a debt of over $140,000 that he began to whittle down before he left office. The Bentsen campaign listed its expenditures as $488,000, but Yarborough and his staff believed they easily spent over $1 million. Many Yarborough supporters blamed their leader for not taking the Bentsen campaign seriously until it was too late to change the outcome. But very few people believed Bentsen could defeat Yarborough until the final few days before the election. Veteran political operative Chuck Caldwell recalled, "it was the only election that I ever went through in my life that I didn't see the wave coming." Bentsen followed and improved on the same themes Preston Smith used two years earlier in his successful race against Don Yarborough. Their efforts also resembled the media campaign utilized by Nixon, which featured oft-repeated televised scenes of urban rioting and siren wailing. In retrospect, Yarborough became the victim of his own overconfidence and his outdated image as an old-time populist leader whose uncompromising attitudes had grown stale. Texas had changed considerably from the days of his nonstop driving from one small-town rally to another. Men in straw hats and women in print dresses no longer flocked to hear political candidates on the courthouse steps. Television, air conditioning, and shopping malls altered life across the state by 1970. Yarborough also became the victim of the political hangover of the 1960's as the electorate shifted to the right during the Nixon years. Al Gore Sr., Yarborough's Senate soulmate, also lost his reelection bid that fall after a similar attack-style campaign. The times seemed to catch up with Yarborough as his defeat left the liberal movement in Texas leaderless and disorganized.[14]

An unresolved issue concerned Lyndon Johnson's role in Bentsen's upset bid. As Yarborough's friends sought answers to the upset, some blamed Lyndon Johnson in spite of earlier stories he discouraged Bentsen's candidacy. "There are some folks who think that LBJ had something to do with Bentsen running," Chuck Caldwell stated. In conversations with the senator after the 1970 election, Caldwell said Yarborough sometimes blamed the former president for playing one final game to settle old scores. But Caldwell and Creekmore Fath discounted any active solicitation or work by Johnson on behalf of Bentsen. Fath said that "Lyndon discouraged two or three people from running against Ralph in 1970." He added, "I never understood why Ralph wouldn't go to Lyndon because Lyndon told everybody not to run, that they couldn't beat Ralph." Whatever his reasons, Yarborough apparently never solicited the support or assistance from LBJ. Connally and Bentsen served as protégés of the legendary president, but they acted on their own in 1970. As Johnson lived out his final years on his Pedernales ranch, he withdrew from most of the battlefields of the Texas Democratic party.[15]

A subdued but still energetic Yarborough and his wife returned to Washington where a crowd of several hundred admirers and friends greeted the veteran campaigners. Senators Eugene McCarthy and Edward Kennedy joined the reception. The only Texas congressman at the airport was his longtime friend Rep. Jack Brooks of Beaumont. Senator Kennedy praised his colleague when he said "no other person has the courage or convictions like Ralph Yarborough." McCarthy, who did not seek reelection, apologized to Yarborough for contributing to his defeat. Senator Thomas Eagleton (D-Missouri) provided the most accurate summation: "Ralph Yarborough would rather be right than a U.S. Senator." Yarborough graciously said that he would leave the Senate at the end of his term "with a heart full of gratitude." He planned to return to Austin and open a private law practice and work to pay off his sizable campaign debt. When Yarborough quickly raised the idea of returning to Texas to run for another office, some of the senator's friends reminded him that his hero Sam Houston returned to Texas to run for governor after he lost his Senate seat because of votes that many perceived were anti-Texan.[16]

Yarborough's final appreciation dinner as a U.S. senator witnessed a grand turnout of nearly 3,000 people and the appearance of many prominent national Democrats. Money from the December banquet at Austin's Municipal Auditorium further reduced Yarborough's campaign debt. Some supporters mentioned the affair was a kickoff for his next campaign. The senator thanked the audience for allowing him to be the "unshackled voice of the people" during his nearly fourteen years in the Senate. Former vice president Humphrey and others expressed their sorrow at losing Yarborough from Washington because of the pointed remarks he easily fired at the Nixon administration. (Only a few days before the dinner, President Nixon announced the appointment of Yarborough's longtime foe John Connally as the new secretary of the treasury.) Yarborough hinted that he wanted to run again, saying he did not plan to come back to Austin and retire. "So much remains to be done and there is so little time in which to do it," he told the gathering. As he returned for the final days in office, senators from both parties recognized the unique role Yarborough played. Senator Harry Byrd (D-West Virginia), who had a reputation for spellbinding oratory, lauded Yarborough as the most eloquent speaker in the body. "I have often said that he could put more words into a period of sixty seconds than could any other Senator," Byrd remarked. Majority Leader Mike Mansfield (D-Montana) said Yarborough was a man of "unimpeachable principle." Senator William Fulbright (D-Arkansas) noted that his name was "attached to more legislation than that of any other Senator in Texas history." Senator John Tower, Yarborough's Republican counterpart, said even though they disagreed on policy issues, the two worked together because of "an attitude of respect." His colleagues noted his commitment and his many legislative accomplishments, but nearly everyone spoke about his honesty, intellect, courage, dedication, and vision. As a final tribute to Yarborough, the Senate passed his Big Thicket legislation calling for a park of up to 100,000 acres in the East Texas woodlands to save the fast-disappearing wilderness.[17]

In his final report to the Senate on January 2, 1971, Yarborough highlighted eighteen major health care bills he authored and one he cosponsored. Most of the legislation went through his Labor and Public Welfare Committee. These included the Hill-Burton Hospital Construction Act of 1970; the Regional Medical Centers—Heart, Cancer, Stroke and Kidney Act; the Family Planning Act; the Alcohol Abuse Act; the Allied Health Professions Act; the Communicable Disease Control Act; the Developmental Disabilities Service and Construction Act; and the Sam Rayburn Memorial Veterans Administration Act. President Nixon vetoed the Hill-Burton Act but Congress voted to override the veto. Yarborough became the first "lame duck" senator to manage a bill which successfully overcame a presidential veto. "I did not let my defeat in the May Primary in Texas defeat the health needs of the people," he told senators. President Nixon made a pocket veto of another Yarborough bill, the Family Medicine Act. Yarborough also pushed for establishment of a National Cancer Authority to combat the dreaded disease as part of the War on Cancer Yarborough inaugurated in 1969. In addition, millions of dollars for medical schools and research came through Yarborough-sponsored amendments. Yarborough also mentioned his legislation to improve public education and libraries, expand veterans training and education, provide compensation for innocent victims of crime, and send millions of dollars in federal funds to the state for defense, construction, agriculture, and other public works programs. "As I leave the Senate I have no regrets," he stated. "In the years ahead I shall continue to devote my time and energy to those causes that will benefit all mankind." [18]

Yarborough's defeat came as a surprise to many and the reaction to his loss took some time. During his final days in the Senate, many editorials praised his service and commitment to the state and the nation over the decades and recognized his many accomplishments. The *Houston Post* editors provided a final salute at the end of his last Senate term. The paper noted that the editors and others frequently disagreed with Yarborough, but no one doubted his sincerity and integrity. No one could question "his abiding love for Texas and his efforts during 13 years in the United States Senate to make it a better place for all its people." Many others praised Yarborough's fights to improve education, expand health care, and for the establishment of two national parks in the state. Although Yarborough was in his late sixties, many writers predicted his return in 1972. Yarborough was such a part of the Texas political scene that few could imagine Texas without him. [19]

14 *The Last Hurrah*

Even before Yarborough returned to Austin in early 1971, many politicos began to speculate about his political plans. Yarborough's imposing presence in Texas politics now spanned several generations, making him one of the most widely recognized figures in the state. He opened a new law office on the seventh floor of the Brown Building in downtown Austin. From behind his desk piled several feet high with papers and books, Yarborough maintained a busy schedule. He talked with friends and provided interviews to reporters, and his supporters debated his chances in running for governor in 1972, possibly against archrival John Connally as the GOP nominee, versus running again for the Senate to challenge John Tower in the general election. Most important to Yarborough, he once again became a focal point of Texas politics.

As the year proceeded, independent polls indicated Yarborough's chances for a return to the Senate were better than his chances for governor. News stories indicated a strong Democrat could defeat Tower because of the growth in voter registration in a state that included many newly enfranchised voters between eighteen and twenty-one, Mexican Americans, and African Americans. Letters also came to Yarborough from many people apologizing for the lack of activity on his behalf in the 1970 primary and promising to work on his behalf in 1972. Yarborough responded that he was truly interested in running again, but as he told his friend and supporter Randy Fitzgerald in August 1971, "I am far from deciding which office to be a candidate for." The lure of the campaign trail coupled with the emerging Sharpstown Bank scandal involving many prominent Texas officeholders encouraged Yarborough's desire for a political comeback. The Sharpstown affair centered on charges that state officials made a quick profit from bank stock furnished by Houston businessman Frank W. Sharp in return for legislation favorable to state banks. Governor Preston Smith, House Speaker Gus Mutscher, State Party Chairman Dr. Elmer Baum, Lieutenant Governor Ben Barnes, and other prominent Democrats were linked to the questionable bank loan and stock purchase deal. Mutscher, his aide Rush McGinty, and state representative Tommy Shannon ultimately received convictions in the case. In the fallout from the Sharpstown case, Smith, Barnes, and other incumbent Democrats saw the end of their careers as elected officials. Reform candidates and new faces dominated statewide and legislative races in 1972. The Texas electorate, in the mood to "turn the rascals out," welcomed some fresh faces.[1]

Yarborough hoped this latest Texas political scandal would work to his advantage. He kept the phone lines busy discussing his future plans. Throughout 1971, he kept the political pundits guessing as he mentioned both the governor's race and the senate campaign in the same breath. To most Texas liberals and labor leaders, his political return was as important as a Second Coming. Undoubtedly many felt guilty for their lack of enthusiasm in Yarborough's 1970 Democratic primary loss. As the acknowledged leader of the liberal faction in the Texas Democratic party, supporters wanted Yarborough back in office to carry the banner for social and economic issues. In addition, many viewed Yarborough as a draw for lower-income and minority voters who voted Democratic and supported more liberal candidates. In the battle for other political offices during the primary, many liberals believed they could capture some of the state's top offices and the legislature. The Sharpstown scandals and a Yarborough candidacy seemed to be the right combination for a liberal resurgence in 1972.

Other rumblings illustrated concerns among many of Yarborough's ideological supporters that time and events made him a relic of the political past. Some feared Yarborough would be too preoccupied with past political battles to focus on a new campaign. Shivers, Connally, and Bentsen still drew his wrath, and Yarborough frequently appeared more concerned with fighting old battles against his longtime foes. One supporter said he was essentially a politician of the old school—more accustomed to long-winded, populist style speeches on the courthouse square—whereas the electorate now concentrated on how a candidate appeared on television. Others believed that Yarborough should serve as the senior spokesman for the liberal movement and step aside for new, younger leadership. Veteran Austin political writer Dave McNeely interviewed dozens of Yarborough's friends whose comments spanned the political horizon. No consensus emerged on whether Yarborough should undertake a race for governor, for senator, or just make a graceful withdrawal. However, nearly everyone agreed Yarborough continued to wield considerable influence since his decision was the one on which the press and aspiring politicians focused. "He is about the most difficult man to help I have ever known," Walter Hall commented to Fagan Dickson as the two Yarborough backers discussed his future. "But what he has done for the people who need help most caused me to respect him greatly and to hope that he returns to high public office." The "old man" of Texas politics believed he had one more race left for a political comeback reminiscent of his first Senate election in 1957.[2]

After consultation with Opal, his brothers Donald and Harvey, his son, Richard, and close friends, Yarborough made his decision for one final attempt. He ended the suspense in early January 1972 when he announced his desire to return to the U.S. Senate. At the age of 68 he entered his ninth statewide political campaign since first running for attorney general in 1938. Yarborough reported his supporters were evenly divided over the senate and the governor's race. He publicly said the deciding factor was his concern for the nation and the threats to the American people he perceived coming from the Nixon administration. He also wanted to vindicate his earlier loss and to complete some of the unfinished business he left behind in Washington, especially the Big Thicket National Park project. From Austin he set off on a five-city tour hoping to gain more television exposure for his announcement. Opposing his bid to return to Washington was Barefoot Sanders, 46, a former aide to President Johnson who previously served in President Kennedy's Justice Department. His first name, Barefoot, was his grandmother's maiden name and turned out to be a plus for the candidate. Three other minor candidates also filed. By this time, most voting Texans knew Yarborough and had either positive or negative opinions about him. He was better known than his opponent, but few observers predicted Yarborough's comeback would be easy. Yarborough's announcement cleared the political decks in Texas. Once his decision was public, other Democratic political aspirants began announcing their intentions. Politicians loved him or loathed him as he continued to command center stage in Texas.[3]

Yarborough stayed involved in the minute details of the campaign as in earlier days. He sent out letters, notes, memos, photographs, and other items he brought home from his years in the Senate. Detailed notes and memos to staff members provide precise instructions. In a directive to one of his campaign aides, Yarborough barked orders like a drill sergeant. He wanted three copies each of the Cancer hearings, the National Conquest of Cancer program, the Big Thicket hearings, the History of the Labor Committee, and the Folklife Foundation Act. He also demanded a whole box of *We The People* books. "I want those 3 boxes, they cost me money, I paid out good hard money for all of these," he said in his typewritten order to Jimmy Bray. Yarborough staff members and volunteers were instructed to provide the senator ongoing information in writing for his review as he campaigned. He campaigned seventeen hours a day, criss-crossing the state just as he had in his earlier campaigns for governor and senator. At a typical Yarborough "banquet," the former senator spoke about Washington corruption while his admirers ate fried chicken and drank iced tea in Dr. Pepper cups. He talked about millionaires who never paid taxes and repeated his complaints against Bentsen, Connally, and Shivers, much to the chagrin of his campaign staff. His campaign produced more television ads for statewide broadcasts. He blasted Republican senator John Tower for his "terrible attendance" and for the high interest rates. (Tower served on the Senate Banking Committee at the time.) Yarborough focused most of his wrath on the Nixon administration's Vietnam policies and the high unemployment and inflation Americans experienced in the early 1970's. His strategy and work nearly paid off. He came within 586 votes of winning the Democratic primary without a runoff, but he led Sanders by nearly a quarter of a million votes out of nearly two million total votes cast. The Senate race was only one of many surprises in the 1972 Democratic primary election. Incumbent governor Preston Smith and Lieutenant Governor Ben Barnes finished behind state representative Frances "Sissy" Farenthold and Uvalde rancher Dolph Briscoe in the gubernatorial race. Voter reaction to the Sharpstown scandal received the credit for ousting Smith, Barnes, and other Democratic incumbents linked to the affair.[4]

Yarborough and his staff challenged the outcome of the election. He maintained that he received enough votes in Dallas, Borden, Delta, Kimble, and Hopkins counties to give him an outright victory. Yarborough campaign manager Ed Wendler attempted to have Dallas County Democratic Chairman Earl Luna conduct a recount, but Luna refused to accept a check, claiming that the deadline for a retabulation had expired. Yarborough also claimed that State Democratic Party Chairman Roy Orr refused to give him access to other returns that would have provided him a majority. Yarborough threatened a court challenge but decided to go into the runoff, where Texans would "bury his opponent." Yarborough said that Texans were ready for political reform and "fed-up with smoke-filled room politics." Sanders claimed that Texans no longer wanted Yarborough's "cry-baby attitude." The situation was not unlike that when Yarborough narrowly lost to Price Daniel in the 1956 governor's election; a change of several thousand votes would have altered the outcome of that election. Yarborough appeared paranoid to his detractors at this time, but the ghosts of past political defeats still seemed very real to him.[5]

In the runoff election, Sanders continued his "cookie" campaign. The candidate's mother baked thousands of cookies shaped like a bare foot. Sanders claimed Yarborough accepted honoraria for speeches, accepted paid overseas trips, and was frequently absent from the Senate. In a face-to-face debate before a Dallas television audience, Yarborough responded to the accusations. He said his attendance record was 80 percent for thirteen years, much better than John Tower's record. He also said he earned nearly $18,000 from his speeches, much less than most other senators, some of whom drew in as much as $80,000 per year. His trips to Europe included attendance at international meetings. On the positive side, Yarborough called for a national health insurance system, increases in aid to Social Security recipients and veterans, and a $1200 tax exemption for middle-class taxpayers. Sanders claimed that Yarborough's proposals would increase taxes and create more federal spending. Both men wanted a quick end to the Vietnam War and an increase in the federal minimum wage. Yarborough expressed concern about a low voter turnout for the runoff, fearing that many voters assumed he would easily win the election. In addition, voters and the media seemed more focused on the governor's race between Briscoe and Farenthold. Many of Yarborough's former supporters worked in Farenthold's losing effort, including longtime advisor Creekmore Fath, who served as her campaign manager.[6]

Sanders pulled off a surprise upset. He defeated Yarborough by better than 70,000 votes out of 1.9 million votes cast. Yarborough's totals declined by over 100,000 from the first election. "It was obvious that Texans were ready for a new senator and liberals were ready for a new hero," stated *The Texas Observer.* Yarborough's staff was composed of nearly all new people, many of whom were young and involved in their first campaign. Many were upset at the loss, especially when it appeared Yarborough won the first election but was denied the victory by the state party. Yarborough gained more votes than Farenthold but trailed her by 32,000 votes in Houston and 24,000 votes in Dallas. She also drew larger and more enthusiastic crowds, indicating that some of Yarborough's liberal support eroded due to his image as an old warrior in comparison with the younger, more charismatic Farenthold and other new Democrats on the ballot in 1972. Many young people were offended by his oratory and his old populist style. Many new reform Democrats ousted conservative legislators and long-prominent officials who were tarred with the Sharpstown brush. The veterans of four decades in Texas politics believed that 1972 was a year to vote such officials out of office and many people mistakenly still perceived Yarborough as an incumbent. Following his loss to Sanders in the runoff election, Yarborough once again pledged his support to the Democratic nominee for the November contest against Tower. Yarborough announced, "I'm fixing to reconvert into the law," and returned to a full-time practice in Austin. At age 69, he faced a large, nearly $100,000 campaign debt. He received many requests to author historical and political works but realized he could not run his law practice or pay his bills "on the royalties from historical treatises."[7]

FINAL BATTLES

Most retired senators enhanced their personal wealth by joining corporate boards and Washington law firms and lobby groups. Yarborough, though, revived his old law practice in Austin, taught classes, and embarked on his favorite activities—making speeches and collecting books. Speculation continued for some time about another campaign, but he announced in 1974 he would no longer be a candidate for a statewide office. He served as a member of the Constitutional Revision Commission in 1973 in the unsuccessful attempt to rewrite the state Constitution of 1876. He commuted to the University of Texas at Arlington once a week for several years to teach a class on government to graduate students. He lapsed into his old patterns when he talked about running for office and enjoyed hearing his name mentioned as a potential presidential candidate in 1976. After Watergate and Nixon's resignation, the country wanted someone with impeccable credentials. Yarborough's legacy of integrity already loomed large only a few years after leaving office. Many Texas liberals wanted him to run as a "favorite son" to counter Lloyd Bentsen's presidential aspirations at the Democratic National Convention.[8]

Yarborough seethed over his defeat by Lloyd Bentsen in the 1970 Democratic primary years after the campaign. He was sharply critical of Bentsen's conduct and the amount of money spent in the campaign. But he reserved his harshest criticism for John Connally. Yarborough believed Connally masterminded the campaign that brought business interests together and raised "millions of dollars" for Bentsen. The money was important, but Yarborough believed that Connally instigated the "worst campaign of defamation and of falsehood in the history of Texas Congressional politics." Yarborough said two items harmed him the most. First, the Bentsen television ads featuring pictures of rioters and fire bombings in Los Angeles and Washington and linking Yarborough to the actions. Second, in the final ten days of the race, Yarborough said the school prayer issue was portrayed as Yarborough voting "against people having the right to pray. Even some preachers . . . preached sermons against me in the pulpit . . . the last Sunday before the election, preying on people's fears that I had voted against the people having the right to pray."[9]

In retrospect, Yarborough recognized the few wealthy, influential Texans who consistently provided him with funds and support throughout most of his political career. They included insurance executive Bernard Rapoport, independent oil producer J. R. Parten, business executive Billy Goldberg, investor and banker Walter Hall, and Yarborough's brothers Harvey and Donald, both of whom worked as attorneys. The lack of funding that continually plagued Yarborough made him even more reliant on the few individuals he could consistently call on for money to support his campaigns. Yarborough realized the small contributors for whom he was the icon of the liberal movement in Texas were his strongest base. Paying off old campaign expenses was not unusual for Yarborough. He incurred debt in his first statewide race for attorney general in 1938 and finished his final Senate campaign with outstanding obligations. He told his friend Rapoport that it took him more than ten years to pay the final costs of the governor's races during the 1950's. Yarborough' 1972 bills amounted to $95,000. A July 1972 "Texas Appreciation Dinner" began his long effort to pay off the balance. He raised all but a few thousand dollars by 1978 mainly from fund-raising dinners and donations from his longtime supporters from around the state. He again called on Hall, Rapoport, Parten, and Goldberg, who continued their contributions even though they realized that Yarborough had run his final political contest.[10]

Yarborough continued his efforts on what he considered his major piece of unfinished Senate business—the Big Thicket. He made dozens of speeches around the state and flew to Washington to press Congress for passage of legislation to protect the disappearing wilderness. Yarborough called further delay "tragic," for more and more acres of trees were cut by large lumber companies. At the 1973 annual meeting of the Big Thicket Association, he called for a massive letter-writing campaign to protect the "wonderful gem of Texas Wilderness" and lambasted Time, Inc. and the Santa Fe Railroad Company, calling them "butchers and destroyers" because of their continued logging operations. Senator John Tower, East Texas congressman Charlie Wilson, and Houston representative Bob Eckhardt sponsored separate bills to create a national preserve but legislation was still held up in committee. Finally,

Tennessee senator Albert Gore Sr., Ralph's closest associate in the Senate, also lost his seat in 1970. Gore and Yarborough, shown in this 1988 photo, visited often and maintained their friendship long after their Senate years. Photo by Tom Daneneau. Courtesy Opal Yarborough.

in 1974 Congress passed and President Gerald Ford signed legislation that established an 84,550-acre Big Thicket National Preserve in twelve sections scattered through five counties. Yarborough's dream at last became a reality, with the Big Thicket Preserve as the final jewel in his crown of environmental accomplishments.[11]

In the 1980's, Yarborough was appointed to the Texas State Library and Archives Commission, on which he served until 1989. When the Texas Library History Colloquium convened at the LBJ Library in 1988, it honored Yarborough for his support of education and libraries. Accepting the award, Yarborough, 84 at the time, talked for over an hour on his years in the Senate interwoven with stories of Texas history and books. Yarborough joined Tom Ferguson as the only two surviving members of the first board of directors of the LCRA when the agency celebrated its fiftieth anniversary in 1985 at the state capitol. Later that year, Yarborough entered Austin's Seton Hospital for a quadruple bypass.

During the 1980's, Texas Land Commissioner Garry Mauro called on Yarborough for assistance involving one of his most historic legal victories. The eighty-five-year-old Yarborough participated in a lawsuit on behalf of the

General Land Office involving a twenty-four-acre Permanent School Fund tract in the Yates Oil Field. Ironically, fifty-four years earlier, as a young assistant attorney general he had faced the same law firm in a case involving the same West Texas lands. Now Yarborough assisted the state's case and sat for three days on the witness stand as he was questioned by the opposing attorneys. The settlement in the dispute brought millions of dollars to the state. More importantly, the decision upheld the interpretations Yarborough set years before on state-owned oil and gas properties. The General Land Office estimated that by the mid 1980's Yarborough's decisions as an assistant attorney general in the early 1930's brought billions of dollars to the public schools and universities. The Permanent School Fund became $1.1 billion wealthier and the Permanent University Fund gained nearly $444 million, about 20 percent of the total value of the fund as of 1985. Yarborough's commitment to education extended far beyond the one-room schools of East Texas where he first taught. He literally earned the title of the billion-dollar father to the public schools and to the components of the University of Texas and Texas A&M systems.[12]

In 1989, Mary Pearl Williams, the Travis County 53rd District Judge, organized a tribute by the Travis County Bar Association to honor Yarborough's service on the bench during the 1930's. His portrait was placed in the 53rd District courtroom where he once presided. Later that year, "The *Texas Observer* Benefit Dinner" featured Yarborough. Tributes by Senator Edward Kennedy, former *Observer* editors Ronnie Dugger and Molly Ivins, and a host of Yarborough's campaign and staff workers lauded and lampooned the aging warrior. Yarborough received the first Frankie Randolph Social Justice Award from the publication. Randolph was one of the founders and the first publisher of *The Texas Observer* and for many years a leader of liberal Democrats in Texas. Yarborough thanked the people of Texas who "just picked me up, and threw me over the fence onto the fertile fields of the United States Senate." The first endowed chair at the University of Texas in his name was created at the College of Liberal Arts. Funding for the chair was provided by his longtime friend and supporter, Bernard Rapoport of Waco. The University of Texas Law School alumni honored Yarborough as one of their founders on their fiftieth anniversary. In 1988 Sam Houston State University also gave him a distinguished alumnus award.[13]

Ralph and Opal suffered a great personal loss with the death of their only son, Richard, in 1986 as a result of complications from arthritis and infections. A graduate of the University of Texas and the School of Law, for nine years Richard served as the legislative assistant for his father in the Senate. President Johnson appointed Richard to the Indian Claims Commission in 1967, where he served for ten years. In 1978 he was appointed chairman of the Foreign Claims Settlement Commission, where he worked until his retirement in 1981. A sudden strep infection was the immediate cause of his untimely death in March 1986. Yarborough's friend and confidant Creekmore Fath credited Dick Yarborough with the legal skills and vision to help his father guide many of the bills for which his father was best known: The Padre Island National Seashore, the Guadalupe Mountains National Park, and the Cold War G.I. bill. Ralph and Opal were both devastated by the unexpected loss of their son. Richard was survived by his wife, Ann, and two daughters, Claire and Elizabeth, and one son, Jefferson. The University of Texas School of Law established the Richard W. Yarborough Native American Indian Scholarship in his honor.

FINAL TRIBUTES

In 1990, when the University of Texas named Yarborough as a distinguished alumnus, Bill Moyers, the former Johnson aide and nationally known correspondent, praised Yarborough for his "determination to accomplish good for his fellow citizens" as a film highlighted his life and career. Thus, the alumni organization finally recognized Yarborough, whose decisions in the Attorney General's office earned the Permanent University Fund hundreds of millions of dollars. In his acceptance speech, Yarborough looked back on his life and his long relationship with the university. He summarized in one brief statement his lifelong philosophy—every individual should make education a lifelong pursuit that bestowed a "faith and belief that is a viable objective to improve the quality of life for all of our People." Yarborough received an orange blazer and beamed with gratitude to the university to which he always remained devoted. Old Yarborough rivals Price Daniel Sr. and, surprisingly, John Connally gave public tributes to Yarborough. Connally told *Houston Post* writer Felton West in 1992 that he and Yarborough "didn't really feud" and "we've never said a cross word to each other to this day." Connally also wrote a letter to the University Ex-Students Association urging Yarborough's induction as a distinguished alumnus. A year after this event the Texas Democratic Women and the National Federation of Democratic Women gave him humanitarian awards, the first man to receive the distinction from those organizations. The University of Texas School of Law established the Ralph W. Yarborough Endowed Presidential Scholarship in Envi-

Democratic leaders and University of Texas officials sponsored the Ralph W. Yarborough Chair at the School of Law in 1992. Pictured are the committee chairs (standing, left to right): UT Chancellor William Cunningham, Lieutenant Governor Bob Bullock, Governor Ann Richards, Land Commissioner Garry Mauro, Ambassador Ed Clark, and Law School Dean Mark Yudolf. Ralph and Opal are seated in front. Courtesy Opal Yarborough.

ronmental and Public Service Law in his honor in 1992. The senator donated his vast legislative and campaign files to the Center for American History as a massive 1,400-linear-foot collection.[14]

Friends from all over Texas gathered at the governor's mansion to celebrate the ninetieth birthdays of Ralph and Opal, born only four days apart in June 1903. The Texas House and Senate passed resolutions recognizing his many accomplishments from his days as an assistant attorney general through those as a U.S. senator. On the lawn beside the Executive Mansion, Governor Ann Richards hosted a tribute attended by thousands of admirers from around the state. "I think I put up more yard signs and more telephone pole signs for Ralph Yarborough than any other candidate in my lifetime, including me," the governor laughed. "The truth is, they should have lived in this house," Richards said, acknowledging Yarborough's efforts to obtain the governor's office during the 1950's. As Ralph and Opal sat by the governor, hundreds of guests passed by to exchange stories, shake hands, and say thanks to the icon

"Two with one shot." Ralph remained an avid sportsman and conservationist his entire life. He bagged these two wild turkeys at age 88 with a single shot. Courtesy Opal Yarborough.

of modern Texas politics. Comments about the "jam on the bottom shelf" and Yarborough's legendary fights against Shivers, Connally, Johnson, and Daniel abounded from those who worked with Yarborough in the early campaigns. A quartet played *The Yellow Rose of Texas* and *Tea for Two*, favorite songs of the couple since their 1927 honeymoon. Governor Richards presented a plaque to the couple recognizing them as "true Texas heroes" and thanked them when she stated "we're better people because of you." There was no flatbed truck or courthouse steps to speak from as the old days, but Yarborough took the microphone to thank his old and new friends. "People are what matters," he said, repeating an oft-stated belief in his softer yet still distinctive voice, and he jokingly declared, "I owe my long life to abstinence from alcohol and tobacco." He shared Opal's order to him shortly before the grand event that he better not lift any boxes of books that cluttered his study because "I don't want you dropping dead the day before your birthday party." The Yarboroughs and all Texans had a lot to smile about that sunny day at the governor's mansion.[15]

Yarborough outlived most of his contemporaries and his best-known political foes. In 1985, he enjoyed an emotional reconciliation with Price Daniel Sr., the man to whom he lost the questionable 1956 gubernatorial race. Daniel praised Yarborough for his many contributions and said he deserved his place in Texas history alongside two of the senator's own heroes—Jim Hogg and Sam Houston. As the old guard faded away, new political leaders took their place. Many of them considered him their political godfather and were inspired to public service by the senator. Most worked on at least one of Yarborough's many campaigns. These included Governor Ann Richards, Land

Governor Ann Richards (middle) honored Opal and Ralph Yarborough at the governor's mansion in honor of their ninetieth birthday. The childhood sweethearts, married for over sixty-seven years, were born only four days apart and a few miles from one another. Courtesy Opal Yarborough.

Commissioner Garry Mauro, Agriculture Commissioner Jim Hightower, Attorney General Jim Mattox, and a host of other legislators and professionals who went to work in state and federal offices.

Yarborough lived his final days at home with Opal at the house in Austin where the couple resided since World War II. His health deteriorated in the waning months of 1995. On Saturday, January 27, 1996, he died in his sleep at the age of 92. Opal, his wife of sixty-seven years, his friend and companion for nearly his entire life, was home at the time of his death. His memorial service at the First Baptist Church in downtown Austin drew the famous, and the not-so-famous people for whom Yarborough labored. His casket, draped with a U.S. flag, was surrounded by yellow roses. His old friend Al Lohman, granddaughter Claire Yarborough, and former aide Alex Dickie praised the leader who served his country at home and abroad. At his request he was buried in his orange University of Texas alumni jacket and law school tie. Interment was on a hillside of the Texas State Cemetery. Yarborough's resting site is surrounded by those of other state leaders and close to the uniform rows of white crosses marking the burial site of Civil War veterans. In his memorial tribute to Yarborough, U.S. District Judge William Wayne Justice wondered how the senator inspired such loyalty among his supporters. "I have become convinced that it was his charismatic personality, absolute honesty, and utter fearlessness, coupled with the moral power of the positions he took—opposition to the misuse of the weak by the powerful—that inspired this loyalty."[16]

Afterword

Ralph Webster Yarborough, who worked continuously to "put the jam on the lower shelf" for people from all walks of life, was a model of liberal philosophy and one of its most eloquent spokesmen. He had many successes, but he also had years of struggle and disappointment. His determination, his fights, and his career personified the nation's battle for social equality based on economic opportunity and justice. Yarborough perceived himself as a link with the people of Texas whose common virtues he considered part of his own. "Smilin' Ralph," as he was sometimes called by both friends and foes, championed the causes of folks from every walk of life. This identification and commitment to representing the people's interests became a fundamental belief as he began his first statewide campaign in 1938. He never departed from this position. In fact, his views intensified during the races for governor and U.S. senator in the 1950's through the 1970's. The outstanding exception was his reluctance to publicly embrace integration following the 1954 Supreme Court ruling. He quickly reversed his role once he entered the U.S. Senate and became the only senator from a state of the Old Confederacy to vote for every major civil rights issue from 1957 to 1970.

As noted by columnist Ronnie Dugger, "the leader of a people's movement is not the movement, the people are the movement, but finally without a leader they rightly trust they cannot consummate their purpose." Yarborough became the foremost successful liberal spokesman in the state "because he understood these things, felt he could lead us, and led us, and because he has been true." His rise to prominence and his record was unique. As senator, Yarborough was a philosophical liberal, more in line with western and northern senators than his southern contemporaries. He was more closely affiliated with John Kennedy, George McGovern, Hubert Humphrey, and Eugene McCarthy—U.S. senators who grew up during the Depression years and became the heirs of the New Deal era. He often stood on the opposite side of the political fence from his fellow southern Democrats who came of age during the 1930's and the great conflict of World War II. He played a critical role in the wars of modernization in Texas, engaging in the conflicts required to break the state and its people away from backward, hidebound traditions and its dominant segregationist culture and to transform it into an active participant in the nation's domestic life.[1]

In order for Texas to become more than just "Mississippi with good roads," social and economic restructuring were necessary to effectively modernize the state. Yarborough became a key figure in this successful transition. His recipe for change included never-before-seen government services and regulation, an end to Jim Crow segregation, and widespread participation in education and the benefits of a managed economy. Texas broke the chains that tied it to its Deep South neighbors during his years, and Yarborough served as the foremost advocate of this role for the state. He dared to defy conventional political wisdom and the entrenched business and political leadership of his era, a move away from most of his conservative southern political brethren that was remarkable in itself. His ideas, once labeled as "wild-eyed liberalism" and "un-American," are now mainstream and part of the nation's economy and culture.

The legacy of the post–World War II era will continue to generate debate among Americans and historians. Before the war, women and minorities consistently trailed the national average in income, education, and access to government services and private sector opportunities. Undisciplined growth also brought on the destruction of irreplaceable natural resources and the environment. Especially in Texas and the rest of the South, the population was mostly made up of "have nots" with little chance for advancement. Yarborough and other reformers confronted all of these contentious issues with new ideas that brought remarkable change and modernization throughout the nation. Many of the laws and ideas created during this time have fallen into disrepute or remain the subject of criticism. From a different perspective, other critics complain that the impulse for reform was too timid and failed to adequately address the fundamental problems of poverty, discrimination, and pollution. But there should be no debate over the role Yarborough played in moving Texas away from its troublesome southern traditions and into the national mainstream. The civil rights measures he pushed corrected over a century of discrimination and disenfranchisement. His advocacy on behalf of education, health care, and environmental protection resulted in a broad-based improvement in the nation's health and well-being. Many doors of opportunity once closed were now open to people regardless of their heritage or economic status. The ideas and the federal programs spawned by Yarborough did not conclusively resolve all of the questions on race relations, the sick and the poor, or the environment. However, Americans will not turn back the clock to restore racial segregation. A vast majority would never give the Guadalupe Mountains or Padre Island back to private owners, disband Medicare or the War on Cancer, or end efforts to improve education. With the passing of Yarborough and his generation, awareness of their impact and contributions becomes ever greater.

Historian Larry Goodwyn, who once worked for the senator, recognized Yarborough's presence as distinct: "Yarborough has been the kind of classical republican that the most committed revolutionaries of the founding generation had in mind when they created the democratic idea we know as America." Yarborough followed his convictions with a religious fervor matched by few public figures of his day. His was a public personality that was long on vision, ability, and knowledge but sometimes short on political judgment. Yarborough's appeal often placed him in conflict with nearly every corporate establishment in Texas. In his mind, the confrontations with establishment figures, corporations, and more-conservative politicians were based on democratic values. He believed that the law and government maintained a duty to defend individuals and organizations from unfair practices and illegal activities. As he always enjoyed stating, "people are our greatest assets." These principles composed the very foundation of Yarborough's public and private persona.[2]

Yarborough's clashes with moneyed interests on policy and legal issues frequently placed him in a position where he was unable to obtain the necessary resources for advancing his interests. Every politician who aspired to a statewide office in Texas faced this dilemma. Lyndon Johnson made his agreements with the oil companies and other business interests to pursue his social agenda. Yarborough, though, was never able to come to any large understanding with any of the major figures in business and the media to reach his goals. With the exception of a few independents and wealthy liberals in Texas, Yarborough fought continuously with the well-heeled establishment. He also dueled with the state's metropolitan newspaper editors in a battle of words he could not win. This contentiousness was evident in every statewide race he entered and cost him at least one and possibly two elections, in the 1950's for governor and in 1970 his race for the Senate. The influence of money and wealthy, vested interests on the democratic process still arouse concerns among the population and elected officials at all levels.

Even with his myriad resume of accomplishments, Yarborough remains the subject of criticism because of his outspoken nature and his unique politi-

"Put the Jam on the Lower Shelf." Memorial tribute from Pulitzer Prize–winning editorial cartoonist Ben Sargent for Senator Yarborough's memorial service, January 7, 1996. Courtesy Ben Sargent.

cal positions. Not unlike their nineteenth-century counterparts, Americans in Yarborough's era faced the dilemma of how to freely express critical or unorthodox political views in an environment which encouraged conformity. In one of the best-known commentaries on American life, Alexis de Tocqueville took note of this tendency during his journeys through the nation before the Civil War. He judged that Americans seemed unnerved by serious criticism because of their lack of experience in this arena. For a nation which prided itself on its ideas of liberty and independence, he wrote, "I know of no country in which there is so little independence of mind and real freedom of discussion as in America." The outspoken Yarborough challenged this tradition in his statewide campaigns as well as by his support for civil rights and criticism of the Vietnam War while in the Senate. Yarborough's own experience and his natural inclinations were to side with the minority who questioned U.S. involvement in Vietnam. When escalation began in 1964, Yarborough and nearly every other prominent politician in the nation supported the war effort as part of their patriotic duty. Similar to his outspoken defense of civil rights a few years earlier, he changed course well ahead of popular opinion in the state and the rest of the nation. His positions were unpopular at the time but have proven correct with the passage of time. Even so, the national penchant for hasty judgment and easy solutions to complex problems is still part of the American character that Tocqueville so accurately observed.[3]

Ralph Yarborough believed that the American justice and democracy in which he placed his love and trust would serve as a foundation for our future. Yet, with all of our achievements, he felt there was always more work to be done—for the people and the nation.

Notes

AP: James Allred Papers
BP: Lloyd Bentsen Jr. Papers
C. R.:   Charles Richard Yarborough, Ralph's father
CAH: Center for American History, Austin, Texas
CP: John Connally Papers
DYPP: Donald Yarborough Personal Papers, papers of Ralph's younger brother
H. J.:   Harvey Jackson Yarborough, Ralph's older brother
HMRC: Houston Metropolitan Research Center
HRC: Harry Ransom Humanities Research Center, University of Texas at Austin
LBJL: Lyndon Baines Johnson Presidential Library, Austin, Texas
LCRA: Lower Colorado River Authority
RP: Bernard Rapoport Papers
RWY: Ralph Webster Yarborough
SCL: Special Collections and Archives, University Library, University of Houston
SP: Allan Shivers Papers, Texas State Archives, Austin
WGH: Walter G. Hall
WGHP: Walter G. Hall Papers
WRC: Woodson Research Center, Fondren Library, Rice University, Houston, Texas
YP: Yarborough Papers, Center for American History
YPP: Yarborough Personal Papers, Yarborough residence, Austin, Texas

I. IT WAS A JOYOUS BOYHOOD

1. Grace Billie Presley, "Yarborough Family History," unpublished, YPP.
2. RWY, "The Yarborough Family," in *Chandler: Its History and People* (Chandler:

Chandler Historical Society, 1981), pp. 204–211. The section on the Yarborough family is one of several authored by Yarborough.

3. C. R. Yarborough marriage license, Smith County, Donald Yarborough scrapbook, DYPP, Tyler, Texas; RWY, *Chandler*, 206.

4. *Texas Almanac and State Industrial Guide, 1903* (Galveston: A. H. Belo, 1904), pp. 288–289. Other local histories of Chandler and Henderson County include Henderson County Historical Society, *Old Homes of Henderson County* (Crockett, Tex.: Publications Development Co., 1982); J. J. Faulk, *A History of Henderson County Texas* (Athens, Tex.: Athens Printing Co., 1929); Chandler Historical Society, *Chandler: Its History and People* (Chandler, Tex.: Chandler Historical Society, 1981); "75th Anniversary Edition," *Athens (Texas) Daily Review*, September 28, 1960.

5. RWY, *Chandler*, 206; Grace Billie Presley to RWY, September 10, 1993, RWY to Grace Billie Presley, September 14, 1993, YPP.

6. Grace Billie Presley to RWY, September 10, 1993, YPP; Michael L. Collins, "Ralph Yarborough," *Profiles in Power: Twentieth-Century Texans in Washington* (Arlington Heights, Ill.: Harlan Davidson, 1993), pp. 150–152.

7. "Has Lived under 19 Presidents," *Athens (Texas) Daily Review*, October 8, 1964. The story was on C. R. Yarborough's 100th birthday celebration.

8. RWY interview by Patrick Cox, April 21, 1993; RWY to Grace Billie Presley, May 18, 1992, YPP.

9. RWY interview, April 21, 1993; E. D. Smith, September 15, 1909, Anti-Saloon League, *The Brewers and Texas Politics*, vol. 2 (San Antonio: Passing Show Printing Co., 1916), pp. 780–785. Chandler voted dry in every local-option election prior to World War I. For information on prohibition in Texas, see Lewis L. Gould, *Progressives and Prohibitionists: Texas Democrats in the Wilson Era* (Austin: University of Texas Press, 1973); Jeanne Bozzell McCarty, *The Struggle for Sobriety: Protestants and Prohibition in Texas, 1919–1935* (El Paso: Texas Western Press, 1980); and Norman D. Brown, *Hood Bonnet and Little Brown Jug: Texas Politics, 1921–1928* (College Station: Texas A&M University Press, 1984).

10. Presley, "Family history," YPP. No records survive of any cases involving African Americans in C. R. Yarborough's justice of the peace court.

11. RWY, *Chandler*, 37; RWY to Howard Peacock, February 11, 1987; RWY to Gladys Yarborough, February 22, 1993, YPP.

12. Presley, "Family History."

13. Ibid. This story was retold by Ralph's brother Donald to the author at the Yarborough family reunion, June 20, 1994.

14. Presley, "Family History."

15. Chandler High School did not go beyond tenth grade, so Ralph went to Tyler High School for an additional year.

16. *The 1920 Howitzer*, yearbook of the United States Corps of Cadets (West Point, N.Y.: 1921), p. 190. Throughout the yearbook, Yarborough's name is incorrectly spelled as "Yarbrough."

17. *Howitzer*, pp. 217, 219.

18. Mark Adams and Creekmore Fath, *Yarborough: Portrait of a Steadfast Democrat* (Austin: Chaparral Press, 1957). According to this 1957 biography, Yarborough left the Academy because of the poor prospects for a military career in the peacetime army. No official transcripts from West Point were located. Members of the Yarborough family, who were reluctant to discuss the issue, indicated that he most likely left the Academy because he was uncomfortable in the surroundings. Yarborough was unwilling to shed any light on this subject during interviews.

19. D. Clayton James, *The Years of MacArthur, vol. 1, 1880-1941* (Boston: Houghton Mifflin Co., 1970), pp. 261-272; Douglas MacArthur, *Reminiscences* (New York: McGraw Hill, 1964); Jacob Devers, "The Mark of the Man on USMA," *Assembly* 23 (Spring 1964).

20. RWY interview by Patrick Cox, October 14, 1993, Yarborough home, Austin, Texas. Yarborough kept his first teaching certificate.

21. Ibid.

22. Ibid.

23. Ibid.

24. Ibid. Annie Webb Blanton, the first woman to be elected to a statewide office in Texas, signed his permanent teaching certificate.

25. RWY interview by Cox, October 14, 1993; RWY to Ernest Dunning, March 27, 1951, Personal Correspondence—1951, RY2R488a, YP, CAH.

26. *The Cactus*, 1927, yearbook of the University of Texas at Austin, CAH, p. 391. Yarborough attended the University of Texas from 1923 to 1927 but only the 1927 yearbook contained a photo or listed any of his activities.

27. "Remarks of Ralph Yarborough on acceptance of the Distinguished Alumnus Award at the University of Texas at Austin," October 19, 1990, YPP; James Hildebrand to RWY, May 17, 1933, YPP. The letter noted receipt of a check for "$17.90 which pays your note in full." Yarborough borrowed money from his father, the University of Texas Law School, and later the First National Bank in El Paso.

28. RWY interview by Cox, October 14, 1993.

29. RWY to Travis County Bar Association, March 20, 1986, YPP. The remarks were delivered to lawyers who practiced in Texas more than forty years.

30. Opal Yarborough interview by Patrick Cox, November 12, 1998, Yarborough home, Austin, Texas; RWY to Travis County Bar; marriage license, Navarro County, Ralph W. Yarborough and Opal C. Warren, June 30, 1928, YPP. The marriage license is recorded in Book 28, p. 119, of Marriage Records of Navarro County, Texas, not their home county of Henderson.

31. RWY to Travis County Bar, YPP. Yarborough and Burges continued their friendship and correspondence throughout the 1930's and until Burges' death in 1945.

32. *Crawford v. White*, 25, *Southwestern Reporter* (2nd), p. 629; RWY interview by Cox, October 14, 1993; Judge Joe Dibrell, Travis County Bar Association speech honoring RWY, February 3, 1989, YPP.

33. RWY interview, October 14, 1993; William Eugene Atkinson, "James V. Allred: A Political Biography, 1899-1935" (Ph.D. dissertation, TCU, 1978), pp. 190-197.

2. THE MILLION-DOLLAR VICTORY

1. "Governor James V. Allred, 1899–1959," program dedication—Texas Historical Marker, Allred files, CAH.

2. Atkinson, "Allred," p. 221. Allred served as attorney general for two terms followed by two terms as Texas governor. Other Allred studies include: Walter B. Moore, *Governors of Texas* (Dallas: Dallas Morning News, 1963), p. 31; Robert Rene Martindale, "James V. Allred: The Centennial Governor of Texas" (Master's thesis, University of Texas at Austin, 1957); George N. Manning, "Public Services of James V. Allred (Master's thesis, Texas Technological College, 1950); Robb K. Burlage, "James V. Allred—Texas' Liberal Governor" (Report for O. D. Weeks, University of Texas at Austin, 1959); Paul Bolton, *Governors of Texas* (Corpus Christi, Texas: Corpus Christi Caller Times, 1947). The James Allred Governor's Papers are at the Texas State Archives and the James V. Allred personal papers and public documents are housed at the Special Collections Library, University of Houston.

3. Thomas Lloyd Miller, *The Public Lands of Texas, 1519–1970* (Norman: University of Oklahoma Press, 1971). Yarborough wrote the introduction to this study on public lands and stated: "It is difficult to imagine how great the educational system of Texas would have been if the state government had shown the vision and leadership to share half of this treasure (as under the relinquishment act) with the surface owners and save just half of it for the school fund. Had Texas done this with all her lands, she would be the wealthiest state this or any other Union ever had." Texas is unique among the other states of the union for it was allowed under its treaty of annexation into the United States to retain ownership of its public lands and mineral estate. Other studies on Texas' public lands include Bascom Giles, "History and Disposition of Texas Public Domain" (Austin: General Land Office Archives, 1945); Jerry Sadler, "History of Texas Land" (Austin: General Land Office Archives, 1961); Octavia F. Rogan, *Land Commissioner Charles Rogan and the Mineral Classification of Texas Public School Land* (Austin: San Felipe Press, 1968)

4. David F. Prindle, *Petroleum Politics and the Texas Railroad Commission* (Austin: University of Texas Press, 1981). For other discussion of problems with oil production in the 1930's, including the fight over proration and "hot oil" in the East Texas field, see Car Coke Rister, *Oil! Titan of the Southwest* (Norman: University of Oklahoma Press, 1949); James A. Clark and Michael T. Halbouty, *The Last Boom* (New York: Random House, 1972); Ruel McDaniel, *Some Ran Hot* (Dallas: Regional Press, 1939); Robert D. Boyle, "Chaos in the East Texas Oil Fields, 1930–1935," *Southwestern Historical Quarterly* 69 (January 1966): 340–352; Texas Railroad Commission Archives, State Archives, Austin, Texas.

5. RWY to Attorney General Allred, "Duties of Attorney General With Regard to Public Land," 1932 Memorandum, YPP. By the 1930's, the Permanent School Fund increased to $70 million and provided about $1.70 per school child, about 10 percent of the total amount of state revenue provided to public education.

6. RWY to Allred memo; Opinions 2904, 2947, 2936, 2932, 2951, *Biennial Report of the Attorney General, State of Texas, September 1, 1932 to August 31, 1934.* All of these

opinions authored by Yarborough involve decisions regarding public lands and the state's mineral interests.

7. *Smith v Turner,* 61 S.W. (2nd) 792; James H. Walker to James V. Allred, February 5, 1931. RWY letter in the *Biennial Report, Attorney General,* YPP.

8. *State of Texas v. Mid-Kansas Oil and Gas Company,* 61 S.W. (2nd), 797; RWY memo, "Outstanding Accomplishments of Land Department from January 1, 1931 to March 1, 1934" and "Memo to the press in Whiteside case," Attorney General, YPP. In a similar case involving the Yates Field, Yarborough defended title to 4,407 acres of state mineral acreage in the Whiteside Case, *State of Texas v. R. B. Whiteside,* 62 S.W. [2nd], 804.

9. "Memorandum to the Press" and "Supplemental Memorandum to the Press," September 23, 1933, Box 240, AP, SCL; *Biennial Report, 1932–1934.*

10. Houston Harte to Attorney General James Allred, October 10, 1933; RWY to Houston Harte, October 10, 1933, Attorney General, YPP; *Houston Chronicle,* September 24, 1933; *Dallas Morning News,* October 1, 1933. Similar stories appeared in the *Austin American,* the *Fort Worth Star Telegram,* and the *San Antonio Light.*

11. RWY, "Outstanding Accomplishments."

12. *State of Texas v. Reagan County Purchasing Company, Inc.,* 65 S.W. (2nd) 353; *The Daily Texan,* November 15, 1932.

13. "Memorandum to the Press," March 17, 1932, Box 240, AP, SCL; *Austin Evening Dispatch,* December 17, 1931. The Board of Regents for the University of Texas engaged the attorney general in many lawsuits with the oil companies from the first strike in West Texas in 1924 through the 1930's. Additional studies of the Permanent University Fund include William J. Battle, "A Concise History of the University of Texas, 1883-1950," *Southwestern Historical Quarterly* 54 (April 1951): 397; Ed Clark, "The Permanent University Fund: A Foundation for Greatness," *The Addendum* 7 (November 1976): 2; Bert R. Haigh, *Land, Oil and Education* (El Paso: Texas Western Press, 1986); David Prindle, "Oil and the Permanent University Fund: The Early Years," *Southwestern Historical Quarterly* 86 (October 1982): 277-298; Martin Schwetmann, *Santa Rita: The University of Texas' Oil Discovery* (Austin: Texas State Historical Association, 1943).

14. RWY to H. J. Yarborough, May 12, 1933, C. R. Yarborough to RWY, October 29, 1933, Attorney General file, YPP.

15. *Magnolia Petroleum Company v. J. H. Walker, Commissioner of the General Land Office,* 73 S.W. (2nd) 526.

16. *Biennial Report of the Attorney General of the State of Texas, September 1, 1934 to August 31, 1936, James V. Allred, Attorney General* (Austin, 1936), p. 240; RWY to Octavia Rogan, February 7, 1969, letter reprinted in Miller's *Public Lands of Texas,* 234. Yarborough stated in 1969 that this was "still my biggest legal victory."

17. *Magnolia v. Walker, Biennial Report,* RWY, Reply Brief, Amicus Curiae, No. C-6008 in the Supreme Court of Texas, *The State of Texas and Wally Scott, Trustee, Petitioners v. Exxon Corporation, Respondent,* October 5, 1987, p. 12, YPP.

18. *Austin American,* May 15, 1935; Garry Mauro, "Honoring Ralph Yarborough," February 3, 1989, Travis County 53rd District Courtroom, Austin, Texas, YPP. Land

Commissioner Mauro said the Magnolia suit made Yarborough "Texas' first billion-dollar lawyer because that case has been worth literally billions for the State of Texas for the Permanent School Fund." The Permanent School Fund was valued at $8 billion in 1989. "Of that amount, conservatively, $2.3 billion can be directly attributed to the legal success of Ralph W. Yarborough," Mauro stated.

19. C. R. Yarborough to RWY, May 18, 1935, C. R. Yarborough file, YPP.

20. Reply Brief, p. 12, YPP.

21. RWY to J. H. Walker, Commissioner of the General Land Office, May 14, 1934, Attorney General Opinions, YPP.

22. RWY interview by Olin Murrell, April 16, 1992, TCTV channel 38, Austin, Travis County; RWY speech, "Remembrances for J. R.'s 90th Birthday, 1986," YPP.

23. RWY, "Remembrances." Parten remained a political supporter and friend to both Allred and Yarborough. For more on Parten and this era, see Don Carleton's *A Breed So Rare* (Austin: Texas State Historical Association, 1998).

24. RWY to Kelly Saylor, August 3, 1933; RWY to Ira P. Hildebrand, H. J. Yarborough, and the Students Memorial Loan Fund, 1933, Personal correspondence—1933, YPP. An entire series of letters involving payment and extension of notes occurred from 1928 to 1934.

25. RWY to C. R. Yarborough, February 3, 1933, RWY to C. R. Yarborough, February 9, 1933, Personal correspondence—1933, YPP.

26. "Ralph Yarborough Round Up," July 25, 1952, 1952 Governor's Campaign, RY2R558, YP, CAH. Yarborough first referenced his father's 1932 county commissioner's campaign in the 1952 Democratic gubernatorial race.

27. Frank R. Kemerer, *William Wayne Justice* (Austin: University of Texas Press, 1991), pp. 4–5. For additional information on Will Justice and William Wayne Justice, see Peter Lawson, "His Honor William Wayne Justice," *Dallas Times Herald*, November 13, 1983; David Maraniss, "Justice, Texas Style," *Washington Post*, February 28, 1987.

28. O. Douglas Weeks, "The Texas Direct Primary System," *Southwestern Social Science Quarterly* 13, no. 2 (September 1932): 5. In his explanation of the Texas election laws and primary system, Weeks said the Democratic primary elections were, in effect, the state, district and county elections." The "all white" primary for the Texas Democratic Party excluded African American voters. Weeks said that in spite of the official ban, "it has been reported that negroes were allowed to vote in an increased number of counties in defiance of the party rule" (p. 25). Texas law also required primary candidates to spend no more than $300 for local elections in small counties. Corporations were forbidden to make contributions to persons running for political office (p. 10). These restrictions on contributions were often ignored.

29. RWY to C. R. Yarborough, April 13, 1932, Commissioner Campaign, YPP.

30. C. R. Yarborough campaign platform (undated), Commissioner Campaign, YPP; Weeks, *The Texas Primary System*.

31. *Texas Almanac*, 1933, pp. 271, 290; *Athens Daily Review*, July 25, 1932, Archives Collection, *Athens Daily Review* newspaper office, Athens, Texas. The archives con-

tain the *Athens Daily Review* and the *Athens Weekly Review* newspapers. With the exception of Sam Rayburn's congressional district in northeast Texas, all other areas voted in favor of repealing the Eighteenth Amendment.

32. RWY to C. R. Yarborough, July 26, 1932, Commissioner Campaign, YPP.

33. Ibid.

34. H. J. Yarborough to RWY, August 24, 1932, Commissioner Campaign, YPP; *Athens Daily Review*, July 29, 1932, August 9, 1932.

35. *Athens Daily Review*, August 29, 1932.

36. RWY to H. J. Yarborough, August 30, 1932; Donald Yarborough to RWY, September 4, 1932; RWY to Donald Yarborough, September 7, 1932, Commissioner Campaign, YPP.

37. RWY to H. J. Yarborough, September 17, 1932; H. J. Yarborough to RWY, September 20, 1932, Commissioner Campaign, YPP.

38. H. J. Yarborough to RWY, September 20, 1932, Commissioner Campaign, YPP.

39. *Athens Weekly Review*, September 29, 30, October 6, 1932. The final newspaper account failed to include any comments from the Yarborough family. No written record of the reaction of the Yarboroughs or any further correspondence survived the case.

3. A MAN WHO HAD TO EARN HIS WAY

1. *The Texas Democrat*, August 17, 1934, Campaign—1934, YPP. For more information on the LCRA's history, see John Adams, *Damming the Colorado* (College Station: Texas A&M University Press, 1990); Jimmy Banks and John E. Babcock, *Corralling the Colorado* (Austin: Eakin Press, 1988); Comer Clay, "The LCRA: A Study in Politics and Public Administration" (Ph.D. dissertation, University of Texas at Austin, 1948); Pauline Mills Edwards, "The LCRA: An Agency of the State" (Master's thesis, University of Texas at Austin, 1982); Jane Anne Morriss, "Board and Staff: An Ethnography of the LCRA of Texas" (Ph.D. dissertation, University of Texas at Austin, 1982); *Years of Progress at the LCRA* (Austin: LCRA, 1956); *The Highland Lakes of Texas* (Washington, D.C.: U.S. Government Printing Office, 1941).

2. *Texas Almanac, 1980–1981*, 92. For a history of flooding on the Colorado, see Adams' *Damming the Colorado*, pp. 1–23. For discussion and analysis on the background and political debate during the formative years of the LCRA, see Robert Caro, *The Years of Lyndon Johnson: The Path to Power* (New York: Knopf, 1982), pp. 284–285, 377–382, and Robert Dallek, *Lone Star Rising: Lyndon Johnson and His Times, 1908–1960* (New York: Oxford University Press, 1991), pp. 120–193.

3. Adams, *Damming the Colorado*, p. 21.

4. Mary Rather, "Memorandum Relative to the Dams on the Colorado River, Texas," April 1, 1975, LCRA Papers, LBJL; Anthony M. Orum, "The Making of

Austin: Taming the River, Part One," *Texas Observer,* December 14, 1984; Caro, *Lyndon Johnson: The Path to Power,* pp. 284–285, 377–382; Dallek, *Lone Star Rising,* pp. 120–193.

5. *Austin Statesman,* February 9, 1935.

6. *Austin American,* February 20, 1935. The group photo with Governor Allred appeared alongside the story of the first board meeting.

7. "Minutes of the Board of Directors," February 19, 21 1935, LCRA archives, LCRA Documents and Records Division, Austin, Texas. For further discussion on the critical role Alvin J. Wirtz played, see Adams, *Damming the Colorado,* pp. 48–70; Banks, *Corralling the Colorado,* pp. 64–87; Caro, *Lyndon Johnson: The Path to Power,* pp. 284–285, 377–382; Dallek, *Lone Star Rising,* pp. 120–193; Alvin J. Wirtz Papers, LBJL.

8. *Fort Worth Press,* March 2, 1935. Similar concerns were expressed in the *Austin American* and *Austin Statesmen* newspapers.

9. Board Minutes, February 21, 1935, LCRA archives.

10. "Alvin Jacob Wirtz," *The New Handbook of Texas,* vol. 6, pp. 1025–1026; Alvin Wirtz vertical files, CAH.

11. Board Minutes, February 21, 1935. Reaction to the selection of Wirtz was generally favorable, although some of the state's newspapers expressed criticism of the board's choice. See *Fort Worth Press,* March 2, 1935. Its editorial staff agreed with Yarborough.

12. Board Minutes, March 27, 1935, LCRA archives.

13. Board Minutes, October 8, 1935, LCRA archives; Banks, *Corralling the Colorado,* pp. 68–69. Banks interviewed LCRA board member Tom Ferguson who noted the friendship between Wirtz and Johnson.

14. *Austin American,* May 20, 1935.

15. *Austin American,* May 17, 20, 1935; Board Minutes, May 25, 1935, LCRA archives. Raymond Brooks, LCRA director and newspaper reporter, wrote many stories of the project.

16. Board Minutes, January 2, 1936, LCRA archives; RWY to Governor James Allred, January 3, 1935, Personal Correspondence—1935, YPP. The minutes of the LCRA Board on January 2 contained Yarborough's resignation.

17. *Austin American Statesman,* December 24, 1935; Yarborough for District Judge, Campaign—1936, YPP; Judith Jenkins Turman, "Austin and the New Deal," *Texas Cities and the Great Depression* (Austin: Texas Memorial Museum, 1973), pp. 189–207.

18. *Austin American,* January 9, 1936; *The Houston Chronicle,* January 10, 1936.

19. *Community Natural Gas Company v. Wichita Falls.* The case is not listed in the *Southwestern Reporter.* No records of the case were kept in the Travis County records.

20. *Austin American,* April 3, 1936; *Austin Statesman,* April 4, 1936.

21. *The State Week,* April 9, 1936.

22. *Dallas Morning News,* April 3, 1936.

23. *Austin American Statesman,* May 24, 1936; *Fort Worth Star Telegram,* May 23, 1936; *State of Texas v. Western Union, et al.* The case was not listed in the *Southwest-*

ern Reporter. The decision was covered in the *Austin American, Dallas Morning News, San Antonio Light, Houston Chronicle,* and other major newspapers.

24. *Austin American,* May 14, 1936.

25. *Austin Statesman,* March 6, 1938; "Lincoln Sesquicentennial, 1809-1959" (Washington, D.C.: Lincoln Sesquicentennial Commission for the National Archives, 1959). Following his own electoral defeats prior to winning the 1957 U.S. Senate race, Yarborough often compared himself to Lincoln.

26. *Houston Chronicle,* November 27, 1936; *Austin American,* July 30, 1939.

27. *Austin American,* July 30, 1939.

28. *Austin American Statesman,* July 12, 1936.

29. *Austin American Statesman,* July 25, 1936; "Ralph W. Yarborough for 53rd District Judge," campaign brochure, Campaign—1934, YPP.

30. *Austin American Statesman,* January 19, 1936; George Mendell campaign card, Campaign—1934, YPP.

31. *Austin American Statesman,* July 24, 1936.

32. "George Mendell as a member of the 35th Legislature of Texas in 1917," Campaign—1934, YPP.

33. *The Austin American,* June 27, 1936; *Daily Texan,* June 25, 1936; *The State Week,* July 30, 1936; campaign endorsement flyer, Campaign—1936, YPP.

34. H. J. Yarborough to RWY, undated (March 1936 and June 1936), Campaign—1936, YPP.

35. "Henry Brooks Radio Address," undated (1936), Campaign—1936, YPP.

36. RWY to H. J. Yarborough, August 10, 1936, RWY to Sam Benbow, August 6, 1936, Campaign—1936, YPP.

37. *The State Week,* July 30, 1936; Ruth Shirley to RWY, August 4, 1936, RWY to Buck Hood, August 11, 1936, Campaign—1936, YPP.

38. "Statement of Expenses of Candidate" Campaign—1936, YPP; *Austin American,* July 27, 1936.

4. THE HAMBURGER CAMPAIGN

1. George Green, *The Establishment in Texas Politics, 1938–1957.* (Westwood, Conn.: Greenwood Press, 1979), p. 15.

2. For scholarly accounts of the 1937 recession and its impact on the economy and politics, see Dean L. May, *From New Deal to New Economics: The American Liberal Response to the Recession of 1937* (New York and London: Garland, 1981); Paul K. Conkin, *The New Deal,* 2nd ed. (Arlington Heights: Harlan Davidson, 1975), pp. 79-102; James MacGregor Burns, *Roosevelt: The Lion and the Fox* (New York: Harcourt, Brace, 1956), pp. 316-357; William E. Leuchtenburg, *Franklin D. Roosevelt and the New Deal, 1932–1940* (New York: Harper & Row, 1963), pp. 231-251.

3. Green, *The Establishment,* pp. 135-137; Sam Kinch and Stuart Long, *Allan Shivers: The Pied Piper of Texas Politics* (Austin: Shoal Creek Publishers, 1973), pp. 37-

40 and 46–49; Allan Shivers Papers, Texas State Archives, Austin, 1977/81-424 and 1977/81-6. Although it is likely that the two men knew each other during the 1930's, no correspondence from the 1930's between Shivers and Yarborough was located in their respective papers.

4. *Texas Almanac*, 1939–1940, p. 358. For information on W. Lee O'Daniel's controversial career, see Claude L. Douglas, *Life Story of W. Lee O'Daniel* (Dallas: Regional Press, 1938); Wayne Gard, *Texas Kingfish* (New York: Editor Publications, 1941), pp. 848–850; Seth McKay, *W. Lee O'Daniel and Texas Politics, 1938–1942* (Lubbock: Texas Tech University Press, 1944).

5. *Austin American,* January 2, 26, June 9, 1937.

6. *Austin American,* May 27, 1937.

7. *San Antonio Express,* July 4, 1937; *Austin Statesman,* November 11, December 1, 1937; *Houston Chronicle,* November 12, 1937.

8. *Austin Statesman,* January 4, 1938; Walter Prescott Webb, *The Great Plains* (New York: Ginn, 1931) and *Divided We Stand: The Crisis of a Frontierless Democracy* (Austin: Acorn Press, 1937). No correspondence in 1938 between Webb and Yarborough existed in Yarborough's papers or in Webb's papers at the CAH. Other correspondence on these issues from 1939 appeared in Webb's collection.

9. "General Charge—Anti-Trust Laws," 1938 Official Correspondence, YPP; *Austin Statesman,* January 4, 11, 1938; *Houston Chronicle,* January 11, 1938; *Dallas Morning News,* January 11, 1938.

10. *Austin Statesman,* January 11, 1938.

11. *Austin Statesman,* March 5, 1938.

12. *Austin Statesman,* March 5, 1938.

13. Ralph Yarborough scrapbook, 1935–1938, YPP. The scrapbook contains dozens of articles and clippings of speeches by Yarborough during 1937 at functions in Central and East Texas. Speeches that received news coverage included speeches at high school graduations, civic clubs, fraternal organizations, Democratic party functions, judicial and legal meetings, and university and law school functions.

14. *Austin Statesman,* August 13, 1937; *Houston Post,* August 22, 1937.

15. J. Frank Davis, *Texas: A Guide* (New York: Hastings House, 1940), pp. 288–290; *Houston Post,* January 15, 1938; *Houston Chronicle,* January 15, 1938.

16. Mike Hogg to RWY, February 25, 1938, Harris County, RY2R555, YP, CAH.

17. RWY to Judge C. A. Leddy, October 7, 1937; RWY to Robert L. Cole, September 19, 1937, Harris County, RY2R555, YP, CAH.

18. "Walter Woodul of Harris County for Attorney General," campaign brochure, 1938 Campaign Scrapbook, YPP; *Houston Post,* August 22, 1937.

19. "Mann's Messenger," campaign newspaper, 1938 Campaign Scrapbook, YPP.

20. State of Texas, *Presiding Officers of the Texas Legislature, 1846–1982* (Austin: Texas Legislative Council, 1982) and *Port Arthur News,* June 1, 1938. Judge Calvert's papers are on file at the state archives, but no information on his early life, legislative career, or attorney general's race is in the collection.

21. "Remembrances for J. R.'s 90th Birthday," YPP; Carleton, *A Breed So Rare.*

22. *El Campo News,* July 15, 1938, Campaign Scrapbook—1938, YPP. The book

contains over 100 clippings from newspapers published where Yarborough appeared during the spring and early summer of 1938.

23. RWY to Ernest Dunning, March 27, 1951, Personal Correspondence 1951, RY2R488a, YP, CAH.

24. *Athens Daily Review,* July 8, 1938.

25. *Athens Weekly Review,* February 24, 1938; *Houston Chronicle,* June 15, 1938; *Fort Worth Star Telegram,* January 27, 1938; H. J. Yarborough to RWY, July 5, 1938, 1938 campaign scrapbook, YPP.

26. Radio speech, July 14, 1938, 1938 Speeches and Materials, RY2R555, YP, CAH.

27. Ibid.

28. "Colonels of Monopoly," 1938 Speeches and Materials, RY2R555, YP, CAH.

29. Sidney Benbow to Elbert Hooper, June 24, 1938, Campaign Debts—1938, RY2R555, YP, CAH.

30. Charles O. Betts to Miss Tylyne Gentry (undated, 1938), Harris County, RY2R555, YP, CAH. As Betts explained, "Judge Yarborough, however, reads all of his mail personally in between trips when he is in his office and having already read your letter, has directed me to answer it."

31. *Austin Statesman,* July 23, 1938.

32. *Texas Almanac,* 1939–1940, p. 358.

33. Ibid., pp. 366–369.

34. RWY to Dudley Hodgkins, January 21, 1939; Tucker Moore to RWY, February 19, 1940; "Campaign Bills 1938—Owed When Campaign Over," Campaign Debts—1938, RY2R555, YP, CAH.

35. RWY to Congressman Lyndon Johnson, December 29, 1939; Congressman Lyndon Johnson to RWY, January 1, 1940, Travis County Bar Association, YPP.

36. RWY to Jefferson E. Smith, August 8, 1938, Travis County, RY2R557, YP, CAH.

37. *Texas Almanac,* 1939–1940, p. 374; "Mann's Messenger," Gerald Mann campaign newspaper, August 1938, 1938 Campaign scrapbook, YPP. None of Gerald Mann's papers are available for research by historians. The CAH Gerald Mann vertical file contains newspaper clippings on his election and tenure as Texas attorney general. Mann was unsuccessful in the 1941 U.S. Senate special election in which Governor W. Lee O'Daniel defeated Congressman Lyndon Johnson in a questionable victory.

5. WE SAW THE WORST

1. *Austin Statesman,* April 12, 1940. Yarborough received many letters of encouragement to run for attorney general in 1942 but he declined all those suggestions and focused his efforts on securing a commission.

2. RWY to Seaman J. R. McDuff, May 14, 1942, Personal Correspondence—1942, RY2R488a, YP, CAH. RWY to Lt. R. H. Spikes, November 23, 1942, Personal Correspondence—1942, RY2R488a, YP, CAH. Russell Spikes was the son of Yar-

borough's older sister Grace. Following his commission as a lieutenant in the navy, Spikes volunteered for submarine duty and was assigned to the Pacific Theater. Lieutenant Spikes along with his entire crew were lost when their submarine disappeared in 1944 off the coast of Okinawa.

3. RWY to Office of Naval Officer Procurement, New Orleans, January 29, 1943, Judge Advocate, RY2R533, YP, CAH. In a letter to Edward Crane of the Office of Price Administration declining the job, Yarborough said that he could not accept the offer because "circumstances are such as to render it practically impossible for me to remove to Fort Worth at this time." Ralph Yarborough to Edward Crane, 15 June 1942, Personal—Business Matters, RY2R488a, CAH.

4. H. J. Yarborough to RWY, January 27, 1943, Judge Advocate, RY2R533, YP, CAH.

5. Judge Advocate files, RY2R533, YP, CAH.

6. RWY to Opal Yarborough, February 18, 1945, YPP. Several other letters addressed to Opal while Ralph was "at sea" were undated.

7. RWY to Lt. Col. Charles L. Decker, July 7, 1943, Judge Advocate, RY2R488a, YP, CAH; Ralph's letters home were mailed from "somewhere in France" or "somewhere in Germany" as soldiers could not disclose any specific information on their location or assignments. Soldiers also were not permitted to keep diaries during wartime. The Ninety-seventh Division, known as the Trident Division, captured over 48,000 German prisoners and fought their way across the Ruhr-Rhine Valley, the industrial heart of Germany. Major German manufacturing cities captured by the Trident Division included Dusseldorf, Soligen, Siegburg, and Leverkusen. When the division captured Cheb, it became the first major Czechoslovakian city liberated by the Allied forces. During the war, Yarborough and Lieutenant Colonel Ward Blacklock forged a friendship that would last for decades after the men returned home to Austin. Yarborough kept the unit's history, a small handbook entitled "Story of the 97th Infantry Division," in his Austin home. He inscribed the back cover with his dates of battle action from March through May 1945.

8. RWY to Opal Yarborough, March 15, April 6, 1945, YPP.

9. RWY to Dr. Alicia Nitecki, September 23, 1993, YPP. This was the most descriptive account recorded by Yarborough of what he witnessed at Flossenburg concentration camp. Numerous biographies and sketches make reference to his participation in freeing the camp as does the history of the Ninety-seventh Division.

10. RWY to Opal Yarborough, April 10, 15, 1945, YPP.

11. RWY to Opal Yarborough, April 1, 1945, YPP. Yarborough stated that the Germans treated the people like cattle "but with far less consideration than the show cattle and horses in this country." He said the German government was committing suicide by continuing the war in 1945.

12. RWY to Richard Yarborough, March 6, 1945, YPP.

13. RWY to Richard Yarborough, April 18, 1945; RWY to Opal Yarborough, April 29, 1945, YPP.

14. RWY to Opal Yarborough, April 21, May 2, 1945; Ward T. Blacklock, "Honor-

ing Ralph Yarborough," Travis County Courthouse, 53rd District Court, February 3, 1989, YPP.

15. Blacklock, "Honoring Ralph Yarborough." Other descriptions Yarborough provided of his service in Japan are described in letters he wrote after returning home: RWY to Donald Yarborough, October 11, 1945, copy of letter given to author by Donald Yarborough; RWY to Howard H. Conaway, May 23, 1947; RWY to Edwin Sale, December 23, 1946, RY2R488a, YP, CAH.

16. Shin Hyun Pill to RWY, March 5, 1946. The inscription from the Korean Association was handwritten on a flag now located at the Yarborough home.

17. Blacklock, "Honoring Ralph Yarborough." Yarborough kept his letters of commendation in his personal library.

18. *Dallas Morning News*, February 22, 1946; *Austin American Statesman*, February 22, June 5, 1946. Ralph and Harvey exchanged letters during the spring of 1946 discussing potential opponents and financing an attorney general's campaign. Other letters came from supporters around the state.

19. Opal Yarborough to RWY, April 19, 1946, YPP. During his assignment in Japan, Opal maintained a steady correspondence on Texas politics. She continuously urged him to make a decision as their supporters were telephoning Opal for instructions for a campaign.

20. RWY to Cooper Ragan, May 29, 1948, 2R488a, YP, CAH. As indicated by his correspondence during the early postwar years, Yarborough received many letters from people around the state who encouraged him to run for office. For a detailed description of the Rainey campaign and the split among Texas Democrats during the 1940's, see Green, *The Establishment*.

21. RWY to Eugene Lankford, December 15, 1950, Personal Correspondence, 2R488a, YP, CAH.

22. RWY to Opal Yarborough, March 6, 1945, YPP; RWY to J. Frank Dobie, November 22, 1944, Dobie Papers, HRC. Yarborough became friends with Dobie during the 1930's and remained a great fan of the Texas writer and folklorist. Yarborough said he read Dobie's columns in newspapers in Europe during the war. He urged Dobie to fight the right-wing movement that threatened to "engulf the educational system of Texas."

23. O. D. Weeks, *Texas Presidential Politics in 1952* (Austin: Institute of Public Affairs, University of Texas, 1953), pp. 1–14; "Tidelands Controversy," *The New Handbook of Texas*, vol. 6, pp. 491–492. Also, in *The Establishment* George Green has an extensive discussion of the Tidelands Controversy, federal policies, racial issues, economic programs, and personal politics during this period.

24. In 1946 the U.S. Supreme Court heard a California case in which the federal government claimed ownership of offshore lands claimed by the state. Congress passed a bill confirming state ownership, but President Truman vetoed the legislation. The next year the court ruled that because oil was valuable for the nation's defense, the federal government had "paramount rights" which overrode state interests. However, Texas officials hoped that federal officials would recognize the state's spe-

cial title retained under the 1845 Annexation Agreement and disregard the California ruling. During the 1948 presidential campaign, on September 20 in Austin, President Truman stated that "Texas is in a class by itself; it entered the Union by Treaty."

After the election, Truman directed the U.S. attorney general to file suit against Texas over the state's claim to oil-rich submerged lands. The U.S. Supreme Court decided in favor of the United States, holding that transfer of national sovereignty to the United States and admission as a state on equal footing with other states accomplished a transfer of the land to the United States. In 1952 Congress again passed a bill restoring to the states submerged lands within their respective boundaries, but for the second time Truman vetoed the bill.

In the 1952 presidential campaign, Dwight Eisenhower campaigned in Texas in favor of state ownership and said he would sign legislation if it were again passed by Congress. In Texas this became the foremost issue in the election. The State Democratic Convention placed Adlai Stevenson's name on the ticket but then passed a resolution urging all members of the Democratic party to vote for Eisenhower. Eisenhower carried the state.

In 1953 Congress made state ownership of submerged lands one of the first orders of business. Price Daniel, then senator from Texas, coauthored the legislation in the Senate, where it survived what was then the longest filibuster in Senate history (twenty-seven days) and finally won a substantial majority in both houses. President Eisenhower signed the measure on May 22. In Texas the three-league boundary included 2,440,650 submerged acres, which, administered by the Texas General Land Office for the Permanent School Fund, earned over $2 billion from leases, rentals, and royalties by 1987.

25. *Austin American Statesman*, April 4, 1952; Weeks, *Presidential Politics in 1952*.

26. *New York Times*, October 14, November 13, 14, 1951, January 13, 1952; *Houston Chronicle*, March 5, 1952; *Austin American*, April 1, 1952; *Dallas Morning News*, April 26, 1952; Weeks, *Texas Presidential Politics*, pp. 16–22.

27. "Ralph Yarborough Round Up," July 25, 1952, Governor's Campaign, RY2R558, YP, CAH.

6. THE STRONG ACID TEST

1. *Texas Almanac*, 1952–1953 (Dallas: A. H. Belo Corporation, 1951), pp. 58–67. See Darlene Clark Hine, *Black Victory: The Rise and Fall of the White Primary in Texas* (Millwood, N.Y.: KTO Press, 1979). In the 1944 *Smith v. Allright* case the U.S. Supreme Court justices ruled 8 to 1 that Texas could not legally exclude African Americans from Democratic party primaries. Minority voter participation increased but remained low because of the poll tax and segregation.

2. V. O. Key, *Southern Politics in State and Nation* (New York: Knopf, 1949), pp. 254–261.

3. Green, *The Establishment*, pp. 141–147; Carleton, *A Breed So Rare*, pp. 410–415.

4. Green, *The Establishment*, pp. 141–147

5. Press release, July 25, 1952, 2R558, YP, CAH.

6. Carleton, *A Breed So Rare,* pp. 410–415. This account is based on interviews Carleton held with both Yarborough and Parten.

7. Ibid.

8. Fagan Dickson, "Texas 1952—Democratic or Dixiecratic?" Radio Address over Texas State Network, March 4, 1952, Fagan Dickson Papers, Box 7, WRC; Weeks, *Texas Presidential Politics,* pp. 22–26; *Dallas Morning News,* June 12, 1952; *Fort Worth Star Telegram,* July 6, 1952; *Houston Chronicle,* July 15, 1952; *Houston Press,* July 16, 1952. Fagan Dickson, the young executive director of the Loyal Democrats of Texas, launched the loyalist attacks on Shivers during a statewide radio broadcast before the Democratic convention.

9. J. Frank Dobie to RWY, July 11, 1952, Dobie Papers, HRC.

10. Opal Yarborough news release (undated), 1952 campaign, 2R558, YP, CAH; Maury Maverick Jr. interview by Chandler Davidson, October 27, 1975, Texas Politics Oral History Program, Woodson Research Center, Fondren Library, Rice University, 36.

11. Kingston et al., *The Texas Almanac's Political History,* pp. 244–247.

12. RWY to Judge Adolphus Ragan, October 2, 1952, 2R558, YP, CAH.

13. RWY to Ragan. Yarborough provided an insightful critique of his campaign to Ragan. The reference to Richard Nixon concerned his emotional Checkers television speech in behalf of remaining Dwight Eisenhower's vice presidential nominee. Charges of a secret slush fund forced Nixon to plead that he had never personally profited from campaign contributions. "Checkers" was the name of the family dog Nixon spoke of during the address.

14. RWY to Ragan; Kingston et al., *The Texas Almanac's Political History,* 244. Dallek, in *Lone Star Rising,* pp. 326–327, gives precise accounts of how money influenced rival factions and groups of voters in San Antonio during the hotly contested 1948 U.S. Senate election between Coke Stevenson and Lyndon Johnson.

15. RWY to Ragan; Green, *The Establishment,* pp. 144–147, and Carleton, *A Breed So Rare,* pp. 416–418.

16. RWY interview by Chandler Davidson, June 26, 1982 (WRC), pp. 70–71; Walter Hall to R. T. Craig, July 10, 1952, General Election—1952, Box 10, WGHP. From 1952 until 1972, Hall provided contributions and raised money for Yarborough in every gubernatorial and U.S. Senate campaign.

17. *Brown v. Board of Education of Topeka,* 347 U.S. 483 (1954).

18. On the racial issue, many significant historical and sociological studies conclude that the South maintained this rigid caste system for social, economic, and political purposes. These include the landmark studies of Gunnar Myrdal, *An American Dilemma: The Negro Problem in American Democracy,* 20th anniversary ed. (New York: Harper and Row, 1962); Key's *Southern Politics;* John Dollard, *Case and Class in a Southern Town* (New Haven, Yale University Press, 1937); Earl Black, *Southern Governors and Civil Rights* (Cambridge, Mass.: Harvard University Press, 1976), and Numan Bartley, *The New South, 1945–1980* (Baton Rouge: LSU Press, 1995). George Green also covers the race issue in Texas in *The Establishment in Texas Politics.*

19. *Dallas Morning News,* July 13, 1954; *Houston Post,* July 16, 1954; James E. Taylor to "Fellow Texans" (undated), 4za45, YP, CAH.

20. Charles R. Graggs, "The Strong Acid Test," *Dallas Star Post,* May 29, 1954, 4za40, YP, CAH. The Graggs commentary appeared to be intended for widespread distribution in the African American community.

21. Stuart Long, ed., *The Austin Report,* vol. 6, no. 34, June 27, 1954. Long edited this well-known political newsletter and often used campaign releases and news accounts on the candidates during statewide elections.

22. RWY announcement, June 7, 1954, Campaign—1954, 4za34, Campaign Speech, Houston, 4za46, YP, CAH; Walter Hall to RWY, September 15, 1953, RWY-WGH Correspondence, Box 10, WGHP, WRC. Hall also advised Yarborough to secure some of Shivers' influential supporters and raise more money. If one of the large daily newspapers broke ranks, that would present the "crack in the line-up" that Yarborough needed. Copies of scripts and other televised productions illustrated the increased efforts made by the Yarborough and Shivers campaigns to utilize television, whose audiences rose significantly after 1952. The number of Texas television stations expanded from five to thirty-five in these two years as the new media reached every corner of the state by 1954.

23. KRLD TV/radio speech, June 28, 1954, YP, CAH; "Texas Frauds and Failures," *Time* 63 (May 31, 1954), pp. 64, 66. Yarborough delivered a series of these attacks on Shivers in the first few months of the campaign.

24. Televised speeches, July 14, 19, 1954, 4za34, YP, CAH; Green, *The Establishment,* pp. 152–153; Carleton, *A Breed So Rare,* pp. 444–446.

25. Televised speeches, July 14, 19, 1954, 4za34, YP, CAH; *Austin American,* July 11, 1954; Carleton, *A Breed So Rare,* pp. 444–446.

26. Palestine broadcast, July 15, 1954, Dallas broadcast, July 16, 1954, "Allan Shivers Governor's Speeches," vol. 4, July 1954–1955, Box 2.325/E467, Shivers Papers, CAH. The "Big Lie" and the East Texas story are included in Green, *The Establishment,* pp. 156–157.

27. "This is Ralph Yarborough" (undated), 4za34, YP, CAH. The Yarborough campaign distributed the material to the media and Yarborough used the statements in some of his campaign appearances in the final days prior to the July 25 primary.

28. Creekmore Fath interview by Patrick Cox, November 10, 1999.

29. "Analysis of voting," Shivers Campaign internal memo, Campaign 1954 Results, AR86-107/4, Shivers Papers, CAH.

30. "Fact Sheet for All Shivers Workers," Propaganda folder, 4za45, Yarborough Papers, CAH. Other Shivers campaign materials illustrating these issues are located in the Shivers Papers at the CAH and the Texas State Archives.

31. "The Port Arthur Story," film #1977/81, SP. Quotations and statements are taken from the film.

32. "The Port Arthur Story," campaign pamphlet, Propaganda Folder, 42a45, YP, CAH.

33. Jake Pickle and Peggy Pickle, *Jake* (Austin: University of Texas Press, 1997), p. 70; *Houston Post,* November 26, 1972. Pickle later disavowed the precedent-setting

negative advertisement and said the film "left a bad taste in my mouth." When he later ran for Congress, Pickle stated that he "never ran another negative, misleading campaign ad." In a 1972 *Houston Post* interview, Robert Heller, a young producer involved with "The Port Arthur Story," recalled, "the instructions, as I remember, were to burn every copy after the election." Heller confirmed that the television ad ran throughout Texas with the exception of the southeast Texas region, "the only area where it could be challenged."

34. D. H. Biggers to RWY, July 31, 1954, Maverick County, 4za37, "Warning" circular from E. T. MacDonald to RWY, August 23, 1954, Presidio County, 4za40, YP, CAH. Many other letters voicing concerns about Shivers' attacks are in these 1954 correspondence files.

35. "Exploding the Big Lie," (August 1954), "An Open Affidavit to the People of Texas," August 4, 1954, Speeches, 2R561, Campaign speech, 4za46, YP, CAH; *Dallas Morning News,* July 15, July 18, and July 31, 1954.

36. Radio spots, August 18, 1954, 2R561, "Statewide TV Broadcast," August 22, 1954, "Ralph Yarborough's Positive Program for Texas," 2R560, YP, CAH.

37. "Statewide radio broadcast by Jack Blacklock of Houston for Shivers," August 25, 1954, "Address to Women's Meeting," August 13, 1954, Shivers, 2R560, YP, CAH; Green, *The Establishment,* pp. 159–165.

38. Secretary of State Reports, 1954, Finances, 2R560, RWY to Adolphus Ragan, December 31, 1954, 2R563, Post-election news release (undated), 1954, 2R563, YP, CAH.

39. Kingston et al., *The Texas Almanac's Political History,* 251; Green, *The Establishment,* pp. 153–165; Post-election news release (undated), 1954, 2R563, YP, CAH.

40. Sam Low to LBJ, January 22, 1954, LBJA Selected Names, Box 25, LBJL; Mark Young, "Lyndon B. Johnson's Forgotten Campaign: Re-election to the Senate in 1954" (Master's thesis, University of Texas at Austin, 1993). Robert G. Baker to Michael Gillette, Oral History. December 9, 1983, LBJL.

7. COONSKINS AND COON HUNTERS

1. For a full review of southern massive resistance after the *Brown* decision, see Dewey W. Grantham, *The Life and Death of the Solid South* (Lexington: University of Kentucky Press, 1988).

2. Bartley, *The New South,* pp. 206–213, 232–233.

3. A 1955 State Auditor's report concluded that over $3.5 million in state money was obtained in 591 transactions judged "fraudulent" and involving 39 different land sellers. A Travis County jury convicted Giles, who also pled guilty on a separate bribery charge. Giles became the first statewide elected official in Texas to serve time in a state prison for a felony committed while in office. O. D. Weeks, *Texas One-Party Politics in 1956* (Austin: Institute of Public Affairs, University of Texas, 1957), pp. 6–13; Green, *The Establishment,* pp. 166–170; Patrick Cox, "Land Commissioner Bascom Giles and the Texas Veteran's Land Board Scandals" (Master's thesis, Southwest

Texas State University, 1988). Ken Towrey of the *Cuero Record* won a Pulitzer Prize for his stories of corruption in the Veteran's Land Board programs.

4. RWY to W. A. Combs, January 1955, W. A. Combs Papers 1:2, HMRC.

5. Weeks, *Texas One-Party Politics*, pp. 15–24; Dallek, *Lone Star*, pp. 491–493; *Austin American*, February 29, March 2, 1956; *Texas Observer*, February 8, April 25, May 2, May 9, 1956. Pro-Shivers newspapers that urged the governor not to run for a fourth term were the *Corpus Christi Caller*, *Amarillo Globe*, *Victoria Advocate*, and *Jacksonville Daily Progress*.

6. RWY to LBJ, March 12, March 24, April 5, July 7, 1955, 2R563, YP, CAH. Johnson replied to Yarborough's letters expressing his thanks but never indicated or implied any support.

7. Carleton, *A Breed So Rare*, pp. 467–470.

8. *Texas Observer*, July 4, 1955; *San Antonio Light*, September 9, 1955. The August 1955 Texas Poll showed that among twelve potential candidates Yarborough led as "first choice" with 23 percent of the respondents followed by Daniel with 14 percent.

9. "Price Daniel—Biography" and "Legal Reviewers on Tidelands Law," *Dallas Morning News*, March 29, 1951; Daniel Vertical files, CAH.

10. Daniel Vertical files, CAH; "Marion Price Daniel, Sr.," *The New Handbook of Texas*, vol. 2, pp. 504–505; *Dallas Morning News*, January 22, March 27, 1956; *Austin Statesman*, March 27, 1956; "Daniel for Governor" campaign brochure. Daniel, who later in life was elected to the Texas Supreme Court, is the only Texan elected governor, U.S. senator, and justice of the Texas Supreme Court.

11. H. W. Brands, "Joe R. Greenhill, Sr. Oral History Interview," *A Texas Supreme Court Trilogy*, vol. 2 (Austin: University of Texas School of Law, 1998), pp. 25–26; *Dallas Morning News*, March 27, April 4, May 10, June 5, 20, 27, July 12, 17, 24, 1956; *Austin Statesman*, March 27, June 5, 7, 1956.

12. *Austin American*, June 2, 1956.

13. James Boren interview by Patrick Cox, January 16, 1999, Austin, Texas. Boren was one of Yarborough's key managers and organizers in the 1956 election. Also, *Dallas Morning News*, July 11, 12, 16, 27, 1956; *Austin American*, June 27, 30, 1956; *Texas Observer*, July 4, 11, 1956.

14. Boren interview; *Texas Observer*, July 4, 11, 1956.

15. *Texas Observer*, March 7, July 4, 11, 1956.

16. *Dallas Morning News*, August 1, 2, 7, 1956.

17. *Dallas Morning News*, August 1, 24, 1956; *Austin American*, August 4, 7, 1956; *Texas Observer*, August 8, 22, 1956.

18. *Dallas Morning News*, August 4, 10, 11, 19, 21, 24, 1956; *Austin American*, August 5, 10, 15, 1956.

19. *Dallas Morning News*, August 6, 10, 12, 14, 1956; *Austin American*, August 14, 20, 1956.

20. Weeks, *Texas One-Party Politics*, pp. 38–39.

21. W. P. Johnson to RWY, August 26, 1956, 4za40, YP, CAH; Boren interview; Greenhill interview by Brands in *A Texas Supreme Court Trilogy*, vol. 2; RWY interview by Davidson, 82–84; *Texas Observer*, August 29, September 5, 1956; *Dallas Morn-*

ing News, August 29, 30, 1956; *Austin Statesman,* August 29, 30, 1956. In primary elections, the state and county parties bore the responsibility for conducting the elections. Totals were phoned in and tabulated at the Texas Election Bureau in Dallas. Totals often changed throughout the counting process as corrections and late changes came in, sometimes days after the election was over.

22. C. F. Booker to RWY, August 27, 1956, 4za40, YP, CAH.

23. Weeks, *Texas One-Party Politics,* pp. 34–37. After the 1956 runoff elections, Attorney General John Ben Shepperd filed a lawsuit against the Texas NAACP and obtained an order to close the offices and its local chapters. Also, Governor Shivers accused the NAACP and other "paid agitators" of creating racial tension during integration of the public high school in Mansfield. The governor supported members of a mob that threatened black students and called in the Texas Rangers to end the efforts to integrate Mansfield schools.

24. Grantham, *The South,* pp. 215–216.

8. PUT THE JAM ON THE LOWER SHELF

1. Edyth Gilbert Barton to RWY, August 1956, Charles Collins to RWY, August 30, 1956, 4za40, YP, CAH; Boren interview; *Texas Observer,* August 16, 1956; "The Garner Act," Article 4.09, *Texas Election Code.*

2. Weeks, *Texas One-Party Politics,* pp. 43–44; *Texas Observer,* September 12, October 3, 24, 1956; Fath interview. At the September Texas Democratic Party Convention in Fort Worth, Johnson and Rayburn forces teamed with Daniel's and Shivers' supporters to elect national delegates at the expense of labor- and liberal-backed candidates. In November, with the state party divided, Eisenhower defeated Stevenson in Texas with more than 55 percent of the popular vote, a gain over the GOP totals in 1952, when the GOP candidate won the state with the support of the Shivercrats. *The Texas Observer,* the liberal Democratic newspaper, painted LBJ as a "vain, arrogant, self-centered politician" and called him a political opportunist who ranked alongside George Washington Plunkett of Tammany Hall.

3. *Dallas Morning News,* February 11, 1957; Dallek, *Lone Star Rising,* pp. 509–510.

4. Dallek, *Lone Star Rising,* p. 510; Green, *The Establishment,* pp. 180–184.

5. RWY interview by Anthony Champagne, April 3, 1992, Austin, Texas, Ralph W. Yarborough Oral Histories, CAH, 16; Dallek, *Lone Star Rising,* pp. 509–510.

6. RWY interview by Champagne, p. 17.

7. Fath and Adams, *Yarborough.*

8. Photos, "Celebration at Yarborough's Election Headquarters, 1957," Russell Lea Photo Collection, 3Y155, CAH; *Austin American Statesman,* April 8, 1957.

9. RWY interview by Champagne, 18. Carleton, *A Breed So Rare,* p. 475.

10. *Dallas Morning News,* April 7, 1957.

11. Caldwell, *Charles Sargent Caldwell Oral History Interview* (Washington: Senate Historical Office, 1996), pp. 62–66; Boren interview.

12. *Senator Ralph Yarborough's Washington Report* (hereafter cited as *Washington*

Report), August, November 19, 1957, Washington Reports, 4JB17, YP, CAH. Yarborough's first Senate newsletters appeared irregularly.

13. *Congress and the Nation, 1945–1964* (Washington, D.C.: Congressional Quarterly Service, 1965), 1622–1624, 74a; *Congressional Quarterly Almanac,* vol. 13, 1957; Dallek, *Lone Star Rising,* pp. 519–527. Gore and Kefauver of Tennessee and Smathers of Florida were the only other southern senators who voted in favor of the bill.

14. *Congressional Record,* 85th Cong., 2nd Session, August 22, 1958, 19085; Committee on Labor and Public Welfare, 100th Anniversary, 1869–1969 (Washington, D.C.: U.S. Government Printing Office, 1970).

15. Ed Clark to Walter G. Hall, November 20, 1957, Box 10, WGHP, WRC; *Austin American,* April 9, 1958.

16. *Austin American,* April 28, 1958.

17. Essin, Emmett M., "The Democratic Senatorial Primary in Texas: Yarborough Versus Blakley (Master's Thesis, Austin College, June 1965), pp. 19–20; "On the Go for Texas," campaign brochure, William Blakley vertical file, CAH. Essin relied on a post-election interview with Blakley for the promises that the candidate believed he had secured prior to making the race. The author maintained that "Shivers made it clear to Blakley that every one of these men would support Blakley in the race." Essin also had a February 22, 1965, interview with Blakley in Dallas, Texas.

18. "The Story of Bill Blakley," campaign brochure, William Blakley vertical file, CAH; O. D. Weeks, *Texas in the 1960 Presidential Election* (Austin: University of Texas, 1961), pp. 3–5; Baggarly, *The Texas Country Editor: H. M. Baggarly Takes a Grass-Roots Look at National Politics,* edited by Eugene W. Jones (Cleveland: World Publishing, 1966), p. 144.

19. *Austin Statesman,* April 29, 1958. Sam Wood and Raymond Brooks, "Capital A," *Austin American,* April 30, 1958.

20. "Story of Bill Blakley"; *New Republic* 138 (April 21, 1958): 4–5; *Austin Statesman,* May 23, 29, June 4, 1958; *Dallas Morning News,* May 29, 1958; *Texas Observer,* May 30, 1958.

21. Essin, "Democratic Primary," 37. Essin interviewed R. C. Slagle on March 1, 1965, and Senator Yarborough on December 30, 1964.

22. "Democratic Primary," pp. 40–42; *Austin Statesman,* July 9, 10, 1958; *Texas Observer,* July 25, 1958; *Dallas Morning News,* July 23, 25, 1958. *Morning News* editorial writer Lynn Landrum was particularly critical of Yarborough and frequently "jammed" him during the campaign.

23. *Austin American,* June 20, July 1, 10, 15, 1958.

24. *Fort Worth Star Telegram,* July 8, 1958; *Texas Observer,* June 6, July 4, 1958; *Houston Press,* July 14. Once the *Observer* broke the story on Blakley's payments to insurance companies and the federal money for Braniff, several of the state's major daily newspapers carried the story.

25. *Fort Worth Star Telegram,* July 23, 1958.

26. Ibid., July 15, 1958. Similar stories appeared throughout the state's daily newspapers on the foreign crisis.

27. *Fort Worth Star Telegram*, July 16, 17, 1958; Weeks, "The Texas Primary System," pp. 48–49.

28. Boren interview.

29. Carleton, *A Breed So Rare*, pp. 481–483; *Fort Worth Star Telegram*, July 25, 26, 1958. The timing of the Blakley donation offended Rayburn, but he eventually accepted it after the election was over.

30. Kingston et al., *The Texas Almanac's Political History*, pp. 134-137, 154-157, *Texas Observer*, June 27, August 15, August 29, September 5, 1958. Yarborough's frequent complaint that the daily newspapers were biased in favor of his opponents has merit. The *Observer* conducted a survey of the Senate race news coverage by four mid-sized East Texas dailies. Blakley received four to five times the number of news stories and photos, and the dailies frequently mentioned Yarborough only in negative terms. Blakley received slightly more favorable treatment from the Houston and San Antonio papers. The *Dallas Morning News* usually mentioned Yarborough as the "liberal-labor" candidate and nearly always mentioned his three losing campaigns for governor.

9. PROBLEMS WITH JOHNSON AND RAYBURN

1. Robert C. Byrd, *The Senate, 1789-1989*, vol. 1 (Washington, D.C.: U.S. Government Printing Office, 1988), pp. 644–645.

2. *Texas Observer*, July 4, 1958. During the 1950's, Texas law prohibited the state parks board from making any expenditures to acquire more lands for public use.

3. "Statewide Texas Salute to Senator Ralph W. Yarborough," October 19, 1963, YPP; *Dallas Morning News*, May 31, 1959, *Houston Post*, June 21, 1959; *Washington Report*, July 23, 1959, 4ze456, CAH.

4. *Texas Observer*, March 14, 1959, *Austin American*, June 7, 1959.

5. *Texas Observer*, August 1, September 16, 25, 1959; *Washington Report*, July 30, 1959, 4ze456, CAH.

6. Ernest M. B. Obadele-Starks, "Ralph Yarborough of Texas and the Road to Civil Rights," *East Texas Historical Journal* 32, no. 1 (1994): 39–48. Robert Mann, *Walls of Jericho* (New York: Harcourt Brace, 1996), pp. 245–246.

7. *Congressional Record—Senate*, January 7, 1960, pp. 113-114.

8. *Dallas Morning News,* June 21, November 8, 1959; *Texas Observer,* September 25, 1959; *Austin American*, November 7, November 12, 1959; *Daily Texan*, December 13, 1959; RWY to Walter Hall, March 25, 1959, Correspondence, Box 11, WGHP. In his letter to Walter Hall, Yarborough said the VFW was the first statewide veterans group he addressed and the "most Democratic of the large organizations." He also belonged to the American Legion, but because he was a "loyal Democrat," he wrote, "I virtually had to shoot my way into their meetings."

9. *Texas Observer*, January 15, January 29, 1960; *Fort Worth Star Telegram*, January 13, 1960; *Dallas Morning News*, January 5, January 13, 1960; RWY interview by

Davidson, 139. In 1959, Yarborough and Johnson agreed on 86 percent of the 215 Senate votes.

10. *Texas Observer,* February 26, 1960. The liberals formed their own organization and called themselves the Democrats of Texas in their ongoing battle with other factions of the state party.

11. Dallek, *Lone Star Rising,* pp. 563–576; *Dallas Morning News,* July 27, 1960; *Texas Observer,* May 13, July 1, 1960.

12. *Dallas Morning News,* October 29, 1960; *Texas Observer,* October 21, November 4, 1960; William G. Phillips, *Yarborough of Texas* (Washington, D.C.: Acropolis Books, 1969), p. 58. Yarborough chaired the Freedom of Communications Subcommittee, which recommended changes in the federal communications law in order to air the televised debates and sponsored the Senate legislation that allowed for the Kennedy-Nixon debates. Only Nixon and Kennedy debated because the legislation excluded dozens of minor candidates from the format. An estimated 75 million people watched the debates, which many scholars believe gave Kennedy the margin of victory in the close race.

13. O. D. Weeks, *Texas in the 1960 Presidential Election* (Austin: Institute of Public Affairs, University of Texas, 1961), pp. 55–57; *Texas Observer,* October 21, November 4, 1960; *Dallas Morning News,* September 29, 1960; *Houston Post,* October 29, 1960.

14. Weeks, *Texas in the 1960 Election,* pp. 63–65; *Dallas Times Herald,* January 25, 1961.

15. Caldwell, *Oral History Interview,* pp. 100–102; *Dallas Morning News,* February 19, 1961; *Texas Observer,* November 11, 1960.

16. Johnson was already at odds with the younger Kennedy due to clashes during the nomination process and the presidential campaign. Woodrow Seals to RWY, February 18, 1963, Folder 16, Box 1, Woodrow Seals Papers, HMRC. LBJ to Robert Kennedy, August 10, September 7, 1961, VP Masters, LBJL; Bobby Baker with Larry L. King, *Wheeling and Dealing: Confessions of a Capitol Hill Operator* (New York: W. W. Norton, 1978), pp. 339–340. Eight boxes of correspondence relating to judicial, marshal, postal, and customs appointments in the Vice Presidential Papers at the LBJ Library have not been opened for examination by scholars.

17. Weeks, *Texas in the 1960 Election,* pp. 78–80; *Texas Observer,* February 11, February 18, 1961. Thanks to a Texas Legislature–approved statute termed the "LBJ law," Johnson simultaneously ran for reelection to the Senate and as the Democratic vice presidential candidate. John Tower gained 41 percent of the popular vote against Johnson in the Senate race in the November 1960 general election.

18. Weeks, *Texas in the 1960 Election,* pp. 78–80; *Texas Observer,* April 22, April 29, May 20, June 3, 1961; Caldwell, *Oral History,* pp. 82–84. The total vote in the runoff was 885,000, about 20,000 votes fewer than in the first election.

19. *Texas Observer,* November 17, 1961; *Austin American,* November 17, 1961; Press release, January 11, 1962, Sam Rayburn, 4Jb21, YP, CAH.

20. *Texas Observer,* January 5, January 19, 1962; *Dallas Morning News,* December 14, 1961.

21. *Austin American,* January 26, 1962; *Texas Observer,* January 26, 1962; RWY statement, January 25, 1962, 1962 Governor's Race, 4Jb21, YP, CAH.

22. *Dallas Morning News,* June 26, 1962; Walter Jenkins to Vice President Johnson and Walter Jenkins to Ken O'Donnell, January 24, 1963, "Ralph Yarborough," LBJA Congressional File, LBJL. Johnson aide Walter Jenkins stated in his memo to O'Donnell that the LBJ staff should repeat that Johnson "has no idea of running anyone against Ralph Yarborough." Jenkins wrote Johnson that Yarborough still complained that he could not "even get a postmaster in a little town without clearing it with the Vice President."

23. *New York Times,* January 25, 1962; *Corpus Christi Caller,* July 4, 1954, April 12, 1961; *Houston Post,* May 1, 1960. Other articles on the debate are located in "Padre Island" scrapbook, CAH. Editorial endorsements for the park legislation came from the *Corpus Christi Caller Times, The Houston Post, The Texas Observer,* and a number of smaller newspapers.

24. *Houston Post,* January 6, 1961; *Texas Observer,* April 8, June 17, July 22, September 9, 1961; Press release, January 11, 1962, 1962 Legislative Aims, 4Jb21, YP, CAH.

25. *Dallas Morning News,* May 2, June 22, 1961.

26. *Dallas Morning News,* March 2, 4, 1962; *Dallas Times Herald,* February 16, 1962. *Houston Chronicle,* March 4, 1962.

27. *Congressional Record,* April 10, 1962, 6256–6257.

28. Ibid., 6258.

29. Ibid., 6259–6261.

30. *Washington Report,* October 5, 1962; *Dallas Morning News,* June 22, 1962; *Texas Observer,* March 9, 30, May 26, 1962; Press release, February 15, 22, April 15, September 18, 1962, Padre Island, 4Jb21, YP; RWY to Walter Hall, September 13, 1962, WGH Papers; "Padre Island National Seashore," *New Handbook of Texas,* vol. 5, p. 8.

31. RWY interview by Davidson, pp. 142–144; "Padre Island National Seashore," *New Handbook of Texas,* vol. 5, p. 8.

32. Martin V. Melees, "Lyndon Johnson and Environmental Policy," in *The Johnson Years,* vol. 2, edited by Robert A. Divine (Lawrence: University of Kansas Press, 1987), pp. 113–120. Passage of Yarborough's 1962 Padre Island legislation occurred the same year as publication of Rachel Carson's *Silent Spring,* considered by many environmentalists as marking the dawn of the modern environmental age. During the 1950's Congress and conservation organizations began to draft legislation that utilized the federal government to extend its powers into newer areas of protection for the nation's land, wildlife, and water systems.

33. *Austin American Statesman,* April 29, 1962; *Lubbock Avalanche Journal,* March 30, 1962; *Dallas Morning News,* May 16, May 22, 1962.

34. Richard E. Carter to RWY, May 16, 1962, and Miscellaneous letters to constituents from RWY, 1962, Texas Political—Billie Sol Estes, 4zd569, YP, CAH. Yarborough stated in most of the letters that "I don't own a foot of land more than I owned the day I was elected, neither have I accumulated any commercial, financial or other interests. I have made the country's welfare my sole concern, and certain newspapers don't like that kind of service."

35. Roy Selman to RWY, May 14, 1962, Gus Garcia to RWY, May 17, 1962, Bonner Frizell to RWY, May 22, 1962, Texas Political—Billie Sol Estes, 4zd569, YP, CAH.

36. Thomas G. Pollard to RWY, June 27, 1962, I. H. Kempner to RWY, May 17, 1962, Texas Political BSE, 4zd569, YP, CAH.

37. "Goldwater Acclaims Yarborough on Estes," *New York Herald Tribune*, May 25, 1962; "Not Beholden," *Washington Post*, May 24, 1962.

38. *Houston Post*, May 28, 1962.

39. Caldwell, *Oral History Interview*, 46.

10. THE RANCID SMELL OF GUNPOWDER

1. Press releases, 1963 Itinerary, 4Jb21, YP, CAH; *Lewisville Leader*, June 20, 1963, Box 3, Frankie Randolph Papers, WRC. "Not once did he complain of the heat nor did he seek shelter from the sun," the Lewisville editor said in amazement. "He was available to all for a handshake and invariably had an appropriate kind remark to make to each person."

2. Elaine Anderson to RWY, September 2, 1963; Larry Tate, President, Texas Junior Chamber of Commerce to RWY, November 7, 1963; Henry Cropper to RWY, October 29, 1963; Civil Rights letters, 4Zd621, YP, CAH; *Congressional Quarterly Almanac*, vol. 19, pp. 189, 192.

3. RWY to Walter Hall, October 29, 1963, Correspondence, Box 11, WGHP, WRC; *Congressional Record*, November 6, 1963, A6897-6898; *Texas Observer*, November 1, 1963. Yarborough told his friend Hall that the dinner ranked just below his marriage and his son's birth. Yarborough wrote, "I enjoyed it even more than getting elected to office."

4. Bill Chamberlain to RWY, October 4, 1963, Mrs. Yarborough Personal Correspondence, 2R491, YP, CAH; *Houston Post*, September 22, 1963; Dallek, *Flawed Giant*, pp. 44-46. The Belden Poll contained telephone surveys of registered Texas voters. Yarborough was not included in the survey.

5. Herbert Parmet, *The Democrats: The Years after FDR* (New York, Macmillan, 1976), pp. 217-219; *Houston Post*, June 23, July 20, 1963; *Dallas Times Herald*, October 4, 6, November 19, 1963.

6. Franklin Jones Sr. to Attorney General Robert F. Kennedy, November 15, 1963, in Ann Adams, ed., *The Itch of Opinion: The Public and Private Letters of Franklin Jones, Sr., 1954-1974* (Oak Arbor, Washington: Packrat Press, 1984), pp. 70-71.

7. John Connally to RWY, November 4, 1963, General Correspondence folder; RWY to Eugene Locke, December 13, 1963, President's Welcome Dinner Tickets and Press Releases: Kennedy Dinner, Series 7, Box 1, CP, LBJL; RWY to Pres. Kennedy, Nov. 18, 1963, 1963 JFK's Trip to Texas, 4C318, YP, CAH; RWY to Walter Hall, November 9, 1963, "Dinner in Austin for JFK," Box 11, WGHP. Yarborough mailed letters to his wealthier contributors and sold his ticket allotment.

8. Maury Maverick Jr. interview by Davidson, October 27, 1975, Texas Politics

Oral History Program, WRC, pp. 33–36; Dallek, *Flawed Giant,* pp. 45–47. After the evening speech in Houston, Kennedy reportedly lectured Johnson about Connally's treatment of Yarborough and told LBJ to correct the situation.

9. *Texas Observer,* November 29, 1963.

10. RWY handwritten speech, December folder, 4Ze351, YP, CAH; *Dallas Morning News,* November 22, 1963; Herbert Parmet, *JFK* (New York: Dial Press, 1983), pp. 342–344.

11. RWY to Opal Yarborough, December 14, 1963, Mrs. Yarborough Personal Correspondence, YP, 2R491, CAH.

12. Ted Bonner, "Don't Swing at a Guy in Dallas—He'll Pull a Gun on You," *The Dublin Sunday Independent,* March 8, 1964. Photocopy in Kennedy, President John F., 2R515, YP, CAH. Yarborough enclosed copies of the article to many friends in Texas who sent him letters regarding the assassination. In *The Vantage Point: Perspectives on the Presidency* (Holt, Rinehart and Winston, 1971), Lyndon Johnson's only extensive discussion of Yarborough is contained in his account of the Kennedy assassination. Johnson wrote that "Senator Yarborough and I had our differences," but that any story that President Kennedy came to Texas "to settle a political feud between Senator Yarborough and me is not true" (p. 7).

13. RWY to Chief Justice Earl Warren, December 16, 1963, Kennedy, President John F., 2R515, YP, CAH. Report of the President's Commission on the Assassination of President John F. Kennedy, pp. 43–48. The published works on the 1963 Kennedy assassination are voluminous. Besides Lyndon Johnson's account, see Lady Bird Johnson, *A White House Diary* (New York: Holt Rinehart and Winston, 1970). For John Connally's version, see John M. Connally and Mickey Herskowitz, *In History's Shadow: An American Odyssey* (New York: Hyperion Books, 1993), pp. 6–7. The official report, best known as the Warren Commission Report, is the Report of the President's Commission on the Assassination of President John F. Kennedy.

14. RWY to Governor and Mrs. John Connally, November 23, 1963; RWY to President Johnson, November 23, 1963, Kennedy, President John F., 2R515, YP, CAH; Dallek, *Flawed Giant,* pp. 54–59.

15. L. L. Chandler to RWY, December 11, 1963; Jack Padgett to RWY, December 4, 1963, Mrs. C. B. Carsey to RWY, January 2, 1963, Lucile Moxley to RWY, December 1, 1963, Kennedy, President John F., 2R515, YP, CAH.

16. *Abilene Reporter News,* December 7, 1963; *Austin Statesman,* December 8, 1963; Dallek, *Flawed Giant,* pp. 46–47; Caldwell, *Oral History Interview,* pp. 108–110.

17. RWY to Leon Green and others, December 11, 1963, Jim Wright, 2R491, YP, CAH; Ann Gough Hunter to Governor John Connally, November 17, 1963, President's Texas Visit, Series 7, Box 1, CP, LBJL. Yarborough asked Green and the seven other attorneys and professors to whom he sent the personal letter that they "not violate my confidence, and . . . not make public in any form what I have said here about our martyred President."

18. RWY to David Miller, December 13, 1963, Jim Wright, 2R491, YP, CAH. Yarborough never said directly that the White House was to blame. But he noted in his letter that the December 8 *Austin Statesman* had announced the appointment

of Leslie Carpenter as the Washington correspondent for the Texas newspaper. At the same time and on the same page of the newspaper, Lady Bird Johnson appointed Leslie Carpenter's wife, Liz Carpenter, as the first lady's press secretary. Yarborough believed that the appointments and the unflattering story were part of a political tradeoff at his expense.

19. John Connally and Mickey Herskowitz, *In History's Shadow*, pp. 6–7.

20. Caldwell, *Oral History Interview*, pp. 107–111; "Car Assignments," President Kennedy's Trip to Texas, Series 7, Box 1, CP, LBJL. In Austin, the schedule called for Yarborough to ride with Congressman Homer Thornberry for the parade that never occurred.

11. THE STRUGGLE FOR THE SOUL OF THE NATION

1. Press release, television interview, December 4, 1963; RWY to LBJ, December 16, 1963; LBJ to RWY, December 20, 1963; press release, December 12, 17, 1963, Press releases (1963); press releases, May 28, June 5, 1964, Press releases (1964), 4Jb21, YP, CAH; *Texas Observer*, January 10, 1964.

2. Caldwell, *Oral History Interview*, 140.

3. Ibid., pp. 140–141; Boren interview; Undated newsclip (1963) on Marian Jean Robinson, Box 3, Frankie Randolph Papers, WRC. Robinson was a Houston native who graduated from Western College for Women in 1961.

4. "The Political Climate in Texas, January 1964," Poll conducted by Louis, Bowles and Grace of Dallas for Allan Shivers, SP, Box 86-107/5, CAH. The statewide poll sampled 527 people January 7–14, 1964.

5. LBJ conversation with Houston Harte, January 20, 1964, transcript of recording #1448; LBJ conversation with Frank Erwin, February 1, 1964, #1805–1806, White House Series, LBJL. Johnson complained about Connally's actions at length to Erwin: "It's unthinkable, that a boy that would work for me for 20 years would do this without ever talking to me, and run off with Shivers. It would just be exactly like if I came down there, and ran off with Price Daniel and put him after John. I can't understand it." Johnson briefly discussed the race with Fort Worth Congressman Jim Wright after Don Yarborough (no relation to Ralph) announced for governor against Connally.

6. Caldwell, *Oral History Interview*, p. 38.

7. Ronald Garay, *Gordon McLendon: The Maverick of Radio* (New York: Greenwood Press, 1992), pp. 177–179; "Gordon Baxter McLendon," *The New Handbook of Texas*, vol. 4, p. 429.

8. *Dallas Morning News*, April 26, 1964; Garay, *Gordon McLendon*, pp. 180–182; *Texas Observer*, March 31, 1967.

9. Walter Hall to RWY, April 14, 1964, and Walter Hall to Robert T. Bartley, Federal Communications Commission, June 1, 1964, Gordon McLendon, Box 11, WGHP; Dave McNeely, "The 1964 Democratic Senatorial Primary" (Master's thesis, University of Texas at Austin, 1965); Carleton, *A Breed So Rare*, pp. 513–514;

Garay, *Gordon McLendon,* pp. 180–182. Walter Hall told Yarborough that Estes' attorney confirmed that Estes lied about the $50,000 donation. An audit of Estes' books indicated no withdrawal in this amount.

10. Walter Hall to RWY, June 24, 1964, Gordon McLendon, Box 11, WGHP; *Dallas Times Herald,* April 29, 1964; Kingston et al., *The Texas Almanac's Political History,* 137. According to official campaign records, Yarborough outspent McLendon by nearly three to one as the senator raised over $300,000 for the Democratic Primary.

11. O. D. Weeks, *Texas in 1964—A One-Party State Again?* (Austin: Institute of Public Affairs, University of Texas, 1965), pp. 14–17; *San Antonio Express,* July 17, 1964; *Austin American,* June 18, 1964.

12. *Congressional Quarterly Almanac,* vol. 20, June 1964, pp. 372–373; Press release, June 19, 1964, Civil Rights, 4Jb21, YP, CAH; John A. Andres, *Lyndon Johnson and the Great Society* (Chicago: Ivan R. Dee, 1998), pp. 25–30. Senator Tower, the only Republican senator from the South, opposed the 1964 Civil Rights Act. The act attacked segregation in public facilities, employment, and schools and allowed federal officials to cut off funds to local school districts if they failed to integrate.

13. Alex Dickie interview by Patrick Cox, April 30, 1999; Press release, June 19, 1964, Civil Rights, 4Jb21, YP, CAH. "Juneteenth" commemorates the official announcement that freed slaves in Texas on June 19, 1865.

14. Caldwell, *Oral History Interview,* pp. 142–145.

15. Ibid., pp. 145–146.

16. *Houston Chronicle,* July 9, 1964; *Los Angeles Herald Examiner,* July 9, 1964.

17. Harold Jones to RWY, July 16, 1964, Mrs. R. Ketterman to RWY, July 10, 1964, "A Texas Voter" to RWY, July 19, 1964, Thurmond-Yarborough Match, 4Zd572, YP, CAH; *Dallas Morning News,* July 15, 1964.

18. Franklin Jones to RWY, July 13, 1964, Oliver Hammonds to RWY, July 13, 1964; Bruce Duncan to RWY, July 10, 1964; V. L. Harris to RWY, July 10, 1964, Thurmond-Yarborough Match folder, 4Zd572, Yarborough Papers, CAH.

19. George Bush and Victor Gold, *Looking Forward* (New York: Doubleday, 1987), pp. 67–73; Nicholas King, *George Bush* (New York: Dodd, Mead, 1980), pp. 43–51.

20. Caldwell, *Oral History Interview,* pp. 127–130.

21. George Bush campaign letter, August 21, 1964, George Bush, 2R508, YP, CAH; Bush and Gold, *Looking Forward,* pp. 77–80. As chairman of the Harris County Republicans in 1963, Bush opened his appeal to conservative Democrats deserted by the "left wing Democrats—the so-called 'liberal' Democrats" in a July 28, 1963 guest column in the *Houston Chronicle.*

22. Jack Howerton, "You Can Still Vote As You Wish," July 8, 1964, *Cuero Record,* George Bush, 2R508, YP, CAH; *Texas Observer,* October 30, 1964.

23. LBJ to RWY, November 3, 1964, Ralph Yarborough Name File, WHCF, LBJL; *Texas Observer,* October 30, 1964; Dallek, *Flawed Giant,* pp. 170–184.

24. RWY, "In Memoriam, Charles Richard Yarborough, Centenarian," October 24, 1964. Pamphlet privately published and printed by RWY, YPP.

25. "Texas Attitudes toward Candidates and Issues," October 1964, statewide survey conducted for the SDEC, pp. iii–viii, Series 2, Box 7; Larry Temple to Martin

Kerner, November 12, 1964, Ralph Yarborough, Series 41, Box 3, CP, LBJL; Caldwell, *Oral History Interview*, pp. 106, 117-118. Chuck Caldwell to Creekmore Fath, July 29, 1964, and Bush campaign letter, August 21, 1964, Folder 18, Box 1, Woodrow Seals Papers, HMRC. Connally's response to Yarborough supporters in 1964 stated his support for the entire Democratic slate but never mentioned Yarborough by name. In his autobiography, Bush believed he was close to defeating Yarborough but lost because of Lyndon Johnson's coattails. Two years later, Bush successfully ran as the GOP candidate for the 7th Congressional District in Houston.

26. H J. Yarborough to RWY, August 14, 1964, George Bush, 2R508, YP, CAH.

27. H. J. Yarborough to RWY, August 19, 1964, George Bush, 2R508, YP, CAH; Frankie Randolph to Alex Dickie, August 24, 1964, Box 3, Frankie Randolph Papers, WRC; *Houston Post*, November 4, 1968; Bush and Gold, *Looking Forward*, pp. 79-81. Bush maintained he opposed the John Birch Society and that he was actually on their "political hit list."

28. *Houston Post*, December 19, 1968; RWY to Frankie Randolph, November 19, 1964, Box 3, Frankie Randolph Papers, WRC. Yarborough claimed election officials in counties using paper ballots improperly discarded as many as 200,000 straight-ticket votes because voters mistakenly failed to eliminate the Constitution Party along with the Republican Party.

29. Richard Morehead, *50 Years in Texas Politics* (Austin: Eakin Press, 1982), pp. 201-204; *Austin American*, December 12, 1967.

30. Mann, *Walls of Jericho*, pp. 453-455; *Houston Chronicle* and *Dallas Morning News*, March 9, 1965.

31. *Austin American Statesman*, August 15, 1965; Caldwell, *Oral History Interview*, pp. 86-89; SDEC Press Release, August 1965, Ralph W. Yarborough, Series 15, Box 6, CP, LBJL.

32. RWY to Frankie Randolph, November 13, 15, 1965, and RWY to Hon. Joe Tunnell and others, November 9, 1965, Box 3, Frankie Randolph Papers, WRC; Walter Hall to RWY, August 20, 1965, Correspondence, Box 13, WGHP, WRC.

33. Alex Dickie Memo to RWY, April 29, 1965, Box 3, Frankie Randolph Papers, WRC; *Dallas Morning News*, December 19, 1965; *Houston Chronicle*, December 19, 1965.

34. RWY to Frankie Randolph, August 8, 1966, Box 3, Frankie Randolph Papers, WRC; *Houston Chronicle*, August 19, 1966; *Fort Worth Press*, March 8, 1966; *Fort Worth Star Telegram*, March 22, 1966; *San Antonio News*, March 9, August 4, 1966; *Washington Report*, October 7, 1965. Yarborough congratulated Randolph, Chris Dixie, Bill Kilgarlin, and others for defeating the Connally-backed amendment "in 70 percent of the counties of Texas." A four-year term would have left Connally in office until 1970 and in prime position to upset Yarborough's reelection efforts.

35. RWY to Walter Hall and J. R. Parten, October 18, 1967, Disaster Relief, Box 12, WGHP, WRC; *New York Times*, March 20, 1966; *Houston Post*, March 28, 1966; *Houston Chronicle*, September 27, 1967; *Washington Report*, October 20, 1967.

36. *Dallas Morning News*, December 1, 1967; *Texas Observer*, August 9, August 23, 1968.

37. RWY to Walter Hall et al., November 4, 1967, El Paso, and RWY to Fagan Dickson, February 2, 1968, Box 12, WGHP, WRC; *Fort Worth Star Telegram,* October 29, 1967; *Dallas Morning News,* November 29, 1967.

38. *Texas Observer,* June 7, 1968.

12. ACTS OF CONGRESS AND ACTS OF MADNESS

1. Jack Campbell, "Senator Yarborough and the Texan 'RWY' Brand on Bilingual Education and Federal Aid," *Education Studies,* 12 (1981-1982), pp. 403-415; Gary Orfield, *The Reconstruction of Southern Education* (New York: Wiley-Interscience, 1969), pp. 4, 27; RWY to Walter Hall, July 28, 1965, Box 3, Frankie Randolph Papers, WRC; *Committee on Labor and Public Welfare, United States Senate, 100th Anniversary, 1869–1969,* 90th Congress, 2d Session (1970), 147-148.

2. Dallek, *Flawed Giant,* pp. 196-202; Phillips, *Yarborough,* pp. 102-104; Campbell, "Senator Yarborough and the RWY Brand," p. 411.

3. RWY to LBJ, May 6, 1965; Bill Moyers, Memo to the President, May 10, 1965, Charles Schultz, Memo to the President, July 22, 1965, VA3, LBJL; Phillips, *Yarborough,* pp. 102-104; *Congressional Record,* October 2, 1966, 28997-29000.

4. Julie Leininger Pycior, *LBJ & Mexican Americans* (Austin: University of Texas Press, 1997), pp. 183-187; *Texas Observer,* April 28, 1967; Campbell, "Senator Yarborough and the RWY Brand," p. 410.

5. *Congressional Record,* January 17, 1967, pp. 21-23; *Texas Observer,* April 28, 1967.

6. *Austin American Statesman,* January 18, 1968; Pycior, *LBJ,* pp. 185-187; *Congressional Record,* December 15, 1967, 37498-37501.

7. *Committee on Labor and Public Welfare,* pp. 75-78; Dallek, *Flawed Giant,* pp. 203-211. Yarborough covered Medicare in the 1965 editions of his *Washington Report* on April 19, May 31, July 9, August 4, and November 16.

8. W. C. Jameson, *The Guadalupe Mountains: Island in the Desert* (El Paso: Texas Western Press, 1994), pp. 1-44.

9. "Guadalupe Mountains National Park," Congressional Hearings, Senate Committee on Interior and Insular Affairs, 89th Congress, July 21, 1965, and August 9, 1966 (Washington: Government Printing Office, 1966), pp. 1-99. *Fort Worth Star Telegram,* September 24, 1964; *Houston Chronicle,* January 23, 1964; *Dallas Morning News,* October 7, 1963; *El Paso Times,* February 10, 1965. Of all the newspapers endorsing the project, only the *San Angelo Standard Times* and the *Houston Chronicle* noted Yarborough's role in creating the park.

10. RWY, *The Guadalupe Mountains: A Congressional Record Bibliography* (undated), CAH; Guadalupe Mountains National Park, *The New Handbook of Texas,* vol. 3, pp. 364-365; *Washington Post,* July 30, 1967; "Guadalupe Mountains Funds Approved by Senate," June 27, 1968, '68 PR folder, 4jb29; RWY to Senator Carl Haden, December 17, 1968, Guadalupe Mountains, 1968, 4C320, YP, CAH.

11. Monte Latimer Monroe, "Lone Star Environmentalist: U.S. Senator Ralph W. Yarborough" (Ph.D. dissertation, Texas Tech University, 1999). Monroe concluded in

his unpublished study that Yarborough's efforts to develop new initiatives and funding altered the national equation for national park selection and acquisition.

12. RWY on Vietnam, August 5, 1964, Press releases (1964); *Senator Yarborough's Washington Newsletter,* May 28, 1964, Vietnam, 4Jb21, YP, CAH. Johnson, *Vantage Point,* pp. 143–153; Dallek, *Flawed Giant,* pp. 268–277. Many historical accounts on Vietnam discuss U.S. involvement and the Johnson administration's policies and their political ramifications. Among these are James S. Olson and Randy Roberts, *Where the Domino Fell: America and Vietnam, 1945–1995* (New York: St. Martin's Press, 1996); Gary R. Hess, *Vietnam and the United States* (Boston: Twayne Publishers, 1990); H. W. Brands, *The Wages of Globalism: Lyndon Johnson and the Limits of American Power* (New York: Oxford University Press, 1995); and Lewis L. Gould, *1968: The Election That Changed America* (Chicago: Ivan R. Dee, 1993).

13. *Houston Post,* July 29, 1965; *San Angelo Standard Times,* November 8, 1965; *Texas Observer,* December 10, 1965.

14. *Texas Observer,* March 18, June 24, July 8, 1966; *Congressional Record,* March 1, 1966.

15. Minutes of Cabinet Meeting, 8/23/67; Cabinet Papers, Box 10, LBJL; Walter Hall to RWY, September 6, 1967, and Yarborough Press Release, August 16, 1967, Vietnam, Box 12, WGHP, WRC; Pycior, *LBJ,* pp. 190–191. In his news release, Yarborough noted that "I have not been one who has expressed criticism of the Administration's conduct of the war in Vietnam. Indeed, I think this statement is my first statement in the Senate on this subject." He said, "Anyone who advocates a land invasion of North Vietnam should be prepared to justify to Congress a formal declaration of war."

16. *Washington Report,* April 19, 1968; '68PR, 4jb29, YP, CAH; Dallek, *Flawed Giant,* pp. 502–517.

17. "Yarborough Supports Lowering Voting Age to 18," May 16, 1968, '68 PR, 4jb29, YP, CAH.

18. Dallek, *Flawed Giant,* pp. 527–532; RWY radio broadcast, April 5, 1968, '68 PR, 4jb29, YP, CAH. The text was also included in the April 11, 1968, *Senator Yarborough's Washington Newsletter.*

19. "Yarborough Cosponsors Right to Counsel in Selective Service Bill," May 20, 1968; "Right to Counsel" release, May 20, 1968, '68 PR folder, 4jb29, YP, CAH.

20. RWY radio broadcast, April 12, 1968, '68 PR, 4jb29, YP, CAH.

21. Tribute to Robert Kennedy, June 14, 1968; Robert Kennedy Funeral, press release and radio broadcast, June 14, 1968; "Yarborough Asks Postponement of Texas Democratic Convention," June 10, 1968, '68 PR, 4jb29, YP, CAH; *Senator Yarborough's Washington Newsletter,* April 19, 1968; *Texas Observer,* May 10, August 23, 1968.

22. *Congressional Quarterly,* October 14, 1968, pp. 32044–32048.

23. "Statement of Senator Yarborough Re the Gubernatorial Race," January 13, 1968; J. R. Parten to Walter Hall, October 25, 1967; RWY to Fagan Dickson, February 2, 1968, Personal Correspondence, 13, WGH Papers.

24. RWY to [William] Wayne Justice and Richard Brooks Hardee, July 10, 1968,

Correspondence, Box 13, WGHP, WRC; "Texas Citizens for McCarthy "(undated, 1968), McCarthy, 2R515, YP, CAH.

25. "McCarthy for President," August 9, 1968, Houston, Texas press conference, McCarthy, 2R515, YP, CAH; *Texas Observer,* September 6, 1968; *Houston Post,* September 12, 1968; Chandler Davidson, *Race and Class in Texas Politics* (Princeton, N.J.: Princeton University Press, 1990), pp. 169–172; Parmet, *The Democrats,* pp. 275–281.

26. RWY to Bernard Rapoport, November 29, 1979, 4C510b, Bernard Rapoport Papers, CAH; *Dallas Morning News,* October 1, 10, 26, 1968; *Texas Observer,* November 1, 15, 1968.

27. Lewis Gould, *1968: The Election That Changed America* (Chicago: Ivan R. Dee, 1993), pp. 142–169.

28. RWY to Bernard Rapoport, November 29, 1979, 4C510b, Rapoport Papers, CAH; RWY to Walter G. Hall, September 18, 1979, Personal Correspondence, Box 13, W6HP, WRC.

29. *Austin American Statesman,* March 13, 1991; Collins, "Yarborough," pp. 172–173.

13. FINAL SENATE YEARS AND ELECTION DEFEAT

1. *Dallas Times Herald,* March 7, 1969; *Dallas Morning News,* April 30, 1969.

2. *Houston Chronicle,* March 3, 1969; *Texas Observer,* March 20, 1970. The *Observer* carried a reprint of the *Medical World News* story.

3. Phillips, *Yarborough; Dallas Morning News,* May 31, June 12, 1969, January 25, 1970; *Houston Chronicle,* May 31, June 13, 1969.

4. *Houston Chronicle,* November 3, 1968, January 5, 1969; *Dallas Morning News,* December 12, 1969, February 6, 1970; *Texas Observer,* February 20, 1970; Caldwell, *Oral History Interview,* 197, 202.

5. "Money Against the People," March 30, 1970, News Releases, 4C321, YP, CAH; *Houston Post,* January 21, 28, 1970; *Austin American Statesman,* January 28, February 1, 1970; *Dallas Morning News,* March 20, 1970.

6. *Austin American Statesman,* January 28, February 1, 1970; *Dallas Morning News,* March 20, 1970.

7. Lloyd M. Bentsen Jr. interview by Dr. Lewis L. Gould, November 27, 1989, pp. 110–129, BP, CAH; Radio Spots, 4C321, YP, CAH; *Austin American Statesman,* January 18, 1970; *Washington Post,* January 19, 1970.

8. *Texas Almanac,* 1972–73 (Dallas: A. H. Belo Co., 1971), pp. 144–146.

9. *Dallas Morning News,* April 5, April 12, 1970; *Houston Chronicle,* April 7, 1970; *The Houston Post,* April 7, 17, 18, 23, 1970.

10. Bentsen interview, pp. 132–138; Bernard Rapoport to Walter Hall, March 31, 1970, 1970 Democratic Primary, Box 13, WGH Papers; *San Antonio Express,* March 22, 1970; *Dallas Morning News,* March 28, 1970; *Texas Observer,* April 17, May 1, 1970.

11. Chuck Caldwell to RWY, Memo (undated), 4C321, YP, CAH; *The Houston Post*, April 25, 30, 1970; *Dallas Morning News*, April 24, 28, 30, May 1, 1970.

12. *New York Times*, April 26, 1970.

13. Fath interview; Caldwell, *Oral History Interview*, pp. 204-211. According to the *Congressional Quarterly Almanac*, vol. 26, 1970, p. 1071, the 1970 campaign was the "most expensive in history" with television and "image making" the instigators of the increase.

14. RWY to Walter Hall et. al., August 17, November 23, 1970, Personal Correspondence, Box 13, WGHP, WRC; Morehead, *50 Years*, pp. 230-231; Caldwell, *Oral History Interview*, 209; *Dallas Morning News*, April 12, May 4, 5, 1970; *Houston Chronicle*, May 8, 1970; *Texas Observer*, May 15, 1970. Walter Hall, J. R. Parten, Bernard Rapoport, Billy Goldberg, and Joe Allbritton sponsored a July dinner in Houston to reduce Yarborough's debt. Walter Hall's records indicated his League City State Bank loaned Yarborough $50,000 the week prior to the May 2 primary election.

15. Fath interview; Caldwell, *Oral History Interview*, pp. 207-208; Bentsen interview, pp. 112-120.

16. *Dallas Times Herald*, May 5, 7, 1970; *Dallas Morning News*, May 5, 29, 1970; *Austin American Statesman*, May 14, 1970; *Texas Observer*, May 15, 1970.

17. "Tributes to the Honorable Ralph Yarborough of Texas," January 3, 1971, U.S. Senate; *Houston Chronicle*, December 17, 18, 1970; *Houston Post*, December 20, 1970. A comprehensive list of Yarborough's accomplishments is located in the *Congressional Record*, 91st Congress, 2nd session, December 22, 1970, 43164, and December 31, 1970, 44372 and 44375.

18. *Congressional Record*, January 2, 1971, pp. 44869-44875; *Texas Observer*, December 25, 1970. Yarborough became the first senator in this category after they were selected by popular vote in 1913.

19. *Houston Post*, December 28, 1970.

14. THE LAST HURRAH

1. RWY to Randy Fitzgerald, August 9, 1971; "Polls," YP, 4Zf279, CAH; *Dallas Times Herald*, March 18, 1971; *Dallas Morning News*, April 18, July 17, 1971; *Fort Worth Star Telegram*, June 27, 1971; *Texas Observer*, September 24, 1971; "Sharpstown Stock-Fraud Scandal," *The New Handbook of Texas*, vol. 5, pp. 997-998.

2. Walter Hall to Fagan Dickson, January 10, 1972, 1972 Democratic Primary, Box 13, WGHP, WRC; *Austin American Statesman*, October 31, 1971; *Houston Chronicle*, November 21, 1971.

3. RWY to H. J. Yarborough, Donald Yarborough and Richard Yarborough, December 20, 1971; Walter Hall Memo, December 2, 1971, Fagan Dickson to J. R. Parten et. al., December 13, 1971, Personal Correspondence, Box 13, WGHP, WRC; *Dallas Morning News*, January 9, 12, 1972; *Houston Chronicle*, January 12, 1972. Dick-

son vainly argued against Yarborough's return and praised Barefoot Sanders as an able, young liberal.

4. RWY to Jimmy Bray, February 18, 1972; "Memo to Staff Members," October 22, 1971, YP, 4Zf279, CAH; *Houston Chronicle*, April 7, 1972; *The Houston Post*, April 20, 1972; *Texas Observer*, April 28, 1972.

5. *Houston Chronicle*, May 16, 28, 20, 1972; *Dallas Morning News*, May 17, 1972; Press release, May 18, 1972, RWY Miscellaneous #1, CAH.

6. *Houston Chronicle*, June 1, 1972; *Dallas Morning News*, June 1, 1972; *Texas Observer*, June 23, 1972. The women's movement was just gearing up at this time. Many younger women of liberal persuasion who ordinarily would have worked in the Yarborough campaign were thrilled to have a female candidate running for the highest office in the state and put their energies into her campaign.

7. *The Houston Post*, June 6, 1972; *Texas Observer*, June 23, 1972.

8. *Houston Chronicle*, June 23, 1973, June 27, 1975; *Dallas Times Herald*, November 15, 1975.

9. RWY to Harold Young, September 5, 1974, 4C510b, RP, CAH.

10. Bernard Rapoport to Walter Hall, February 28, 1973, and RWY to Walter Hall, August 13, 1973, Personal Correspondence, Box 13, WGHP, WRC; RWY to Bernard Rapoport, January 25, 1978, RP, CAH. Rapoport told Hall that dinners in Bryan, Houston, Austin, and San Antonio after the 1972 primary loss reduced Yarborough's debt to $72,000. Yarborough eventually paid off the entire amount.

11. *Texas Observer*, June 29, 1973; Monroe, "Lone Star Environmentalist."

12. Press release, General Land Office, June 13, 1985. By the late 1990's, the Permanent School Fund totaled over $10 billion and the Permanent University Fund contained over $5 billion.

13. *Austin American Statesman*, May 24, 1989.

14. Bill Moyers transcript, RWY Remarks, and Distinguished Alumnus Award Program, University of Texas Ex-Students Association, October 19, 1990, YPP. *Houston Post*, October 18, 1992. Portions of Senator Yarborough's library and personal papers remained at his law office and residence at the time of this accession to the Center for American History.

15. *Dallas Morning News*, June 11, 1993.

16. *Texas Observer*, February 23, 1996.

AFTERWORD

1. Ronnie Dugger, "What He Has Done," *Texas Observer*, July 14, 1989, p. 8.

2. Larry Goodwyn, "Energy from the People," *Texas Observer*, July 14, 1989, p. 6.

3. Alexis de Tocqueville, *Democracy in America* (New York: Alfred A. Knopf, 1966), vol. 1, pp. 263, 265.

Bibliography

A NOTE ON THE RALPH W. YARBOROUGH ARCHIVES AND PAPERS

The Center for American History in Austin, Texas houses the Ralph Yarborough collection which contains documents on the latter part of his career. Senator Yarborough donated his papers and files on his campaigns for governor in the 1950's and his records as U.S. Senator from 1957 through 1970, all of which totals over 1,400 linear feet. Finding aids are available for these manuscripts. The collection has a small number of documents from his earlier legal career in the 1930's and some correspondence from the 1940's, but very little information on Senator Yarborough is available from these decades in the Center for American History.

When he donated his papers to the Center for American History, Senator Yarborough retained all of his personal files and papers from his early legal career through the 1940's in his law library in Austin. These materials, which subsequently moved to the Yarborough residence, include letters, memos, documents, newspaper clippings, scrapbooks, and photos from his earlier life beginning with his year at West Point in 1919 through his campaigns of the 1930's. Documents cover his early legal career in El Paso, four years as assistant attorney general, one year on the board of the LCRA, four years as 53rd District Judge, his private law practice, and his service in the U.S. Army during World War II. The law library files also contained information on numerous political campaigns in the 1930's in which Senator Yarborough participated. These included the campaigns of James Allred, those of his father, Charles R. Yarborough, and Ralph Yarborough's own races for district judge and attorney general.

When I began the original research, Senator Yarborough informed me that he had kept the vast majority of his papers from these early years and restricted access to his staff and family members. Fortunately, Senator Yarborough granted me unlimited access to all files and papers. These general files contained no guide or index. Some were well organized while others contained information covering a variety of subject areas. Very little overlap was noted between the files and records at the Center for American History and the senator's personal papers. The family intends to provide the wealth of data the latter represents as an addition to the Yarborough Collection at the Center for American History. Needless to say, I am extremely grateful to the late senator and his family for providing me access to these manuscripts from his early career. In the future, this valuable source of information will be available to historians of the twentieth century. All items that were part of Ralph Yarborough's personal collection are noted as "Yarborough Personal Papers" or "YPP" in the notes.

MANUSCRIPT AND PHOTO COLLECTIONS

AUSTIN HISTORY CENTER, AUSTIN PUBLIC LIBRARY

Ralph W. Yarborough Biographical file

CENTER FOR AMERICAN HISTORY

James V. Allred Biographical file
William Blakley Biographical file
Richard F. Burges Papers
The Cactus, yearbook of the University of Texas at Austin
John Connally Biographical file and Scrapbooks
Price Daniel Sr. Biographical file and Scrapbooks
Ira P. Hildebrand Papers
Russell Lea Photo Collection
Gerald Mann Biographical file
Bernard Rapoport Papers
Allan Shivers Papers and Scrapbooks
Walter Prescott Webb Manuscripts and Papers
Walter F. Woodul Biographical file
Ralph W. Yarborough Biographical file and Scrapbooks
Ralph W. Yarborough Manuscripts and Papers, 1936–1940
Ralph W. Yarborough Manuscripts and Papers, 1936–1990

HENDERSON COUNTY HISTORICAL SOCIETY, ATHENS, TEXAS

Charles R. Yarborough file
Ralph W. Yarborough file
Yarborough family file and clippings

HOUSTON METROPOLITAN RESEARCH CENTER

W. A. Combs Papers
Judge Woodrow Seals Papers

HUMANITIES RESEARCH CENTER, AUSTIN

J. Frank Dobie Papers, HRC

INSTITUTE OF TEXAN CULTURES, SAN ANTONIO

Ralph W. Yarborough Biographical file and Photo Collection

LYNDON B. JOHNSON LIBRARY

John Connally Papers
LBJ Archives: Subject Files
Lyndon B. Johnson House Papers
LCRA Manuscripts and files
Presidential Papers
Senate Papers
Telephone Tapes
Vice President Masters
White House Central Files
Alvin Wirtz Papers

RALPH W. YARBOROUGH RESIDENCE, AUSTIN, TEXAS

Yarborough Family History
Yarborough Family Papers
Yarborough Papers and Manuscripts, 1903–1952

SPECIAL COLLECTIONS AND ARCHIVES, UNIVERSITY LIBRARIES,
UNIVERSITY OF HOUSTON

James V. Allred Papers and Manuscripts

WOODSON RESEARCH CENTER, FONDREN LIBRARY, RICE UNIVERSITY,
HOUSTON, TEXAS

Chandler Davidson Papers
Fagan Dickson Papers
Walter G. Hall Papers
Frankie C. Randolph Papers
Bernard Rapoport Papers
Texas Politics Oral History Program

GOVERNMENT DOCUMENTS AND SOURCES

FEDERAL

Committee on Labor and Public Welfare, United States Senate, 100th Anniversary, 1869–
1969. 90th Congress, 2d Session. Washington, D.C.: U.S. Government Printing
Office, 1970.

Congressional Quarterly Almanac
Congressional Record—House
Congressional Record—Senate
Lincoln Sesquicentennial, 1809–1959. Lincoln Sesquicentennial Commission. Washington, D.C.: National Archives, 1959.
The 1920 Howitzer. United States Military Academy.
Senator Ralph Yarborough's Washington Report: Senate Newsletters
Tributes to the Honorable Ralph Yarborough of Texas in the United States Senate, January 3, 1971. Washington, D.C.: U.S. Government Printing Office, 1971.

STATE OF TEXAS

Texas General Land Office

Report of the Commissioner of the General Land Office, 1928–1930, 1930–1932, 1932–1934, 1934–1936.

Texas Law Library, Tom C. Clark Building, Austin, Texas

Attorney General's Opinions: 1930–1932, 1932–1934, 1934–1936
Reports and Opinions of Texas Attorney General: 1930–1932, 1932–1934, 1934–1936.
Southwestern Reporter—Texas Cases
Southwestern Reporter (2nd)—Texas Cases

Texas State Archives, Austin, Texas

Attorney General Reports, Briefs, Opinions and Correspondence, 1930–36
Governor James V. Allred Papers
Robert W. Calvert Papers
Governor John Connally Papers
Senator Lloyd M. Bentsen Papers
Governor W. Lee O'Daniel Papers
Secretary of State Reports, 1938—Campaign Expenses
Governor Allan Shivers Papers

Texas Legislative Library, Austin, Texas

Presiding Officers of the Texas Legislature, 1846–1982
Reports and Opinions of Texas Attorney General: 1930–32, 1932–34, 1934–36
Speakers of the Texas House of Representatives

Lower Colorado River Authority (LCRA), Austin, Texas

Minutes of the Board of Directors, 1935–1936, LCRA Archives

COURTHOUSE RECORDS

Birth Records, Henderson County Clerk's Office, Athens, Texas.
Henderson County Court Records, 1900–1932, Athens, Texas.
Minutes of the Henderson County Commissioners Court, 1920–1932, Athens, Texas.
Marriage Records, Navarro County, Texas

INTERVIEWS

Anthony Champagne interview with Ralph Yarborough, April 3, 1992, Austin, Texas. Ralph W. Yarborough Oral Histories, Center for American History, Austin, Texas.
Patrick Cox interviews:
  James Boren, January 16, 1999.
  Alex Dickie, April 30, 1999.
  Creekmore Fath, November 10, 1999.
  Joe Pinnelli, May 6, 1999.
  Grace Billie Presley, June 10, 1994.
  Donald Yarborough, June 10, 1994.
  Opal Yarborough, October 12, 1998.
  Ralph Yarborough, April 21, 1993.
  Ralph Yarborough, October 14, 1993.
  Ralph Yarborough, June 8, 1993.
Chandler Davidson interviews, Texas Politics Oral History Program, Woodson Research Center, Fondren Library, Rice University, Houston, Texas:
  Chris Dixie, January 17, 1977.
  Walter Hall, December 27, 1982.
  Maury Maverick, Jr., October 27, 1975.
  Ralph Yarborough, June 26, 1982.
Lewis L. Gould interview with Lloyd M. Bentsen Jr., November 27, 1989. Lloyd Bentsen Jr. Papers, Center for American History, Austin, Texas.
Olin Murell interview with Ralph Yarborough, April 16, 1992. TCTV channel 38. Video recording. Austin, Travis County general media services production.

NEWSPAPERS AND NEWSLETTERS

Abilene Reporter News
Amarillo Daily News
Athens (Texas) Daily Review
Athens (Texas) Weekly Review
Austin American
Austin American Statesman

Austin Citizen
Austin Evening Dispatch
Austin Report
Austin Statesman
Austin Times
Chandler (Texas) Times
Corpus Christi Caller Times
The Daily Texan
Dallas Morning News
Dallas Times Herald
The Dublin Sunday Independent
El Campo (Texas) News
The Ferguson (Texas) Forum
Fort Worth Press
Fort Worth Star Telegram
The Gladewater (Texas) Journal
The Highlander (Texas)
Houston Chronicle
Houston Post
Houston Press
Los Angeles Herald Examiner
Lubbock Avalanche Journal
New York Herald Tribune
New York Times
Port Arthur News
San Antonio Express
San Antonio Light
South Austin News
The State Week (Texas)
The Texas Democrat
The Texas Observer
Tri Cities Labor Leader
Tulia (Texas) Herald
Tyler (Texas) Courier Times
Tyler (Texas) Morning Telegraph
Washington Post

OTHER SOURCES

Adams, Ann, ed. *The Itch of Opinion, the Public and Private Letters of Franklin Jones, Sr., 1954–1974.* Oak Arbor, Washington: Packrat Press, 1984.
Adams, John. *Damming the Colorado.* College Station: Texas A&M University Press, 1990.

Adams, Mark, and Creekmore Fath. *Yarborough, Portrait of a Steadfast Democrat.* Austin: Chaparral Press, 1957.

Alexander, Charles C. *The Ku Klux Klan in the Southwest.* Lexington: University of Kentucky Press, 1966.

Alibates Flint Quarries: A National Monument. Amarillo, Tex.: Potter County Survey Commission, 1963. A copy resides in Alibates Flint Quarries, 3W193, YP.

Anders, Evan. *Boss Rule in South Texas.* Austin: University of Texas Press, 1982.

Andres, John A. *Lyndon Johnson and the Great Society.* Chicago: Ivan R. Dee, 1998.

Anti-Saloon League. *The Brewers and Texas Politics,* vol. 2. San Antonio: Passing Show Printing Co., 1916.

Atkinson, William Eugene. "James V. Allred: A Political Biography, 1899-1935" (Ph.D. dissertation, TCU, 1978).

"Ayes of Texas." *Time* 69 (1957): 33.

Baggarly, H. M. "The Story of Ralph Yarborough." *The Tulia Herald* (June 29, 1972): 3.

———. *Texas Country Democrat.* San Angelo, Tex.: Anchor Publishing Co., 1970.

———. *The Texas Country Editor: H. M. Baggarly Takes a Grass-Roots Look at National Politics.* Edited by Eugene W. Jones. Cleveland: World Publishing, 1966.

Baker, Bobby, with Larry L. King. *Wheeling and Dealing: Confessions of a Capitol Hill Operator.* New York: W. W. Norton, 1978.

Banks, Jimmy, and John E. Babcock. *Corralling the Colorado.* Austin: Eakin Press, 1988.

Bartley, Ernest. *The Tidelands Oil Controversy: A Legal and Historical Analysis.* Austin: University of Texas Press, 1953.

Bartley, Numan. *The New South, 1945–1980.* Baton Rouge, La.: LSU Press, 1995.

Battle, William J. "A Concise History of the University of Texas, 1883–1950," *Southwestern Historical Quarterly* 54 (April 1951): 397.

"Birthday Celebration of Democratic Proportions." *Texas Alcalde* 82, no. 1 (September/October 1993): 73.

Black, Earl. *Southern Governors and Civil Rights.* Cambridge, Mass.: Harvard University Press, 1976.

Blacklock, Ward T. "Honoring Ralph Yarborough," Tribute delivered in Travis County Courthouse, 53rd District Court, February 3, 1989, Transcript in Yarborough residence.

Bolton, Paul. *Governors of Texas.* Corpus Christi, Texas: *Corpus Christi Caller Times,* 1947.

Boyle, Robert D. "Chaos in the East Texas Oil Fields, 1930–1935," *Southwestern Historical Quarterly* 69 (January 1966): 340–352.

Bourgeois, Christie Lynne. "Lyndon Johnson and Texas Politics, 1937–1945." Ph.D. dissertation, University of Texas at Austin, 1992.

Brands, H. W. "Joe R. Greenhill, Sr. Oral History Interview." *A Texas Supreme Court Trilogy,* vol. 2. Austin: University of Texas School of Law, 1998.

———. *The Wages of Globalism: Lyndon Johnson and the Limits of American Power.* New York: Oxford University Press, 1995.

Brown, Norman D. *Hood, Bonnet and Little Brown Jug: Texas Politics, 1921–1928*. College Station: Texas A&M University Press, 1984.

Burlage, Robb K. "James V. Allred: Texas' Liberal Governor." Report for O. D. Weeks, University of Texas at Austin, 1959.

Burns, James MacGregor. *Roosevelt: The Lion and the Fox*. New York: Harcourt, Brace, 1956.

Bush, George, and Victor Gold. *Looking Forward*. New York: Doubleday, 1987.

Byrd, Robert C. *The Senate, 1789–1989*, vol. 1. Washington, D.C.: U.S. Government Printing Office, 1988.

Caldwell, Charles Sargent. *Charles Sargent Caldwell Oral History Interview*. Washington, D.C.: Senate Historical Office, 1996.

Calvert, Robert A., and Arnoldo De Leon. *The History of Texas*. Wheeling, Ill.: Harlan Davidson, 1996.

Campbell, Jack. "Senator Yarborough and the Texan 'RWY' Brand on Bilingual Education and Federal Aid." *Education Studies* 12 (1981–1982): 403–415.

Carleton, Don. *A Breed So Rare*. Austin: Texas State Historical Association, 1998.

———. A Red Scare! Right Wing Hysteria, Fifties Fanaticism, and Their Legacy in Texas. Austin: Texas Monthly Press, 1985.

Caro, Robert. *The Years of Lyndon Johnson: Means of Ascent*. New York: Knopf, 1990.

———. *The Years of Lyndon Johnson: The Path to Power*. New York: Knopf, 1982.

Clark, Ed. "The Permanent University Fund: A Foundation for Greatness," *The Addendum* 7 (November 1976): 2.

Clark, James A., and Michael T. Halbouty. *The Last Boom*. New York: Random House, 1972.

Clark, Joy, ed. *Chandler: Its History and People*. Jacksonville, Tex.: Jayroe Graphic Arts, 1981.

Clay, Comer. "The LCRA: A Study in Politics and Public Administration." Ph.D. dissertation, University of Texas at Austin, 1948

Collins, Michael L. "Ralph Yarborough." In *Profiles in Power: Twentieth Century Texans in Washington*, pp. 150–152. Arlington Heights, Ill.: Harlan Davidson, 1993.

Congress and the Nation, 1945–1964. Washington, D.C.: Congressional Quarterly Service, 1965.

Conkin, Paul K. *Big Daddy from the Pedernales*. Boston: Twayne Publishers, 1986.

———. *The New Deal*. 2nd ed. Arlington Heights: Harlan Davidson, 1975.

Connally, John, with Mickey Herskowitz. *In History's Shadow: An American Odyssey*. New York: Hyperion Books, 1993.

Cotner, Robert, et al. *Texas Cities and the Great Depression*. Austin: Texas Memorial Museum, 1973.

Cox, Mike. "Yarborough Is Gentleman, Book Collector." *Austin American Statesman*, June 10, 1984, 6f.

Cox, Patrick. "Land Commissioner Bascom Giles and the Texas Veteran's Land Board Scandals." Master's thesis, Southwest Texas State University, 1988.

———. "'Put the Jam on the Lower Shelf': The Early Career of U.S. Senator Ralph Webster Yarborough." Ph.D. dissertation, University of Texas at Austin, 1996.

————. "What in the Name of God Am I to Do?" *East Texas Historical Journal* 37, no. 1 (1999): 47–61.

Crawford, Ann Fears. *Frankie: Mrs. R. D. Randolph and Texas Liberal Politics.* Austin: Eakin Press, 2000.

Dallek, Robert. *Flawed Giant: Lyndon Johnson and His Times, 1961–1973.* New York: Oxford University Press, 1998.

————. *Lone Star Rising: Lyndon Johnson and His Times, 1908–1960.* New York: Oxford University Press, 1991.

Davidson, Chandler. *Race and Class in Texas Politics.* Princeton, N.J.: Princeton University Press, 1990.

Davis, J. Frank. *Texas: A Guide.* New York: Hastings House, 1940.

Devers, Jacob. "The Mark of the Man on USMA." *Assembly* 23 (Spring 1964).

Divine, Robert A., ed. *The Johnson Years.* 2 vols. Lawrence: University of Kansas Press, 1987.

Dollard, John. *Case and Class in a Southern Town.* New Haven, Conn.: Yale University Press, 1937.

Douglas, Claude L. *Life Story of W. Lee O'Daniel.* Dallas: Regional Press, 1938.

Doyle, Judith Kaaz. "Out of Step: Maury Maverick and the Politics of the Depression and the New Deal." Ph.D. dissertation, University of Texas at Austin, 1989.

Dugger, Ronnie. "Ralph W. Yarborough — More than Any Other Single Texan of the Last Hundred Years." Speech at Ralph Yarborough appreciation dinner, July 27, 1972, Houston, Texas.

————. "Texas' New Junior Senator." *National Review,* April 22, 1958, p. 8.

————. "What He Has Done." *Texas Observer,* July 14, 1982, p. 8.

Eagles, Charles, ed. *Is There a Southern Political Tradition?* Jackson: University Press of Mississippi, 1996.

Edwards, Pauline Mills. "The LCRA: An Agency of the State." Master's thesis, University of Texas at Austin, 1982.

Essin, Emmett M., III. "The Democratic senatorial primary in Texas: Yarborough versus Blakley." Master's thesis, TCU, 1965.

"Fair Deal for the Cold War Soldier." *Harpers* 230 (1965): 82.

Faulk, J. J. *A History of Henderson County Texas.* Athens, Tex.: Athens Printing Co., 1929.

Faulk, John Henry. "Slanders and Lies for Sale." *The Highlander,* February 10, 1972, p. 4a.

Foley, Michael. *The New Senate: Liberal Influence on a Conservative Institution, 1959–1972.* New Haven, Conn.: Yale University Press, 1980.

Foner, Eric. *The Story of American Freedom.* New York: W. W. Norton, 1998.

Garay, Ronald. *Gordon McLendon: The Maverick of Radio.* New York: Greenwood Press, 1992.

Gard, Wayne. *Texas Kingfish.* New York: Editor Publications, 1941.

"Gerald C. Mann." *Texas Parade,* March 1939, 18.

Gertsle, Gary. "The Protean Character of American Liberalism." *American Historical Review* 99 (October 1994): 1043–1073.

Giles, Bascom. "History and Disposition of Texas Public Domain." Austin: General Land Office Archives, 1945.

Goodwyn, Larry. "Energy from the People." *Texas Observer,* July 14, 1982, p. 6.

Gould, Lewis L. *1968: The Election That Changed America.* Chicago: Ivan R. Dee, 1993.

———. *Progressives and Prohibitionists: Texas Democrats in the Wilson Era.* Austin: University of Texas Press, 1973.

Grantham, Dewey. *The Life and Death of the Solid South.* Lexington: University of Kentucky Press, 1988.

———. *Recent America: The United States since 1945.* Wheeling, Ill.: Harlan Davidson, 1998.

———. *The South in Modern America.* New York: Harper Collins, 1994.

Green, George Norris. *The Establishment in Texas Politics, 1938–1957.* Westwood, Conn.: Greenwood Press, 1979.

Haigh, Bert R. *Land, Oil and Education.* El Paso: Texas Western Press, 1986.

Hardeman, D. B., and Donald Brown. *Rayburn: A Biography.* Austin: Texas Monthly Press, 1987.

Henderson, Richard. *Maury Maverick: A Political Biography.* Austin: University of Texas Press, 1970.

Henderson County Historical Society. *Old Homes of Henderson County.* Crockett, Tex.: Publications Development Company, 1982.

Hendrickson, Kenneth E., Jr., and Michael L. Collins, ed. *Profiles in Power: Twentieth Century Texans in Washington.* Arlington Heights, Ill.: Harlan Davidson, 1993.

Hess, Gary R. *Vietnam and the United States.* Boston: Twayne Publishers, 1990.

Hine, Darlene Clark, *Black Victory: The Rise and Fall of the White Primary in Texas.* Millwood, N.Y.: KTO Press, 1979.

Howerton, Jack. "You Can Still Vote As You Wish," *Cuero Record,* July 8, 1964.

Ivins, Molly. *Nothin' but Good Times Ahead.* New York: Random House, 1993.

James, D. Clayton. *The Years of MacArthur, vol. 1, 1880–1941.* Boston: Houghton Mifflin Company, 1970.

Jameson, W. C. *The Guadalupe Mountains: Island in the Desert.* El Paso: Texas Western Press, 1994.

Johnson, Lady Bird. *A White House Diary.* New York: Holt, Rinehart and Winston, 1970.

Johnson, Lyndon B. *The Vantage Point: Perspectives on the Presidency.* Holt, Rinehart and Winston, 1971.

Jones, Armand. "Senator Ralph Yarborough." Unpublished ms. Yarborough residence.

Kemerer, Frank R. *William Wayne Justice.* Austin: University of Texas Press, 1991.

Key, V. O. *Southern Politics in State and Nation.* New York: Knopf, 1949.

Kinch, Sam, Jr. "Yarborough Isn't Through Yet." *Dallas Morning News Sunday Magazine,* October 11, 1970, pp. 1–4.

Kinch, Sam, and Stuart Long. *Allan Shivers: The Pied Piper of Texas Politics.* Austin: Shoal Creek Publishers, 1973.

King, Nicholas. *George Bush.* New York: Dodd, Mead & Co., 1980.

Kingston, Mike, Sam Attlesley, and Mary G. Crawford. *The Texas Almanac's Political History of Texas.* Austin: Eakin Press, 1992.

Lawson, Peter, "His Honor William Wayne Justice." *Dallas Times Herald,* November 13, 1983.

Leuchtenburg, William E. *Franklin D. Roosevelt and the New Deal, 1932–1940.* New York: Harper & Row, 1963.

MacArthur, Douglas. *Reminiscences.* New York: McGraw Hill, 1964.

Maraniss, David. "Justice, Texas Style." *Washington Post,* February 28, 1987.

Mann, Robert. *The Walls of Jericho.* New York: Harcourt Brace, 1996.

Manning, George N. "Public Services of James V. Allred." Master's thesis, Texas Technological College, 1950.

Mark, Carol Bengtson. "Smiling Ralph: I Don't Have Time to Mope." *Austin Citizen,* October 4, 1978, p. c5.

Martindale, Robert. "James V. Allred: The Centennial Governor of Texas." Master's thesis, University of Texas at Austin, 1957.

Mauro, Garry. "Honoring Ralph Yarborough." February 3, 1989, Travis County 53rd District Courtroom, Austin.

May, Dean L. *From New Deal to New Economics: The American Liberal Response to the Recession of 1937.* New York and London: Garland, 1981.

McCarty, Jeanne Bozzell. *The Struggle for Sobriety: Protestants and Prohibition in Texas, 1919–1935.* El Paso: Texas Western Press, 1980.

McDaniel, Ruel. *Some Ran Hot.* Dallas: Regional Press, 1939.

McKay, Seth S. *Texas Politics, 1906–1944.* Lubbock: Texas Tech University Press, 1952.

———. *W. Lee O'Daniel and Texas Politics, 1938–1942.* Lubbock: Texas Tech University Press, 1944.

McNeely, Dave. "Hero of Texas Democrats." *Onward,* March 15, 1983, pp. 4–5.

———. "The 1964 Democratic Senatorial Primary." Master's thesis, University of Texas at Austin, 1965.

Miller, Thomas Lloyd. *The Public Lands of Texas, 1519–1970.* Norman: University of Oklahoma Press, 1971.

Monroe, Monte Latimer. "Lone Star Environmentalist: U.S. Senator Ralph W. Yarborough." Ph.D. dissertation, Texas Tech University, 1999.

Moore, Walter B. *Governors of Texas.* Dallas: Dallas Morning News, 1963.

Morehead, Richard. *50 Years in Texas Politics.* Austin: Eakin Press, 1982.

Morriss, Jane Anne. "Board and Staff: An Ethnography of the LCRA of Texas." Ph.D. dissertation, University of Texas at Austin, 1982.

———. *The Highland Lakes of Texas.* Washington, D.C.: U.S. Government Printing Office, 1941.

———. *Years of Progress at the LCRA.* Austin: LCRA, 1956.

Moyers, Bill. "Presentation Depicting Events in the Life of Ralph W. Yarborough." Speech from 1990 Distinguished Alumnus Award, University of Texas at Austin, October 19, 1990. Transcript at Yarborough residence.

Myrdal, Gunnar. *An American Dilemma: The Negro Problem in American Democracy.* 20th anniversary ed. New York: Harper and Row, 1962.

"Neck and Neck." *Newsweek* 44 (1954): 18.

The New Handbook of Texas. Edited by Ron Tyler. Austin: Texas State Historical Association, 1996.

Obadele-Starks, Ernest M. B. "Ralph Yarborough of Texas and the Road to Civil Rights." *East Texas Historical Journal* 32, no. 1 (1994): 39–48.

"Office of Attorney General." *Texas Pioneer* 1 (July 1932): 3.

Olson, James S., and Randy Roberts. *Where the Domino Fell: America and Vietnam, 1945–1995.* New York: St. Martin's Press, 1996.

Orfield, Gary. *The Reconstruction of Southern Education.* New York: Wiley-Inter-science, 1969.

Orum, Anthony M. "The Making of Austin: Taming the River, Part One." *Texas Observer,* December 14, 1984.

———. "The Making of Austin: Taming the River, Part Two." *Texas Observer,* January 11, 1985.

Parmet, Herbert. *The Democrats: The Years after FDR.* New York: MacMillan, 1976.

———. *JFK.* New York: Dial Press, 1983.

Phillips, William G. *Yarborough of Texas.* Washington, D.C.: Acropolis Books, 1969.

Pickle, Jake, and Peggy Pickle. *Jake.* Austin: University of Texas Press, 1997.

Porterfield, Billy. "Yarborough: Making the World a Better Place." *Austin American Statesman,* March 13, 1991, p. b1.

Presley, Grace Billie. "Yarborough Family History." Unpublished manuscript. Personal papers of Ralph W. Yarborough. Ralph Yarborough Library, Austin, n.d.

Prindle, David F. "Oil and the Permanent University Fund: The Early Years." *Southwestern Historical Quarterly* 86 (October 1982): 277–298.

———. *Petroleum Politics and the Texas Railroad Commission.* Austin: University of Texas Press, 1981.

Provost, Norma Matlock. "Issues in the Texas Gubernatorial Race of 1954: Shivers versus Yarborough." Master's thesis, Lamar University, 1981.

Pycior, Julie Leininger. *LBJ & Mexican Americans.* Austin: University of Texas Press, 1997.

Ralph Webster Yarborough at 80: A Gathering of Tributes from Several of His Book-loving Friends. Austin: Jenkins Publishing, 1984.

Report of the President's Commission on the Assassination of President John F. Kennedy (the Warren Commission Report).

Rister, Car Coke. *Oil! Titan of the Southwest.* Norman: University of Oklahoma Press, 1949.

Rogan, Octavia F. *Land Commissioner Charles Rogan and the Mineral Classification of Texas Public School Land.* Austin: San Felipe Press, 1968.

Sadler, Jerry. "History of Texas Land." Austin: General Land Office Archives, 1961.

Schendel, Gordon. "Something Is Rotten in the State of Texas." *Collier's,* June 9, 1951.

Schulman, Bruce J. *Lyndon B. Johnson and American Liberalism.* Boston: Bedford Books of St. Martin's Press, 1995.

Schwetmann, Martin. *Santa Rita: The University of Texas' Oil Discovery.* Austin: Texas State Historical Association, 1943.

"Senator Ralph Yarborough." *Texas Observer,* April 17, 1964, pp. 1–9.

Shesol, Jeff. *Mutual Contempt: Lyndon Johnson, Robert Kennedy and the Feud That Defined a Decade.* New York: W. W. Norton, 1997.

"Story of Bill Blakley." *New Republic* 138 (April 21, 1958): 4–5.

"Symposium on the Texas Tidelands Case." *Baylor Law Review* 3 (Winter 1953).

Texas Almanac and State Industrial Guide, 1904. Dallas: A. H. Belo, 1905.

———, *1933.* Dallas: A. H. Belo, 1934.

———, *1939–1940.* Dallas: A. H. Belo, 1940.

———, *1972–73.* Dallas: A. H. Belo, 1971.

———, *1980–81.* Dallas: A. H. Belo, 1981.

"Texas Chooses Up for a Runoff." *Life* 37 (1954): 22–23.

"Texas Frauds and Failures." *Time* 63 (May 31, 1954).

"Texas Salute: An Appreciation Dinner Honoring United States Senator Ralph W. Yarborough, Austin, Texas, October 19, 1963." Program.

"A Third Time, Maybe." *Texas Observer,* July 4, 1955, pp. 1–2.

"Tidelands Controversy." *The Handbook of Texas Online* <http://www.tsha.utexas.edu/handbook/online/articles/view/TT/mgt2.html>

The "Tidelands" Decision of the Supreme Court of the United States. Austin: State of Texas, n.d.

"Trouble in Texas." *Time* 64 (1954): 17.

Tocqueville, Alexis de. *Democracy in America,* vol. 1. New York: Knopf, 1966.

Turman, Judith Jenkins. "Austin and the New Deal," *Texas Cities and the Great Depression.* Austin: Texas Memorial Museum, 1973.

Webb, Walter Prescott. *Divided We Stand: The Crisis of a Frontierless Democracy.* Austin: Acorn Press, 1937.

———. *The Great Plains.* New York: Ginn, Company, 1931.

———, ed. *The Handbook of Texas.* 3 vols. Austin: Texas State Historical Association, 1952.

Weeks, O. Douglas. "The Texas Direct Primary System." *Southwestern Social Science Quarterly* 13, no. 2 (September 1932): 1–5.

———. *Texas in 1964: A One-Party State Again?* Austin: Institute of Public Affairs, University of Texas, 1965.

———. *Texas in the 1960 Presidential Election.* Austin: Institute of Public Affairs, University of Texas, 1961.

———. *Texas One-Party Politics in 1956.* Austin: Institute of Public Affairs, University of Texas, 1957.

———. *Texas Presidential Politics in 1952.* Austin: Institute of Public Affairs, University of Texas, 1953.

"Winner at Last." *U.S. News and World Report,* April 12, 1957, pp. 20–22.

Woods, Randall Bennett. *J. William Fulbright, Vietnam, and the Search for a Cold War Foreign Policy.* New York: Cambridge University Press, 1998.

Woodward, C. Vann. *The Burden of Southern History.* Baton Rouge, La.: LSU Press, 1993.

Woodul, Walter F. "Texas Must Continue to Advertise." *Texas Weekly,* August 15, 1936, p. 4.

Yarborough, Donald. "Remembrances." Unpublished manuscript.

Yarborough, Ralph. "The Bounty of Nature." *Texas Observer,* December 27, 1962, p. 3.

————. *Christmas in El Paso.* Austin: Carl Hertzog, 1973.

————. "C. R. Yarborough Home." In *Old Homes of Henderson County.* Athens, Tex.: Henderson County Historical Commission, 1982, pp. 187–188.

————. "Duties of the Attorney General's Office." *Texas Pioneer Magazine,* July 1931, p. 3.

————. "Early Histories of Chandler." In *Chandler: Its History and People.* Jacksonville, Tex.: Jayroe Graphic Arts, 1981.

————. "Federal Government Has Beneficial Role to Play in Education." *Houston Chronicle,* April 1, 1984, pp. 3, 11.

————. "The First Continental Congress to the Formation of the Federal Union." In *The Two-Hundredth Anniversary of the First Continental Congress 1774–1974.* Washington, D.C., 1974.

————. Foreword to *The Big Thicket of Texas: A Comprehensive Annotated Bibliography* by Lois Williams Parker. Arlington, Tex.: Sable Publications, 1977.

————. Foreword to *Congressional Medal of Honor Recipients, 1863–1963* by the Subcommittee on Veterans Affairs, United States Senate. Washington, D.C.: Government Printing Office, 1964.

————. Foreword to *Defenders: A Confederate History of Henderson County, Texas* by Leila Reeves Eads. Athens, Tex.: Henderson County Historical Survey Committee, 1969.

————. Foreword to *The Education of American Indians: A Survey of the Literature* by the Special Subcommittee of Indian Education of the Committee on Labor and Public Welfare, U.S. Senate. Washington, D.C.: Government Printing Office, 1969.

————. Foreword to *Freedom of Communications: Final Report of the Committee on Commerce, U.S. Senate.* Washington, D.C.: Government Printing Office, 1961.

————. Foreword to *Outlaws in the Big Thicket* by Wanda A. Landrey. Quanah, Tex.: Nortex Press, 1976.

————. Foreword to *The Public Lands of Texas, 1519–1970* by Thomas Lloyd Miller. Norman: University of Oklahoma Press, 1971.

————. Foreword to *Red Granite for Gray Heroes: Partial History of Woods Brigade* by Col. Harold B. Simpson. Hillsboro, Tex.: Hill Junior College Press, 1969.

————. Foreword to *Three Men in Texas: Bedichek, Webb and Dobie* by Ronnie Dugger. Austin: University of Texas Press, 1957.

———. *Frank Dobie: Man and Friend.* The Westerners. Washington, D.C.: Potomac Corral, 1967.

———. "General Custer Learned Sign Language at Texas State College." *Frontier Times,* February 1952, p. 124. Reprinted in *Custer in Texas: An Interrupted Narrative* by John M. Carroll. New York: S. Lewis, 1975, 143–146.

———. *The Guadalupe Mountains: A Congressional Record Bibliography.* Washington, D.C.: Government Printing Office, 1961.

———. "In Memoriam, Charles Richard Yarborough, Centenarian," October 24, 1964. Privately published and printed. Booklet at Yarborough residence.

———. Introduction to *Alibates Flint Quarries and the Texas Panhandle Pueblo Culture (circa 10,000 B.C. to 1300 A.D.); the Source of Tools and, at the Same Time, the Factories of the American Indian.* N.p.

———. "Lincoln as a Liberal Statesman." In *Lincoln for the Ages* by Ralph G. Newman. Garden City, New Jersey: Doubleday, 1960, 279–283.

———. "Opportunities in the Field of Texas History." *The Junior Historian,* December 1946, p. 12.

———. "Passenger Pigeons over Chandler." In *Chandler: Its History and People.* Jacksonville, Tex.: Jayroe Graphic Arts, 1981.

———. "The Pinckard-Askew Duel: Two Brave Men." In *Chandler: Its History and People.* Jacksonville, Tex.: Jayroe Graphic Arts, 1981.

———. "Remarks of Ralph Yarborough on Acceptance of Distinguished Alumnus Award of the University of Texas Ex-Students' Association," October 19, 1990. Transcript at Yarborough residence.

———. "Remembrances for J. R.'s 90th Birthday, 1986." Transcript at Yarborough residence.

———. "Rich History of Texas Mail Reviewed." *Austin Statesman,* May 4, 1939, p. 12.

———. "Salute to the American West." *American West* (Winter 1965): 78.

———. "Sam Houston: Giant on a Postage Stamp." In *Texas Avenue at Main Street: The Chronological History of a City Block in Houston, the Most Significant Block in the History of Texas,* by A. Pat Daniels. Houston, Tex.: Allen Press, 1964, 57–62.

———. Signed Conference Opinions by Assistant Attorney General Ralph W. Yarborough. In *Biennial Report of the Attorney General of Texas, 1930–1932.*

———. Signed Conference Opinions by Assistant Attorney General Ralph W. Yarborough. In *Biennial Report of the Attorney General of Texas, 1932–1934.*

———. "Talk on J. Frank Dobie." *Corral Dust* 12 (Spring 1967): 2.

———. "Teaching Society How to Listen." In *Proceedings of the National Conference of Educational Opportunities for Mexican Americans.* Austin, Texas, April 25–26, 1968.

———. "Texas Frauds and Failures." *Time* 63 (May 31, 1954): 64, 66.

———. "Three Yarborough Myths." *Yarborough Family Quarterly,* June 1992, p. 14.

———. "Tiger Jim." *Texas Observer,* January 28, 1977, pp. 21–23.

———. "The Totem Trees of Chandler." In *Chandler: Its History and People.* Jacksonville, Tex.: Jayroe Graphic Arts, 1981.

———. "The Yarborough Family," in *Chandler: Its History and People* (Chandler: Chandler Historical Society, 1981), pp. 204-211.

———. "Yarborough Family of Chandler, Texas." In *Family Histories of Henderson County, 1846–1981.* Dallas: Taylor Publishing Company, 1981.

"The Yarboroughs at 90." *Texas Observer,* July 2, 1993, p. 2.

Young, Mark. "Lyndon B. Johnson's Forgotten Campaign: Re-election to the Senate in 1954." Master's thesis, University of Texas at Austin, 1993.

Young, Nancy Beck. "Wright Patman: Congressman to the Nation, 1893-1953." Ph.D. dissertation, University of Texas at Austin, 1995.

Young, Roland. "Lone Star Razzle Dazzle." *The Nation* (June 21, 1941).

Index

Italic page numbers refer to illustrations or their captions.

(1952), 102, 104; (1954), 110, 111, 118,
120–121; (1956), 126, 131; and Guadalupe Mountains National Park, 236;
and integration, 221; and Johnson-
Yarborough relationship, 146, 167–
168; and Kennedy's Texas trip, 197;
and Mann's possible appointment to
Supreme Court, 80; and oil and gas
industry cases, 24, 26, 27; and Padre
Island National Seashore, 177; and
presidential race (1964), 216; and race
issues, 107; and Shivers, 98, 124; and
Sputnik, 151; and Texas Democratic
party, 209; and Thurmond wresting
match, 213; and Tidelands Controversy, 98; and Travis County district
judgeship, 49, 51, 53–54, 58, 59, 62, 63,
66–67; and U.S. Senate race (1958),
152–153, 156–157, 161, 306n.24, 307n.30;
(1961), 174; (1964), 187–188, 216; and
Vietnam War, 240; and Yarborough as
senator, 185–186, 251, 266
Progressives, 38
Prohibition, 5, 33
Proxmire, William, 162
Public lands, xvi, 19, 20–28, 29, 30, 178–
179
Public Works Administration (PWA),
42–43, 44–45

Race and racism: and *Brown v. Topeka
Board of Education*, 106; and governor's
race (1952), 104; (1954), 108, 111–113,
115–120; (1956), 130, 136; and Great
Society, 229; and politics, 97, 123; and
presidential election (1968), 249; and
Texas Democratic party, 91; and Travis
County district judgeship, 63; and U.S.
Senate race (1958), 154, 159
Radio: and attorney general race (1938),
72, 74; and Estes affair, 184; and gov-
ernor's race (1952), 99, 101; (1954),
118; (1956), 128, 129–130, 132, 135;
and McLendon, 207–208, 209; and
O'Daniel, 61; and public service announcements, 183–184; and Travis
County district judge race, 57; and
U.S. Senate race (1958), 154; (1970),
260
Ragan, Cooper, 91

Rainey, Homer, 92, 97–98
Ralph W. Yarborough Chair at University
of Texas School of Law, 277
Ramsey, Ben, 126, 141, 176
Randolph, Frankie, 225, 275
Randolph, Jennings, 162
Rapoport, Bernard, 250, 261, 273, 275
Rayburn, Sam: death of, 174–175; and
governor's race (1952), 99, 100, 101;
(1956), 126; and patronage, 172; and
presidential election (1952), 93–94,
104; (1956), 124, 125, 140, 305n.2;
(1960), 153, 170, 171; and Shivers, 124,
125, 140, 153–154, 168; and U.S. Senate
race (1957), 140, 141, 145; (1958), 153–
154, 159; Yarborough's relationship
with, xv, 121, 158, 164, 167–168, 175
Reagan, Ronald, 162
Red Scare, 106
Reinhard, A. J., 42
Relinquishment Act (1919), 21
Republican party: and Cold War G.I. bill,
232; and education, 151; and governor's race (1954), 118, 119; (1956), 122,
136; growth of, 226–227; and Johnson opposition, 226; and presidential
elections, 169, 215, 218, 249; and Sen-
ate control, 162; and Shivers, 252; and
Thurmond, 212; and U.S. Senate race
(1957), 139, 140; (1958), 154, 161; (1961),
173, 174; (1964), 214, 215–216, 219
Repurchase Act (1926), 27
Richards, Ann, 277–278, 279
Rivera, Carlos, 205
Roberts, Oran M., 55
Robinson, Marian, 205
Rodriguez, Armando, 234
Roosevelt, Eleanor, 150
Roosevelt, Franklin D., xvii, 19, 33, 40, 41,
55–56, 60, 91, 102
Russell, Richard "Dick," 108, 149, 210

Sadler, Jerry, 177, 178, 182, 236
Sanchez, George, 232
Sanders, Barefoot, 269, 270–271, 272
Sandlin, George, 177
Saylor, Kelly, 30
Saylors, J., 33
Scaggs, Jack, 178
Seals, Woodrow, 173

283, 302n.22, 318n.14; governor's race
(1952), 99–104, 248; (1954), 108–121,
109, 114, 124, 182; (1956), 124, 126,
129–138, 139, 270, 279; (1958), 152–153,
155; (1962), 175–176; (1966), 222, 223;
(1968), 227–228, 247–248; (1972), 267,
268; and personal contact, xvii–xviii,
56, 59, 70–71, 74, 78, 101, 126, 130,
147, 155, 263; presidential race (1960),
164, 166–176; (1964), *217;* (1968), 246,
249–250; and statewide strategies, xv–
xvi, 75–76, 78; support for, 29–30, 37;
Travis County district judge race, 49,
54–59; U.S. Senate race (1957), 138,
139–143, *142, 144, 145,* 269; (1958), 146,
152–161, *156, 160;* (1964), 187, 190, 197–
199, 203, 206–209, 214–216, 217–220,
258; (1970), 228, 246, 254, 256–258, *259,*
260–262, 268, 272–273; (1972), 267,
268, 269–271
—public service: Allred's influence on,
20; and ethics/integrity, 44, 46–47,
76, 181–184, 209, 265, 266, 272; family
history of, 1–2, 4–5; final tributes to,
276–280; legacy of, 281–285; as Texas
liberal, xv, xvi–xvii
—as Travis County district judge: and
antitrust law, 64–65; appointment to,
47, 48, 57; and Community Natural
Gas Company case, 49–51; and history interests, 51–54; and New Deal,
61; and political campaigns, 49, 54–
59, 80; and Roosevelt's programs, 60;
Yarborough as activist judge, 62–67
—as U.S. Senator: and civil rights

issues/legislation, 149–150, 154, 175,
186–187, 210–212, 222, 246, 282, 284;
committee assignments, 146, 162,
190, 252, 254; and education, 151–152,
162, 163, 164–165, 185, 229–235, 239,
246, 265, 266, 282; and environmental
issues, 162–163, *180* (*see also* Environmental issues; Padres Island National
Seashore); and Estes affair, 181–184,
208–209, 218–219; and farmers, *238;*
and Great Society, xvi, 201, 226, 229,
234, 241, 242; and Hurricane Beulah,
225; and Kennedy assassination, *192,*
193–198, 201, 202, 246, 253; and Robert
Kennedy, 173; and patronage, 172–173,
174, 176, 190, 245, 309n.22; and presidential race (1960), 169–176, *170, 171;*
and Southern Manifesto, 147–149, 154,
211; and Thurmond, 212–214, 215; and
Vietnam War, 226, 239–244, 246–247,
255, 257, 260–262, 284, 316n.15; work
habits of, 204–206, *244,* 254–255
— *See also* Johnson-Yarborough relationship; Speeches; World War II
Yarborough, Richard: as child, 30, 54,
82, 89, 145, 155; death of, 275–276; as
Indian Claims Commission attorney,
255, 276; and Supreme Court certification, *252;* as Washington aide, 180,
204, 216, 275
Yates, Ira, 23
Yates Oil Field, 22–24, 26, 28, 49, 275
Young, John, 8, 177–178
Youngblood, Rufus, 192, 193